Pacific
Coast High

Pacific Coast High

Tracy Amos

authorHOUSE®

AuthorHouse™
1663 Liberty Drive
Bloomington, IN 47403
www.authorhouse.com
Phone: 1-800-839-8640

First published by AuthorHouse   02/03/2012

ISBN: 978-1-4685-5159-4 (sc)
ISBN: 978-1-4685-5158-7 (ebk)

Library of Congress Control Number: 2012902180

Printed in the United States of America

Any people depicted in stock imagery provided by Thinkstock are models, and such images are being used for illustrative purposes only.
Certain stock imagery © Thinkstock.

This book is printed on acid-free paper.

DEDICATION

To my son, Ryley. Write your own life story.

PROLOGUE

FROM THE MOMENT she pressed the plunger, white-hot heat shot through her body; ferocious and alarming in its intensity.

Something's not right, her mind yammered, panicked, and she felt her heart pounding against her ribs.

"Doesn't matter," her voice was slurred, barely audible. "This time's the last time."

The room went from normal to watery and translucent in a matter of seconds. The air around her turned into thick syrup, forcing itself down her throat with the invasion of a reptile. She watched the world fade towards black, and then it sped away with the velocity of a mach-ten missile.

Her head exploded towards the ceiling, even as her stomach dropped through the floor. The pounding of her heart intensified until her ribs felt like they were vibrating with every thud.

This time's the last time, her mind whispered, relieved.

This time's the last time.

CHAPTER 1

KEITH LAMONT TOOK off his lab coat and hung it on the hook behind his office door with a tired sigh. It had been a long day, physically demanding and mentally exhausting, and he was ready to go home. Emily, the woman he hoped to maybe marry one day, was staying at his house for the weekend, and had promised him a homemade dinner, and now he was anticipating that.

He rode the elevator down to the first floor and started to wave goodbye to the nurse on duty when the gasps and exclamations of those in the crowded emergency room forced his attention to the automatic doors . . . and the young woman collapsing just inside of them. The sound of her head hitting the tile was like a gunshot through the shocked room and inwardly Lamont winced even as his feet carried him swiftly across to where she lay.

One perfunctory look told him she was merely a hairs breadth from dying right there, but beyond her torn and beat up body there was the most pressing matter, up at the forefront and so far ahead of her physical wounds . . .

The girl wasn't breathing.

Lamont let his professional training take over and lead him as he tilted her head back and poked a finger in her mouth, searching for any debris. He shot a look at the nurse before commencing CPR on the unconscious girl; the nurse nodded and snatched up the phone, mumbling instructions into it as Lamont forced his air into the girl's lungs.

"Breathe," he muttered, straddling her and pressing her thin sternum down with his closed fists. "Breathe, goddamnit."

Again he forced air into her lungs; again he pressed on her sternum, over and over, thinking he was probably going to break her ribs with each compression . . . a thought secondary to the fact that she was going to die right here on the floor. A presence beside him made him reach up without looking, and paddles were shoved into his hands. Another pair of hands cut smoothly through the girl's oversized sweatshirt, revealing an emaciated torso that looked like it had come directly from a concentration camp.

His eyes taking in everything, Lamont saw the teeth marks along her small breasts, the cuts and gashes across her sunken stomach and sides. One massive bruise covered her left side from armpit to hip and he had to wonder if any of her ribs were already broken.

Even with extra holes punched in the worn belt, her baggy jeans hung low enough on her skinny waist that he could see the protrusions of her hip bones, the hollows of her pelvis, and the still-fresh wounds that were slashed randomly across her abdomen.

He gritted his teeth, growled *"Clear!"* and pressed the paddles against the girl's chest.

The bolt of electricity made her upper body jump off the floor and he grabbed a wrist, searching for a heartbeat. There was none. Again, *"Clear!"* and her body jerked once more. This time he detected a heartbeat, thin, barely there, but *there, thank God*.

Handing off the paddles, he lifted up an eyelid and noted the eye rolled back to the white. Shaking the girl's head slightly, he muttered,

"C'mon, kid. Don't die on me now."

A small cough issued from the girl's mouth, followed by a thin stream of bile. Lamont found the wrist again and this time the heartbeat was minimally stronger. With the help of others he lifted her on the gurney that suddenly appeared beside him and without looking back he wheeled her into the nearest elevator.

Lamont stood beside the girl, now identified as Kyler Maddox, and watched as she lay, still lost in the drug-induced coma. It was three days later and he was awaiting the results of the toxicology tests that had been done on her. He'd had his intern perform a pelvic and vaginal examination on her, mainly because his intern was a woman, and also because she was studying primarily gynecology.

He looked up as she now came through the doors carrying a manila folder, and his heart sank at the look in her eyes . . . vicious, unforgiving. Inwardly he sighed, knowing another intern was about to resign; her personal morals and values too much for the type of lifestyle this girl had apparently been living.

"Don't judge," his voice came out sharper than he'd intended, but suddenly he was angry.

"She's clean," his intern ignored his statement but her eyes were hard as she handed him the folder. "No current STDs, but she'll need to be tested again in a couple weeks. Substantial vaginal damage, some tears, massive bruising. Not pregnant. Negative for Hep C, but again, she'll need to be tested again in case it decides to show up."

She paused, gauging the emotion shining from her boss's eyes. "Multiple sexual partners, none who were apparently gentle with her. Drug of choice presumed to be heroin, although cocaine, speed, and Quaaludes were found, along with a miscellaneous of various over the counter stuff. Probably swiped when she was out of money and needing a quick high."

"Sarcasm's not necessary, either," Lamont snapped, glaring at her.

"It's not sarcasm," the intern sneered. "It's wondering how the hell someone can sink that low, do apparently what she'd been doing."

Lamont laid the folder gently on the bed and shot his intern a thin glare. He shoved his hands in his pockets and tried to rein in his anger.

"You sure you wanna do this? This type of work? Judgments are made for God and the judicial system, you know; not for people who help others. This line of work has lots of opportunities for judging others, but you can't do your job well if all that stays in your mind is morality."

The intern just shook her head. "I can't understand it. How can someone do this? Live this way, run themselves into the ground like this?"

Lamont stared at her. "Our job is to save lives," he mumbled. "Not condemn how they're lived."

"Morality and values are the core of why I chose this profession," the intern stated. "To teach others the importance of health and life. Not to . . . to condone this . . ." she gestured at the prone body on the bed.

Lamont clenched his jaw. "You're not condoning anything. You don't have to understand why a sick person ended up sick, or condone it or depict it against your version of morality. Your job is to just find a way to heal the sick, fix what's broken. You want ethics, try for the hospital administrator's job."

The young intern just stared at him, anger shooting from her hard gaze. Finally she gave a slight shake of her head and turned towards the door. "My resignation will be on your desk," she said as she slipped out the door. Lamont didn't even watch her go; he just turned back to the girl in front of him, picked up the folder and leafed through it with a fury shining from his eyes.

Later on he heard the door to the room open and then felt gentle arms circle his shoulders. Emily's familiar smell enveloped him for a moment before she pulled away and circled around to the other side of the bed.

"How's she doing?" She asked, laying two fingers along the inside of the girl's wrist.

"Same," Lamont watched as she took a penlight from the pocket of her lab coat and lifted one eyelid, monitoring the dilation of the pupil. "No better, no worse. Withdrawal's harsh . . . couple seizures earlier. I've got her on methadone and Librium."

Emily raised her eyebrows. "Bad?"

"They're all bad," Lamont sighed. "Doing what I can but I'm not sure she's gonna make it."

Her eyes were calm and sympathetic on his. "Don't lose the faith yet, Keith, all right?"

He nodded but didn't answer.

Emily pulled up a chair and looked at him over the girl's prone body. "Saw your intern earlier. Didn't look too happy."

"She resigned. Morals too high, I guess, for her to be objective on . . ." he gestured at the girl on the bed, "her lifestyle."

Emily looked at him for a moment and then silently held out her hand for the folder. She was quiet for a few long minutes as she looked through it, and then cleared her throat, handing it back to him.

"Not exactly been leading a boring life." She gently traced a finger down the infected tracks on the inside of Kyler's right elbow. "You knew she'd been shooting up?"

Lamont shrugged. "Somewhat, I guess. I didn't know it was heroin, but yeah, I'd've bet money she'd been shooting *something* for quite a while."

He looked at her. "On the very rare chance that I manage to save this kid's life, you think there's a possibility chance you can save her future?"

Emily leaned back and rubbed her eyes, then let her gaze rest on Kyler's still form. "She's done a lot of shit, broke a lot of laws . . ." she shook her head. "Let's just go slow, all right?" She looked back at him. "Get her better first." Standing up, Emily walked back around the bed to him and put a gentle hand on his neck.

"Call me if there's any change."

"I will," Lamont stroked her arm. "You goin' home tonight?"

"Probably."

He nodded. "Call me, all right? I can be there in minutes."

"I know," Emily sighed. "But I should be ok. I'll let you know if I hear anything." She left him without waiting for an answer, and he felt it when she walked away, letting the door swing shut quietly behind her.

The beeper on his belt went off at the same time he heard his name being called urgently over the PA. Bolting up from his chair in his office, Lamont rushed out the door and towards the nearest stairway. He was being summoned to Kyler's room and knew from experience that running up four flights or more was still a lot quicker than waiting on the hospital's notoriously slow elevators.

Running into her room he found chaos mixed with fear and anger. A nurse stood to his left, holding a towel over a bleeding gash on her arm while another fought with Kyler on the floor.

The girl was wild, showing more strength and animation than she had for the past few days. Fueled by violence and addiction as she was, it took less than half a second for Lamont to realize that she'd tried to jump through the window in an effort to end her life.

Running to the nurse's side, he added his strength and together they managed to pin Kyler to the floor.

"Fuck," the nurse spat as he tried to pull a syringe from his pocket. "Just went fucking berserk. Tried to give her a shot . . ." he jammed the needle into the side of Kyler's neck and Lamont winced as she yelped.

"Easy," he snapped. "We got her, ok? Don't hurt her more than you have to."

The nurse shot him a barely-concealed glare and then glanced back at Kyler as she slowly relaxed beneath them. The drug, a heavy sedative, worked quickly through her body and both men warily eased their weights off of her as she succumbed to a deep sleep.

"Jesus," the nurse said shakily. "Sorry, Doc, it's just . . ."

"It's all right," Lamont said. "Just help me get her back on the bed." He looked at the other nurse, still holding the towel to her arm. "You ok?"

"Yeah. Might need a stitch or two, but it's not bad."

"What'd she cut you with?" Lamont gently took the nurse's arm and gave it a perfunctory examination.

"The first shot we tried to give her. She was kind of awake but then turned violent when I tried to catch a vein in her arm. Grabbed the needle and stabbed me with it."

"Then jumped out of bed and ran for the window," the other nurse cut in. "Surprised the shit outta both of us."

"Ok," Lamont rubbed his eyes. "Go get that checked out, and you, I guess, go with her. I'll take care of her," he flapped a hand towards the bed.

"You sure?" The male nurse looked at him. "Hell, Doc, she's fucking cra—" He stopped at the look on Lamont's face. "She just . . . watch her, ok?" He muttered.

Lamont nodded curtly and then waited while they walked out of the room before turning back to Kyler. The girl's breathing was shallow but steady, and her heartbeat was stronger than it had been.

"Shit," he muttered. Plopping down in the chair beside the bed, he regarded her for a long moment before pulling his cell phone from his pocket. He spoke a few quiet words and then hung up, watching her.

Kyler had curled up into a ball, her muscles tight, straining against the very air in the room. Her hands were clenched, the knuckles white, and he saw thin streams of blood sliding down the edges of her palms.

Having watched her for nearly a week, Lamont now knew the telltale signs of an oncoming seizure. Quickly he pulled a clean syringe already full of a clear liquid from his pocket and inserted it into the vein on her inner wrist. Kyler gave a small jerk and a moan but he saw the methadone instantly start to work its magic. She relaxed into the bed and her muscles loosened their death grip on her body.

Gently he opened up her hands, finger by finger, and noted the deep, bloody crescents imbedded into her palms from her ragged fingernails. Taking a deep breath, Lamont let it out slowly and reached for the button to call the nurses' station.

While he waited he did something he'd never done before: he reached out a hand and brushed her hair back from her forehead, leaned close and muttered,

"You don't wanna die, Kyler. You're not ready to. Hold on, kid. Just hold on."

There was no response but he didn't expect there to be. Between the sedative and the methadone, the girl was pretty much out of it. Lamont was content though, that somewhere she heard him and he just hoped she could recognize that truth.

He'd caught a glimpse of the steel inside of her the night she'd collapsed in the ER, when she should have been dead by any stretch of the imagination. Yet here she was, and somehow getting stronger by the day, despite the extensive damage she'd done to her body.

The door opened behind him and a nurse walked in carrying gauze pads and surgical tape.

"Thanks," he muttered, taking them from her. As gently as he could, he wiped the cuts on Kyler's palms with antiseptic wipes and then taped pieces of the gauze on them. He figured if anything it would prevent her from doing any more damage.

The door opened again and in walked a police officer. Lamont felt his stomach clench but managed to nod at the man.

"You want me to cuff her to the bed?"

"Yeah," Lamont nodded. "Just one hand. Just to keep her from attacking anybody else."

The cop raised his eyebrows as he snapped a handcuff on Kyler's wrist. "She attacked somebody? No offense, Doc, but it looks like she might better benefit from jail."

"That'll probably happen in due time," Lamont growled. "Right now, though, you wanna be the one pulling her out of seizures on the concrete floor?"

The cop looked first at him and then at Kyler. Finally he shrugged and walked towards the door. "Just make sure I get that back."

Lamont didn't answer. He gave a heavy sigh and rolled his head on his neck, feeling exhausted throughout his whole body.

CHAPTER 2

OVER TIME, SHE became aware of muttered voices around her. Words and phrases slid into her ears and were just barely registered by her exhausted, numb brain, before sliding back out again.

"*Coma . . .*"

"*Don't know why . . .*"

"*. . . medically speaking, should be dead . . .*"

"*Poison of some kind.*"

"Poison, common enough to buy over the counter," this time the voice cut through loud and clear, right next to her head. It was a male voice, not too old. "We got it narrowed down to a type of drain cleaner or similar chemical."

"And it shot straight to her heart," a female voice, from the other side of her. "Fucking amazing. She should be dead, if not a complete vegetable. Should have most of her insides eaten up from that shit."

"But I don't?" Her voice came out a thin croak. Silence dropped like a bomb around her, and she opened her eyes to see astonishment on the face of the man standing next to her bed. "I don't?" She repeated.

He gazed at her, his eyes narrowed as they stared hard into hers.

"Hello, Kyler," he offered a small smile. "Welcome back to the land of the living."

More silence as she wondered how they knew her name. And then it didn't matter as the first few tendrils of panic seeded by need began to work their way through her.

"I didn't die," Kyler muttered flatly, and gazed around the hospital room in which she found herself. She struggled to sit up, but the handcuff on her right wrist limited her movements. She brought her eyes back up to the doctor's beside her.

"What's with this?" She growled.

He gave her a level look and then glanced up at the woman on the other side of the bed. "Emily, you want to start?"

The woman gave a small nod and looked at Kyler. "My name is Emily, Kyler, and I'm a drug and alcohol counselor here at the hospital. You mind if we talk for a few minutes?"

"Doesn't look like I got a choice," her voice cracked and she cleared her throat. The sweat was beginning to gather in her temples and on her sides, and she felt the sniffles high up in her sinuses, working their way down.

Emily pulled up a chair, watching her. "This is Doctor Lamont, and between the two of us, we are rather ... uh ... amazed at the recovery you seem to be making. Do you remember anything at all?"

Kyler stared at her, her mind working. The panic was increasing and she swallowed back sudden fear and the urge to vomit. "No."

"Nothing?" Lamont's eyes bored into hers.

She looked away, feeling the shaking start to overcome her body. "A fix," she murmured. "I fixed with something that wasn't all smack, I think. There was something wrong with it."

Emily nodded, waiting, as Kyler took a deep breath, and then another.

"You said drain cleaner?"

"Or something similar," Lamont's voice was unreadable. "Was it on purpose?"

Kyler glanced at him, her brow furrowed. "No . . ." she responded slowly. "No, it wasn't, but . . ."

"But you were looking for a way out anyway, right?" Emily asked quietly.

"Yeah." She now felt the legs of a million crawling bugs working their maddening way over her, and she laid back, her stomach rolling up in a hard knot. She felt Lamont's searching eyes on her, and met his gaze as steadily as she could.

"How long have I been here?"

"Little over a week."

"How long am I staying?"

He and Emily shared a glance, and then he said softly, "Probably for a little longer. You may still be alive, but your body is in pretty rough shape . . . even without that poison you shot into it." He paused. "We wanna monitor you for awhile."

Kyler felt a drop of sweat roll down her cheek and she wiped it away with a badly trembling hand. "And then jail, right?" She wiggled her cuffed right hand as a way of explanation.

Emily cleared her throat. "That . . ." she gestured, and then faltered, trying to find the right words. "That is for your protection as well as ours, and . . . yes, it *is* to keep you restrained."

Kyler arched an eyebrow. "Your protection? Mine?" She paused, trying to get her panicked mind past the incredible need for a fix in an effort to remember *something*.

"You went ballistic one night," Lamont offered. "Uh . . . you attacked a nurse and tried to jump through the window."

There was a deep silence for a moment as Kyler let his words sink in.

"And then, lemme guess, people started showin' up with charges against me."

Emily's gaze was neutral, meeting her own, as she slowly nodded.

Kyler nodded back and felt the exhaustion battling with the panic, feeding the need for a fix.

"Shit," she gritted her teeth.

"Can I ask you a question?" Emily's voice was soft.

Kyler didn't answer, but Emily went on anyway.

"How bad do you want to die?"

"Very badly."

Emily regarded her with understanding eyes. "Let us help you."

She shut her eyes and didn't answer. Her mind was a hurricane of thoughts and emotions run rampant, and a horrible seemingly depthless amount of self-loathing weighed down on her.

Kyler rolled into the bed as far as the handcuff would let her, feeling the panic and shaking escalate with each breath.

"I need a fix," her voice was barely audible. "Christ, I need a fuckin' fix."

Lamont stared at her for a moment, and then shot Emily a look. She shrugged, nodding grimly.

"Here," he muttered, reaching for her arm. "This'll help." He inserted a syringe into the IV going into the back of her hand. Kyler had no idea what he was putting in her, but for a split second it seemed to ease back the horrible dipped-in-glass feeling her body was going through.

Kyler had just enough time to take a relieved half-breath, and then her jaw clamped down on her tongue, hard, and her head felt like it exploded. Shakes blasted through her limbs like she'd just grabbed hold of a live electrical wire, and she wrenched back on the bed, feeling her shoulder as it strained in its socket from the handcuff still locked around her wrist.

"Shit!" Lamont snapped, grabbing her and holding on tight. *"She seizing! Get me some help in here!"*

Emily pried her jaw apart and inserted a block into her mouth. Blood flowed down, spattering Kyler's gown and the bed around her. *"Unlock this cuff!"* She barked at the patrol officer who'd just run in the room.

He whipped out the key and released the handcuff in one quick motion, and then Kyler was strapped securely down in the bed. Lamont placed two fingers on the thin inner skin of one wrist, counting off pulse beats with one eye on the monitor.

Slowly the shakes abated; Kyler lay on the bed unconscious and barely breathing. Emily peeled back an eyelid and determined that her eyes had rolled up, showing the whites.

"Christ," Lamont wiped a shaking hand across his forehead, not surprised when it came away wet with sweat. "That's four in two days."

"Up the methadone," Emily said quietly. "Another dose per day, but keep the Librium the same." She gently opened Kyler's mouth, and with a gloved finger slowly moved her tongue around. "Took a good chunk out of it, but it's already starting to clot. It doesn't need stitches."

He nodded and took a ragged breath. "I shoulda gave it to her sooner, I guess."

Emily gazed at him, her eyes unreadable, and shrugged. "I don't know if that would've prevented it. Her body's just gotta figure it out on its own."

Lamont sighed and shook his head. "Yeah. Look, you mind if I run a little late? I want to make sure she's stable before I leave here."

"No, I don't mind," she walked over to him and slipped an arm around his waist. "I figured you'd wanna stay. Take as long as you need, all right?"

He nodded and leaned into her, deriving comfort from the shape of her body against his. "Sure. I'll try not to be too long."

Emily nodded against his shoulder and gave his neck a soft squeeze before walking out the door. Lamont felt her go without looking, and gazed down at Kyler with his brow furrowed. He reached for the nurse's button and pressed it; when a nurse appeared he instructed her to change the bedclothes and Kyler's gown, and to call him with any change . . . good or bad.

CHAPTER 3

KYLER TENTATIVELY SLIT one eye open and then the other. She felt the straps across her shoulders, hips, thighs, and calves; tight, holding her down. But the handcuff was gone. She took a breath that was somewhat restrained as the strap pressed into her sternum, and felt it when the panic of claustrophobia started to claw at her brain.

Emily came into the room carrying a mug of something steaming. Her eyes were concerned and alert, and widened slightly when she saw what looked like terror in Kyler's gaze.

"Hey," she said quietly.

"Hey," Kyler responded hoarsely, licking her dry lips. "Will you do me a favor?"

"If I can," Emily set the mug on the table by the bed and bent to loosen the straps. As they fell away one by one, Kyler ran shaking hands through her hair, feeling like her sanity was held by just one loose thread. The steel of the needle from the IV in the back of her hand jiggled sickeningly just below the surface of the skin, and she felt her stomach roll over.

"What do you need?" Emily gazed at her.

"Just that," she swallowed. "The straps. I'm claustrophobic and . . . and they were really starting to get to me."

"Yeah, they can do that." Pulling over the bedside table, Emily set the mug within arm's reach of her. "Chicken noodle. I know you're probably not hungry, but you gotta eat."

Kyler felt the hard knot her stomach had become, but grimly reached for the spoon, regardless. She gritted her teeth when the needle from the IV wiggled again.

"Can you take this out?" She gestured. "It . . . feels like I'm tryin' to shoot up through my hand. Kinda makin' me sick."

Emily favored her with a long, level look. "I know it's uncomfortable, but . . ."

"Please," Kyler met her gaze. "I think . . . I can do better without it."

There was a deep silence between them for a moment, and then Emily raised an eyebrow. "Do you want to? Do better? Get better?"

Words and phrases tried to form suitable responses in Kyler's brain, but none seemed viable or believable. Finally she settled on a certain truth she felt in her heart.

"I don't know right now."

Emily's eyes searched hers, and then she gave a small nod and reached for the needle in Kyler's hand. "Fair enough. That's better than the answer you gave me yesterday. I'll take it out for now, but we may need to use it again later, ok? Just be prepared for that."

"Ok," she tried not to flinch as the needle was pulled smoothly from her vein. "What happened to me?"

"You had a seizure. And it wasn't the first."

Kyler absently stirred the soup. "No," she muttered. "It wasn't." She took a deep breath and let it out slowly. "How many'd I have?"

"Total so far is four. It's the heroin, obviously, but the methadone helps."

"Methadone," her voice was a soft mutter.

"Yeah."

"What else?"

"Librium."

Kyler was silent, staring past Emily towards the window. Her forehead creased with the amount of emotions flooding through her.

"Can I talk to you for a few minutes?" Emily asked, watching her, and Kyler nodded.

"Ask you a few questions?"

"Yeah."

"Most of these I already know the answer to, ok? My main point here is to determine how much *you* know, and if the seizures have had any impact on your memory."

Kyler shot her a sidelong glance. "Why?"

"I just told you."

"No, why do you care? And why should *I* care if my memory's fucked up if I'm not sure I wanna live to see another sun rise?"

Emily regarded her silently for a moment. Kyler's dark eyes staring into hers were exhausted and full of self-loathing.

"Because," she started slowly, "my job is to help you get better, and even though you may not want to right now, I want to follow you through every aspect of your life—past, present, future—to hopefully find something you still want to hang on to."

"There's nothing," Kyler sighed, looking away.

"You sure?"

"Yeah."

Emily was quiet for a minute, absently tapping her pen against her notebook. "You worried about your legal troubles?"

Kyler shot her a sarcastic look. "No."

"No?"

"No."

Emily sighed and gazed at her. "Then what?"

"Then what what?" Kyler's eyes hardened.

"Then what is it that is making you just so absolutely want let go of everything without even trying to find something to live for? Besides getting high, I mean?"

"I don't live to get high."

"Right. You wanna die *because* of that," now it was Emily's voice that was heavily-ladened with sarcasm.

Kyler swallowed and shifted her eyes away. She flapped a hand in a vague gesture and said softly, "Go ahead, ask your questions."

Silence again, and then Emily grunted. She put the notebook and pen back in her bag and stood up. Kyler glanced at her, watching as she walked over to the window. She leaned against the wall, staring out at the sunny day. The sun played across her face in light and shadow, and for just a second Kyler recognized that Emily was right smack in the middle of her own hell and her own pain.

She drew her knees up to her chest and glanced at the monitor again. She felt it coming; a deep, harsh need that started in the back of her head, at the base of her neck, and made its way with the sharpness of barbed wire to the pit of her stomach.

Kyler ran her hands through her hair, locking her fingers behind her neck, and took a deep, ragged breath. She stared at the spot of sheet between her knees, locking her throat against the scream that wanted to come out.

"Gimme some methadone," she managed to mutter. "Please give me some more methadone."

Emily glanced at her, hooded eyes focused inward even as she watched Kyler roll into a ball and hug her knees against the pain beginning to wash over her.

She walked over to her and sat down beside the bed. Grasping one of her shaking, sweat-soaked hands, she said softly, "Hold on, Kyler, ok? Work through this, breathe through this."

Kyler squeezed her eyes shut and groaned, feeling the crushed glass in her bones, the pin-pricks of a million needles stabbing at her muscles. The withdrawal of the heroin and various other drugs had always been bad, but before she'd always managed to score even just a little bit to keep it from getting this far.

This time was the worst ever; the pain coming on her in waves that roared over her with the scream and velocity of a hundred freight trains.

Emily dialed her cell phone without looking and spoke a few soft brief words, never letting go of Kyler's hand.

"Easy," she murmured. "You're ok. Just breathe, breathe through this."

The pain spiked, fueled by the harshest need Kyler'd ever known; a need for *anything* to get her as high as she needed to be; *anything* to keep from feeling like her brain was trying to claw its way out of her ears, like her stomach was wrapped in barbed wire, like her skin was being scraped off with sandpaper.

She buried her face in the pillow, dimly feeling Emily's fingers wrapped around hers. Before she could so much as turn her head, the vomit was halfway up her throat, and then it was out of her mouth, on the pillow, in her hair.

She smelled it, felt it in the back of her throat and sinuses, and puked again.

Another pair of hands on her shoulders, helping to steady her, and all Kyler wanted to do was give up the fight; sink into the bed and let her life go.

"Stay with us, kid," Lamont's voice was soft in her ear. "C'mon, Kyler, hold on."

"Fuck that," she managed. "Just lemme go."

"No," he said firmly. "Hold on."

"Lemme go, Doc," she moaned. "I'm tired of this shit."

Over her shoulder, Emily's eyes met Lamont's, and she raised her eyebrows. *Was this the surrender she'd been waiting for? Was this the surrender of wanting to give up the drugs and embrace life . . . or was it the surrender of life. Was she giving up or letting go?*

"Breathe, Kyler," she said grimly. "Just breathe."

Kyler's body was a tight, thrumming ball of electricity, drawn up and shaking from the withdrawal and need. She gripped the sheets in tight fists, clenched her jaw, and waited to see if her heart would explode . . . and what she was going to have to do if it didn't.

Little by little the pain faded. Kyler sank back into the bed, wishing for sleep, for release, for a fix, for anything that would make this hell end . . . one way or another.

"Easy," Emily repeated softly. "How do you feel?"

"Like shit," Kyler answered weakly. "Fuck, I don't wanna do this anymore."

Lamont gently picked up a wrist, feeling her thin, unsteady pulse. "Least it didn't go into another seizure," he muttered. Her dark eyes stared into his, but she didn't answer.

Emily poured a glass of water from the pitcher on the table and held it to her lips. Kyler managed to take a small sip, relieved it seemed to be staying down. It washed the vomit back some, but she was still surrounded in it.

Lamont pushed the button, summoning a nurse, and quietly instructed a cleanup when one arrived. Kyler lay back, breathing deeply, feeling her heart pounding painfully against her sternum. She felt gentle hands on her, peeling off her filthy gown, moving her towards the bathroom. She kept her eyes closed, feeling the exhaustion in its totality wash over her, pushing her down.

"Just a quick shower," Emily's voice was comforting, "and then we'll get you back to bed, all right?"

Kyler didn't answer; it was almost too much for her to remain standing on her own.

She was led back to the bed, where she collapsed gratefully onto it. Almost immediately, sleep overtook her, forcing her far down deep inside herself.

CHAPTER 4

"What's your full name?"

"Kyler Maddox."

It was two days later, and there had been plenty of pain, but no more seizures. Almost two weeks had gone by without Kyler having any kind of drug in her system . . . the longest stretch she'd had in a good long while.

Slowly, it seemed like her was sanity trying to return.

"Parents?"

"Not that I know of."

"Address?"

"The streets of San Diego."

"Age?"

Kyler opened her mouth but was hesitant. Emily patiently waited, watching her.

"Eight . . . Eighteen . . . ?"

"Are you asking me or telling me?"

"I . . . don't know."

"You're birthday was a week and a half ago, Kyler. You're nineteen, now."

She nodded silently, and in the back part of her mind she felt the beginnings of the withdrawal, coming back to haunt her again. She shot a glance at the beeping monitor next to the bed, but couldn't get all the lights and buttons to make any kind of sense.

"It'll kick in in about a half an hour," Emily's voice was quiet, reading her mind. "You gotta hang on 'till then."

"And then what?"

"Then you get another dose in about five hours or so. Two doses a day on the methadone; three for the Librium."

"I need more for the methadone," Kyler scrubbed a hand hard across her face. "Two ain't gonna keep me from going into convulsions."

"Trust me, ok?" Emily stared at her, forcing her to meet her eyes. "Two doses of methadone are enough for you right now. And you need to be aware that, over time, we're gonna decrease that amount in order to wean you off of it."

"So why even bother with it at all?" Kyler said sharply, glaring at her. "Why tease me with it?"

Emily leaned down and brought a hardcover book from the bag at her feet and handed it to her. "A thorough non–fiction account of heroin addiction in a certain individual's life," she said. "It's honest, complete, and true, and it'll help answer any questions you have."

Kyler drew her eyebrows together in a sign of aggravation. "You want me to read this?"

"Only if you want answers to questions I know you're gonna have. You can talk to me anytime, day or night, but I'm not a heroin addict. I know the drug and I know my job, but I can recognize the fact that I'm not inside where you are.

"Just look it over, ok? I think you can relate to it."

Kyler's eyes hardened but she laid the book off to her side.

"Birth date?"

"May seventh, nineteen-seventy-four. But just answer that question for me, ok? Why even start me on the methadone in the first place?"

"Because," Emily glanced down at the notebook in her hand, "it helps ease back the withdrawal, and it's close enough to heroin that the body thinks it *is* heroin. On the methadone you won't feel like hammered horse shit all the time."

"Family?" She looked back up at Kyler.

"I . . . what? No, no family," Kyler felt her mind reaching out to the ones who at one time were the only family she'd ever had, and she slammed a mental door on that so hard that its echo reverberated against the sides of her skull. "Methadone's addictive, too?"

"Yes."

She took a deep breath and pressed the heels of her hands against her eyes. "Christ," her voice took on a hoarse mutter.

"One day at a time, Kyler. That's all you gotta think about. Right now, today, ok? Tomorrow may or may not come, so why even waste time worrying about it?"

Kyler shot her a look that was unreadable but didn't answer.

"How long have you been getting high?"

"Most of my life," she muttered. "But it only got to be an everyday thing when I started shooting smack."

Emily grunted and wrote down a few quick notes, and then she leaned back and regarded Kyler with a steady look. "What do you think about rehab?"

"I think it'd be a waste of money since I'm not even sure I wanna get better." Kyler lay curled up in a ball, holding back as much of the pain as she could.

"Uh huh," Emily nodded. "I agree with you. Unfortunately, the court system doesn't care whether you want to live or die. Right now there are a lot of people who want to see you behind bars for the crimes you've committed. And they want to see it happen ASAP, you know what I mean?"

Kyler shut her eyes and sighed. "So what're you saying? I'm headed to jail like tomorrow?"

Emily was silent for a few minutes and Kyler waited her out, eyes still closed against the world, pain racing through her body, brain buzzing from the tremendous need for a fix.

"No," she finally answered slowly. "Not tomorrow. But soon, if you don't let me help you."

Now it was Kyler's turn to remain quiet as she thought about her options. Finally she took a deep, deep breath and let it out slowly, trying to exhale the pain as well as all her reservations and fear.

"Ok," she muttered. "Tell me what I need to do."

Putting her pen and notebook away, Emily leaned close to her and met her exhausted eyes. "Part of what I do here is to negotiate with the courts and try to cut certain deals depending on the charges committed and both the patient's mental and physical state.

"In your case, the charges aren't really too serious. You didn't kill anybody, anyway, right?" Her eyes bored into Kyler's, searching for an alternate truth, but there wasn't one.

"Right."

"Couple B and E's, a GTA, possession, possession with intent to sell, and prostitution, if I'm correct."

"Right again," Kyler felt the accusatory weight of her crimes pressing down on her. Emily was right; they weren't as bad as they could have been, but the Kyler who did them was a far cry from the Kyler who used to be as pure as the power of the ocean, and as wild as the air that ran across it.

Emily regarded her silently, sensing concrete similarities between this young woman on the bed in front of her and her own son who was at this moment God only knew where, forcing more poison into his system.

She leaned back and sighed, shifting her gaze to the window for a brief instant before turning back to Kyler. "I've made some calls and I can get you into Harmon's Rehab for a six month program." She waited for a protest, but Kyler remained silent, watching her.

"Upon completion of the program, you'll move into a halfway house, find a part-time job, and begin rebuilding your life." She waited again, but there was still no comment from Kyler.

"A drug test is required once a week for the following three months, and then twice a month after that for a year. You do all this, and the charges against you will be dropped on the basis that you're aware you did wrong, and that you're actually trying to get better."

Kyler cleared her throat and Emily waited for the explosion. There was none, though, as Kyler said quietly, "And it doesn't matter what I want, right? Whether I wanna live or die?"

"It matters to me," Emily responded seriously, "because it's my job and my job matters a lot to me. I like helping people and it really hurts me when I'm not able to do that." She paused, thinking, and then admitted, "With you, it would really hurt because I've seen the poison you put in your body. You should be dead right now, Kyler. You shoulda been dead two weeks ago when you shot up whatever it was that was in that heroin.

"A lot of people don't even get to where they do that much damage; they die long before. You ask me, I think you got very, very lucky in this case. You wanna still go ahead and kill yourself, I think it would be a huge waste, and a huge shame."

Her eyes burned with an intensity that suggested other, more personal, reasons for her wanting Kyler to go on living. In her gaze, Kyler read a certain hope and optimism that seemed directed towards the positive aspect of her own case, and of her body's own seemingly miraculous strength to continue with life even when it was loaded with certain death.

"It matters to you," Kyler stared at her, trying to see past the wall that she sensed was there. "Why?"

"I just told you."

"Yeah, but there's more," she sat up on one elbow, consciously pushing the pain and withdrawal to the back burner for a moment. Being able to read people had always been a natural gift for her, and she did it with ease and a certain patience that enabled her to whittle away walls of distrust until there was nothing left but exposure to whatever secret one may be hiding.

"What makes *me* so special to *you*? Besides the fucking poison, I mean, and the fact that I'm still alive. What is it about *me* that gives *you* hope?"

Emily regarded her for a long, long time, trying to feel angry but feeling only drained and exhausted. She took a deep, haggard breath and stared out the window again, sorrow and fear—her main constant companions for the last year or so now—once again by her side, invading her with their negativities.

Finally she looked back at Kyler, her eyes hooded and unreadable. "My son," her voice came out as soft as the touch of feather on one's skin, but Kyler could read all too well the immense amount of anger, frustration, fear, and hatred behind that softness; the same emotions that Josh had conveyed both in his body and in his speech over the last few horrible roller coaster-like weeks they were together.

"My son has a drug addiction that's gonna end up killing him before too much longer, I think," Emily's voice was now gruff with the sound of unshed tears. "And watching how close you came to the edge, only to step back at the last minute . . . well, it gives me hope. Let's me know it's ok to hold on just a little bit longer, even though every day he's out there tears away another little piece of me."

Kyler sat up in bed, crossing her legs Indian-style in front of her. The sudden movement caused the pain to spike, but now, watching Emily in her pain, she suddenly felt unworthy of the hell her own body was going through.

To see it from someone else's point of view for once—the way Josh had seen her—told her how selfish she'd been, and how much undue pain and suffering she'd caused him.

And then immediately on the heels of that came a thought, *Christ, just one fucking fix*, and the contradiction of the emotions, reeling from one end of the spectrum to the other, was just a hair short of being enough to drive her completely fucking insane.

"Fuck," she muttered, and ran a hand through her hair. Two feet away, Emily was taking a deep breath of her own, and then bent down to gather up her things. "I'm sorry," Kyler offered.

Emily gave a small, absent smile. "Everybody's got their demons, right? So what should I tell the courts?"

"Tell 'em I'll take the deal."

Emily regarded her, eyes serious. "But not for yourself, right?"

"No," Kyler met her gaze. "Not for me. Maybe one day it will be, but right now it'll be for you. You need the hope more than I do."

Giving a slow shake of her head, Emily sighed, and then not finding a suitable answer, turned and walked out of the door.

Emily lay with Lamont's arms around her, feeling like her heart was being ripped apart. Curtis was in jail again . . . she'd gotten the call not more than half an hour before. He was high and being charged with robbery and attempted murder. Bail hadn't been set as of yet, and it didn't matter anyway, because this time she wasn't going to pay it.

Same as how she wasn't going to pay it last time or the time before . . . and then ended up forking over the cash.

"Christ, this hurts," she murmured into his shoulder. Lamont didn't answer as he pulled her closer, trying by the sheer presence of his body against hers to expel the demons in her.

After a while, he felt her breathing slow and her weight settled more firmly against him. He stared at the ceiling as he gently stroked her shoulder, wondering at the enormous strength drug addiction has on its victims; both who used the drug and those who had to stand by and watch their loved ones succumb to it.

Jesus, if we could get that kinda strength in some of the good things on this planet . . .

He sighed, and turned over on his side, facing her. She burrowed her face into his chest, allowing sleep to help her escape, if even just for a little while.

CHAPTER 5

IT WAS EARLY evening when Lamont walked into Kyler's room. The TV bolted to the wall across from her bed was on, tuned to a local station that was broadcasting an amateur skateboarding tournament in Venice Beach. He opened his mouth to say hello, when her eyes turned to meet his, full of an alarming intensity that he'd never seen before.

"Hey," he offered slowly, pulling up a chair. "What's up?"

She shook her head and looked back at the screen. "I forgot about that . . . about that tournament up in Venice Beach. I used to go there every year."

He chanced a glance at the screen and saw young kids competing for trophies and awards, doing tricks with their skateboards on the ramps and on the concrete of the boardwalk. It was a circus, a media-frenzy that made all the skaters crazy around this time of year, and as always, he was thrilled he resided in a city a hundred miles away.

Kyler, though, was staring at the TV like she wanted nothing more than to jump through it. The handcuff, still daily more on her wrist than off, pulled her arm back behind her, straining her shoulder, but she appeared not to notice.

She was as close to the TV as she could get, eyes narrowed and brow furrowed as she seemingly glared a hole through the screen.

"You're gonna dislocate your shoulder," he muttered. She favored the cuff with an irritated look and backed up an inch or two, allowing for a small amount of slack. Lamont watched her watch the skaters, her face showing for the first time an emotion besides anger or the desire to die.

Slowly an idea began to form, and he wondered if this—this show on the screen and this intensity with which she was watching it—might not be the key to giving her something to live for.

"You skate?"

For a second Kyler's eyes dropped to the needle marks on the inside of her elbows and he saw deep sorrow cross her face. Then her eyes once more found the screen and her shoulders straightened in what could only be resolve.

She turned her dark eyes back on his, still burning with that intensity, that desire, and gave a slow nod. "Used to. Before the smack."

He grunted and looked at the TV again. "Any good? Like them, maybe?"

For the first time in the two and a half weeks he'd known her, Kyler smiled, and it was the most beautiful thing he could've seen at that moment. She jerked her head back towards the skaters, and gave a somewhat self-conscious shrug.

"I held my own."

"You competed?"

"Sometimes. Sometimes I just went to watch. TV doesn't do it any justice. You have to see it to get the feel of it."

"Really," he was skeptical but he hid it from his voice. He could only imagine the horror of the traffic in the area around Venice Beach at this moment.

"Really," she grinned. "And you have to *skate* it to *really* feel it."

Lamont saw that the heroin wasn't with her right now; neither was the coke or any other drug she'd lived off of for the past God only knew how long. Right now, her heart and soul was with those skaters who were riding those little boards in hopes of winning something, anything to show they were just a little bit better than their fellow skaters. Or luckier. Watching the dangerous tricks and perilous moves those people made, luck had to have more than just a little to do with it.

Otherwise, he thought sardonically, *this place'd be full of banged up kids.*

The show cut to a commercial and Kyler looked back at him.

"Think you can pick me up one of those?"

"What?" He stared at her in surprise.

"A board," her voice was almost comically patient.

"Kyler," he sighed, "no offense, but you're about as beat up as anybody I've seen in a long time. I know you're feelin' better, but . . . shit, kid, that don't mean your body's a hundred percent, you know?"

"No," she agreed, but there was a small smile playing around the corners of her mouth, "but my soul is, and it's wantin' like hell to skate again, Doc. Even if I don't step foot on a board for the next couple of months, it'd be good just to have, you know?"

He regarded her for a long moment, his eyes searching hers. He recognized this all too well as potential progress, and knew that if her mind was free to think about something other than getting high, then maybe her body would have shot at getting better.

She must have seen this in his eyes because her smile became a grin.

"You know where the Swale Surf shop is down at Third and Broadmore?"

"Not exactly," he shrugged. "I can probably find it, though."

"Just go in there and ask for Michele or Dan and tell 'em I need a board. They owe me a favor and just say I want to cash it in."

"This ain't got nothin' to do with drugs, does it?" His voice came out sharper than he intended, but she merely shook her head.

"No," she said seriously. "I helped them out of some trouble one time . . . perfectly *legal* trouble."

"I don't wanna know," he held up his hands.

"Ok," she responded easily, "but will you do that for me? They probably won't even believe I'm still alive."

"You want me to just walk in there and ask for a free board?"

"Relax," that grin again, the one bright spot he'd seen for days. "They're not gonna shoot ya."

The look in her burning gaze finally convinced him, albeit reluctantly. He figured if a skateboard could make her forget even just for a little while the hell she'd been through, then yeah, sure, he'd get it for her.

"Just so long's I don't get shot," he grinned back and stood up. "I'm off work now . . . what time they close? I can pick it up tonight if they're still open."

"Last I knew they stayed open till eleven."

Lamont checked his watch and saw he had a good three hours or so. "Ok. I'll see if I can get it, and if I do, you want me to bring it back by tonight?"

"Yeah, if you don't mind," Kyler said. "Thanks, Doc."

"Sure. Guess I'll see ya in a bit."

She nodded and turned back to the TV as the program came back on. In her heart she felt that great desire threaten to counter and even jump ahead of the constant need that seemed to have been with her her whole life.

"But it hasn't," she muttered quietly. "It *hasn't* been with me my whole life because *this* was here long before I took my first fix. Way, way long before."

Briefly, Josh's face floated across her mind and she clenched her jaw against the very real physical pain it caused.

"Just get me back on a board again," Kyler's voice was a hoarse whisper as she finally fell back on the bed, giving her straining shoulder a break. "Please just lemme skate again."

Lamont parked outside the small shop and surveyed the entrance before giving a sigh and pushing out of the car. He walked in the open door of the skate/surf shop and stood a minute, looking around at the merchandise, cluttered here and there, and at the various groups of young people scattered about.

"Hey," an attractive blond walked up to him with a smile. "Help ya with somethin'?"

He cocked an eyebrow, offering an easy smile. "Either you just helped all these other people, or you're putting me to the front of the line."

She cocked her head and gave a small laugh. "Sorry. It's just that . . ."

"I'm the only one here who looks outta place, right?"

"Yeah," she shrugged. "They . . ." she gestured vaguely "are skaters and surfers. You, on the other hand . . ." the woman gave a slow shake of her head, "I don't know."

"Am a doctor," Lamont offered his hand. "Keith Lamont."

"A doctor," she repeated, shaking his hand. "Never had one of those in here before. Police, yeah, but no doctors."

He grinned. "No, I guess you probably don't have much of a demand for people like me. Actually, I'm here to see either Michele or Dan."

"Well," the woman crossed her arms in front of her. "I'm Michele. Dan's in back. What can I do for you?"

"I'm here," Lamont started reluctantly, "because a young woman named Kyler Maddox wants a skateboard, and she said she wants to cash in a favor you and Dan owe her."

Michele stared at Lamont for a minute and then said softly, "Kyler, huh? Jesus, I figured she'd died a long time ago." She chewed on a fingernail and then glanced back behind the counter. "Hang on a sec, all right?"

He nodded and watched her walk behind the counter and into a back room separated from the front by a curtain of hippie beads. There was muttered conversation for a brief second, and then a young man came out, followed by Michele.

He regarded Lamont as he shook his hand, offering his name as Dan. Lamont nodded and waited with raised eyebrows.

"Kyler back in the circuit?" He asked. Michele had disappeared back in the back and now came out with a brand new skateboard. Wordlessly she handed it to him and then knelt down in front of a counter filled with wheels, skate tools, pads, and other such equipment.

Lamont watched as she selected a key from a ring on her belt, unlocked the glass case and started sifting through the stuff.

"What circuit?" He asked, looking back at Dan.

"The skating circuit. She was awesome there for awhile, but the dope got to her quick."

"I don't know if she's back or not. She just asked me if I could pick this up for her."

Michele stood up with a grin on her face. She had a bunch of gear that she began putting into a plastic sack with the Swale Shop's logo on it. "If she's wanting a board again, she's definitely back. Finally get off the dope?"

"Trying to, I guess," Lamont said neutrally. He took the bag Michele handed to him with raised eyebrows. "She still cashing in that favor?"

Michele gave a small shrug. "Just a welcome back gift bag, if you will. Tell her we'll be lookin' for her come competition time."

Dan grinned, leaned over and kissed his wife, and then walked Lamont out to his car. "Nice to meet ya. Tell Kyler to come by when she's better. Hell, we all thought she was dead, laid up in some alley somewhere with that fuckin' needle in her arm."

Lamont nodded. "I'll tell her. And it was nice to meet you, too." He started to get in his car but Dan stopped him with a hand on his shoulder.

"You get a chance to watch her skate, she'll change the way you feel about the sport. She's good, man; she can make that fucker walk and talk."

Lamont smiled and got in the car. As he pulled out of the lot he glanced over at the skateboard lying on the passenger seat, and wondered just how much it took for somebody to make a piece of fiberglass with four wheels walk and talk.

The look in Kyler's eyes as he handed her the skateboard was one of gratitude, and—he was very glad to see—life. There was more life in her in that moment than he'd seen in the past two weeks, and as she held that board in her hands, it was obvious that it was so much more to her than just a piece of fiberglass with four wheels.

CHAPTER 6

KYLER WAS SITTING up in bed early the next morning, knees drawn up to her chest, arms wrapped around her knees. She was staring absently out the window, but turned to look at Lamont when he walked in the room.

The skateboard was on the bed beside her, and he raised his eyebrows.

"Hey, kid," he offered a weary smile. "You sleep with that thing?"

She smiled back, somewhat sheepishly. "It was hard to sleep. All I wanna do is skate." Then she glanced away and rested her chin on her knees. "But treatment first, right?"

"Well," he pulled up a chair and sat down beside her, eyes on hers. "Emily talked to you." It wasn't a question, but Kyler gave a small nod. "Treatment's your only option right now, regarding these charges."

"Yeah."

He started to say more, but stopped and glanced down at the board. "You really love skating that much?"

"Yeah," she said again, this time with an anticipatory glitter in her eyes.

He looked at her with his brow furrowed. "So? You wanna live now?"

Kyler stared at him for a moment, and then gave a shrug. "I wanna skate. Right now I can't get past that."

Lamont gave a slight nod. "Whatever you ultimately decide is completely up to you." His eyes found hers and locked in on them. "But we hope you decide to live. Seriously. Life's good, if you give it a chance."

"I know," she sighed, and stared down at the bed for a second. Then she looked back up at him, face open and concerned. "How's she doing?"

Lamont gazed at her for a long time, and then gave a small shrug. "Ok. Why?"

"'Cause she told me about her son. We talked, and . . . it gave me a new perspective, seeing this shit from her end."

He raised his eyebrows, surprised that Emily had shared her problems with Curtis with Kyler; even more surprised that she hadn't told him.

"Yeah," he agreed slowly. "It makes a difference, seeing it in a different light."

Silence fell between them for a minute or two, and then Lamont cleared his throat. "You feel up to traveling today?"

"Takin' me to rehab, huh?" She sighed, feeling a new emotion—fear—override the constant pain and this new sudden desire to get on her board again.

"Yeah. It, uh . . . it's better if you get into a program as soon as you can. Legal-wise, you know?"

Kyler nodded silently. She thought a few minutes and then asked, "What about the halfway house Emily was talking about? Where's that gonna be?"

Lamont reached for the nurse's button and pressed it, saying, "I'll work on that while you're up there. I'll keep in touch with you, ok? And I'll let you know probably in a month or so where's it's gonna be."

Kyler gave another nod, feeling her stomach knot up. "They gonna detox me?"

"Maybe," he muttered, "but it won't be near as bad as here. Most of the shit's out of your system, and actually they'll probably just give you a piss test and send you on to class. Eventually, they'll wean you off the methadone."

"Ok," she sighed, and looked up as a nurse walked in the room.

"Hey," Lamont said standing. "Will you help her get dressed and get her things together?" He looked back at Kyler looking at him. "I'm gonna drive you up there myself, is that all right?"

"Yeah," she muttered, allowing the nurse to help her off the bed. He nodded and left the room, shutting the door behind him.

Lamont drove steadily across the state with Kyler sleeping the sleep of the dead in the backseat.

Or rather, the sleep of one who's been up for four or five days, loaded up on speed, he thought.

Except she hadn't done any speed. Hadn't done any coke or heroin or anything else for the past seventeen days. For the first time in a long time, her body was completely free of any drug, and the sleep she was now wrapped in came from the total exhaustion of the life she'd been living for the past God only knew how long finally catching up with her.

He kept the radio down, listening for the more than occasional bits and pieces of conversation as she talked to someone she was only seeing in her dreams. The name 'Josh', familiar enough to him now, surfaced more than a few times, and he had to wonder once more just who this kid really was, where'd she come from, and how'd she ever managed to get roped into the life she'd been leading when she'd collapsed on the floor right in front of him over two weeks ago.

He glanced in the rearview mirror at her as he pulled off the exit and saw she was sitting up now, staring out the window.

"Hey," he said quietly.

"Hey," Kyler favored him with a quick glance. "Did I sleep the whole way here?"

"Just about," Lamont pulled into a space and looked back at her. "You ok?"

Her brow furrowed and he sensed the uncertainty and fear in her. She shrugged and pushed open the door. "Gonna hafta be, I guess."

One hundred and thirty-five miles east of San Diego and Kyler found herself in the parking lot of Harmon's Rehab. Surprisingly, her heart was aching for the familiarity of the hospital room she'd left behind, and the thought of getting through even one day here without the doc or Emily or any kind of drug just about terrified her.

She was signed in and was being led down a hall when she stopped and looked back at him. He was still there, watching her, and offered an encouraging smile when his eyes met hers.

"Hey," Kyler started, and then faltered as her pride tried to rear up. He waited, eyebrows raised. "Call me, ok? Let me know how things are going. And tell Emily to call me, too. I . . . I'd like to talk to her."

"Sure," Lamont gave a slow nod. "I will. And you can call me, too. Anytime, day or night. Lemme know how *you're* doing."

"Yeah, ok," Kyler answered, and then turned and plodded on down the hall, not looking back.

CHAPTER 7

THE DAYS TURNED into weeks turned into a month and Kyler found herself slowly getting better. The classes were extensive; focusing on drug addiction in general, and the heartbreak and despair it causes both the addicted and those who love them. Some showed the far-reaching damage different kinds of drugs did to the human body, while others spotlighted the lengths to which some people would go to in order to get the drugs they needed so bad.

Kyler found herself filled with self-loathing any time prostitution was brought up, and so she, in turn, pushed back her fierce pride and opened up to her counselor about her feelings on this subject. She still didn't know if whether or not she wanted to live, but every time she thought she wanted to die, she remembered Emily's words about how not many people got as bad as she did without dying.

And every time she looked at her board stashed beside her bed, she felt the desire within her grow another notch.

Won't be long now, she thought each night, as each night her body was just a little bit stronger. Walking through the halls and rooms of the treatment center, she found herself looking out the various windows to the parking lot . . . and at all that asphalt stretching out into the California sun, just screaming to be skated on.

A month and a half in Kyler found herself with a new roommate. Barbara was barely a week clean, strung out as hell, and on her knees in front of the toilet puking her guts out when Kyler first met her. Wordlessly, she handed her a wet wash cloth when she was done, and Barbara gave her a grateful—if somewhat distrustful—look when she took it.

"Thanks," she muttered, and got shakily to her feet.

"Yeah," Kyler responded, and left her alone, knowing she'd probably want to fight if forced into a conversation at this point in her life. She vaguely remembered her first couple of nights clean, and how she'd felt like if she didn't get something soon, she was going to rip her own head off.

Laying down on her bed, staring at the ceiling, Kyler wondered how Emily was doing with her son, and if he'd finally gotten enough of himself back to check into someplace like this. Movement out of the corner of her eye caused her to glance towards the bathroom door. Barbara was standing there looking at her through shell-shocked eyes.

"You wanna be alone, I can go somewhere," Kyler sat up and reached for her shoes.

"No, that's all right." She hesitated and then muttered, "I'm Barbara, by the way. Barb."

"Kyler."

They stared at each other for a minute, and then Kyler lay back down. "I don't sleep too good, so I'm gonna apologize in advance if I wake you up."

Barb gave a short, gruff laugh and lay down on her own bed. "I'll be lucky if I sleep at all." There was silence for a beat, and then Barb shot her a glance. "Can I ask you something?"

"Yeah."

"You shoot up?"

"I did." She offered a sarcastic grin. "What gave it away, the body art I got?" She held out her arms for emphasis, the deep-seated needle marks barely healed, despite the time that had elapsed since her last fix.

"Takes one to know one," Barb offered her own gruesome arms, both covered in what looked like hundreds of mosquito and spider bites. "Legs're covered, too. Fucking veins keep collapsing . . . *kept* collapsing." She bit her lip and shifted her eyes away, and Kyler recognized the thick fear in her gaze.

"Why'd you quit, court?" She asked.

"Yeah. That and . . ." Barb trailed off and brought her eyes back to Kyler's. "Can I tell you something, but . . . but I don't want anybody else to know just yet, ok?"

Kyler shrugged and sat up, reaching for her cigarettes. She held up the pack with raised eyebrows and Barb nodded. She tossed it to her and lit a cigarette; one eye squinted against the smoke.

Barb lit one of her own and tossed the pack back with a nod of thanks. Kyler watched her take a deep, deep drag and let the smoke bite hard into her lungs before letting it out.

"I think I might be pregnant," Barb muttered softly. Kyler gazed at her with controlled emotion, knowing that with the condition Barb was in right now, odds were already well against the fetus she may be carrying.

"I don't know who the father is, and I couldn't even begin to guess."

Kyler was silent, smoking her cigarette, and didn't have to reach very far to see herself in Barb's shoes. It was only by sheer luck that she'd never gotten pregnant during all the months she was hooking for that high.

She met Barb's eyes, so full of fear and that all-too-familiar hatred. "How far along, do you think?"

"Anywhere from three to five weeks is my guess, but my mind's so fucking shot right now it's hard to keep anything straight."

More silence, and then Kyler asked quietly, "So why're you tellin' me? What makes you think I care enough to not go runnin' out and open my mouth to the first person I see?"

"You probably couldn't give two shits about me," Barb lay back on her bed, ribs and hip bones prominent against the loose fabric of her clothes, "but I got nobody else and I just wanted to tell somebody." She shrugged. "Maybe you'll tell and maybe you won't. Gotta come out sometime, I guess. Can't really hide something like this forever."

She crushed out her smoke and rolled over, facing the wall. Kyler watched her for a minute and then did the same, knowing she would hold Barb's secret, if only for the reason that there was still one person left who was willing to put any kind of trust in her at all.

And because of her trust, over the next few weeks Barb and Kyler began to form a tentative friendship, built on the distrust and paranoia of the addicted, but concreted by the courses that had led them both to that same place, and cemented by the experiences they both shared that mirrored the other's.

Heroin had drawn them along paralleled paths, and because of this, Kyler was able to form a trust in Barb more easily than in anyone else for a long, long time.

As Barb's pregnancy became a reality, and as her rehab began to take a subtle turn—mainly towards no longer doing what she needed to do just for herself, but also for her unborn child—Kyler began to experience the rewards of sharing in something that wasn't exclusively geared towards either constantly searching for that next high, or thinking about searching for it. For once in her life, she began to feel comfortable, both in herself and in her surroundings.

Having Barb as a roommate helped her along in her own recovery, as she helped Barb in hers. The decision to have the baby was a difficult one to make—Kyler made sure she did not sway Barb's choice one way or the other—but she was able to be there for comfort, if nothing else.

Like Kyler, Barb had no one else to turn to, and so they turned towards each other, reaching for a friendship and understanding. Ironically, their mutual drug of choice, and all the experiences that came with it—both good and bad; some funny, most just really, really sad—helped to seal this friendship.

CHAPTER 8

Barb was in their room when Kyler walked in, curled up on her bed, head buried under the pillow, shoulders shaking with the huge sobs that racked her thin body.

Kyler wordlessly sat down on her bed and stretched out a tentative hand to touch her shoulder. Barb sat up and wiped her eyes, and then glared at Kyler with a burning anger that she knew wasn't directed at her.

"Those fuckers," Barb growled. "You know what they told me?"

"Who?" Kyler reached for her smokes and lit one, handing her the pack.

"That idiot doctor and my counselor and a couple others. They told me to abort, you believe that? *Abort,* for Christ's sakes. Said physically I can have a kid, but that without me knowin' who the father is and being just barely two weeks clean, the kid won't have a shot 'cause I'll probably be right back at it as soon as I can."

Kyler was quiet for a minute, thinking. "They said all that?"

"Well," Barb took a deep drag on her cigarette, "not in those exact words, but I got the overall meaning. And then there's the aspect of AIDS or hepatitis—which I don't have as of yet, but . . . you know . . ."

She sighed and stared out the window. Kyler saw her shoulders slump in indecision and defeat. "Maybe they're right, fuck, I don't know. I mean, how can I raise a kid, when I don't even have a place to live? How'm I gonna get money, other than the way I've always gotten it?"

A million questions, Kyler thought. *A million decisions.*

"I'm barely old enough to legally drink," Barb muttered softly. "No education, no family. Been shootin' dope since I was twelve, and I don't know anything else." She gave another heavy sigh and repeated, "Maybe they're right."

Kyler stared at her skateboard lying on the floor a few feet from her. Its mere presence calmed her, and she wished Barb had something like that to lean towards and hold on to.

"Baby aside, what were you gonna do when you leave here?" She asked her.

Barb looked at her and gave a small shake of her head. "You mean if I wasn't pregnant?"

"Yeah."

"I don't know, Kyler. I honestly don't know. I mean, my counselor says there're programs that can help me get on my feet, move into a halfway house and get a job, maybe. Maybe get a little bit of education, try to do something with the time I got left."

She shrugged. "But I don't see anything *ahead* of me, if you know what I mean. They say once I get my head cleared and my body starts to feel better, then maybe I can find something better in life than gettin' high. Maybe I'll start to believe that it can only get better, and all that other shit they've been tellin' me since day one."

"You believe that?"

Barb was silent for a long time, staring out the window. "No," she finally said. "No, I don't. Because I know how I am, and how I am is I'll do ok for awhile, and then it won't matter how many meetings I go to or how many times I call my sponsor.

"Sooner or later it's gonna come on me in the middle of the night like it always does and I'll get up and get dressed and head on out the door. Back out to get high, back to the business of slowly killing myself, 'cause truth be told, Kyler, I really don't think I got nothin' to live for."

She took a last big draw off her cigarette before crushing it out and turned to look at her. "I don't think I wanna die, but there's just nothin' out there for me to hold on to, ya know?"

Kyler leaned back against the wall and drew her knees up to her chest. She remained silent, not allowing her words or thoughts to influence Barb's in any way, but she could feel the hopelessness emanating off her friend like waves coming in from the ocean. She glanced down at her board and felt her heart flutter with desire, with hope, with the power and weightlessness that comes from being free.

She shut her eyes, feeling Barb's trembling through the thin mattress. *Hopelessness,* she thought. *Christ, what a motherfucker.*

"Come with me," she said quietly, "outside." She gently pulled Barb up by her hand and gave her a gentle shove towards the door. "Parking lot."

"Jesus, Kyler, what the fuck's in the goddamn parking lot?" Barb ran the heels of both hands under her eyes, watching her.

"For me, everything," Kyler muttered, and picked up her board. "I'm gonna try to help you get through this, but I gotta think, and I can't do that in this small-ass room. Come on."

Barb shot her a thin glare, but turned to walk alongside her. There was silence all the way down the long hallway until they pushed out into the bright sunshine. The parking lot was only partly full and Kyler stopped for a minute surveying it. Barb watched her eyes narrow as her gaze trailed the lot from one end to the other.

"All right," she glanced at Barb. "Gimme a minute, ok? There's a way outta this for you, I know."

Barb shook her head and turned away. "Whatever, Kyler. If you think of something, make sure you let me know, ok? I'll be right over there under that tree—"

She stopped and looked back at the spot where Kyler had been just a mere second before. Now she was halfway across the parking lot, riding her board like she was born with it under her feet.

Barb's jaw dropped as she watched Kyler maneuver, twist, and turn the skateboard across the hot asphalt, never missing a beat, never faltering in any way. She skimmed across the hoods of cars, used the handrails for massive grinds, and jumped the steps flawlessly.

Kyler used the whole parking lot, feeling freer than ever before. Her mind was lighter, her body stronger, her spirit cleaner, and her heart one hell of lot happier. As usual when she skated hard, she felt all the heaviness of her troubles lift off like a dozen doves, soaring higher until there was nothing left but the board under her feet, the wind in her hair, and the sun warm on her face.

Finally, she headed towards where Barb sat, still slack-jawed and in awe. She came fast, jumped the curb, and then just let the board go as she hit the ground hard two feet from her friend, knocking the wind out of her.

Kyler lay there, breathless, staring at the brightness of the day until the sun's rays were blocked by Barb's worried face, bending over her.

"Christ, Kyler, are you ok?"

"Never . . . better," she gasped, grinning. "It . . . ain't been . . . that good . . . in a long fuckin' time." She felt the peace that always came with skating wash over her, like she'd just shed a bad skin and now a cleaner one was growing back.

Kyler let the world spin around her with Barb beside her for a few long, luxurious moments, and then finally looked up at her. Barb met her gaze with peace in her own eyes, and understanding, and most importantly, with a decision.

"You know what you should do?" Kyler asked quietly.

"Yeah," Barb answered. "I should keep the baby."

Kyler sat up and stared at her. "Why?"

Barb gazed at her for a long time, and then shifted her eyes to the parking lot. "Because," she started, then shook her head as if to clear it. "Because I want what you have. I want something to hold on to, something like that," she pointed towards Kyler's board, lying a few feet away.

"You've got that, Kyler, and it's got you. It's got you in a huge way, and why the fuck you ever quit that for smack, I'll never know."

Kyler shook her head. "Me neither."

"But now you got it back, and it's gonna carry you through this. I want that, Kyler; I want this child to be my reason for living. I wanna give everything to this kid like you just gave everything you got out there."

Kyler looked at her a minute "Well," she said, "there you have it. You've made the decision, and if you're willing to stick by it, just know that I'll be with you, ok? I may not be much, but at least I can at least be one person you can lean on."

Barb's eyes stared into hers, and Kyler saw a grudging trust in them.

"Yeah?" She asked.

"Yeah."

Barb cleared her throat and stared at Kyler's skateboard for a few minutes, and then shot her a look. "It always comes for you? The answer?"

Kyler reached over and snagged it off the grass, running her fingers down the new deck, absently spinning a wheel. "Yeah." She paused, thinking. "For me it does . . . when I skate. When I'm not skating and I got a needle stuck in my vein and I try to make a decision?" She stood up, stretching her back, feeling the new soreness in her muscles from landing hard on the grass.

"When I'm like that I can really fuck a whole lotta shit up."

Barb offered a bitter grin and stood up beside her. "You ain't the only one, Kyler. Shit, I could fuck up a wet dream in a heartbeat."

CHAPTER 9

BARB LAY AWAKE in her bed in the early hours of the morning, listening to Kyler as she worked her muddled way through what sounded like one fuck of a nightmare. There were mumbled phrases and words, sometimes a moan or a sharp cry. Just as Barb started to wonder if she should wake her up, Kyler rolled out of bed and staggered into the bathroom.

The door shut and then the light clicked on, and then came the retching sounds; horrible gut-twisting gasps . . . the kind that come from the very core of the stomach and fight every step of the way coming out.

"Shit," she muttered, and got out of bed. She knocked on the door, but Kyler didn't answer. She went on in anyway and saw Kyler in the space between the tub and the toilet, sitting up with her head back against the wall.

Her eyes seemed faded and washed out as they looked into hers, but the emotion was high, with fear being prominent.

"Hey," Barb said quietly, "you ok?"

Kyler shook her head and spit into the toilet. "I think . . ." her voice was hoarse and she cleared her throat. "I'm not sure, but I think I mighta opened a door today when I skated that lot."

"Why?" Barb sat down beside her.

"'Cause," Kyler scrubbed a hand hard across her face, "I think I let out the bad dreams . . . memories . . . shit I shoulda left buried."

"Heroin?"

Kyler shrugged and leaned against the toilet, feeling drained and exhausted. "Some, but not much. This was before the heroin, before I let go of the only person I've ever loved."

Barb was silent, staring at the tile between her feet. Then she looked at Kyler with raised eyebrows. "Josh?"

Kyler offered a small, bitter smile and pulled herself to her feet. "I talked, huh?"

"Just a little."

Kyler rinsed her mouth out and stumbled back to bed. Barb followed in silence, and lit a cigarette from the pack on the nightstand. Her eyes tried to catch Kyler's but they slid away.

"Wanna talk?" She asked.

"No," Kyler mumbled, lighting a cigarette of her own. "It was just a bunch of bad dreams. I've had 'em before and I'll have 'em again."

Barb grunted and lay back on her bed, blowing smoke rings at the ceiling. The silence settled around them for a few minutes, and then she looked over at Kyler, staring up at her own ceiling and seemingly lost in thought.

"Who was he? Your boyfriend?"

Kyler sighed. "Yeah, I guess you could say that."

"What happened to him?"

She pressed the heels of her hands hard against her eyes. "Thought I said I didn't wanna talk?"

Barb sat up and met her gaze. "You don't hafta talk. I can just sit here and guess all night."

"What's wrong with sleep?" Kyler asked wearily.

"Nothin, 'cept it ain't comin'. Not in this room tonight."

Kyler rolled over on her stomach and crushed out her half-smoked cigarette in the overflowing ashtray. She let her arm dangle over the side of the bed, her hand resting on the deck of her board.

Closing her eyes, she tried to will sleep to come, but was rewarded a flash of deep sea-blue eyes, a strand of shaggy blond hair instead.

"I met him when I was twelve," she muttered. "When we both were twelve. We latched onto each other quick . . . and hard. A few days after I met him I realized there wasn't a whole lot I wouldn't do for him."

She sighed and felt the ache in her heart. "That wasn't like me, you know. I'd been alone my whole life up till then, and I did good by myself. Didn't need nobody, didn't want nobody."

"But you fell for him, huh?" Barb asked quietly, staring at the ceiling with a lost look in her eyes.

"Hard," Kyler repeated. She paused, feeling the calm presence of her board beneath her fingertips, trying to work that calm up through her hand and into her heart.

"He taught me how to skate, and I fell almost as hard for that as I did for him. Skating's the complete opposite of smack for me, but I needed 'em both just the same. Sometimes I needed smack more, sometimes I'd skate for days and not think about shooting up.

"But after awhile it was more shooting up and less skating."

Barb shot her a sidelong glance. "And when that happened, he split, right?"

Kyler took a deep breath and let it out slowly, feeling the hurricane of emotions raging within her. She loved skating, loved heroin, didn't want nothing more than to skate as hard and as far as she could, felt she couldn't take another breath until she had more heroin thrumming through her veins.

"Yeah."

"Talked to him since?"

"No," she rolled over on her back and stretched out, trying to straighten the knot her stomach had become. "He's only in my dreams now."

That statement cut her harder than she expected, and she felt the pain in her throat, sharp as a fishhook.

"Can we try to sleep now?" She asked, looking at Barb.

"Yeah," Barb put her cigarette out and turned off the light. "I'm sorry."

Kyler seemed not to hear her, as she turned again on her side and reached for her skateboard. "All I wanna do is skate," her voice came out a soft mutter. "If I can just do that, then maybe the nightmares'll go away and maybe I won't wanna get high so much anymore."

CHAPTER 10

THE NIGHTMARES DIDN'T go away; Kyler had one or two increasingly bad ones each night, followed by a miserable few minutes of puking up what little food she had in her system. The weight once more started to drop off her, but she barely noticed as she was wrapped up in surreal images from these nightmares that stayed with her throughout the day.

It was a little after two a.m. one morning when she bolted awake, shaking, gasping for breath. She rolled out of bed and barely made it to the toilet before everything came up in a steaming rush. Her knees buckled and she fell hard on the cold floor.

For a long moment she just lay there, trying to grab hold of some kind of control, but her mind returned again and again to the pictures in her mind that the nightmare had left her with.

Finally she was able to gain her feet a little at a time, and managed to stagger out of the bathroom. Barb's bed was empty; Kyler was alone in the room and her eyes found the partially-opened window.

She thought of Lamont, who'd promised to call and so far hadn't. That hurt more than a little bit, and Kyler surveyed the empty room and clenched her jaw against the wave of despair that threatened to wash over her.

Turning, she pulled open the door and stepped out into the hallway. Holding onto the wall as much for balance as a way to keep reality from fading back, she walked slowly towards the payphone near the cafeteria.

Finding some change in her pocket, she dropped it in the slot and punched in the numbers from memory with a badly shaking hand.

Lamont answered on the third ring. "Hello?"

"Doc," Kyler's voice came across the line sound exhausted and trembling. "Sorry I woke you up."

"You didn't," he tossed his keys on the table and fell heavily into a chair. "Just walked in the door." He paused and scrubbed a hand across his own tired eyes. "What's wrong?"

Kyler slid down the wall and hugged her knees to her chest. She gave a heavy sigh and he heard the hopelessness in it. "I just needed to hear a sane voice for a minute."

Lamont was quiet, hearing the hurt in her voice, and feeling his own hurt in his heart. "What's wrong, kid?" He repeated quietly.

She was silent, trying to hold her slippery rein on the wild emotions that threatened to tear her apart.

"I can't help you if you won't talk to me."

"Doc," a tear slid down her cheek and she wiped it away absently. "Why the fuck didn't you just let me die? Jesus, I'm no good at this, and there ain't no way in hell I can stay clean when I get outta here."

A brief flash of anger reared up in him and he savagely pushed it back. "Yes, you can, Kyler. I know you can, and so do you."

She shut her eyes against the remnants of the nightmare still pulsing around her. "I can't sleep," she muttered. "I haven't slept in like a week, Doc. My stomach's a wreck . . . can't keep nothin' down. I keep . . . keep havin' these bad dreams about . . . shootin' dope, and about this . . . friend I had once. And about . . ." she swallowed and pulled a battered pack of cigarettes from her pocket. "About all that shit I did to get the smack I needed and I swore that was the lowest point of my fucking life and how I'd *never* go back to that, *never* do that shit again.

"And then I wake up shaking, thinking if I could just get one fix all this shit would get outta my head and I'd be ok again, you know, even if it's just for a little while."

Lamont was silent for a long time, his own heartache battling for attention over Kyler's voice, filled with fear, exhaustion, and a never-ending hunger coming across the wire to his ear.

"It's just instant gratification, kid," he finally said quietly. "One fix *will not* stop the nightmares, you know that. It'll only make them worse. And it won't make *you* better, either, because one's not enough for you. In a matter of hours, probably, you'll be right back out there, doing the same shit you always did just to get that next taste. Chasin' that next high, and the one after that, and the one after that.

"It's a circle that won't end unless you *hold on* and *keep* holding on. You're strong enough to do that, Kyler. You're strong enough to hold on and hold on and hold on until you can stand on your own and go an hour without thinking about getting high.

"And then that hour will turn into a day, and the day will turn into a week. And you just keep holding on and doing what you need to do to stay clean, and then you hold on some more."

He stopped and took a deep breath, glancing around his kitchen, bare now, without Emily's things. "Eventually you'll find some happiness again. Some reason for living."

Kyler leaned her head back against the wall and swallowed heavily. Another tear slipped from the corner of her eye and she brushed it away, thinking she deserved all this; thinking of Josh and his deep, sea-blue eyes; the heat of his body next to hers; the love she felt from him as he held her.

"Hold on," Lamont's voice was soft in her ear. "Hold on, Kyler, ok? I *promise* you it'll get better."

"Yeah," she responded. "Ok. Thanks, Doc."

"No problem. You can call me anytime you need to, ok? Did I give you my cell number in case I'm not here?"

"I think so," she said. "I got it written down somewhere, I think. Emily's, too." She paused and took a deep, shuddering breath, willing back some control. "She doin' all right?"

Lamont was silent and across the line Kyler sensed something. "Shit," she muttered.

"Look, kid, I'll call you tomorrow, ok?" He had to work hard to keep his voice even and neutral. "I got some things I need to go over with you about that halfway house and whatnot."

"Yeah," Kyler answered. "Ok. Talk to you tomorrow." She hung up without waiting for an answer, and then just stood there for a minute, feeling her own hurt, sensing Lamont's, worried for Emily and her son, wondering where Barb had taken off to . . . and if her friend maybe gave it all up for one last hit.

CHAPTER 11

"Hey," Barb slid into a chair across from her in the cafeteria early the next morning. Kyler sat with barely enough food on her tray to feed a small dog, and none of it had been touched.

"Hey," she murmured wearily. "What's up?"

"Two things," she passed Kyler a small hardback Twenty-four Hour book and a candy bar that had been opened. "Got this from a friend of mine; thought it might help you. I took a bite; hope you don't mind." Barb's eyes drilled into hers and Kyler picked up the message.

"Ok," she said slowly. "Thanks. You coulda left it by my bed."

"That's the other thing," Barb lit a cigarette and looked across the table at her. "You got a visitor. He's waiting in the room."

Kyler's eyebrows shot up. "He?"

Barb nodded. "Older guy, nice looking."

Pushing her tray away, Kyler grunted and stood up. "Probably either a cop or my doctor," she sighed. Gently she picked up both the book and the candy bar, being especially careful with the open end, and slid them into the loose pockets of her baggy jeans.

"Thanks. I'll catch ya later, all right?"

"Yeah," Barb nodded and reached for her tray. "I'll finish this off, if you don't mind." Kyler flapped a vague hand and headed out the door.

Lamont was sitting on her bed when she walked in the room, and she gave a heavy sigh, leaning against the doorjamb.

"Doc," she said softly, "you didn't have to come. I just had a bad night and things look pretty fucking dramatic at two in the morning, you know?"

He nodded and offered a small smile. "I just thought you'd like some company," he shrugged. "Even if it *is* only me."

Kyler smiled back and walked over to Barb's side of the room. She pulled both the candy bar and book from her pockets and set them on her dresser, then lay down on her bed. "You're 'bout the only person I got left who'd wanna come see me, anyway, and I appreciate it."

She pressed the heels of her hands hard against her eyes, and Lamont's brow furrowed as he looked at her. Her jeans were real loose around her waist; hanging low on her hips. He noticed her ribs sticking out and the concavity of her sunken stomach.

"Shit," his voice was somewhat of a growl, "you weren't lyin' when you said you weren't eating much."

Kyler shrugged and sat up to light a cigarette. "I told ya the food's not staying down too well here lately. Nightmares are gettin' too it, I guess." She met his gaze with her exhausted, bloodshot eyes and took a long draw off her smoke.

"Emily left, didn't she?"

Lamont gazed back at her for a long moment, his eyes hard. "Yeah."

"What happened?"

He shook his head and clenched his jaw. "Curtis . . . uh . . . he OD'd a week and a half ago. But before that, he shot up a liquor store and wounded the girl working the counter. Took less than sixty bucks from the register."

Lamont's gaze burned into hers. "They're pushing for armed robbery and attempted murder, but he already had three years on the shelf. If he lives, he's headed to prison for a long time."

Kyler took a deep draw off her smoke and regarded him. "He got a good shot at makin' it?"

"No," Lamont shook his head. "Coke and speed . . . wired to the max. He had a massive heart attack that did major damage. Right now he's on a ventilator." He shifted his eyes away towards the window.

"Emily's . . . been vague, from what I've gotten from her. And she's got a right to be. He's her son. Each detail she tells me she has to *feel*, you know?"

Kyler nodded and crushed out her cigarette. "Yeah," she muttered softly.

"Anyway," he took a deep breath and cleared his throat, looking back at her. "How you doing?"

She shrugged. "Wanna go for a walk? Get outta here? These walls kinda close in on me sometimes."

"Sure," he stood up. "Claustrophobic?"

Kyler offered a small nod. "Yeah." She started out the door but stopped and looked back when he called her name.

"Wanna take this?" He held up her skateboard. She hesitated for so long that he wasn't sure she would. But then she reached out a hand and took it from him.

"You act like you don't," Lamont fell into step beside her as they walked down the hallway.

She glanced briefly at her board. "I've only skated once since I got here, and it was that night that bad dreams started. I told my roommate I mighta opened up a door that's better left closed."

Lamont grunted. "Maybe. Or maybe it's just something in you that's gotta get out, and it was gonna come out later anyway." He paused, considering his words as he pushed the door open for her and followed her out into the bright sunshine.

"Are you skating in these dreams?"

"Some of them," Kyler answered quietly. "Sometimes it's . . . that friend of mine. He . . . taught me to skate, and skating's one of the three things I've ever really loved in this life."

She stopped and slid onto the top of a picnic table, resting her board across her knees. Lamont sat beside her, close, but aware of distrust she still had of him. He felt her distance and sat far enough away to respect it.

"What're the other two?"

Kyler swallowed and gently spun a wheel, seeming to take comfort in its easy revolution. "Him," her voice was soft, barely audible. "And heroin."

There was silence between them for a few long minutes. She felt that familiar ache in her heart, thinking of Josh, and felt a rare kindred spirit in Lamont, knowing he was missing Emily.

"I got ya something," he said finally, reaching into his pants pocket. Kyler looked at him with an eyebrow raised and that distrust again in her gaze. He pulled out a length of silver chain with a medallion dangling from it.

"It's—"

"Saint Christopher," she gave a small smile, taking it gently in her hands. Her fingertips traced another form on the back, and she turned it over to reveal another saint. "And . . . ?"

"Saint Anthony," he responded. "Finder of the lost. I figured you probably travel a lot, and Chris, there, will keep you safe. And if you get lost along the way, Tony'll lead ya back." He stopped and stared at her. "Are you Catholic?"

"No," Kyler reached behind her head, trying to hook the lobster-claw clasp. "But I was in a Catholic orphanage the first seven or eight years of my life. I still remember some of it."

"Here," Lamont reached for her, and without thinking, she flinched away from him. He saw a look of hardness come into her eyes and she clenched her teeth.

"Sorry," she muttered. "Reflex."

"S'ok," he said quietly and gently hooked the clasp with his fingertips, being careful not to touch her. Kyler took the medallion in her hand and let it slide off to hit gently against her shirt.

"Thanks," she said, gazing at him.

"You're welcome," Lamont nodded. "Maybe they'll help keep your demons at bay."

"Maybe," she responded. She stared out over the parking lot for a minute and then looked back at him. "Wish I had something to give you to keep yours away."

"Ah," Lamont took a deep breath and let it out slowly. "Everybody's got 'em, kid. Mine'll probably go away eventually."

Kyler swallowed and reached for the necklace on her chest again. "I really am sorry, Doc. And what I said last night makes me sound like an ungrateful bitch, I know."

He shook his head. "It's no big deal, Kyler, really. You were hurting, and I'm just glad I answered the phone, gave you somebody to talk to."

"Yeah," she said softly, and gave a wheel on her skateboard another spin. Lamont watched for a second and then took a deep breath. Kyler shot him a look, eyebrows raised in question.

"Emily was, uh . . . acting as a sort of liaison between me—your primary physician, as of this time . . . hope you don't mind," he offered a quick smirk, "and the court system." She watched his smile fade a bit as he gathered his thoughts.

"She had to step aside, you know . . ."

"Yeah," Kyler nodded, watching him.

"So now it's just me, going back and forth with the court on the charges against you." Lamont ran a hand through his hair. "There's a halfway house down on Kennedy Street with a spot open for you in four months. It's on the bus line between the hospital and Beaumont, and there's about four or five places within walking distance where NA meetings are held."

Kyler gave a slow nod, staring absently across the lot. "Women only?"

"Women only," Lamont agreed.

"And these NA meetings . . . I guess I gotta go to 'em, right?"

"Two meetings a day for two months, mandatory. Once in the house, you'll be assigned a drug counselor who'll give you a weekly paper to get signed at the meetings. This'll be submitted to the court as a way of showing you're serious about getting straight."

She nodded again and pulled her cigarettes from her pocket. Lamont watched her light one and then her eyes met his.

"Community service?"

"One thousand hours."

Kyler let the smoke filter out of her nose and he could see her mind working.

"What's on Beaumont?" She asked.

He smiled and reached into his jacket pocket. "Got something else for you." He handed her roughly a dozen four by six photographs and watched as her eyes widened a bit when she stared at the first one.

"What do you see?" He asked.

Kyler felt her heart beating steadily against her ribs, excitement and fear mixing in her eyes.

"This what I think it is?"

"What do you think it is?"

"A ramp," she muttered softly. "Tore up as hell, probably warped and rotted . . ." she trailed off, looking through the stack of pictures. "Mini ramp," she said absently, mainly to herself. "Something that looks like it mighta once been a flatland . . ."

Lamont watched as she slowly sifted through the pictures, and then went through them again. Her eyes were narrow and intent, seemingly staring a hole through each glossy.

"Where's this at?" Kyler asked quietly.

"Beaumont Avenue," he responded. "Right now it's being managed by a friend of mine. I gave him a call when I found out you skated, and for the past month the three of us—me, him, and Emily—have been back and forth with each other, the court . . . you name it.

"John—my friend—is a horse trainer and lives in Kentucky. He's usually only here when he's got a race, but . . ." he paused, sorting out his words. "You can see the park's in pretty bad shape. He's been trying to put it back together, but it's hard 'cause he doesn't live here, you know?"

"So why's he got it?"

"Tax write-off, mainly. It kinda fell into his hands a couple years back and he thought he could do something with it, but now it's getting to be too much."

"And he'd let me work off my thousand hours there?" Kyler looked at him with something like incredulity and a huge amount of distrust in her eyes. "Why? He doesn't even know me."

Lamont met her gaze and shrugged. "You want to?"

"You know I do," she muttered, staring at him.

"He's got to get back to Kentucky. This skate park's been around for years, kid, but it's been passed off to so many people that eventually most people, I guess, pretty much forgot about it. It's behind a locked fence and the grass is so fuckin' high that it's hard to even see what's back there.

"John wants to keep it, if only for the tax write-off. But like I said, it was getting to be too much so he was just gonna go ahead and let the city have it back."

"Where it would no doubt be turned into a Seven-Eleven or something," Kyler said, somewhat bitterly.

"Basically, you came along at the right time," Lamont looked at her. "No offense."

She shrugged, flipping through the pictures again. "None taken. Actually, I'm a little floored right now."

He gave a soft laugh. "I imagine." He paused and glanced down at the top picture. "You think it can be saved?"

"Oh, yeah," Kyler answered immediately. "Everything that I can see right here is salvageable. It's just a matter of doing the work. Which," she glanced up at him, "I can do."

"Really?"

"Yeah," her eyes were back on the pictures again, and he saw again that mixture of excitement and fear.

"Ok," he grinned. "I'll tell him. He'll probably call you sometime soon, I guess, just to go over some things. Then once you get in the house, he said he'd meet you over there one day and show you exactly what needs to be done." Lamont met her gaze. "How good are you on a computer?"

"Actually," Kyler gave him a somewhat sheepish smile. "Not bad at all. I, uh . . . used to, on occasion, jump into a hard drive here and there."

"Oh, yeah?" Lamont raised his eyebrows. "This one of those things I don't wanna know about?"

"Probably," Kyler said, standing up and stretching. "What I was doing wasn't exactly legal."

"Then I don't wanna know."

"No," she said smiled, but it didn't quite touch her eyes, "you don't."

They started back towards the building, but Lamont stopped and faced her. "You won't do that there, will you? Stupid illegal shit on the computer?"

"No," she said seriously, meeting his eyes. "That illegal shit always had to do with the drugs. Skating was always better for me . . . cleaner." Kyler sighed and stared down at the skateboard she carried. "I'm tired of getting high, you know?"

Lamont stared deep into her dark eyes, trying to see behind the screen. Finally he nodded and shoved his hands in his pockets. "Ok, kid. I'm gonna hold you to that."

"I know you will," she said quietly.

There was silence for a minute, and then he cleared his throat. "Ok, well, I'm gonna head on outta here, all right? Call me if you need anything."

"I will," Kyler promised. "Thanks again, Doc, for everything."

"You're welcome." He reached out to shake her hand, but Kyler awkwardly gave him a brief hug. He gently folded his arms around her, still feeling her resistance, distrust, and fear.

He had to wonder at all she'd been through, and how much it would take to get her to trust him . . . or at least not have fear in her eyes every time she looked at him.

Barb was lying on her bed with the NA book when Kyler walked back in. She raised her eyebrows and grinned.

"Been out skating?"

"No," Kyler shook her head and walked over to Barb's dresser and gently picked up the open candy bar. "Thought about it, but I was just out talkin' to my doctor." She cautiously peeled back the wrapper and poured seven small blue pills into her hand.

Her eyes met Barb's and she felt huge relief pouring through her. "Valium."

"I got tired of both of us not sleeping," Barb said. "And when I do manage to sleep, you talk the whole night through and that just wakes me up."

Kyler grinned and dry-swallowed two of the pills. "Yeah, I know. Sorry." She paused, considering. "How much?"

"Don't worry about it," Barb flapped a hand. "Just consider it a thank you for hangin' out with me and being my friend." Her eyes were serious as they stared into Kyler's. "Don't have too many of them, you know?"

"Yeah," Kyler pulled the cellophane from her cigarette pack and carefully wrapped the remaining pills in it, and then put them back in the far corner of her dresser drawer, behind her socks. "I know. Me, neither."

She crawled up into her bed and stared at her with one eye visible from under the pillow. "Who from?"

Barb hesitated and then said quietly. "I've been seeing that guy from the men's unit, the one with the long dark ponytail?"

Kyler thought, and figured she maybe knew who he was.

"Anyway, his name's Jimmy, and . . . well, you know . . . he kinda makes me happy." Barb's eyes turned accusatory for a brief moment as she thought Kyler would say the same thing about the brief relationships that rarely make it past the time spent in treatment.

"If he makes you happy," Kyler looked at her, "then I think you should hold onto that. There's not too much for people like me and you that can make us happy beyond a needle full of heroin." She paused and fingered the silver necklace against her skin. "Not yet, anyway."

Barb smiled, relieved. "Thanks, Kyler."

"Yeah," Kyler burrowed deeper into the bed. "Thank *you* for the pills. And thank Jimmy, too. No sleep was really starting to get on my nerves."

Barb didn't answer as she watched Kyler succumb to the magic of the valium. Once her light snores began to fill the room, she gave a small smile and then turned back to her book; occasionally making notes in the margins or on the notebook beside her.

CHAPTER 12

TWO DAYS LATER, Kyler was sent to talk to her counselor. She thought it was yet another attempt to try to convince her to convince Barb to go ahead and have an abortion. Kyler had been in to talk to both hers and Barb's counselors multiple times in the past month because of her friendship with Barb. But that friendship was also used as a leverage to push Kyler into talking with Barb—seriously—about the effects her previous heroin abuse would have on her unborn child; the risks and problems that were predicted, and the handicaps her child would most likely face . . . if it even survived.

Kyler never told Barb about these meetings with the counselors and never intended to. She was being used and she knew it, and it pissed her off. It also pissed her off that they just could not accept Barb's final decision, and they were determined to do whatever it took to abort the baby.

In the deep hours of the night, when neither one of them could sleep, they had talked about the baby, and the risks, and the hardships of single motherhood without drug addiction, and the almost-impossibility of it with a monkey strapped to your back.

Kyler knew that Barb had thought everything through, and then thought it through again. She was well aware of what she was getting in to, researching it extensively and exhaustively through books, magazines, and newspaper articles she'd managed to get from God knows where. She didn't say and Kyler didn't ask.

But Kyler *did* ask her about potential baby names, and what she thought the baby might look like. She asked her what Jimmy thought about it all, and if there was a chance the three of them might make it as a family outside the walls of the treatment center.

She asked her about the things that were important to Barb at that particular time in her life, and kept on being her friend above anything else.

On this certain day, though, it was not about Barb. To Kyler's surprise, it was a meeting about her drug use, about her attempt at getting clean, about her legal problems and the back-and-forth negotiations with the court, and about the half-way house, the thousand hours community service, and the five grand it had taken to get all the charges lessened.

"What?" Kyler asked her counselor, eyebrows raised.

"You've been in some kind of legal trouble or another for the past year or so," her counselor consulted a piece of paper in front of her. "And your actions were gradually escalating. You went before a certain judge on more than one occasion, and with this last possession charge, she was more than willing to put you away for a long time."

She glanced up at Kyler. "Legally, we have to direct your progress here towards the case—or *cases*—against you, and thus far, we've done that. We've also been communicating somewhat with your doctor . . . the one who was here two days ago?"

It seemed like her counselor was expecting something, so Kyler gave a slight nod, and then asked, "Why?"

"Our original negotiator was a woman named Emily. Due to some personal problems, she had to step aside and so instructed us to liaise with this Doctor Lamont. The charges pending are based first on your total cooperation—which you've established you're willing to do, correct?"

Again, Kyler nodded, the wheels in her mind turning. "Doc didn't say nothing about talking with you guys. He just told me he'd taken over talking to the courts."

Her counselor nodded. "That's not really surprising. We try not to overwhelm our patients with legalities. Our main purpose here is to help you get clean, and then show you how to live life outside these walls without drugs."

Kyler was silent for a long time, regarding her counselor. It was not her nature to readily trust many people, and with this new information regarding both her attempt to stay clean and her current legal troubles, she felt even less trust than just a mere fifteen minutes ago.

"What about the five grand? What's that about?"

"That money is in lieu of reduced charges and fines for past crimes. It was an amount established by the court system that goes hand in hand with the reduced amount of community service hours you're to serve once you leave here."

Kyler swallowed, her mouth dry, her mind working. "What was the original amount of hours?"

"Twenty-five hundred."

"Reduced why? 'Cause my doctor forked over five grand?" Her voice was bitter and angry. She watched her counselor raise her eyebrows, which spiked her anger even more.

"That and you seem to be willing." She paused, pen tapping against paper. "Are you?"

"Yeah," Kyler snapped, standing up. "But it might help me feel more willing if you guys would quit doing all this secretive bullshit behind my back. Fuck, it's *me* you're talking about. Why don't you just fucking talk about it *to* me, instead of *about* me?"

"Kyler," the soothing voice was more irritating than anything, "just calm down, ok? This wasn't done behind your back. We just felt it was in your best interest to focus more on you staying clean than—"

"Forget it," Kyler snapped. "Do me a favor, all right? Don't think you can fix me by holding out on me. Next time you wanna talk, talk *to* me. Otherwise, don't even fucking bother sayin' hi."

She left the room, slamming the door hard behind her. She felt her heart hammering hard against her sternum, anger thrumming thickly through her veins. Without thinking, she grabbed her board out of the room, briefly meeting Barb's startled gaze, and then left, headed down the hallway and out into the warm air of the early morning.

Brain buzzing, rage burning through her soul, Kyler hit the parking lot skating hard. She rode her board aggressively, anger and rage lending speed and maneuverability to her run. She wasn't aware of the slowly gathering crowd on the edge of the concrete; focused only on skating the poisonous rage out of her system before it burned a hole in her sense of reality.

Christ, her mind moaned, *I'd give anything for a loaded spike right now. A line of coke or a shot of speed. Any kind of pill to get me off. Fucking anything to get me up there.*

The more she thought, the harder she skated, pulling every turn, every trick, every twist and flip from her dusty memoirs; intentionally thinking of Josh in order to lend more anger to her heart.

Across the parking lot, from one end to another, Kyler skated hard and fast, willing the calming sensation of the rubber wheels on hard concrete to soothe her jagged emotions. Finally, exhausted and worn out, she stepped off her board and collapsed on the grass.

Barb knelt beside her, concerned, as Kyler took one ragged breath after another. "What happened?" She asked quietly.

Kyler shook her head and struggled to her feet with Barb's help. "These fuckers here . . ." she shook her head and glared at the building. "Fuck, I don't know if they're actually tryin' to help us or just piss us off."

"Probably piss us off," Barb gently led her back inside. "But I'm havin' my kid, Kyler, and they can't stop me. Whatever they did to you, don't let 'em beat you, ok?"

Kyler sighed heavily and stared at the floor. "Fuck," she muttered tiredly.

"Hey," a new voice came from behind them, easy and male. "You ok?"

She glanced back, eyes narrowed. Barb gently took the young man's hand and looked at Kyler with a raised eyebrow.

"Jimmy, this is Kyler. Kyler, Jimmy."

"Hey," she muttered. "Thanks for the . . . candy bar."

Jimmy smiled and offered his hand. "No problem. Barb said you guys were havin' a rough time."

Kyler shook his hand automatically, eyes on his, trying to see past the screen. This was the guy Barb had taken a liking to, and this was also the guy who just might break her heart and send her right back to the needle.

Right now she was clean, and getting better day by day. But she was an addict, plain and simple, and she was an addict first, before anything else . . . including a mother.

Kyler hoped he wouldn't bolt, leaving her to choose between her kid and that fucking monkey on her back.

"You were pretty good out there," he jerked a thumb over his shoulder. His eyes were soft on hers, trying to read her as much as she was trying to read him.

She shrugged. "I was angry, and I tend to skate better that way. It motivates me, I guess."

He nodded and grinned. "Don't I know it. But, listen, guys, I gotta head on back over. It was nice to meet you, Kyler."

"You, too."

They watched him walk out the door and then Barb turned to her. "You wanna get something to eat?"

"No," Kyler said. "I gotta make a phone call. I'll see you later, ok?"

"Sure," Barb nodded, and watched as Kyler headed towards the pay phone down at the end of the hall.

When the phone on Lamont's desk rang, he absently picked it up instead of letting it go into voicemail.

"Doctor Lamont."

"Doc," Kyler's voice, shaking with rage, came across the wire. "You didn't tell me anything about the five grand you put up for me."

"What?" He asked slowly.

"Five thousand dollars, Doc," she snarled. *"I don't have that; you* know *I don't have that."*

"Kyler," he muttered, "stop for a second, all right?"

"Why?" And now he heard fear as well as rage in her voice. "Why the fuck'd you do it?"

"Look," he said quietly, "I did it because at the time it was all or nothing. That judge you pissed off? She wanted the money right then or there were not going to be any negotiations on your behalf, get it? It was a reduced fine and a reduced amount of hours that I was asking for, and between me, Emily, and the people there at Harmon's, we got it for you."

"I don't like owing people," she growled softly. "And I don't like not knowin' what the hell's goin' on with my own life."

"I know," Lamont responded. "Believe me, I wanted to tell you, but your counselor and a few others thought it'd be better if I didn't. But I never thought *they'd* tell you, and the money was never supposed to've been brought up at all."

"Doc," Kyler leaned against the wall, "I don't *have* the money."

"Don't worry about the money, ok, Kyler? Shit, right now that should be the least of your worries."

There was silence for a long moment. In the hallway, Kyler was shaking, now more from fear than rage. The prospect of owing that much money threw panic into her system and made her stomach twist up in a hard knot.

"I'm sorry," Lamont said softly. "I'm beginning not to like some of their, uh, methods up there at that treatment center."

She didn't answer, although she couldn't agree more.

"Kyler, you there?"

"Yeah," and now her voice was so quiet it was hard to hear. She murmured something, and Lamont strained against the ear piece but couldn't catch it.

"What?" He asked. "I missed that."

"I said . . ." Kyler swallowed heavily, her stomach twisting even tighter, "I don't want to have to pay you back in trade. I don't want that, Doc, all right?"

Silence dropped like a bomb on the line, thick and suffocating. Kyler absently wiped away the tears running from her eyes, stomach twisted, heart pounding. In the back of her mind, she knew she didn't have too much longer before her stomach revolted and uploaded everything in it.

"Oh. Jesus, Kyler," Lamont said softly. He ran a hand through his hair and began to recognize the hate in his gut for these people who were getting this kid clean by throwing a bunch of shit in her head.

Across the wire she heard him take a deep breath and let it out slowly. "Listen to me, ok?" His voice was hard with a rage of his own. *"I will never ask that of you. I will never ask you to do any of that, all right?"*

He took another deep breath, trying to get a hold of his anger. "The money went to help you and I'm sorry I didn't tell you about it, but I didn't do it so you'd have to . . ." he stopped, unable to finish.

"Christ, those idiots up there don't know what the fuck they're doing," he said angrily.

Silence again. Kyler wanted to believe him, but the past eight months or so of her life had led her to believe the worst in people, had taught her that people lie, and that men were usually after just one thing and would do anything or tell any certain lie just to get it.

"You don't have to believe me, kid," his voice was quiet in her ear, seemingly reading her mind. "But just remember that *I* didn't tell you about that money, ok? *They* did. Don't you think if I wanted a . . . repayment . . . I'd've told you myself? Wouldn't that make more sense?"

Kyler took a deep, shuddering breath and then had to swallow back the bile that rose in her throat. "I don't know, Doc," she said shakily. "I'm just . . . I'm just tired, and I just . . . wanna be able to look in just one person's eyes and be able to find at least a little trust, you know? But, Christ, it's just so fuckin' hard . . ."

"I know," he said softly. "And I'm not asking for your complete trust, ok? But I *am* asking that you believe me on this one thing. *I will* not *ever ask you to do anything like that.* I promise you that with everything I got."

"All right, look, Doc, I gotta go. I'll talk to you later." Kyler hung up the phone, her stomach churning, and pushed open the door to the restroom. The first empty stall she came to, she collapsed in front of the toilet and miserably heaved up acid and a small amount of food.

She hung her head and closed her eyes against the spinning walls, feeling the sweat on her body amid the acres of goose bumps that covered every inch of her skin.

"Christ," she mumbled and drew her knees up to her chest. She wrapped her arms around her legs and laid her forehead on her knees, wishing—just wishing just this one wish—that the pain would stop for one minute. That she could walk through this world for sixty seconds without feeling any kind of pain or fear.

Barb was gone from the room when Kyler finally made it back. Without thinking, she quickly popped three valiums and sprawled across her bed, willing them to work fast and hard. At that moment, she wanted nothing more than to sleep long and solid, and with no dreams whatsoever.

CHAPTER 13

THAT ENDLESS DAY finally came to an end, and eventually, so did the rest of the week and the rest of the month. Kyler was able to relax a little bit more, and as Barb's belly started to grow and Jimmy started coming around more, the three of them formed a reluctant friendship that swiftly became tight-knit and protective.

Barb's pregnancy helped to bring them together, and as the weeks became months the excitement of a newborn child, coupled with the anxiety of its condition from the heroin use, quickly became the center of their bond.

Kyler soon began to realize that Jimmy was in it for the long haul, and because of that, her respect for him grew tremendously, as well as her trust that he wasn't going to leave Barb anytime soon.

Her last day in rehab was bittersweet, and she was apprehensive about her chances out in the world without any drugs. The three of them—her, Barb, and Jimmy—were sitting at the picnic area in the back of the complex. Barb reached over and hugged her friend and felt her fear in the shaking of her body. She pulled back to look at her . . . almost *glare* at her.

"You're gonna be ok," she growled. "You got numbers, right? Mine, Jimmy's? Your doc's? Use 'em, and it don't fuckin' matter what time it is. Day or night, call me, ok? Don't try to fight this battle on your own."

"You gotta help us raise this kid, Kyler," Jimmy pitched in quietly, and Kyler could see the fear in his eyes, as well. Fear for her or for the kid or for having to raise the kid without dope, she had no idea. But it helped that they needed her, and needed her straight for it all to work out right.

"Yeah," Kyler muttered. "I know. I will."

"And the house . . . your doctor's got you all set up in that?" Barb asked.

"Yeah. And the job, too."

"Ah, right," Jimmy grinned. "Workin' off your time, doin' the one thing you love most? Shit, Kyler, wish I could get that lucky."

"You don't like doing anything," Barb smiled at him.

He arched an eyebrow and winked at Kyler. "Sure, I do. I love doin'—"

"Don't say it," Barb grinned. "This is about Kyler, ok? She's leaving and she doesn't wanna take your freakish sexual ideas with her."

"Yeah, Jim, I'd really rather not have to have that shit in my head," Kyler smiled but it was strained and distant. Both Jimmy and Barb could see their light banter wasn't doing much for the apprehension she was feeling.

"You're gonna be fine," Barb said, more gently now. "Ok? You and your doc back on good terms?"

"We were never on bad terms," Kyler gazed across the parking lot and took a deep drag on her cigarette. "Just a misunderstanding, I guess."

"But you're ok now, right? He's not gonna leave you hanging?" She persisted.

"No . . ." With her fingertips she gently touched the Saint Christopher's medal hanging around her neck. Taking a deep breath, Kyler pitched her cigarette out into the grass and stood up. "I'll be ok," her voice held conviction she didn't really feel.

"Yeah," Barb stood up with her. "You will. And you're gonna still call? Even if you don't really need nothin' except to bitch about life on the straight side?"

Kyler grinned. "Life on the straight side's already too good to bitch about, you know that. No more gettin' beat up or driving my self-respect into the ground, right? I got this . . ." she gestured to her skateboard lying in the middle of the table. "Got you guys."

She took another deep breath and stared across the lot again. "A whole new life out there . . ."

Jimmy lightly squeezed the back of her neck. "Call, though, ok? Sometimes . . . maybe just every once in a while."

"I will," she smiled a somewhat sad smile. "Done lost too many people in my life. I'd like to keep in touch with you guys so I don't lose you, too."

"Ok," Barb agreed. "And I'll call you, too."

Kyler nodded. "I'll get you the skate park's number when I get there. And you got Doc's?"

"Uh . . ." Barb pulled a piece of paper from her pocket. "Yeah. Both the place you're staying at and your doctor's."

"Ok, then . . ." Kyler hesitated, looking at her friends. "Ok." She ran a hand through her hair. "I'll be all right."

"Yeah, you will," Jimmy pulled her into another gruff hug before giving her a gentle shove towards the end of the building and the street beyond. "And you need to get going before you miss your bus."

She gave another small nod and started off down the sidewalk before the fear she felt froze her in place. She tried to keep the last six months of being drug-free at the forefront of her mind . . . how it felt to have finally gotten over the shakes, convulsions, the feel of ten million bugs eating her alive.

Walking again, with her head held up, not having to worry about her next fix . . . where she'd get it, what she'd do for it . . . and how long before she had it.

Kyler stuck another cigarette in her mouth and sat down on the graffiti-covered bus stop bench; five minutes to spare and having to wait with her stomach churning.

"Fuck, how'm I gonna do this?" She whispered to herself, scrubbing a hand hard across her face. "How'm I gonna even last one day out here?"

She looked up as the bus rounded the corner and when it stopped she climbed aboard wearily, already exhausted with her day just barely started.

"Kyler Maddox?" The woman greeted her at the front door of the halfway house with a thin smile. "We expected you a half hour ago."

"I got lost," Kyler mumbled, feeling guilty for an unknown reason . . . and angry, as well, at the look of suspicion on the woman's face.

"Sure," she said. "That happens. I'm Wanda Simms. Here," she handed Kyler a plastic cup and pointed down a hallway. "Just so we start off on the right foot, ok?"

Now she felt shame mixed with the anger, and tried to calm it down by telling herself she'd gotten her own self into this . . . nobody else stuck a needle in her vein.

"Sure," she muttered and started down the hall.

"Wait," Wanda put a hand on her backpack. "I need to check this."

Kyler swallowed back rage and shrugged out of her pack, letting it fall to the floor. "Might wanna check this, too," she dropped her skateboard next to it. "Might be drugs hidden in the wheels."

For a long moment the two women glared at each other; Kyler, angry and scared; Wanda, angry and suspicious. Finally Wanda jerked a finger down the hall.

"You gonna piss in that cup?"

Without answering, Kyler turned and walked towards the bathroom, anger churning in her gut.

She was shown to her room and instructed to attend at least three NA meetings a day. She was given a meeting schedule, along with a bus schedule, and, overwhelmed and utterly exhausted, Kyler fell into bed, backed up against the wall, and tried to let sleep overtake her.

Lamont was supposed to pick her up early the next morning and take her to her new job—perhaps the only thing she was looking forward to—but even that wasn't enough to take the fear and apprehension from her.

They hadn't talked at all since the night she'd called him, and the last remaining weeks had been long. Kyler was scared, thinking about a million things, her mind jumping from one thing to another, and after about an hour of tossing and turning she gave up on sleep and just lay there, staring at the ceiling.

Around her came the snores and shifting of the other women, each lost in her own demon-filled hell; the monkeys on their backs waxing and waning depending on their various stages of recovery.

She tried to remember her time in treatment . . . meeting Barb and Jimmy, having Doc and Emily to look out for her, if only for a little while. The slow recovery. The painful release of the drug on her body. The valiums that eased her through the worst of those nights.

Skating across the parking lot.

At the thought of skating Kyler reached down and ran a hand along the deck of her board, deriving peace from it.

Tomorrow, she thought. *Doc's gonna take me to my new job where I can get the chance to build something from the ground up . . . repair the ramps . . . build new ones . . . work off the city's time doing what I love . . .*

Kyler shut her eyes as her heart gave a squeeze . . . Josh's sea-blue eyes once again invading her mind.

I miss you.

Josh and skating were always synonymous with her: with one there was always the other. It was hard to imagine him not being with her, next to her on his own board, as they skated together through life . . . and love . . .

Life. Survival. Love.

Fuck, her brain muttered. *Just shut up. Fuck. Get some sleep.*

She shoved her head under the pillow and forced her mind to be still and to quit jumping from one random thought to another. Finally, as dawn was beginning to break over the horizon, Kyler was able to fall into a light doze.

CHAPTER 14

LAMONT GAZED AT her as she walked into the front room of the house. She was haggard . . . thin . . . eyes bloodshot from lack of sleep.

Kyler nodded to him. "Hey."

"Hey. See you made it here ok."

"Yeah." There was a pause, followed by an uncomfortable silence. Lamont reflected back on their last conversation—a stilted, shocking exchange over the phone—and wondered how much his buying her a get out of jail card had hurt her.

He wasn't *that* comfortable with his lifestyle to realize that the five grand was indeed a lot of money to her; perhaps too much . . . maybe more than she could ever expect to see in her lifetime. Yet he'd dealt it out with no other thought than trying to help this kid . . . and he'd never expected to hear that flat-out terror in her voice at the prospect of repaying him . . . or rather, at the *way* she'd thought he'd expect repayment.

"I thought about calling you . . . tell ya I'd pick you up."

"That's ok," she shrugged. "I took the bus."

Lamont nodded. "You . . . uh . . . you ready?"

"Yeah." Kyler slid by him, not looking at him. Slipping into the front seat of his car, she rested her hands lightly on the board across her lap.

"Hungry?" He got behind the wheel and started the engine. "We got time to eat."

"Nah, I'm ok."

He grunted and pulled away from the street. The radio was off and the silence pressed like a stone between them. Finally he cleared his throat and glanced at her.

"Look . . . Kyler . . . I'm sorry about . . . before. When you called me . . ."

"Forget it," her voice was hoarse. "I was just . . . mad, I guess. It came outta left field and I wasn't expecting it. I . . . actually thought they wanted to talk to me about something else . . . and . . . uh . . ." she shook her head and stared out the window. "I don't know."

Lamont didn't respond and they drove for a little while longer in silence. He pulled into a drive-thru and ordered two coffees, giving her one.

"Thanks." The coffee's warmth was heaven to her, washing away the cold and fatigue.

"Sure."

He pulled up into a parking lot on the edge of the beach and without a word, put the car in park and got out. Kyler watched as he walked across the sand to a picnic table and sat down, staring at the ocean. She debated a minute with her hand on the door handle before finally stepping out.

She slipped around the table and sat down at the far end of the bench he was on. He shot her a glance as he took a sip of coffee.

"I come out here sometimes . . . watch the dolphins."

"Don't you live by the ocean?"

"Yeah. But I still stop by here some days. You know, if I'm runnin' early and got a few minutes to spare. It's relaxing."

Kyler watched the waves pound the packed sand and thought about what it would be like to walk along in the early morning surf.

Relaxing. Comforting. The water washing away all the fear and doubt.

"The house ok?"

She shrugged. "Yeah. Sure."

"Still not sleeping, though, right?"

Kyler sighed. "It was my first night. No, I didn't sleep good. I usually don't sleeping four to a room, surrounded by people I've only known for about ten minutes."

Lamont regarded her for a long moment. "They tested you, right?"

She shot him a thin glare and he held up his hands.

"I'm not here to fight."

"I'm not using," she growled.

"I know. I just figured that's what you're pissed about."

She lit a cigarette and didn't answer.

"You were a half hour late and—"

"I got lost."

He smirked in a way that irritated her. "I doubt that."

Kyler pinched the bridge of her nose and took a deep breath, feeling anger thread through her veins.

"Somehow I'm thinking you know this city like the back of your hand. You didn't get lost."

"What's your point, Doc?"

"Talk to me. Tell me what's on your mind."

She stood up and turned on him. "What, you mean like having this five fucking grand held over my head? Like fucking walking in the door of this halfway house and the first thing I gotta do is piss in a cup? Searching my bag is one thing, ok?

But goddamn, just 'cause I was late it's automatically assumed I went out and got high?"

"I'm not holding that money over your head," he said quietly.

Kyler dropped her eyes and ran her hands through her hair. "Shit," she muttered.

Lamont waited a beat and then said gently, "Why were you late? And no, you didn't get lost."

She remained silence, staring out across the water.

"C'mon, kid, talk to me."

"What's it matter?" Her voice was low . . . nearly inaudible against the sound of the waves.

"It doesn't, I don't guess," he sighed. "Just curious."

Kyler sank back down on the bench and rested her elbows on her knees; head between hunched shoulder blades.

"I was scared," she said softly. She turned to him with hooded eyes. "Ok? Jesus, Doc."

He looked at her for a long moment. "Ok."

She didn't offer any more and he didn't ask. Finally he touched her shoulder with a gentle finger and gestured back to the car.

"C'mon, I told John I'd have you there by nine."

Silently Kyler got back in the car, more exhausted than ever. Lamont slid in behind the wheel and turned the key, but then paused and glanced over at her.

"You're gonna be fine, kid, all right? Trust me."

She didn't answer as she looked out the window, watching the world flow by in the early morning sunshine.

"Kyler? I'm John Carter," the man held out his hand and she shook it somewhat reluctantly. Lamont stood beside her and shook his hand with more warmth and with the comfort of old friendship.

"As you can see . . ." John gestured around as they walked through the knee-high weeds, "it's pretty bad. I used to keep it up—or try to, anyway, but . . ." he shrugged. "I live in Kentucky. When I'm out here I'm running horses, and that keeps me pretty busy."

Kyler didn't answer as they walked around what used to be the pool. The concrete was pitted and cracked, shot through with weeds. She stared into it for a long time before hopping down and walking it, front to back, side to side. John shot a glance at Lamont, who shrugged and shook his head.

"The flat's the same way," Kyler looked up at them with her hands on her hips, and it wasn't a question.

"Uh . . . yeah. Basically."

She nodded and jumped up, grabbed the lip and pulled herself up. "Ok," she said with a small decisive smile. "If I can skate this pool I can salvage this place."

"If you can . . . what? Kyler, look at that thing," Lamont stammered. "It's . . . rocks . . . and chunks of concrete. And weeds. You . . . can't . . ."

"Relax," now her smile became a grin. "I'm that good."

"Good at what, breaking your neck?" Lamont tried again but not very hard. That grin of hers was addictive and much-needed. She was going to skate that death trap and he was going to let her, even if it his heart wouldn't beat for the next few minutes due to fear of her splitting her head open or yes, even breaking her neck.

"She always this crazy?" John leaned over and whispered.

Lamont gave another shrug. "I haven't known her very long, but . . . I'm thinking yes."

The two men watched as Kyler went on a seemingly jagged suicidal run down into the pool, back up the other side, and then down again. Incredibly she never missed a beat, never once faltered. Lamont winced and found it hard to breathe.

Jesus Christ, and she's straight, his mind moaned. *I'd hate to see how reckless she is loaded up on smack.*

Finally she flew up one side and snagged her board effortlessly out of the air. She stood for a moment, breathing hard, staring down into the weed-choked pit she had just skated.

John walked over to her, eyebrows raised. "Did it pass the test?"

"Yeah," Kyler started back towards the building that served as the office/storage room. "It may take some time, but—"

"This place ain't on a time schedule. I mean . . ." he gestured around them. "It's a shithole, really, and I don't want you to think you *have* to do it."

She stopped and offered a small, bitter smile. "What, and work a garbage detail along a highway somewhere? Relax, John. I can do this . . . and I *want* to do this, ok?"

He looked at her and gave a reluctant shrug. "Ok."

Kyler rubbed a finger along her left eyebrow and gave him a questioning look. "One thing, though . . ."

"You're gonna need money," he responded. "How much, you think?"

She shot Lamont a quick look before resting her eyes on John's again. "I . . . don't know offhand. If I do this a little bit at a time, you think you can just give me enough for what I need at the time? And I can get you receipts on everything."

John regarded her for a moment, and then gave a slow nod. "Yeah. I'll need those for tax purposes. Uh . . . how much you think you'll need to start off?"

"Enough for a lawn mower. And wood. Lumber for the ramps." She paused, thinking. "I'm gonna need a computer."

"Yeah, I figured that. I think I can find an extra one laying around somewhere, but it'd be a good one. Have all the programs on it you'll probably need."

"Ok." She pulled a cigarette from her pack, noticed the hunger in his eyes and offered it to him.

"Uh . . ." John hesitated.

"You're trying to quit," she stuck the smoke in her mouth and lit it. "Sorry."

He shrugged. "No big deal."

Lamont stood off to the side watching them silently. This was a pivotal moment in this kid's life, he knew, and the impact she could receive from this would be instrumental in her recovery. He knew this both as a doctor and as the mere human who'd had the good enough luck to pull her from the brink.

"What about the concrete?" John gestured towards the pool, and then to the flatland beyond.

"Concrete's expensive. Lemme get the ramps first."

"O . . . k," he said slowly. "But there . . . you know . . . aren't any ramps. None that aren't much more than rotted wood, anyway."

"No, not yet." She offered a broad grin. "But there will be."

Kyler started back towards the office again with the two men trailing her. She stopped just inside the door and flicked on the overhead light. The bulbs were dusty and covered in cobwebs, but they gave off enough light for her to see there was a desk—solid wood and scarred from many years of use—and not much else.

Lamont began to feel the first implications of skepticism in his gut. Maybe he'd been wrong; it'd actually been months since he'd stepped foot in the park, and he'd never been inside the office. Its dilapidated appearance depressed him.

"Hey . . . um . . ." he began, but John cut in, obviously swimming in his own doubt.

"Kyler, look . . . I mean . . ."

She turned and regarded both men, eyebrows raised in question.

"So . . . what?" She muttered. "Either neither of you guys think I can do this or you really do think this is a shithole that can't be saved."

The two men glanced at each other, then at her. Kyler sat on the edge of the desk and waited, watching them.

"It's not that, kid . . ." Lamont started.

"I just . . . haven't been here in awhile . . . and it's . . . really bad," John offered.

"Look, I wouldn't say I could do it if I couldn't, all right? I can do this. It's gonna take some time, yeah, and a little bit of money, but I can get it done."

John stared at her, then raised his hands in surrender. "Ok, Kyler. But I'm gonna hold you to that."

"Wouldn't ask you to do anything less," she hopped off the desk. "That a bathroom I see back there?" Kyler pointed to a small room off the office that had either a bathroom or a small closet at the far end. She was hoping it was a bathroom.

"I can't guarantee its condition," he smiled. "But, yeah, it is."

"Great, hopefully we won't need to add a plumber to the list of shit we need money for."

Lamont watched her walk back to the bathroom before turning his eyes to John. "So nobody's really been here since the last time you brought me here? Not even you, I guess?"

John shook his head. "Fuck, Keith, if she can't bring it back I guess I'll have to turn it over to the city. I think this is the worst I've ever seen it."

Lamont sighed and scrubbed a hand across his face. "She said she can do it. I guess we'll see, right?"

CHAPTER 15

LESS THAN A month later Kyler had managed to change the park's appearance from something merely waiting for a flock of bulldozers to a place that could be noticed again from a positive view. The huge expanse of grass, previously buried under mounds of weeds and scrubland, was again visible and thriving under the care of the part-time lawn service she'd convinced John to hire.

"Just to get it back under control again," she'd stated. "After that I can do all the mowing and landscaping myself."

A new fence had been erected around the property; replacing old, warped boards with industrial-strength steel and iron. The front gate was new, as well, and she'd even talked John into contracting out an electrical company to install huge arc-sodium lights across the property.

The office itself had taken on a whole new look, too, but this was from John's appreciative standing. Kyler came in one morning and found new wall-to-wall carpeting laid over the previously bare concrete floor. The new computer on the desk hummed quietly and the mini-fridge standing where trash and spider webs had been just the day before was stocked with bottled water and cokes.

The note stuck under the keyboard made her smile.

> *Just wanted to make it feel less like a run-down shithole and more like a place of business. Didn't know about the desk . . . thought about a new one but something told me you might like this old beat-up thing. If not, let me know and I'll buy a new one.*
>
> *Thanks for doing this. It's huge, I know, but you've already made a difference. I'm back to Kentucky in a few hours. Here's my numbers if you need anything . . .*
>
> *John*

Kyler sat down in the chair behind the desk (the leather so new it creaked under her weight) and stared across the office. On a whim she got up and went through the storage room and into the bathroom.

The carpet extended even back this far and the cabinet under the sink was stocked with toilet paper, soap, and paper towels.

"Damn," she said. "So this shit really is for real."

"You thought it wasn't?" A voice came from behind her, and she whirled, heart in her throat.

"Sorry," Lamont held up his hands. "Didn't mean to scare you."

"That's . . . all right," she said shakily. "Nerves're still pretty bad, I guess."

He gave a small nod, watching her. "Just thought I'd stop by, see how things are going."

"Good," she managed a small smile. "Going good. You notice the office?"

"Yeah. Looks respectable now. He wanted to surprise you."

"Well, he did," Kyler led the way back to the office. "Toilet paper in the bathroom and drinks in the fridge." She pulled two waters from the fridge and handed him one. "Got lights out there now and a couple ramps all the way done. It's getting there."

"So . . . yeah . . . it's real, then, right?" He gazed at her.

"Yep," she leaned against the door jamb and looked out over the park. "I didn't mean that like it sounded. I mean, I know it's real, but . . . it's just still hard for me to believe I'm standing here, doing this, you know? After all that shit . . . laying in too many gutters . . . and now . . ." she waved a hand in front of her, encompassing the park. "I'm doing this."

"You seem awed," he took a drink of water and sat down in the chair behind the desk. "Not as confident as you were when you said you really were that good on that thing the day you skated that death trap out there."

"What, the pool?" Kyler smiled. "That's probably the only self-serving comment you'll ever hear me say, and I said it mainly for my benefit rather than yours. It was scary," she admitted. "I was trying to talk myself up."

"Glad you're telling me that now," Lamont muttered. "And here I thought you really *were* that good. I was runnin' on faith that I wouldn't have to drag you outta that thing and to the hospital for a couple hundred stitches in your head."

She shrugged and grinned. "No stitches. I didn't get hurt. And the concrete's coming in a few days so the next time I skate it it'll be smooth as glass. No worries."

Lamont grunted and stood up. "Easy for you to say. But listen, I'm gonna head on into work. You ok?"

"Yeah," she stared at him. "I'm fine."

"House and things still going good?"

"Same as ever," her eyes shifted away and his brow furrowed.

"Sure?"

"Yeah . . . I mean . . ." Kyler gestured absently. "It's a halfway house, right? The people there are ok and I'm going to meetings. Still testing negative for any drugs. I'm doin' all right, Doc, really."

His gaze bored into hers but he couldn't see past the wall that was in them. "Ok," he said quietly. "But you know my numbers, right? You can call anytime; day or night, it doesn't matter. I'm usually either working or awake anyway."

She didn't respond and he saw the pride in her dark eyes. Without waiting for an answer he slipped out the door. Kyler sat down in the chair he'd just vacated and ran her hands through her hair. Things were fine . . . better than ever, actually, but all of that was the park. When she was there it wasn't about NA meetings where there were more drugs around her than sometimes seemed possible; it wasn't about reading the NA book through and through, again and again, and struggling to work the twelve steps.

And it definitely wasn't about the halfway house and the conflict she'd been in there since that first day. Where every day was a gauntlet of misplaced rage and addiction that fueled anger and spite among the eight women who were currently residing there.

Kyler sighed and lit a cigarette, staring absently out at the park. "At least I got this," she muttered. "This keeps me sane."

Two weeks later insanity tore through her world with the destruction of a thousand earthquakes, driving her to the brink and nearly beyond.

CHAPTER 16

KYLER CAME TO in an alley just a block or two up from the beach. Her entire body had that feeling where it seemed like it had been dipped in crushed glass, and between her stomach wanting to crawl out of her throat and the shakes that racked her body, she felt complete and total despair begin to overcome her.

For the first time in a long time she began to check her body for fresh needle marks. She checked as slowly and methodically as her shattered mind would allow, feeling her stomach roll into a tighter and tighter ball with each location. She found none, anywhere, but only felt thin relief.

Because I sure as hell did something, her mind shrieked in a somewhat insane tone. *I know I snorted a shitload of coke and just* what the fuck did I do to get it? *How'd I pay for it, with what, and how much of my body was used by another psycho john just so I could get enough of what I needed to get me outta that hole?*

She moaned thickly and pulled herself shakily to her feet. Spotting a gas station on the corner, she ducked into the bathroom around the back, and only felt just a little bit safer with the door locked between her and the outside world.

Leaning against the wall, Kyler stripped off her clothes until she stood naked in front of the mirror. Her body was dirty, but not filthy, and there were no signs of blood anywhere. Sliding a shaking, exploratory hand between her legs, she encountered no new pain or bruising—nothing newer than two days old, anyway—and allowed herself one tiny bit of hope.

"Maybe I didn't fuck anybody for it this time," she muttered softly. "But if I didn't, how else did I get the cash for the coke?"

She used the tepid water and commercial soap to wash off as well as she could, and then slowly got dressed. Standing there in front of the dirty mirror, Kyler studied her own eyes and hated what she saw in them. Gruffly she turned and yanked open the door, staggering out into the bright early sunshine of the day.

The air played soft and warm against her skin, and the air she breathed in smelled strongly of the water that she currently stood so close to, and that she'd once loved as much as life itself.

Kyler turned in that direction and walked, trying to find solace deep within her soul as each step took her closer to her beloved ocean. She plopped down in the sand, alone amidst the hordes of sunbathers, surfers, and beachcombers, and just stared out at the waves as they came crashing in, one by one.

Piece by piece her heart was breaking. She felt it going, tried to stop it, but her mind insisted on repeating over and over that there was nothing—*nothing*—to hold onto anymore, and to just let it go.

Kyler took a deep breath and thought of Barb and Jimmy, and this controlled the helplessness a bit. She thought of the skate park and how she finally felt a part of something when she was there.

She thought of Josh again, and a huge chunk of her heart broke off. Tears rolled down her face, and she absently wiped them away.

And then she thought of the doc, who'd put so much faith into her already; faith that she knew she didn't deserve, but he'd given it willingly and without reservation.

Kyler gave a heavy sigh and ran a hand under her nose. It came away smeared with blood and she ground her hand into the sand, trying in vain to scrub it clean.

"If I could do the same to my fucking soul, I'd rip it out myself," she growled.

Abruptly, she stood and headed back the way she came, not allowing herself to think until she stood outside his front door, hand poised to knock. Briefly she hesitated, and then slid a finger down to the doorbell, pressing it hard.

Lamont opened the door and Kyler managed to look at him. For a split second there was a kind of dull acceptance in his eyes; a look that said *This is not really all that surprising to me . . . didn't really expect her to go all the way straight, anyway.*

It was enough to send her weak heart shattering, and Kyler crumpled to the ground. Tears poured from her eyes even as blood seeped from nose, and she was faintly aware that she'd never felt so alone; so hopeless.

And then, dimly at first, she felt his arms around her, helping her to her feet. Lamont half-carried her in, supporting most of her weight, and led her to his couch. Without a word, he laid her down and gently tilted her head so that it caught the light coming through the living room window, staring intently at her bleeding nose.

"I'll get a towel," he muttered, and he was gone before Kyler could reach out and grab him, to tell him it wasn't a towel she needed, but a bullet to the head. Another spike loaded with drain cleaner. Another two-hundred lines of coke so that hopefully she'd O.D. for good this time.

She pressed the heels of her hands hard against her eyes and never wanted to die so much as she did right then.

"Easy," his voice came soft, off to her side, and Kyler felt a gentle hand slide under her neck, easing her head back over the arm of the couch. He laid towel-wrapped ice along the bridge of her nose, held it there with one hand, and with the other began to wipe off the partially-dried blood from under her nostrils.

"What happened?" Lamont's voice was still soft, soothing. It was meant to calm her, and Kyler knew that, but never in her life had she felt less calm. Part of it was the coke still in her system and part of it was because of what had happened down at the house on Kennedy.

But most of it came from the despair and self-loathing that swamped her each time she thought about that look in his eyes when he'd opened the door. The same look that Josh had had right before he split, and it made her hate herself a little bit more with every memory.

"Kyler."

She remained silent, eyes closed, trying to dispel the demons raging inside her.

"Who did this to you?" The tip of his finger gently touched the scrape beneath her eye and then traced the purple bruise across her windpipe. Immediately the massive fear engulfed her, forcing her to remember jagged pieces of the terror and pain that had followed her for the past two days. In an instant she was up and off the couch, backing away from him, eyes wide and frightened.

Lamont gazed at her, his brow furrowed. Slowly comprehension dawned on him, and a burning anger that quickly turned to rage surfaced in his eyes.

"Who?" He growled softly.

Kyler shook her head, her whole body trembling.

"Who?"

She slid down the wall and put her head in her hands. "Doc . . ." her voice was barely audible, and Lamont, not wanting to scare her more by getting too near to her, had to strain to hear.

"Nobody. Nothing happened."

"Bullshit," he snapped. "Talk to me."

Kyler swallowed and looked away, not meeting his gaze.

With a huge effort Lamont reined in his anger, and then deliberately walked over and sat down in front of her. She flinched back, but was stopped by the wall. He saw the fear in her eyes, but also an intense anger that was borderline hatred.

"I can't help you if you won't talk to me."

The anger in her eyes hardened. "I don't need your help. I've been getting along just fine by myself for awhile now, Doc."

He regarded her with a long, level look, his own fury at what had happened to her countering hers. "Then why're you here? Why'd you show up on my doorstep at eight in the morning with a bloody nose from too much coke and a bruise around your neck like somebody tried to fucking choke the shit outta you?"

Kyler met his furious eyes steadily, but she couldn't stop the shaking in her body; shaking that came more from fear than from coke.

"Talk to me."

She took a deep, haggard breath and put her head in her hands. "I left the house," she said quietly. "Two days ago."

There was heavy silence between them for what seemed like hours to her. Finally Lamont took a deep breath and let it out slowly.

"Why?"

Kyler just looked at him with hooded eyes, feeling that fear still walking hand in hand beside her.

"At the house." It wasn't a question, and his voice was soft and full of raging anger. *"Who was he?"*

"I don't know," she swallowed and dropped her eyes to the floor. "It . . . it was dark, late at night. I had to take a leak and . . . and he was there . . . in a stall." Kyler scrubbed a hand hard across her face.

"I never even saw him coming."

"Jesus," Lamont murmured, feeling like somebody had sucker punched him. Without thinking, he reached for her, but Kyler pulled away and stood up, eyes full of that fear again, along with distrust as she stared at him. He pulled back and held his hands up.

"I'm sorry," he said quietly.

Kyler just looked at him, and then edged along the wall away from him. She fell heavily down on the couch again and sat with her elbows on her knees, staring at the floor.

"I don't know what to do," she admitted softly. "I'm probably headed to jail since I went out and got loaded again. Probably 'cause I left the house, too." She gave a heavy sigh that was almost a moan. "Fuck, I'm just so goddamned tired, Doc."

He stared at her for a minute, then shook his head slightly, trying to think past the huge things looming front of him—the rape (*rape??*, his mind wanted to skitter away from the thought), jail time for her, the coke in her system—to the smaller, more presently important things.

Lamont gazed at her, seeing the incredibly fragile balance of her emotional state shining from her dark eyes. Physically, she seemed fine, though a bit skinny. But what he saw on the outside gave no indication of the condition of her insides; what she might be carrying right now, maybe the beginnings of a fetus or a potentially fatal immune or venereal disease.

She needs to be checked, he thought, somewhat wearily. *Again.*

But still before that, she needed something even simpler, more basic. Human trust (*I gotta get her to trust me*), and yet one step closer was human need. Basic simple human need. Food. Water. Shelter.

Lamont stood, watching her, wondering how much simpler he had to get with her before she could even begin to find her way again.

"I'm gonna walk in here," he jerked a thumb over his shoulder towards the kitchen, "and make a pot of coffee. You want some?"

Kyler was quiet for a minute, and then slowly gave a small nod. "Yeah. That . . . that'd be good."

He nodded back and abruptly walked in the other room. Behind him, he sensed Kyler's indecision on whether or not to follow him. This decision, he realized, would go a long way in determining the depth of her trust in him.

Christ, he thought, *this kid's been through so much that it's come down to this: whether or not she can trust me enough to come in the kitchen with me for a cup of coffee.*

He pulled the can out of the fridge and scooped eight cups into the percolator. He filled it up with water, turned it on, and then turned around to meet her eyes as she stared at him from the doorway. He gestured towards the table.

"You can have a seat. Won't be but a minute or two. You hungry? I can make some soup real quick."

Kyler edged along the far wall and sat down, shaking her head. "No thanks. I'll . . . I'll get something later."

Lamont grunted and glanced back at the coffee pot. "You workin' today?"

She nodded, needing a cigarette, but couldn't get up the nerve to light one, or to ask to light one, or to walk past him to go outside to light one. She gnawed on a ragged fingernail, thinking how much she'd already been through, with the dope and the johns and the abuse and everything else. But also realizing just how much more had been taken from her two nights ago in that bathroom.

There was no more trust in her; it'd been replaced by a bone-chilling fear she'd never felt before, and she had to wonder if it would ever come back. If there was enough backbone left in her to be able to put even a small amount of trust in anyone ever again.

"Yeah," she glanced at the clock on the wall. "At five."

He regarded her silently for a minute, then turned and pulled two cups out of the cabinet. "Cream? Sugar?"

Kyler shrugged. "Whatever. I can drink it any way."

Lamont pulled both from a shelf and walked towards her. Kyler realized she was flinching as he got closer to her, awaiting the inevitable blow, and made herself stop. He was well aware of her turmoil, and stayed as far away from her as the little four-person table would allow.

He carefully set her cup as close to her as he dared, and then sat down at the chair farthest away from her. Kyler poured both cream and sugar in her coffee, and then wrapped her hands around the cup, relishing in its warmth.

"Want me to give you a ride?" He asked, gauging the reaction in her eyes.

Kyler glanced at him with raised eyebrows, fighting the fear to find some trust for this man. She was quiet for a long time, thinking, and then finally gave a slow, reluctant nod.

"Sure . . ." her voice came out hesitant. "If you don't mind."

"Nah," he shook his head. "I don't mind. I'm off all day." Lamont paused a moment, trying to get his words together. "You work yesterday?"

She nodded, staring down at her cup.

"Day before?"

Another nod. "John's been busy. Asked if I could pick up a couple extra days."

He cleared his throat. "Where . . . uh . . . where've you been staying?"

Kyler shot him a quick glance. "Wherever."

Lamont met her eyes. "Safe places?"

"Not really. I mean, you know . . ." she shrugged and looked away. "That house was supposed to be safe, but . . ."

He absently poured a little more sugar in his cup, his mind working. "Been with other people?"

"God, no," she stared at him. "I'm better on my own."

"Yeah?"

"I don't trust anybody enough to sleep in the same place with them."

"Not now."

"No," she agreed, and took a deep, haggard breath. "Not now."

There was silence between them for a few minutes, and then Lamont asked quietly, "Does John know you left?"

"No," Kyler looked at him. "Not unless they called him." She shrugged. "Maybe they did, I don't know." She paused, and then asked softly, "You think . . . you think he'd fire me if he found out?"

Lamont was quiet for a minute. "I don't know, Kyler. He may not have a choice, you know, with the deal you got with the court system. It may not be so much a matter of you leaving the house . . . that can be explained, you know . . ." his eyes bored into hers, "but more of the fact that you were using again."

Kyler felt her stomach knot up and she sighed heavily. "That . . . job, Doc . . ." her voice cracked and she stopped to clear her throat. "It's given me more hope than I've had in a long time. It . . . gives me a purpose, you know . . . something to try for other than trying to kill myself with dope."

He watched her, feeling somewhat helpless. "You were raped, Kyler. That's enough to push you back out."

She winced slightly and stared out the window. *The ocean's out there,* her mind whispered, and just the mere thought of that vast amount of water in all its power and ability was enough to send a thin thread of calm through her.

"Can I walk out there?" She pointed towards the back door.

"Yeah," he said quietly and watched as she got up and headed out onto the deck. Lamont followed at a slight distance, aware that she was aware of just how close he was to her. Kyler bypassed the lawn chairs and sat on the steps leading down to the beach. He watched as she pulled a crumpled pack of cigarettes from her pocket and lit one with a slightly shaking hand.

"It was more than that," she said softly, watching the waves as they crashed along the sand. "But that was a lot of it." She sighed and dropped her head, thinking.

"I had a friend, once, Doc, who meant everything to me. He . . . he taught me how to skate, and besides this ocean here," she gestured with her hand; the cigarette smoke making lazy swirls in the mild air, "besides this, skating's the one thing that always calms me."

Kyler took a deep draw off her smoke, her brow furrowed as waves of memories hurtled into her. "Working at the park is probably the best thing that could've happened to me right now, but it also brings back a lot of . . . memories of good times I had with this friend. *Skating*, itself, reminds me so much of him, and it's really hard, you know . . . remembering him all at once like this again."

Lamont watched her for a minute, and then asked quietly, "Josh?"

Kyler shot him a sharp look, eyes narrowed. "How'd you know?"

"You told me . . . a couple times. When you were in the hospital right after you'd O.D.'d. It seemed like the only time you were somewhat coherent was when you were talking about him."

"Oh," she nodded, and stared back out over the ocean. "How much'd I tell you?"

"Enough," he answered truthfully. "I got the gist of everything. How good you guys were together until the drugs tore you apart and what you went through when he left."

Thick silence fell around them for a few minutes, until Kyler broke it with a soft voice. "I love my job, Doc, and I hate that I mighta fucked it up like this. I got no credible excuse," she got up and turned to face him, her dark eyes staring hard into his, "and I'm not gonna lie, ok? I *wanted* to get high; I know I did because if I didn't, why spend the money, right?" *If I did spend money*, her mind insisted on adding.

"I guess I was just looking for an excuse to do it. Josh . . . seems like he became a fixture, a constant thought in my head, and . . ." she rubbed her eyes, trying to hold back the tears. "I *hate* what I did to him, and I *hate* that the drugs tore us apart. But they're such a big part of me that by me thinking of him all the time, I just kept getting closer and closer to picking an excuse to go out and get high again.

"That make sense?" Kyler looked at Lamont with hooded eyes, and he nodded silently.

"The rape," she flapped her hand and turned away, but not before he saw the wild fear jump up into her eyes, "was like you said . . . just the thing that pushed me over the edge."

"*Just the thing?*" He asked softly. "It wasn't *just the thing*, Kyler. I know . . . I can tell by the look in your eyes. It took more away from you than the drugs or losing Josh or anything else ever has, right?"

Kyler hung her head between her hunched shoulder blades. Her head was beginning to pound with a sickening thud, and her stomach—knotted up the way it was—wasn't doing too much better.

"All the shit I've been through, Doc, and I don't think I've ever been raped," her voice came out in a barely audible mutter. "And if I did, I don't remember it and I wouldn't've cared anyway, 'cause I always got what I was after."

"Dope or money," he said quietly.

"Right. Dope or money." She felt the shaking increase throughout her body as she thought of the thumbs pressing into her windpipe, and then the incredible *tearing* sensation between her legs as she was forced to take in something that had never penetrated her unwillingly before.

As the air in her lungs faded, it seemed the pressure inside her grew. It was more gruff and more abusive than anything she'd ever encountered, and as fear faded with her consciousness, her hatred mounted to a white-hot spike of motivation that allowed her reach up with one badly shaking hand, find what felt like an eyeball, and use her ragged fingernails to do as much damage as possible in the split second she felt was all her own.

A deep howl of pain and then Kyler was released; she was up like a shot, down the stairs and out of the house before her pants were even back up. And then the crushing feeling of being turned, guided with a mind that wasn't her own, and after that came the overwhelming need to find **something, anything** to get higher than she'd ever been; so high there wasn't a chance in hell of ever coming back down.

She heaved a heavy sigh and gave a soft, muttered, "Fuck." Across the deck he saw her shaking and wanted to go to her, but held back. The fear raging through her was fierce and was probably more than enough to send her back out into the streets, but Lamont knew that by her just coming here to his house that there was at least a small amount of sanity left.

Kyler sank back down on the steps, facing the ocean. She put her head in her hands and slowly ran her fingers through her hair until they locked at the back of her neck. If it was possible to be curled up in a ball sitting on a wooden step, she was doing it.

Lamont's heart twisted and he broke down and walked softly across the deck to her. Tentatively, he sat down beside her; Kyler sank back against her side of the railing, but with a width of about two feet on the stairs, there wasn't much room to move away from him.

He sighed. "Kyler."

The sound of her tears hitting the wood was barely heard above the roar of the waves, but he heard them just the same. She took a haggard breath and let it out, wishing for an end to the fear and anger, even if that end meant death for her.

Too much of this shit, she thought. *And, Christ, I am just so fucking tired.*

"Kyler."

"What?" Her voice came out in a sighing moan.

"I want to help you if you'll let me."

Kyler raised her head and stared out over the ocean. Her eyes were filled with a hopelessness so deep it seemed to go on forever. Lamont saw the exhaustion and defeat in those eyes, and hoped to God he had enough strength of his own to pull her back from that edge.

"Will you let me?"

She sighed and leaned her head against the supports of the railing. She was still shaking; the boards trembling minutely with the force of her shudders.

"I'm no good at taking help from people, Doc," she said quietly. "I don't have the trust it takes to let people in that much."

Jesus, he thought. "I'm not asking for your trust . . . not right now. I'm just talking about letting me help you so you can make it through the next five minutes, ok? And then the next five after that. A step at a time, kid, all right?"

Kyler closed her eyes for a brief second, giving her fatigued mind a blessed spurt of rest. She felt his hand touch her shoulder gently and instinctively pulled away, stopped once again by the railing at her side.

And then suddenly she was just so goddamned tired of hurting, of running, of always being so fucking afraid it seemed every little noise wanted to explode in her brain, send her heart hammering and her body shaking.

"I didn't used to be like this," she murmured, eyes still closed. "Christ, what the fuck happened to me?"

"Let me help you, ok?" He asked softly. "And I'm not gonna ask you for anything in return." Briefly he felt anger again for the way the people at Harmon's handled her case, making her believe every good deed had a price tag.

Kyler rubbed her forehead, trying to dispel the headache. Her body, coming down from the coke, was just now feeling the pain caused by the beating she took at the house and by the beating she instilled upon it the two days she was back out on the street.

"Tell you what," Lamont started in a hesitant voice, "why don't you go upstairs and take a hot bath. I'll find you some clothes you can wear and I'll throw yours in the washer, ok?"

Kyler flinched away from the thought of her lying naked in this man's tub, picturing him barging in on her and pulling her out of the water, throwing her on a bed—

"I'm gonna leave, ok?" He muttered, as if reading her mind. "I'll come back in about a half an hour and I'll leave the clothes outside the bathroom door for you."

She felt shame wash over her; another emotion to add to her growing list of negativities.

"No," her voice came out in a croak as she stood up. "You don't have to leave. Just . . . just promise me you won't . . ." she stared into his eyes, trying desperately to find enough trust to believe him, if only for this one thing.

"I promise," he stared back at her. "I promise you, Kyler, I will *not* come anywhere near you."

Kyler took another deep, shuddering breath and finally gave a reluctant nod. He still saw the massive amount of fear in her eyes, and knew she probably wouldn't fully trust him for a long, long time . . . if ever.

"Upstairs?"

"On the right," he jerked a thumb back over his shoulder towards the house.

"Ok," she said softly, and headed towards the door, her steps tentative and her shoulders hunched as if expecting a blow from behind.

Lamont turned back to the water and stared out at the waves. His face was troubled, his thoughts heavy with Kyler's sketchy future, her more than uncertain mental and emotional state, and her highly questionable physical state.

"Shit, I hope I can do this," he muttered softly. "Hope I got it in me to get her through this."

Kyler was still shaking as she turned on the water in the tub. The door had a lock on it, but it was flimsy at best, holding more considerate deterrent power than stopping power.

Still, she'd felt an unshakable urge to lock it, and she did.

The hot water felt good to her sore body, and she allowed herself to let her guard down just a little bit, to relax for once. She shut her mind down hard and lay back in the tub with water up to her chin, letting the heat and steam wash as much of her demons away as possible.

She was drying off with the towel when Lamont's voice came from outside the door. Her heart leapt up into her throat and she felt the fear tying her stomach in knots.

"Hey, Kyler? I'm gonna leave these clothes out here, ok? They may not fit perfect but I think they'll get you by."

"Ok," she swallowed around the lump in her throat. "Thanks." With her eyes focused on the doorknob, Kyler waited to see if it would turn, or try to turn. Without thinking in any conscious way, her entire trust in the doc—thin as it was—rested on the movement of a single doorknob.

It didn't move, and she heard his steps on the stairs outside the door, going down. She hadn't been aware she'd been holding her breath until it whooshed out in a gasp. Shaking all over, Kyler sat heavily on the closed toilet and put her head in her hands.

After about five minutes she slowly opened the door and peeked out. The hallway was empty; no sign of the doc, and the clothes were folded neatly at her feet. Slowly Kyler bent to pick them up and then backed into the bathroom, once more locking the door between her and the world.

The sweats were a men's small; the shirt the same, and they hung low and loose on her skinny frame. But the doc was right: they'd get her by.

Kyler found Lamont back out on the deck, drinking another cup of coffee. He gazed at her as she sat down on the lawn chair across from him.

"Thanks," she gestured towards the clothes.

He nodded easily, meeting her eyes. "They're the smallest I had, sorry."

She shrugged and shifted her gaze away. He glanced at his watch and saw that it was just a little past ten.

"You said you don't have to be at work till five?"

"Yeah."

Lamont nodded and stared back out over the ocean before taking a deep breath and glancing back at her. She raised her eyebrows, feeling the shift in her stomach.

"What?"

He cleared his throat and faced her, his eyes soft on hers. "I want you to come to the hospital with me, ok?"

Kyler met his gaze with a defeated one of her own. She took a deep breath and let it out slowly, then pulled her battered pack of smokes from her pocket. Lamont watched her chase the tip of one with the lighter for a brief moment before the flame caught, and she took a deep draw. Her eyes settled on the ocean again and she allowed a small amount of calm from it enter her battered soul.

"All right," she finally muttered, knowing why he wanted her to go, and feeling the fear hit her all over again like a bowling ball to the stomach.

Lamont assessed her scrawny body, protruding bones, and the deep, deep exhaustion in her eyes. "It's gonna be ok, kid," he said quietly.

"I guess," Kyler sighed and stood up. "Either way it goes, it's gonna hafta be, right?"

He grimaced and reached for her without thinking. She gave a small shake of her head and backed up a step.

"I'll be out front, ok?" She gently opened the screen door and disappeared into the kitchen. Lamont gave a soft growl of self-disgust for his forgetfulness, and then slowly followed her.

CHAPTER 17

LAMONT PARKED DOWN in the parking garage, and in the dim light Kyler felt the pressure of the low ceiling and thick walls closing in on her. Her heart slammed against her rib cage and she took one deep breath after another, trying to calm it down.

He pulled into a space and waited outside the car as she slowly got out, looking like she wanted nothing more than to bolt back out into the sunlight . . . which was exactly what she wanted to do.

"You ok?" He asked.

She shrugged easily, but didn't answer. He noted her pale face and trembling hands and stopped in front of her, forcing her to meet his gaze.

"You're not," he answered for her. "Trust me, kid, all right? *Can* you trust me?"

Kyler looked at him and then gestured vaguely around her. "It's . . . it's nothing, really, Doc, just feelin' a little bit claustrophobic down here."

He considered, searching her face. Finally he gave a brief nod and motioned ahead of them. "Two minutes, Kyler, and we'll be in the hospital, ok?"

She didn't answer as she followed behind him. When he stopped in front of the small elevator and hit the button, Kyler felt her stomach drop.

"Just up to the fourth floor," he said, stepping inside. When he turned to look at her, she was still well outside the doors, holding onto an iron railing. Her face had grown even paler, and he noted the sheen of sweat across her forehead and across her upper lip.

"I'm sorry," her voice came out a hoarse mutter. "I can't go in there, Doc. I . . . I can't . . ." She took a step back and looked at him with terrified eyes. For a moment Lamont read in her gaze that it was completely plausible to her for him to reach out and drag her in, forcing her to ride the elevator up the four flights.

"Jesus," he murmured, and stepped out just as the doors started closed. "Kyler . . ."

She took another step back and swallowed. Lamont didn't think it was possible, but now her body was shaking even harder, close to the convulsion point. In a flash, he realized that if he didn't get her out of the garage quick, she would most likely pass out from pure terror.

"Can you walk?" He asked gruffly. "Up the stairs?"

Relief showed on her face and then she was already headed towards the iron steps on the other side of the elevator. Without waiting for him, claustrophobia and real fear driving her, Kyler bolted up the stairs two at a time, barely noticing the straining in the muscles of her legs or the breath gasping in and out of her smoke-ladened lungs.

When she pulled open the heavy wooden door marking the fourth floor, she rushed through it, coming to a hard stop as she collided with the wall across from the stairwell.

"Fuck," she muttered, and slid down to the floor and put her head in her hands. The world pulsed in and out of focus with every beat of her pounding heart; making her wonder if she really was going to pass out.

Lamont came through the door seconds later, breathing hard, concern on his face as he spotted her. "Shit, kid," he squatted down in front of her. "I'm sorry, Kyler."

She shook her head, finally getting her breath back in the openness of the bright hallway. "It's my fault, Doc. I . . . I hate spaces like that . . . closed up, it . . . it presses in on me, you know?"

"Yeah," he nodded.

"And then . . . and then the elevator . . ." Kyler swallowed and slid her eyes away. "I felt . . . like I couldn't breathe. Like it was . . . like that guy was there again, you know, choking me . . . and I couldn't breathe . . . and I guess I . . ." she ran a hand through her hair. "I guess I just panicked."

"It's ok," he said softly. "It's my fault, anyway. You told me you were claustrophobic, but I really didn't think when I headed to the elevator."

She took a deep breath, trying to ease the stitch in her side. "It's never been that bad. I've been in elevators before, and it was never that bad because of the access hatch in the ceiling, you know?"

Lamont gazed at her, wondering again at all this kid had been through, where she'd been, what she'd done . . . what she'd been after when she crawled out the access hatch of whatever elevator she'd been in.

"It was just . . ." she shook her head, her voice growing softer, "the walls closed in and I felt that hand on my throat again . . ."

He looked at her and took a slow, deep breath. "Ok. Ok, Kyler. We'll take the stairs down, all right? Better yet, I can just pick you back up in front of the hospital. That way you don't even have to go down to the garage."

Kyler met his eyes, gauging him, trying to see the deceit hidden in there somewhere. Usually really good at reading people, she detected none of that. Her gut instinct—the one thing she'd relied on for the whole nineteen years of her life—told her not to give up on him quite yet. To maybe throw just a tad bit more trust his way.

Lamont held out a hand, and she regarded it for a moment before hesitantly taking it and allowing him to help her to her feet. For a moment, the hallway tilted and turned colors, and he slipped an arm around her waist, holding her steady.

"Breathe," he said quietly. "Stay with me, kid."

Kyler put her other hand on the wall and hung her head, breathing deeply. Eventually the hallway and colors both righted themselves and Kyler was able to pull away and stand on her own. She started down the hallway in silence with Lamont beside her, ready to catch her if she stumbled or fell.

"What're you gonna test me for?" She asked, pulling herself up on the table in the exam room he led her to. "Drugs, I know." She met his eyes directly. "What else?"

"You already told me coke," he replied, pulling up a stool for himself. "Was there anything else?" His eyes searched hers.

"No-o-o," Kyler answered hesitantly. She held out both her arms to the light, displaying the old, half-healed scars and no new wounds. "Nothing here," she sighed and folded her hands together. "But that don't mean nothin', really. There's a hundred places I coulda fixed."

"You think you did?" Lamont pulled on a stethoscope and gently placed the round metal end on one lung in her back. "Deep breath."

She took a deep breath and let it out slowly. "I don't know," she answered honestly. "The coke, definitely. Smack … I really don't know. Pills? Maybe. Don't know that, either."

She felt the end of the stethoscope move to her other lung and took another deep breath. She tried to remain still and not flinch away from him, but it was getting harder to do by the second. Lamont sensed this and pulled back.

His eyes were dark and direct, gazing into hers. "I'll test you, if you want me to."

Kyler nodded and swallowed heavily. "Yeah, ok." She paused, then repeated, "What else?"

"STDs, mainly," he slid back on the stool and reached inside a drawer, pulling out a disposable thermometer. "Pregnancy," his eyes pierced hers before he motioned for her to open her mouth. Kyler felt her heart pounding steadily against her sternum, but opened her mouth and slid the thermometer under her tongue.

"Physical damage, both internal and external," Lamont counted out seconds on his watch, then gently removed the thermometer. "Little bit high," he muttered.

"How much is a little bit?"

He shrugged. "A hair over a hundred." Dropping the thermometer in the trash, he turned back to her. "So. That's about it. Just doing what we need to do to make sure you're all right physically."

Kyler gave a reluctant nod and chewed on her bottom lip. Exhaustion was eating at her, making it hard to think, but she knew she couldn't afford to sleep right now.

"I've got a friend who's gonna examine you, ok?" Lamont said softly. "She's a good doctor and she knows what she's doing."

"Not a shrink," Kyler muttered.

"No. She's friendly, so she might just wanna talk, but she won't pick your brain."

She took a deep breath and scrubbed a hand across her face. "All right."

"Try to relax, ok?"

"Sure."

"Here," he reached into another drawer and pulled out a small plastic cup. "There's a bathroom right next door. Just leave it in that little door in the wall."

Kyler nodded and hopped off the table. She started out the door, but turned to look at him. "You'll test for other stuff besides the coke?"

"Yeah."

"Ok," she started back out but stopped when he called her name.

"When you get back, put this on, ok?" He laid a cotton hospital gown on the bed.

"All right."

Lamont waited until he heard the bathroom door close, and then eased out of the room. He walked across the hall and entered an office; the woman sitting behind the desk offered a small smile and gestured with her head towards the general area of the exam room.

"She ready?"

"Yeah. See if you can get her to vent a little bit. She's got a lot inside her."

"But she knows I'm not a therapist."

"Right. I just told you were gonna examine her, and that you like to talk but that you won't press her."

The young doctor nodded and stood up. "Ok. But rape is no little thing, Keith. She can carry this around for years, and no matter how much she's already been through, it might come crashing down on her even years from now."

"Yeah," Lamont sighed and sat down in a chair. "I know."

Kyler was sitting on the table with the gown wrapped tightly around her, gnawing on a ragged fingernail when the doctor walked in. She met her eyes briefly, her gaze giving away nothing while her trembling body giving away everything.

"Kyler," the doctor held out her hand, "my name's Jane Jericho."

Kyler shook her hand and gazed at her, saying nothing. The doctor smiled and pulled up the stool.

"Don't worry. I'm not a shrink. I'm just a regular doctor, specifically OBGYN." She rolled to the end of the bed and pulled the stirrups up. Kyler grimaced and felt her stomach roll over.

"First of all, I need to know if you're hurting anywhere," the doctor laid a hand on her shoulder, pushing her gently down on the bed. Her gloved hands were cold against Kyler's bare chest, and she gritted her teeth.

"No, not really," she muttered. "It . . . not now, but it was real bad when . . . after . . ."

Doctor Jericho's eyes were soft on hers as her hands worked first one breast and then the other. She pressed along both sets of ribs and then the stomach that was rock hard despite the sunken-ness of it.

"Any current pain in the abdominal area?"

"No," Kyler stared at the ceiling, hating this. She felt her feet being lifted one at a time and placed in the stirrups, and now she hated it even more as the cool air of the room played around her exposed vaginal area.

Doctor Jericho's voice was meant to be calming, but all Kyler heard was the noise of various metal instruments being pulled from a drawer.

"I'm not gonna grill you on anything. I just need facts, all right?" The doctor's eyes were sharp on hers above her mask.

Kyler nodded, feeling sicker with each passing second.

"How bad did you hurt?"

"Very bad."

"Did you bleed?"

"Yeah, a lot."

Doctor Jericho's voice came from the end of the bed. Kyler felt a soft hand on one ankle, adjusting her legs. "This is gonna be cold and it'll probably hurt. Let me know if it hurts too much and I'll stop."

Kyler swallowed and didn't answer. Then she had to bite back a gasp as the cold metal instrument was inserted in her. And then the pain came, spiking high quick. She clamped her jaw shut hard against the moan, locking it in her throat. She couldn't hide the tension in her body, though, or that fact that every muscle she had suddenly went rock hard.

The doctor looked up at her, eyes sharp and concerned. "Is it hurting? Want me to stop?"

"No," Kyler managed. "Just hurry up and get it over with."

"Twenty seconds, Kyler. I'm hurrying."

And then, blessedly, the instrument was removed, leaving her with a slick, slimy feel of exposed flesh. She took a deep breath and pressed the heels of her hands hard against her eyes, feeling the betrayal of a few teardrops running down her cheeks.

"One more time, ok? But this time I'm just gonna feel around your uterus and ovaries, make sure everything's ok."

Kyler felt the doctor's fingers enter her, and pain followed by self-loathing and disgust swamped her. The urge to crawl deep inside herself was strong and commanding, insisting that heroin was the only answer to this hell.

"It's over," Doctor Jericho said softly. She scooted back from the table as Kyler sat up, wiping her eyes. "I'm sorry I hurt you."

Kyler shook her head and took a ragged breath, avoiding her gaze. "It's not your fault. Shit like this always hurts."

Doctor Jericho gazed at her for a long moment, and then asked quietly, "When you say you bled a lot, how much is a lot?"

There was silence for a few minutes as Kyler tried to gather her thoughts. "Probably a pad every fifteen minutes or so. It soaked right through to my underwear at first, but then I started using two at a time. That lasted a little longer, but I still went through a forty-four pack almost within an hour."

"How long did the bleeding last?" The doctor's eyes were on Kyler's again, wide and concerned.

"Maybe two, three hours."

She nodded and stood up, stripping off her gloves. "All right. From what I just saw, you're gonna be fine. You have a little tear that's healing well, and if you're not having any other pain, you're good to go. Just come back and let me look at you if you do start hurting anywhere, ok? Either in the abdomen or vaginal area. There's not much of a chance of that tear getting infected if you keep it clean and dry, but you never know," she shrugged.

"Ok," Kyler sighed. "Thanks."

"No problem." Doctor Jericho gazed at her. "You know, Kyler, you can have ten guys pay you to have sex with them, but that still does not give that eleventh guy a right to rape you."

"I know that," she growled softly.

"Do you? Because your eyes are telling me something else."

Kyler stared down at the floor and didn't answer.

"This is not your fault, and what you've done in the past doesn't warrant this happening to you."

She gripped the edge of the table and swallowed hard. "Don't judge me," her voice was barely above a whisper.

"Oh, I'm not," the doctor responded mildly. "Believe me, I am not judging you; I'm just giving you facts. That's what we said, right? Just the facts?"

"Sure," Kyler sighed, meeting her eyes. "But I thought you said you weren't a therapist."

"I'm not," Doctor Jericho answered. "But this isn't therapy. This isn't gynecology, either. This is just me, ok? This is me talking to you as a woman, from a woman's standpoint. And you don't have to believe me . . . but those are the facts."

There was silence in the room for a few long minutes. Finally Kyler took a deep breath and let it out slowly.

"I believe you," she murmured. "And . . . and I don't think I deserved this shit, you know? But . . . it kinda makes sense that even if I don't deserve it, I've done enough stupid shit in my life for it not to surprise me if I *did* deserve it."

She looked at her and shrugged. "Probably makes absolutely no sense to you, though."

Doctor Jericho shook her head. "No, actually, it does, Kyler. I can see where you're coming from."

Kyler gave a slight nod and scrubbed a hand hard across her face, trying to vanquish the demons by sheer force alone. She was feeling the total exhaustion even more now, and with the effects of the coke worn off, the lack of sleep over the past sixty hours was catching up quick.

"Ok, here's what I'm gonna do," the doctor said. "I've got a couple phone numbers I'd like you to take; one's for a support group and one's for an actual rape therapist."

Kyler regarded her with hooded eyes but remained silent.

"You don't have to call either one," her eyes showed that she knew what Kyler was thinking. "But my motto is better to have it and not need it, you know?"

And Kyler, who had somewhat the same motto, nodded reluctantly.

"And I'm gonna give you this," Doctor Jericho handed her a card. "It's got my work and cell on there. Call me if you have any pain or problems, ok?"

"Ok."

"Doctor Lamont wants to get a blood sample, wanted me to stick around for a few minutes to help him. I'll see if I can track him down and we'll be right back in. You can go ahead and get dressed if you want. And here," she opened a drawer and pulled out a sanitary napkin. "I may have aggravated your tear, and it might bleed a little bit more, but it won't be much."

"Sure," Kyler took the pad from her and then waited until the door shut before sliding off the table and reaching for her clothes.

"She's got a tear, Keith," Doctor Jericho's eyes were hard on his when she walked back into the office. "It's healing well, but if she'd've come to me when it happened, I would've put a few stitches in it."

"How long?" Lamont asked quietly.

"'Bout an inch or so. She said she bled a lot, and I can see why." She opened a desk drawer and pulled out a pack of cigarettes, lighting one. "I believe her," she said softly, almost absently. "I believe she was raped. It's in her eyes," she glanced at him.

Lamont swallowed and gave a small nod.

"I gave her some numbers, but I doubt she'll call them," she shrugged. "I think it's gonna take time for her . . . maybe a lot. She didn't really say a whole lot."

He looked at her and then glanced towards the door. "All right," he sighed. "You gonna help me?"

"Yeah," Doctor Jericho crushed out her smoke and stood up.

Kyler was sitting back on the bed, feeling the slight blood soak into the pad in her underwear. Every part of her body cried for even just a few minutes of sleep, even as that one part of her brain screamed for more and more and more of anything to keep her as fucked up as possible.

She was gnawing on a ragged fingernail, shaking and feeling the wild currents of conflicting emotions raging within her when both doctors walked back in. For a brief instant her eyes met those of the doc's and then she slid her gaze away.

Lamont pulled up the stool and looked at her. "Hey, kid, I'm gonna take a blood sample, ok?"

"Sure," Kyler muttered. "Testing for more drugs or what?"

"Hepatitis, HIV, things like that," he responded, pressing gently with his thumbs along the inside of her right elbow, trying to find a usable vein.

"Shit," she hissed and gritted her teeth against the sudden itch that rose from the scar line of her tracks.

"Kyler . . ." he started.

"Don't," she pulled away, breathing hard, unable to catch her breath. Against her will, her body scooted back on the bed, pulling her arm out of his hands. "Christ, Doc, please don't touch it."

Lamont's eyes were sharp as he stared at her, raising his hands in surrender. "I'm sorry, Kyler," his voice was quiet. "Does it hurt?"

She shook her head, her left hand clamped hard against the scars, trying to still the maddening itch that seemed more in that one part of her brain than in her skin.

"No, it . . . it just . . ." she swallowed and shut her eyes against the sudden tilt of the room. "Just don't touch it, ok?"

"Ok," he muttered. "Ok, Kyler." Gently, he took her left hand in his and glanced up into her eyes, open now, and filled with a deep, cold fear. "This arm ok?"

"Um . . . I don't know. I guess." Kyler felt her heart pounding hard against her sternum, sending sharp pains down her ribs and across her back. She felt the fear eating at her, tasted the hot copper tang of it in her mouth. She watched Lamont's thumbs work along the nearly wasted veins in this arm and felt Doctor Jericho's eyes on her.

More than anything she wanted to appear sane and in control in front of these people, but the fear was mounting, filling her with a bone-chilling cold from the inside out, and she felt the telltale trembling in her rock-hard muscles.

"Ok?" Lamont asked, looking up at her.

She shrugged and swallowed heavily. "Just do it, Doc, ok?" Her voice was shaking and she hated it, hated all of this.

Lamont glanced over at Doctor Jericho, who gazed back at him with a furrowed brow as she handed him the syringe. He nodded and set it beside Kyler before tying off the vein with a length of rubber tubing.

Kyler felt the familiar pressure in her arm, could almost believe it was her own belt stopping the blood flow, could almost feel the cold glass of the syringe between her teeth as she prepared to fix.

"Easy, kid," he said quietly, and as gently as possible, slid the needle smoothly into her swollen vein.

In an instant Kyler was back, sitting on the wet concrete of some dank, dark alley, her works beside her, the needle in her arm, sending the heroin through her body. Her eyes were closed and she slumped against the brick wall behind her, wasted and getting more wasted; the smack taking her to that fabled place where there was no fear, where there were no johns ready to beat her just because they could and she always let them because there was always more dope or money at the end of it all.

Down where nobody could touch her or hurt her, where there were no sharp-edged memories of better times, ready to come back and haunt her over and over as she passed out in a thin miserable sleep time after time.

With the smack roaring through her veins, soaking her heart, racing up to that place in her brain that always screamed for more, Kyler was always *exactly* where she needed to be in this world, in her mind, in her body.

Heroin was her demon, her angel, her salvation and damnation, and sitting on the table in the hospital room in the cold, fear-filled present, she knew that; knew that with her entire being and Kyler, for the first time, seriously could not see herself living without it.

And Jesus Christ, how that scared her. There was nothing in this world she wanted more than to never **ever** fix again, just like there was nothing in this world she wanted more than heroin . . . and seemingly never so much as right at this moment.

Her heart jumped into her throat as she stared at the needle sticking from her arm. She loathed it, needed it, hated it, loved it. In an instant, Kyler was off the bed and back against the wall, her hand over the inside of her elbow, covering the few drops of blood seeping out, breathing hard, her heart slamming inside her chest.

The vomit rose up unexpected, and she turned and bolted out of the room, hitting her knees hard in front of the toilet in the bathroom, letting everything come up on its own, powerless to stop it.

Waves of bone-chilling cold washed over her, and she gripped the porcelain with white-knuckled hands, feeling the worse case of withdrawal she'd ever known crash down on her.

Dimly, from behind her, she felt Lamont's hands on her shoulders, steadying her.

"Easy," his voice was quiet in her ear. "It's ok, Kyler."

She shuddered and laid her head on her arm. He could see the dark rings of exhaustion beneath her eyes when she closed them and felt bones and the little meat of her back and shoulders beneath the tips of his fingers.

"Jesus, this has just gotta stop," she mumbled. "This has gotta stop, Doc."

"Hold on," he said. "Just hold on, kid, ok? You're stronger than this, and if you hold on, I promise you it'll get better. This'll stop and it'll get better."

Kyler took a deep, ragged breath and let it out slowly. She stayed there for another minute, trying to find the strength to stand up, wondering how she could now possibly convince both of them that she was ok, in control, sane and normal.

Gritting her teeth, she willed strength into her legs—just enough to hold what little weight she had—and pulled herself to her feet. Turning, she met first the doc's eyes and then Doctor Jericho's . . . and then felt more than saw the room tilt at an alarming angle.

Kyler, exhausted and defeated, fell with it, not caring anymore, and barely felt it as her head connected solidly with the hard tile of the floor.

Slowly, she opened her eyes, squinting against the harsh glare of the fluorescents above her. Her head pounded with a sickening force, and Kyler brought a shaking hand up to her temple, briefly disoriented and feeling slightly sick to her stomach.

"Hey, kid," Lamont's voice was soft, but it reverberated from one side of her skull to the other.

Kyler winced and managed to look at him, noting the concern in his eyes. "What happened?" Her voice came out hoarse.

"You passed out," he responded.

"How long?"

"Just a couple minutes."

She took a deep breath and held it for a minute, trying to get her bearings, wishing for a cigarette. "Shit."

He helped her sit up and she stared at him dully. "You gotta let me go to work, Doc."

Lamont didn't answer as he shined a small light into her eyes, monitoring the equal dilation of each pupil. "Follow my finger," he moved a forefinger slowly in front of her face, watching her gaze follow.

"Work's the only thing I got," she muttered, trying to focus around the pounding in her head. "If I don't go, I'm headed back to jail."

"We'll worry about that in a minute, ok? Right now I'm more concerned about whether or not you got a concussion and why you passed out to begin with." His eyes bored into hers. "Been dizzy lately? Double vision?"

"Doc," Kyler shook her head gently, looking away. She ran her hands across her face, pressing her palms against her forehead. "Lemme go to work, ok? Please? Just lemme go."

"Kyler," Doctor Jericho's voice was quiet from off to her side. "You can't even walk by yourself. You're weak, you're exhausted, and I know you're hurting. Let us help you and we'll worry about the legal stuff, all right? Let us take that and you just lay there and relax for once."

"I can't," she slid off the bed before either of them could stop her. "I can't relax." For a moment a wave of dizziness ran over her, but it was gone almost before she realized it was even there.

"Kyler…" Lamont started, and then just stopped, watching her. He glanced at Doctor Jericho and she shrugged.

"It's your call, Keith. If she thinks she can do it, I guess you better let her."

"I can do it," Kyler said softly.

There was silence for a few minutes, and then the pager on the young doctor's belt beeped. She looked down at it and then back up to Lamont. "I gotta take this . . ."

"Yeah," Lamont nodded. "All right, Jane. Thanks for your help." He let her walk out of the room and then looked back at Kyler.

"You can't sleep," he muttered. "I know that's all you wanna do but you might have a concussion, and . . ."

"I won't sleep," her exhausted, bloodshot eyes rested on his.

He regarded her for a long moment, then reached up and ran his thumb gently over the bump on the side of her head. She winced but remained still and finally he gave a small sigh.

"I'll make you a deal, Kyler, all right? I won't keep you here, and I'll let you go to work, but five o'clock's still six hours away. You're crashing hard 'cause you've been up for, what, two, three days?"

She shrugged, still trying to focus around the pain in her head.

"Come home with me and you can sleep in my spare bed for a couple hours. I'll wake you up every half hour just in case you *do* have a concussion, and other than that I won't even come in the room."

Kyler wanted to shake her head, wanted to back away and not have him see the true pain she was in, but true pain was what it was, and without some kind of sleep she knew her body would just shut down on its own.

Which wouldn't be bad, except that most of those places it chose to shut down weren't the best in the world, and in her current upheaval of emotions, she didn't want to be anywhere near any kind of drug for at least the next day or two.

She swallowed around the lump in her throat, trying to focus, trying to grasp reality. It was hard, and the more she tried, the more she just wanted to lie down for a little while, for even a just a few minutes.

Just as much time as she needed to forget for a moment all the fear, hatred, and that overwhelming need that had been her main emotions for too long now.

"All right," she finally said. "Just . . . just promise me you won't . . ."

"I promised before and I'll promise again, and I'll keep promising for as long as it takes," he said seriously, his eyes on hers. "And I mean it every time, Kyler."

She stared at him for a long time, and then finally gave a small nod and pushed herself away from the bed. He helped steady her as they walked out to the front entrance, and although she wanted to back away from his touch, she was grateful for the support and the strength he lent her.

"Wait here and I'll get the car," he said, stopping in front of a bench outside the main entrance.

Kyler gave a tired nod and sat down, pulling her cigarettes from her pocket. She lit one and gazed out over the parking lot, feeling old, tired, and scared. When Lamont pulled up in front of her, she pushed herself off the bench and staggered towards the car. He watched her fall heavily into the seat, noting the sheen of sweat across her forehead and in her temples.

"Thanks, Doc," she muttered.

"Don't thank me yet," he growled softly. "I'm still about halfway to changing my mind and keeping you here."

She managed a wan smile. "That why we're headed out of the parking lot?"

He grunted and glanced at her. "You don't look so hot, kid."

"I'll be all right," Kyler leaned against the door and stared out at the passing roadside. "Just need time to regroup, is all."

"Yeah?"

"Yeah," she sighed.

Silence descended between them as the miles rolled by. Kyler felt the warm wind blowing her wet hair back from her forehead and it felt like heaven. She closed her eyes and smelled the salt in the air and tried to let the ocean's presence sooth her battered body.

"Sorry about before," she murmured quietly. "About freaking out like that."

Lamont didn't answer for a minute, and then he said, "It's ok. It was my fault, I guess. I just . . . wasn't thinking about everything, you know, that you've been through. I draw blood everyday out of people, and to me it's routine. I didn't stop to think how it would affect you."

Kyler let a few minutes slip by and then responded, "It wasn't you, really. I mean, if you want my blood, you can have it. It . . . it's not you I'm afraid of, I guess. Maybe just the needle, maybe the needle in my vein . . ." she raked a hand through her hair. "Shit, I don't know."

"Don't worry about it," he said, pulling into his drive. "One step at a time, ok? You know where the spare bedroom's at? Up the stairs, across from the bathroom?"

"Yeah," she got out of the car and waited while he unlocked the door. At the foot of the stairs she paused and looked back at him. Lamont read the fear again in her eyes and gave a slow shake of his head.

"I promise, kid, once every half hour. Other than that I won't come near that door, ok?"

Kyler nodded and started up the steps. Inside the bedroom, she closed the door but didn't lock it, and then stood, regarding the full-sized bed in front of her. It looked warm and inviting and finally she allowed herself to give in to her body's extreme exhaustion.

Crawling under the light cover, she felt the mattress absorb her body, soothing against the rock-hard muscles, cradling the multiple sore places on her back and legs. She looked over and stared at the door, scared still that it might open, but the fear wasn't enough to hold back the much-needed sleep.

She was still staring at the door when her eyes slipped closed moments later, her mind retreating back in on itself, and her body—for the first time in months—was able to completely relax.

CHAPTER 18

"DON'T DO THIS again, ok?" Josh's breath whispered against her ear and she felt his arms wrapped tight around her body. "Kyler, please don't do this anymore."

Kyler shook her head, gripping the toilet seat with sweaty palms. She felt the sweat on her forehead, sides, and running down her back. There was a high ringing in her ears and the point of entry—a pinprick-sized hole on the inside of her right elbow, barely visible—was just now starting to itch.

"I won't," she muttered, believing everything about those two words. "I won't do it no more, Josh. This shit kicked my ass." And she believed it, actually really and truly believed it, because the heroin was too strong, too venomous, too fucking harsh on her mind and body.

The massive vomiting was only the start of it. Her bones felt brittle, her muscles felt stretched and strained beyond what they could possibly be. Her stomach was a small, hard knot wrapped in barbed wire, while the head on top of her fragile neck seemed huge and ready to explode.

"No more," Josh said softly, and she heard fear in his voice. It tore at her heart and because of that, she agreed instantly and wholeheartedly.

"No more," Kyler repeated and leaned back against him, using his heat and strength to hold back her own fear of what she'd discovered. Even now, swearing and promising vehemently over and over, the memory was still with her; the memory of the way the heroin had made her feel, the weightlessness and non-feeling and incredible heights to which she'd flown while on that one ride.

"No more."

And no more became just one more, and one more became another, and then another. Because the seed had been planted and the monkey had a good, strong hold on her from the very first.

"No more," Kyler murmured, deep within her dreams. Lamont stood watching her, getting more bits and pieces of her previous life from her sleep-induced confessions. Briefly, he debated on waking her, but the concern for a concussion won the argument and he reached out to her, touching her shoulder lightly.

"Kyler."

She gave a soft moan and drew away.

"Kyler."

This time his voice cut through the thickness of the dreams surrounding her, and Kyler snapped awake, immediately alert but for a moment unable to focus or keep the world from tilting to the side.

"Doc," she muttered, trying to bring reality back in check.

"Just the half hour wake up call," he said lightly. "You ok?"

Her eyes were bloodshot and still exhausted as they stared into his. "I guess."

"Still got a headache?"

"Some, not much," she sat up and ran her hands through her hair. "I've only been asleep a half an hour?"

Lamont gave a slight shrug. "More like forty-five minutes. You needed it so I let it go a little longer."

Kyler nodded and shifted her gaze to the window. "Ok."

"Sure you're all right?"

"Yeah."

He watched as she slid back down underneath the covers. "Ok, I'll be back in another half hour or so."

She watched him shut the door behind him, feeling the dream still wrapped around her like a python around her neck. It seemed so real because it actually happened, just not even a year ago, when she'd discovered heroin for the first time.

Pulling her legs up to her chest, Kyler rolled into a ball, shutting her eyes against the world and trying to shut her heart against the wall of emotions pressing into her.

Sleep came harder the second time around, but once it did it covered her completely. The dreams were more detailed this time, more terrifying, pushing against her, toying with her fragile emotions and haunted memories.

The first time she fixed she knew she was in deep shit. Heroin grabbed a hold of her like no other drug she'd ever used, and it opened up a floodgate that up until then Kyler hadn't even been aware of.

"No more," Josh's voice echoed in her brain, now as it did then, as it always did whenever she crumpled again, finding herself lying to him more and more just for one more taste.

And then his voice merged into hers, both of them saying the same thing: *no more no more no more.* Josh was saying no more heroin, but both his voice and his arms around her faded as her own voice became more urgent, more filled with fear.

In her darkest memory, Kyler was saying *NO MORE NO MORE NO MORE* to her attacker . . . that nameless, faceless male being that so horribly and completely invaded her in a dumpy bathroom stall in the middle of the night in what was supposed to be a women's only halfway house.

"No more!" Kyler spoke aloud in her sleep, and the sound of her own voice made her bolt upright in bed. She was shivering and covered in sweat, and immediately, with the dreams and memories still so close they were nearly suffocating, her stomach clenched up. She fought her way out of the twisted bedclothes and once again raced for the bathroom.

On her knees before the toilet, Kyler silently begged for forgiveness, redemption, some peace and maybe a little bit of sanity. Reaching blindly for the flush, she pushed it, smelling the clean water as it filled the bowl.

"Christ, again?" Lamont asked gruffly from the doorway. Kyler turned her head and looked at him with her intensely burning gaze.

"Just the dreams again," she muttered thickly, forcing herself to her feet. She reached for the sink and managed to rinse her mouth out with blessedly cold water. "Fucking dreams."

Kyler shook her head and tried to slide by him, but Lamont took her arm lightly, stopping her. He felt the heat baking off her as he stared into her shell-shocked, terrified eyes.

"You're burning up," he said softly.

She pulled away, reaching for the banister at the top of the stairs. "We had a deal, remember? I held up my end . . . you gonna hold up yours and let me go to work?" Kyler's eyes bored into his.

"That was before your fever spiked."

She ran a hand across her face, then turned and stumbled down the stairs, praying for balance as the banister tried to turn to rubber and the stairs moved liquidly beneath her feet. It sort of reminded her of the one trip she'd taken long ago on a couple hits of acid, only now there was no acid—no drugs at all—and either she was as sick as the doc thought or she truly was losing her mind.

"You can barely even walk down the steps," Lamont said from behind her. Kyler stopped just inside the kitchen door as a monstrous bolt of pain ripped through her head.

"I can walk," she pressed her hand hard against her left eyebrow. "I just got a helluva headache."

"Kyler—"

"Doc," she turned to face him, and now it was just her own dark eyes again, staring imploringly into his. "Please, ok? You can take me, you can stay with me . . . but please just give me this, all right?"

Lamont stared at her for a few long minutes before finally giving a small shake of his head. "Jesus," he muttered. "You just that fucking stubborn or just that goddamned full of pride?"

Kyler grunted and sat heavily in a chair at the table. "Probably a little bit of both, I guess."

"What time's the park close, nine?"

"Yeah," she had her head in her hands and was gently massaging her temples, trying desperately to relieve the pressure.

"Come back here when you close up," his voice was firm. "Better yet, call me when you're almost done and I'll come get you."

She remained silent, staring at the tabletop while the headache pounded and screamed against the sides of her skull.

"You promise me you'll do that, and I'll take you to work instead of the hospital."

She raised her heavy eyes to meet his. "Really?"

"Yeah," he agreed reluctantly. "Promise me."

Kyler swallowed, trying to think past the pounding in her head, trying to rationalize a way out of this, but nothing came. She finally took a deep breath and nodded at him.

"All right, Doc. I'll call you."

"Promise?"

"Yeah," she said wearily, glancing up at the clock. It was just a little past two and she was running on empty, but couldn't imagine trying to sleep just a little bit more. The nightmares were still around her, taunting her with their truth and intimate detail, and Kyler strongly suspected it might be quite a while before she was able to fully sleep again.

"Coffee?" He asked.

"Um . . ." she debated, trying to gauge the condition of the stomach. "No, I guess not."

"Soup? Might help your stomach."

Kyler shook her head, staring dully out the window. "No thanks."

Lamont poured himself a cup and sat down across from her, measuring her with his sharp eyes. "Josh again?" He asked, taking a small sip of the coffee.

"No," she pulled a bent cigarette from her mangled pack and straightened it as best as she could with a trembling hand.

"Drugs?"

"Kinda," she shrugged, applying a flame to the wavering tip and avoiding his eyes.

"Was it the rape?" Lamont asked deliberately, seeing the fear and rage jump up a notch in the brief glare she gave him.

Kyler took a deep drag and held the smoke in, letting it bite hard into her lungs. She let it filter slowly out of her nose as she stared out the window, feeling the cutting edges of the terrifying memories still digging into her.

"Kyler."

"I don't wanna talk about it, all right?" She snapped. "Christ, Doc, just leave that one alone."

"That's the one that gonna kill you if it *is* left alone," he responded mildly.

The fight was gone out of her as quickly as it came, and Kyler dropped her gaze to the floor, exhaustion and fear weighing her down.

"Leave it alone," she muttered. "It's over."

"Not for you, it's not," Lamont said gently, and then felt his heart give a surprising little twist as she gave a heavy sigh and brought her eyes up to his. The skin across her cheeks and forehead was stretched taut, her eyes sunken and her cheeks hollow.

Little food, little sleep, and too much of the fear and anger were starting to take a toll on her, and he strongly suspected she was way beyond running on empty; to his physician's-trained eyes, Kyler looked very much on the verge of collapse.

"Mind if I use your shower real quick?" She asked.

"No," he shook his head. "Go ahead; you don't have to ask."

She nodded tiredly and pushed herself up from the table. He watched as she shuffled out of the room, head hung between hunched shoulder blades as if she expected either a blow from behind or was carrying an enormous burden.

He briefly thought about taking her to the hospital after all, but then quickly dismissed the idea. He knew without a doubt that if he did that, Kyler would take off and he'd most likely never see her again.

Somehow, in some way, that hurt him a little bit.

Later that evening as nine o'clock came and went, Lamont sat in his car across the street from the skate park and watched as Kyler came slowly to the gate and locked it between herself and the world outside the fence. She was stumbling a bit, and even from this distance he could see the haggardness in her face.

He waited until she was back in the office before picking up his cell phone and dialing the number.

"Beaumont Skate Park," her weary voice came thin across the line, and he pictured her sitting at the desk with her head in her hands.

"You didn't call," he said quietly.

"Doc," she sighed, "where are you?"

"Home."

Kyler was indeed sitting at the desk and holding her pounding head gently in the palm of one hand. The phone was in the other, slightly away from her ear because even his soft voice was enough to send shrieking pain through her skull.

"I just got done," she mumbled. "I was gonna call."

Lamont was silent, watching the park through the window of his car.

She swallowed thickly and reached for the bottle of water on the desk with a badly shaking hand. "I'm a lotta things, Doc, but I'm not a liar. I was gonna call."

"Ok," he responded mildly. "You all right?"

"Yeah. Just busy . . . lotta paperwork."

"Thought you said you were done."

"With the repairs. Still got the invoices and everything. I'll be here . . . probably awhile."

He was silent again, thinking. "You gonna stay there?"

Now it was her turn to pause as she tried to put her words together. "Doc . . ." Kyler faltered. "I . . . you know . . . I just . . ."

"Don't trust me, I know," his voice was neutral. "And I'm ok with that, Kyler. You've been through a lot and I can't expect you to just latch onto me."

"I normally don't latch onto people anyway," her voice held tired amusement, and for that he was somewhat glad. If she could find even a little humor, then she wasn't too bad off . . . yet.

"So? You gonna stay there?"

"Yeah," Kyler answered reluctantly. "At least tonight. I won't get done till real late anyway."

"Where you gonna sleep?"

"The storage room," and now her eyes swept that way as her body anticipated the sleep that would hopefully come and that it so desperately needed.

"On the floor?"

"Doc," she sighed and scrubbed a hand across her forehead. "I'll be all right. I'm gonna stay here, I'm not gonna go wandering the streets, and I'm not gonna go get loaded, ok?"

Lamont was silent for a minute or two, and then she heard him give a heavy sigh of his own. "Ok," he muttered. "But just know that the spare bed is open if you want it. And if you want it at two in the morning, that's fine, Kyler, ok? I don't care if you wake me up. I just . . . you know . . . want you to know that you don't *have* to sleep there on the floor."

"I appreciate it, Doc; I really do," her voice was hesitant, almost timid. "But right now . . . right now it's just really hard for me, and . . . I think I could sleep better . . . here, ok?"

"Yeah," he said. "Ok."

"I'll call you tomorrow."

"Sure. Be careful."

"I will," Kyler hung up the phone and dropped her head to her arms. The room was swinging lazily around her, and she was all too aware of just how hard her heart was beating.

With an effort she pushed away from the desk and staggered over to the storage room. Inside she had a pillow and an old Army blanket, and she fell into these with the total and complete exhaustion that only the amount of pressure she was carrying could produce.

CHAPTER 19

TWISTED IMAGES WRAPPED themselves around her, strangling her with their horrific embraces. Kyler was lying on the floor, backed against the wall with the blanket tight around her, breathing hard and shaking, lost in her deep nightmares.

Again it was that hand closing around her throat, shutting off her air. Claustrophobia swamped her harder than ever before and Kyler was dimly aware she was fighting a losing battle to get oxygen in her body and sanity in her brain. The fingers dug into her flesh, throttling her windpipe; tremendous pain in itself, but nothing compared to the tearing sensation of being split wide open in her groin.

Kyler felt the blood start to flow, heard his harsh breathing in her ear. She smelled his horrible breath and felt the weight of him like a ton of rocks on her chest, crushing her from the top, splitting her from the inside, cutting her off from the world.

It was so much more than she'd ever experienced and in the most awful, negative way. Worse than all the lows heroin had brought her to; worse even than the day Josh had walked away from her.

Easily the worst thing she'd ever gone through, and it was bitterly ironic that it was happening now, when she was finally starting to get her life back together.

"*. . . kyler . . .*"

Her name, being spoken from a long way off, but she barely heard it as she fought with everything she had left to get this monster off her.

"*. . . Kyler . . .*"

He wasn't going. *He wasn't going.* Kyler fought the panic and pain, reaching way down deep for one final bout of strength.

"*Kyler.*"

She felt her ragged fingernail dig hard into an eyeball, and she twisted it, raking it across flesh and bone, trying with everything she had to drive it all the way into the eye socket.

"Kyler."

A hand on her shoulder, and then Kyler was up against her attacker with a gun pointed between his eyes.

"Not this time, motherfucker," she said softly.

Lamont stared into the end of the blue-steeled barrel and felt his mouth suddenly go dry. His heart leapt into his throat and fluttered there like a wounded bird.

Talk! His mind yammered helplessly. *Talk! Let her hear your voice, and please, God, let her recognize it!*

"Kyler . . ." he croaked. "Jesus, kid . . . it . . . it's me, Lamont. Doc."

For a second the gun stayed steady as a rock . . . a second that lasted more than a lifetime to him.

"Kyler, you know me. Wake up and look at me." Her eyes were wide open in the dim darkness, but they were unfocused and lost, still living that nightmare.

"It's ok, kid, it's ok, it's gonna be ok." Realizing he was close to blubbering, Lamont made himself stop and take a deep shaky breath. "You know me, kid."

The gun was still pointed at him, but now it wavered just a bit, and looking into her eyes—*Jesus Christ, thank you*—he saw they were slowly coming back to life.

"Doc?" Kyler asked tentatively.

"Yeah, Kyler."

Her arm dropped and he heard the sweet-blessed sound of the gun thumping to the floor.

"Oh, God," she moaned, and then lunged towards him. Lamont caught her easily and held her tight against him, his arms around her frail, skinny body. Her shirt was soaked with sweat and her skin was burning against his. He smelled the fever on her, as well something else; something medicinal.

Her arms were locked in a death grip around his neck and he felt her heart slamming out an erratic rhythm against his own.

"Shh," he murmured. "It's ok. It's ok, kid."

"No," he felt her shake her head on his shoulder. "It's not, Doc. None of this shit's ok."

"It's gonna be," he whispered. "I promise you that. It's gonna be ok."

He held her for a long time, until both of their hearts quieted. Kyler finally pulled away and leaned back against the wall with her head in her hands.

"Help me," she pleaded. "Help me, Doc." The tears pouring down her cheeks tore at his heart and he nodded.

"I'll help you, Kyler."

She dropped her forehead to her knees and wrapped her arms around her legs. "It won't stop," she muttered. "These dreams won't fucking stop."

Lamont dropped down beside her and put a hand gently on the back of her neck. "Hold on, kid," he said softly. "Just hold on."

Kyler took a deep breath and let it out in a gush of air. "Fuck, I didn't used to be like this."

For the first time Lamont noticed a slight slur in her words and his brow furrowed. "You're strong, kid," he muttered. "You're gonna get through this." He waited a beat and then offered her his hand.

"C'mon," he pulled her gently to her feet. "Let's go."

"Where?" Kyler struggled to stand on her own, but her sense of balance was way off. She put one hand on the wall and hung her head. Lamont slipped an arm around her waist and took on most of her weight. The sharpness of her rib cage startled him, as did the bagginess of her jeans, riding low on her skinny waist, that he was sure had fit just fine only a week ago.

"To the hospital," he answered gruffly. "Where you shoulda been two days ago."

Kyler allowed him to guide her towards the door, but stopped suddenly after only a step. "I gotta get the gun, Doc. I can't leave it here."

Lamont took a deep breath and let it out in a mumbled, "Shit."

"I can't have one of these kids comin' in here and findin' it," she pulled away from him once more and staggered towards the gun.

He stood where he was for a brief second and then went to her. "Is it loaded?"

"Yeah." He watched as she ejected the clip and pulled the slide back, releasing the one bullet in the chamber. "But not now, it ain't."

"Ok, then," he reached for it. "Let me take it, all right?" Kyler willingly handed it over to him, feeling the world shift sharply to the side.

"Don' lose it, k?" her voice was becoming more slurred. "It ain't mine."

"I won't," Lamont promised, slipping it into his jacket pocket. "C'mon, we gotta get you outta here." He reached for her again and led her out into the night. Kyler stumbled along beside him; her head hung low and her breathing becoming more ragged with every step.

That medicinal smell coming off her seemed sharper in the warm air, and he felt his mind struggling to place it.

At the car Kyler crawled into the back seat, utterly exhausted and slightly sick, with the world spinning freely around her now. Lamont caught a brief glimpse of her face before she fell back on the seat, and felt his heart jump at her eyes, dilated as far out as possible.

He got behind the wheel and started the car, his mind working.

"Kyler," he said quietly, pulling out onto the street. "You still with me?"

"Yeah," she answered. "How'd you get in there? I locked the gate."

"John gave me a key," he shot a quick glance over his shoulder at her in the back seat, but with the arc-sodiums of the park falling behind them, it was hard to see her. "Awhile back."

Kyler was quiet for a few minutes, trying to pull her brain past the weight of the dizziness and the fog it seemed to be under. Finally, she grasped the back of his seat and pulled herself into a sitting position. Lamont just had time to look over and then she was crawling between the seats to plop heavily into the passenger beside him.

Her eyes looking into his were dull and unfocused, and her voice held bitter amusement. "He doesn't trust me."

Lamont waited a beat and then admitted reluctantly, "Not at first, no, he didn't. But he does now."

"Why?" She muttered, leaning against the window and staring blearily out at the night. "Lookit me, Doc," her hands fluttered vaguely over her torso. "I ain't nothin' but a junkie and a thief." She paused and then murmured softly, "And a whore."

There was silence in the car for a mile or so and then she sighed and scrubbed a hand across her face, trying to force reality to reassert itself. "Jesus," her voice was barely audible.

Lamont glanced at her, his hands tight on the wheel, still seeing that blue-steeled barrel pointed between his eyes. "Kyler," he started, swallowing hard. He waited but she didn't answer. "Kyler, I need you to tell me what you're on."

Slowly she pulled her head away from the window and turned to stare at him. "What?" Her voice was definitely slurring now, countering any denial she might give him.

"You heard me," he said gruffly. "What're you on?"

"Nothin'," Kyler gave a slow, drunken shake of her head. "Nothin', Doc, since the coke."

"Yeah?" He stared hard at her. "Nothin' at all?"

"No, noth—" she stopped mid-sentence and he saw her mind trying to reach back. "Nyquil," her voice was sudden and abrupt. "I took Nyquil."

"Nyquil?" Not what he expected to hear. "The cough syrup?"

"Yeah," she leaned her head back against the window. "I . . . couldn't sleep . . . an' I was cold. You said I had a fever so I thought I was probably gettin' sick."

"Nyquil," he repeated quietly. "How much?"

"Uh . . ." Kyler fought to remember. "Two, I think."

"Teaspoons? Tablespoons?"

She shot him a look that he couldn't read in the dim light. "Bottles," her voice was very quiet, and he sensed the shame in it.

"Two *bottles*?" He asked sharply. "*Christ*, Kyler."

She heaved a heavy sigh and turned back to the window again. The fight was gone from her now, along with any peace she'd hoped to derive from the medicine. There was nothing left but an empty shell, lost in a deep fog of codeine overdose.

"Leave it alone, Doc," he read the massive defeat in her soft voice. "Please just leave it alone."

Lamont remained silent and gripped the wheel even harder. The rest of the drive to the hospital was buried under a mountain of stone-cold silence.

He helped her out of the car and into the hospital. By this time Kyler was well on her way to passing out hard. The Nyquil was definitely doing its job and she welcomed it.

Lamont put her on a gurney and savagely hit the button on the elevator, his face stoic against the roar of emotions inside of him.

"You'd be getting on this elevator even if you *weren't* half-comatose," he muttered softly, and to his surprise, she answered back.

"Yeah, Doc, I know," her voice was exhausted. "Just try not to get us stuck, ok?"

He sighed and pushed her in when the doors opened. "When you gonna stop doin' this shit to yourself, kid?"

Kyler just shook her head and pressed the heels of her hands hard against her eyes. The deep, dark hole she was standing just on the edge of opened up wider, and without hesitation she stepped into it, passing all the way out.

CHAPTER 20

KYLER FELT THE pounding in her head before she even opened her eyes. Easily one of the worst headaches she'd ever had, it was par for the course for a Nyquil binge, if her memory served. Although of all the times before when she drank it, never had she downed more than one bottle.

She let out a groan and slit her eyes open against the blinding fluorescents above her.

"Welcome back," a quiet voice said beside her. "Again."

Kyler gently turned her head and saw Emily sitting in the chair beside the bed. Her eyes looked dull and worn, and Kyler had a brief moment to wonder what her own roller-coaster drug use was doing to this woman's emotional state.

"I could say the same to you," her voice came out in a hoarse croak, "but I get the feeling you're not stayin'."

"No," Emily admitted, pouring a glass of water from the pitcher on the nightstand. She held it to Kyler's lips, allowing her a small drink. "Keith asked me to come, but no, I'm not staying. Can I get you anything?"

"Excedrin," Kyler answered immediately. "Four of 'em. Extra strength if you got 'em."

Emily nodded to the nurse and held up two fingers. The nurse nodded back and left the room, arriving back in a minute and handing Kyler two caplets.

"Sorry," Emily shrugged. "Two's the recommended dosage." She paused, watching Kyler down the pills with another swallow of water. "You *do* know what a recommended dosage is, don't you?"

Kyler looked at her with hooded eyes. "This about the Nyquil?"

"Not really," she responded. "I think Keith wants to talk to you about that."

Sighing heavily, Kyler laid back down and looked towards the window. "What do *you* wanna talk to me about?"

"You."

There was silence for a brief second, and then Kyler asked quietly, "About goin' back to jail?"

"I'm working on that, but yes, your legal problems are a concern of mine right now. As well as you personally."

Kyler was quiet, regarding her closely. Her eyes wore dark circles of exhaustion around them, and she could see Curtis weighing heavily on her, rounding her shoulders and dropping her head as if she carried a physical burden.

"How's your son?" She asked softly.

Emily gave a slow shake of her head. "It's day to day, Kyler. He's on the transplant list for a new heart, but it's gonna be awhile . . . if ever. And even with the new heart, I'm not sure if he'll fully recover. That heart attack did extensive damage to his whole system and right now he's on a ventilator."

Kyler swallowed hard, hating herself for her own helpless drug addiction and what it was doing to constantly remind Emily of her dying son.

"I'm sorry," she mumbled.

Emily nodded and took a deep breath. "Yeah. It ain't good, but like I said, it's just day to day."

The silence between them was brief this time and then Emily cleared her throat and met Kyler's eyes directly.

"Tell me what happened."

Kyler stared at her for a moment and then shifted her gaze away. "I'm sure Doc told you."

"He did. But now I want you to tell me."

Kyler stared at the ceiling, feeling the blessed relief of the Excedrin start working, but also the weight of depression and self-loathing as well.

"Talk to me, Kyler."

The quiet of the room was nearly suffocating, and finally Kyler turned to look at her. "What I tell you won't make any difference, Emily. You have to know that."

"Why won't it?" She asked mildly.

"Because I'm a junkie," Kyler snapped. "I spent the last year of my life lying on my back just so I could score some dope. *It's what I do.* Tellin' you what happened to me ain't gonna make the court see it any other way than that."

"Let me worry about that part, ok? You just tell me what happened."

"They're not gonna see rape," Kyler persisted. "They're gonna see it as I was tryin' to score, and then see that I did. They're just gonna see I left the house to get loaded up on coke."

Emily pulled out a notebook from her briefcase on the floor beside her. She opened it up to a specific page and withdrew a pen from her purse. Her eyes were sharp, staring into Kyler's.

"You still going to meetings?"

"Yeah. Two a day. Still getting that fucking paper signed."

"AA or NA?"

"Both, sometimes. Mainly just NA."

Emily nodded and jotted a few notes. "You think they'll overlook that when reviewing your case?"

"I don't know," Kyler growled softly and ran her hands through her hair.

"Because why even bother with the meetings if you're just looking to score?"

"I don't know," she repeated. "I just don't expect anything positive to come outta this, and I really don't deserve anything positive. I fucked up. In the course of one day I let five fucking minutes get out of hand and, in turn, gave up everything I've gained in the last seven months."

Emily was silent, regarding her. Finally, she leaned forward and pinned Kyler's eyes with her own. "Listen, kid. I'm going to do everything in my power to keep you from going to jail, all right? I think the case is there, and I think they'll have to listen to it. All I need from you right now is no bullshit and all facts, ok? Just tell me what happened."

Kyler took a deep breath and let it out slowly. She badly needed a cigarette and just as badly (or even more) needed about five lines of coke laid out in front of her. Better yet, just one syringe filled with the demon of her choice; just one quick fix in a near-collapsed vein to send her flying way above all this.

"It was . . . dark," she started. "I . . . it was late at night—I don't know what time—and I woke up and had to take a piss. I mean, the fucking bathroom's just down the hall from my bedroom, you know?"

Emily nodded, watching her closely.

"I didn't even think . . . about . . . about there being a man in there. The house is for women only, and . . . I don't sleep much anyway, and there were tons of times I'd gone to the bathroom late like that."

Kyler shook her head and stared out the window. She felt the fear building inside again, making her hands shake and her stomach twist up.

"He . . ." she swallowed and hung her head. "He came from behind me and . . . and threw me into a stall. I didn't expect it and I hit the toilet hard on my shoulder. I think that's what let him get to me. The wind . . . the breath got knocked out of me and for a second I couldn't move."

Emily wrote as she talked, listening intently to every word. She was aware of Kyler's fear and her heart went out to her. But she also knew she had to keep her talking until she had everything. The smallest detail would probably be what would keep her out of jail.

"Do you know him?" She asked.

"No."

"If I showed you pictures, do you think you can pick him out?"

"No," Kyler raised her eyes to hers. "I never saw him." She was quietly flooded with the cold, damp fear again, remembering the events of that night.

"It doesn't matter anyway," her voice was soft. "Like I told you, the court won't see it as rape."

Emily reached down and pulled a manila folder from her briefcase. "Kyler, in the past month the police have been called to that neighborhood six times. Two peeping Tom cases in ground-level apartment windows, three attacks that were reported as attempted rapes." She stopped and looked at her. "The last was a rape that occurred a week and a half ago."

Kyler furrowed her brow, thinking, and then gave a slow shake of her head. "What's all that got to do with me?"

"The police believe they have a serial rapist in that area . . . the area within a three-block radius of the house on Kennedy."

Kyler was silent, waiting.

"The one woman who was raped got a good look at the suspect and the police drew up a sketch." Emily pulled a piece of white paper from the folder and handed it to her. Kyler looked at it but shook her head and shrugged.

"I never saw him," she repeated.

"Listen," Emily's voice was calm. "The sketch matches the mug shot of a man who was in prison two years ago for aggravated rape and assault." Now she pulled out another picture—a mug shot—of a short, stocky man and handed it to her. Kyler's eyes were confused as they stared into her own.

"Go on, kid. Tell me what happened next."

"I . . ." Kyler swallowed, "I don't know. He . . . raped me . . . there in the stall. My shoulder . . . where it hit the toilet, you know, it was numb . . . and . . . and actually my whole arm was numb and it wasn't working and I couldn't use it to get him off me. He . . . I couldn't see him but I felt him . . . his face . . . with my other hand."

Emily's sharp eyes drilled into hers, waiting.

"I . . . think I . . . well, I mean, I found his eye with my thumb and I scratched it as hard as I could. He . . . kinda yelped, I guess, and rolled off me. That's when I got up and ran and I . . . you know, I just kept goin'."

Kyler drew her knees up to her chest and locked her arms around them. The light caught the unshed tears in her eyes as she shifted her gaze to the window.

"And I didn't wait. Didn't sleep, didn't go to the cops. Didn't pass go, so to speak," now her voice held bitter sarcasm. "Just went out and got high."

Deep, heavy silence dropped between them for what seemed like an eternity. Kyler felt that old need raging inside of her, demanding that she leave this place and these questions and find the solace she'd been finding for far too long in a needle in a dark alley somewhere.

She sighed and pressed the heels of her hands hard against her eyes, trying to find enough inner strength to just make it the next five minutes . . . or even maybe just the next two.

"Two days ago, Kyler, a man was arrested one block over from Kennedy Street, trying to break into the basement window of a house," Emily's voice was soft, seeming to come from far away. "Here," she laid yet another sheet of paper on the bed beside her. "His new mug shot."

Kyler shifted her eyes to stare down at the paper. It was definitely the same man as in the other picture, only this one was sporting a gauze bandage over his right eye. For a minute her stomach plummeted and she felt nauseous. The sweat gathered on her sides and temples and slid down her back.

"Oh . . . shit," her voice was barely audible.

"They caught him, Kyler, and this is the proof you need, and circumstantial though it is in your case against *him*, it just might be enough to keep *you* outta jail."

Kyler took a deep breath and let it out slowly, wanting to believe, to hope, but not quite able to. She thought of Josh . . . again . . . as usual . . . and wondered about him, where he was, how he was doing. If he'd finally found the peace he was looking for and if that peace had come in another woman.

The hard weight of regret and too many wasted days, months, years, carried heavily on her shoulders, and instead of hope what she really felt was a lost, bitter, hopelessness.

I wouldn't even be in this fucking situation if I'd never fucked it up with him, her mind whispered wearily.

She laid her head on her knees and silently begged him in her heart for forgiveness.

"Kyler."

She turned and met Emily's gaze. "Ok," she said softly. "What now?"

"Now," Emily gathered up her papers and stuck them all back in her briefcase, "you just relax. I'll worry about the legal stuff and where it's goin' from here, all right?" Her eyes bored into Kyler's. "And quit doin' all this stupid shit. It ain't gonna get you back all the stuff you lost; you know that, don't you?"

Kyler gave a slow nod and laid back on the bed. "Yeah," she sighed. "I know."

"Ok," Emily offered a small smile. "Take it easy and I'll talk to you later. Don't worry, I'll keep you up to date on everything." She started out of the room, but Kyler's voice stopped her.

"Hey . . . Emily?"

She turned, regarding her with raised eyebrows.

"Thanks . . . for doing all this," Kyler said quietly. "Thanks for coming."

Emily shrugged noncommittally, but there was a sadness in her eyes. "It's my job, Kyler, and right now it's keeping me grounded, you know?" She paused, almost looking like she wanted to say more, but then shrugged and left the room, closing the door gently behind her.

CHAPTER 21

KYLER WAS UP again, arms wrapped around her drawn up knees, when Lamont walked into the room a few hours later. For a moment his eyes drilled into hers, and she saw exhaustion and weariness in them.

"Hey," he said quietly.

"Hey," she responded. She gestured towards her left ankle, where an IV was embedded in a vein, slowly drawing blood out. "Guess you got your blood, huh?"

He nodded and pulled the chair up close to the bed. "Doesn't hurt, does it?"

"No."

"Got some good news. Your urinalysis from Monday came back clean . . ." He paused, brow furrowed. "Not clean, really. I mean, the cocaine showed up, but . . ." he shrugged, looking at her. "There was nothing else."

She was quiet, watching him. "And this?" She pointed to the IV. "This'll help show if I got hepatitis or AIDS?"

Lamont offered a slow nod. "Over a period of time. The AIDS test will take at least six months."

Kyler swallowed and glanced towards the window. Something was sticking in her head . . . a sharp thorn . . . that was just out of the reach of her reasoning. She gazed out at the bright sunshine, wishing she was at work or on her board. Or down by the ocean. She always wished she was down by the ocean.

As she stared out the window, the thorn in her brain got just close enough for her to reach out and work loose, and she turned back to Lamont with confusion in her eyes.

"You said my urinalysis was done on Monday."

"Yeah."

"That was . . . yesterday . . . right?" Her brow furrowed in thought as she struggled to remember.

He took a deep breath and let it out slowly. "No, kid, it wasn't. Yesterday was Wednesday. From the time I dropped you off at work on Monday until I dragged you out of that office late last night, I didn't hear from you."

Kyler stared at him, trying to reach back in her muddled brain to figure out just how the hell she could've lost two days. He saw faint fear in her gaze and quickly answered her unspoken question.

"No, I tested you when I brought you in here last night. Nothin' but the Nyquil, Kyler."

"Then, how the hell . . ." she trailed off, confused and scared.

"My guess is . . . well, you had a virus, for one thing. Kinda like the flu only . . . not, you know? That's where your fever came from, and by the time I got to you, and between the two bottles of Nyquil, you were pretty far out of it. The fever finally broke around one a.m. this morning, but before that it spiked up close to one oh three.

"You were about damn-near delirious and incoherent. For about an hour you couldn't even remember your own name. I've been flushing your system for the past six hours or so, and fed you an IV to re-hydrate you."

He stopped, watching her. "When's the last time you ate?"

Kyler stared back at him, having absolutely no clue. Food had never really been that important to her, even without the drugs, and on the drugs she'd been known to go weeks without eating.

"I don't know. Been awhile, I guess."

"Yeah," he muttered.

Kyler shifted her gaze back to the window. "I feel fine now. Stomach's kinda iffy, but otherwise . . ."

Lamont gave her a long, level look; his eyes measuring. "Good. I'm glad to hear that, Kyler. You up to talking to me for a while?"

"Sure . . . ok . . ." she muttered slowly, and he saw the suspicion rise up in her again. Reaching for the stethoscope in his pocket, he put it on and placed the cold, steel end on her inner wrist. He counted off a few beats and then slung the stethoscope back around his neck.

"Emily told me about your shoulder," he said. "Mind if I take a look?"

Kyler gave a little nod and he gently slipped the hospital gown down past her upper arm. She tried to sit still but found herself pulling away. Lamont felt her shaking as he slowly examined the area of the huge black and yellow bruise that covered her entire left shoulder blade.

The knobs of her spine were obvious and distinct down the length of her back, and her shoulder blades and collar bones protruded along her pale skin.

"Easy," he murmured, his brow furrowed. "Does this hurt?" He gently pressed along her spine closest to the edge of the bruise. She hissed in a breath and flinched away.

"I take it that's a yes," he said. Pulling her gown up, he slid back around and gazed at her. "How's your arm? Working all right now?"

"Yeah," Kyler muttered, not looking at him. She tried not to show it, but he saw the fear—more prominent now—in her eyes.

"I'd like to get an x-ray, all right?"

She sighed and ran her hands through her hair. Finally she met his eyes with an imploring stare. "Can't you just let me go, Doc?"

He sat back in the chair and watched her for a minute. "Where would you go?" His voice was soft. "Empty building? Vacant lot? Back to the storage room at the park?"

Kyler swallowed heavily and offered a slow shake of her head. "Does it matter?"

Lamont took a deep breath and let it out slowly. "Yeah. It kinda does, kid."

"Why?"

He contemplated for a minute and scrubbed a hand across his face. "They, uh . . . legally, Kyler, you're supposed to be in a halfway house. They *want* you in a halfway house, as per the terms of your deal."

She stared at him for a long moment, feeling her heart pounding against her sternum. "Doc . . . I can't . . ." her voice was shaky. "I can't . . . you know . . . that . . . that . . . *shit*." She wrapped her arms around her knees again dropped her head.

Lamont saw the shaking in her body increase and without thinking reached out a hand to comfort her. Kyler drew away, not looking at him.

"It's ok," he said softly. "We'll figure something out."

"Just lemme go, Doc. Please?"

"I can't. You're still sick, and barring the fact that you've got no place to go, legally . . . I can't."

Kyler pinched the bridge of her nose, feeling the seeds of a potentially bad headache starting. "Ok," she nodded. "All right, Doc."

Sliding her gaze to his, he saw ultimate defeat in her eyes. "But don't do the x-ray. I can't pay for it."

Lamont gave a slow shake of his head. "You've got insurance, kid, through the park. Didn't you know that?"

She stared at him. "What?"

"Didn't John ask you to fill out some papers when you first started?" And once again Kyler found herself fighting for recollection in her scattered memories.

"Yeah, I think so. If I can remember, yeah, he did."

"Those were insurance forms . . . health insurance, actually, paid for by the park in a roundabout tax write off kinda way."

Kyler offered a raised eyebrow in question.

"It's a given you're going to get hurt," he said in a way of explanation. "So because it's a community park and paid for by the city, and because you work there, the city is ultimately paying for your health insurance."

She was quiet a minute, thinking. "I thought John owned the park."

"No," Lamont shook his head. "He's just sole operator, and up 'till recently, he just had it for a tax write off."

"Why just 'till recently?" Kyler was having a hard time processing that somebody was actually paying for her to have health insurance.

Lamont offered her a measuring look. "Because you went to work there. You've turned that place around, and now it might just be profitable for the city to keep it instead of razing it like it was previously suggested."

She stared at him for a few minutes, and then laid back down, stretching out her stomach. "I ain't really done nothin', Doc, 'cept try to stay occupied."

"I wouldn't call twenty-thousand dollars nothing," a gruff voice came from the doorway. They both turned to see John Carter leaning against the door jamb with his hands stuffed in his front pockets.

"Besides," he offered a grin, walking into the room, "I couldn't close that place down now. I'm liable to get shot with all them young kids runnin' around everywhere." He offered his hand first to Lamont and then to Kyler.

"Done a helluva job, kid, and it's keeping those kids outta trouble," he drawled in his thick Kentuckian accent.

"Thanks," she gave a small smile of her own and sat back up. "What're you doin' here?"

"I called him, Kyler," Lamont said quietly, "when I brought you in here."

"And I'm glad he did," John's eyes were somewhat stern as they stared into hers. "Otherwise, I'd've never got to see my twenty-thousand dollars worth of concrete poured."

"They poured it?" Kyler's smile became a genuine grin . . . the first one Lamont had seen on her in days, and he was really glad to see it. "How's it look?"

"How's *what* look?" He asked, staring from one to the other.

John lifted an eyebrow and gestured with his head towards Kyler. "Apparently, Keith, she designed this huge ramp out in the middle of the grass, went and bought the concrete for twenty grand, and today they poured it." He shot her a somewhat sharp look.

"You're gonna keep on, right? I mean, you ain't gonna just leave this big patch of concrete sittin' there, are you?"

"Relax," Kyler said mildly. "I've got the plans all drawn up and I'll do most of the work myself so it'll save you from getting another big bill."

"Good," he muttered. "Hey, Keith, you mind if I talk to her alone for a minute?"

"Nope," Lamont got up and walked out the door without a look back. For a minute Kyler felt her stomach shift, and as she stared into John's hard eyes, she was wondering if he was about ready to fire her.

"So you're really doing ok?" He sat in the chair Lamont had vacated and gave her a pointed look.

"That's what they tell me," thinking, *Just how much does he know? The coke? Probably. The Nyquil? The rape?* She had no answer to these but wasn't about to offer up any information.

He grunted and leaned forward, resting his elbows on his knees. "Listen, kid . . ." John paused and purposefully focused his gaze on a hangnail on his left ring finger.

"What?" Kyler muttered.

He looked up at her. "You like workin' there? At the park?"

"Yeah, John, I do."

He favored her with a long, level look. "What about after your community service is up? Got any plans?"

Kyler gave a slow shake of her head. "Haven't really thought about it."

"Wanna stay there? Full time?"

Her eyebrows shot up in surprise, and for a minute all she could do was stare at him.

"Well?" John allowed a small smile.

"Are you serious?"

"Sure. I need somebody . . ." he paused, thinking. "Actually, I need *you*. You've done more in the past month to that place than's been done in the past two years. I know, because I've been the one there, struggling with it."

Kyler took a deep breath, wondering if she could dare to believe in this little bit of good luck.

"You look kinda sick. You're not gonna throw up, are you?" John asked somewhat apprehensively.

"No," she shook her head. "It's just that I woulda bet money you were only about two seconds away from getting rid of me."

"Oh, yeah?" He leaned back and folded his arms across his chest. "Why would you think that?" And now his eyes were hard again, drilling into hers.

'Cause of the coke, her mind whispered.

"I don't know," she muttered. "Maybe 'cause you're pissed about the concrete?"

"Kyler, you got a shitload of concrete for that amount of money . . . they cut you a deal or what?"

"Just talked 'em down, I guess." A thought occurred to her and she shot him a sharp look. "Not all of it was supposed to go out in the grass."

"It didn't," John shook his head. "The rest went in the pool."

"Good," she smiled, relieved. "That's where it was supposed to go."

"Besides," he flapped a hand vaguely, "you're still way under budget."

This was something Kyler already knew because she'd been damn-near obsessing over the numbers for the past couple of weeks, and she took a certain amount of pride in knowing everything was balancing out.

"So, no, I'm not gonna fire you," he said. "You're good there, and you got the place really lookin' good. And it helps me out 'cause I'm only supposed to be out here maybe three, four times a year . . . or whenever I got a horse running."

He looked at her and shrugged. "Gets tiring flying three-thousand miles every coupla weeks to check on the place."

"Yeah, I guess it would."

For a second she regarded him, picturing his life as a horse trainer in some town in Kentucky, and wondered why the fuck a man like him would've ever hooked up with a place like the skate park to begin with.

"So?" John asked with raised eyebrows. "Yes or no."

"You know it's a yes," Kyler murmured.

He grinned. "Good. How's thirteen seventy-five sound?"

"An hour?" Kyler shot him an incredulous look.

"Just to start," he said quickly, misunderstanding the expression on her face. "You know, and then I'll raise ya up over time."

"Thirteen seventy-five an hour," her voice was soft. Unlike what John was thinking, it wasn't too little of an amount . . . it was actually more than she'd ever contemplated.

"Of course, the hours are long . . . nine to nine, and I know it sucks but it's seven days a week . . ." John trailed off, giving a half-hearted shrug. "But it's up to you."

Kyler looked at him. "I told you yes. The hours don't bother me, 'cause . . . you know . . . sometimes I get to thinkin' too much, and the work'll make sure that don't happen."

"Yeah, that's what I figured."

There was silence for a minute and then she shook her head. "You tell Doc to let me outta here and you can head on back home tonight."

John gave her a hard look. "I'll try, Kyler, but he'll probably keep you for at least another day or two. In either case, I actually *do* have a horse out at Del Mar this week so I'm here 'til Sunday."

"Ok," Kyler gave a tired nod. "But ask him anyway, all right? I ain't doin' nobody any good stuck here in this room."

"Sure," he stood up and offered her his hand. "But don't overdo it. You wouldn't be doing anybody any good if you wind up back in here." He started to leave but paused at the door and looked back at her. The look in his eyes was unreadable as he said,

"And lay off the powder, ok? That shit *really* ain't doin' nobody good . . . not you, not them kids, not me or Keith . . ." He trailed off and then added gruffly, "And eat something for Christ's sakes. You look like a fucking bone rack."

Kyler watched him walk out the door and felt the shame in her gut. "Shit," she muttered, "I don't deserve for these people to keep on having faith in me." She lay back down and pressed her hands hard against her eyes, reaching desperately to find some solace *somewhere*.

A few minutes later Lamont came back in the room and sat quietly in the chair beside her bed. Kyler turned her head and gazed at him.

"He didn't fire me."

"You thought he would?"

"Yeah."

He waited a beat and then said softly, "Lemme get that x-ray, ok? Then you can come outside with me while I eat my lunch. I know you need a cigarette."

And Kyler, though hating the prospect of the x-ray, found that she definitely needed a cigarette, and in a desperate way.

She sighed and rolled out of bed. Lamont stopped her with a hand on her shoulder and gestured back towards the door.

"I've got a wheelchair right outside. Let me get it before you fall and crack your head on the floor."

Kyler leaned against the bed and waited in silence, and then plopped heavily into the chair when he rolled it in. He wheeled her out of the room and down the hall with the silence thick around them. Finally she cleared her throat and said softly,

"The shoulder ain't really that bad, Doc. Don't even hurt much now."

"Yeah," Lamont pushed her into the x-ray room, "but one side of that bruise is damn close to your spine, Kyler. You may not feel any pain, but I just want to make sure it didn't damage anything major, ok?"

She sighed and pushed herself out of the chair. "Fuck, when's this shit gonna stop?" She mumbled, not really expecting an answer. Lamont gently helped her up on the table and arranged her face-down with the huge eye of the machine over her left shoulder.

"Just keep on holding on, kid," he responded quietly. "It's gonna get better." He pulled the heavy blanket over her and told her to hold still for just a couple of seconds. Kyler heard him walk behind her to the wall that separated him from her, and then felt rather than heard the machine start to hum above her.

She closed her eyes and wished desperately for Josh's arms around her, feeling her heart ache with a regret that was fiercer than any withdrawal she'd ever gone through.

"Ok," Lamont's voice was beside her again, and she felt the blanket leave her body. "Done."

"Any damage?" She managed as she half-fell off the table. He caught her and eased her back into the wheelchair.

"I'll know in a minute. You still feeling all right?"

"Yeah, I guess," Kyler rubbed her forehead. "Headache, but it ain't too bad."

Lamont grunted and glanced towards the machine as it beeped. "Hold on a sec." He walked back behind the wall and pulled the results from the printer near the floor. Kyler watched him through the small window as he held her x-rays up to the light. When his eyes met hers he gave a shake of his head.

"No damage," he walked back over to her. "Just a bad bruise, but it completely missed your spine. No damage to your shoulder or arm, either."

Kyler nodded. "That's good."

"Yeah," he grasped the handles of the wheelchair and pushed her back out into the hall. "Wanna go outside with me for some fresh air?"

"And a cigarette?" She glanced hopefully back at him.

"Yeah," he smiled. "And a cigarette. You got any or do you need me to get you some?"

"I think I got some . . ." she paused, thinking. "I did, anyway, in my jeans pocket."

Back in her room he pulled her clothes from the top shelf of the closet and handed them to her. Kyler went through the pockets of her jeans until she found a battered pack of Marlboros and a nearly-empty lighter.

Just the feel of them in her hand brought on the anticipation of a nicotine rush. It seemed like it'd been months since she'd last had one, and she found her body crying out for it.

"You wanna get dressed, you can," Lamont said. "I take it you don't want to ride the elevator down?"

Kyler shot him a look that he read all too well.

"Ok," he held his hands up in mock surrender. "As long as you don't fall down the stairs. I'll be outside."

She waited until the door closed behind him before pulling herself out of the chair and struggling into her clothes. Her jeans were baggier than ever, and she figured she'd have to pick up a belt sometime soon.

Lamont was waiting for her outside the door, and the look on his face told her he could tell she'd lost another few pounds.

"I'm gonna grab something from the cafeteria and figured we could sit out by the lake. You want something? I'm buying. They got good sandwiches."

Kyler held the door to the stairs open for him, avoiding his eyes. "No, thanks, Doc. I'm not really hungry."

He didn't answer as he started down the stairs slightly ahead of her. Kyler knew he was aggravated, and felt slightly guilty, but she'd always had a hard time accepting charity, even if that only included a two-dollar sandwich from a hospital cafeteria.

And after all, she'd told the truth when she'd said she wasn't all that hungry.

Silently she walked behind him as he went through the line, and giving in, gave a slow nod when he pointed to a coke cooler filled with twenty-ounces.

"Mountain Dew," she answered his raised eyebrows. Lamont put a Mountain Dew and a Diet Coke on his tray, paid the cashier, and gestured with his head towards the door. Kyler followed him out into the bright southern California sunshine, and the feel of it on her skin was like liberation.

For once she was feeling halfway decent and the warm rays on her skin and the smell of salt in the air forced her demons to the back burner for the moment.

Lamont headed over to a picnic table on the edge of the man-made lake. Kyler pulled her smokes from her pocket and lit one, took a deep drag and held it far down in her lungs for as long as she could. She let the smoke filter slowly out of her nose as she twisted the top on her Dew.

Between the nicotine and the caffeine, the warm sun and the breeze coming in off the ocean, she felt like it could be possible to maybe love being alive again; to hopefully forget all the bad things that had happened, all the bad choices she'd made, and maybe someday be able to let go of all the regrets that were still so heavily on her shoulders.

Lamont pulled his sandwich from its plastic container and wordlessly handed her half. Kyler only reluctantly took it because she knew how much he wanted her to eat, and right then she was feeling too good to turn away from him.

It was chicken salad, and actually pretty good, but her stomach was slowly turning in circles. Kyler chewed mechanically and swallowed each bite completely before taking another, praying silently for her stomach to accept this first real food in God only knew how long, and to not send it racing back up her throat.

It was a little rough, but eventually the sandwich was down and her stomach seemed stable enough to keep it there. Kyler took a big drink of her Mountain Dew and nodded thanks to Lamont.

"You didn't have to give me half your food."

He shrugged and popped the last bite of his sandwich into his mouth. "You need it more than I do."

Kyler didn't answer as she lit another cigarette. For a few minutes the only sounds around them were the birds out on the lake. She absently chewed on a ragged fingernail and stared out across the water.

Finally Lamont cleared his throat and turned to look at her. Kyler felt her stomach roll over once more as she tried to read his eyes.

"You wanna tell me about the gun?"'

Something squeezed hard against her heart and lungs, making it hard to breathe. She remembered the hot, oily panic she'd felt as she became aware that the gun was held centered between her doctor—her *friend's*—eyes instead of the man who'd raped her. Everything had been fueled by terror and hatred, yes, but that was enough to force her along a road that almost ended in total destruction for her soul and sanity . . . not to mention Lamont's own life.

Even now she felt her finger, trembling and hard against the cold steel of the trigger; felt the pressure both inside and out as the hair's-breath more poundage needed to send a bullet into Lamont's brain became a very real possibility.

He saw her begin to shake beside him on the picnic table and knew she was reliving that night much like he'd done every night since then.

"It belongs to a friend of mine," Kyler murmured, forcing herself to meet his eyes. "You still got it?"

"Yeah," he sighed. "You're gonna give it back, right?"

Kyler ran her hands through her hair and locked her fingers behind her neck, staring back down at the ground. "Yeah."

She wished she could take that night back, maybe stick with just one bottle of Nyquil instead of guzzling two, or maybe (even better) she could've told him the nightmares just weren't going away—and were, in fact, getting worse—long before she pulled a gun on him with a barely-conscious state of mind.

"I'm sorry," she said softly. "I know that don't mean much, but for what it's worth, it wasn't you I was trying to kill that night."

Lamont grunted and gathered up his trash. She watched him walk it over to a garbage can and waited as he stared across the water, seemingly lost in deep thought.

"I know it wasn't me," he shot her a glance. "But I'd've still been dead."

Kyler swallowed and dropped her eyes, feeling the exhaustion start to wind its way through her body her again.

Lamont sat beside her and waited for a moment, searching for the right words.

"Kyler," he started gently, "if you ever want to talk about it . . . the rape—"

"I don't," she responded sharply.

"But if you do," he pressed, "we have an outpatient therapy program here that I think would help you out a lot."

Wonderful, she thought. *First I'm feeling like pounded horse-shit—not to mention scared outta my fucking mind—'cause I almost killed him, and now I'm pissed 'cause he won't just leave this shit alone.*

"Yeah," Kyler gave a bitter laugh. "Lemme walk in and tell a total stranger I was raped, and once it's out in the open I've been whoring for dope for the past year, they're gonna wonder why the fuck it didn't happen sooner."

"Jesus, Kyler," Lamont said angrily. "You can't really think that."

"Why not?" Her gaze drilled into his and he saw the immense rage in it. "Living the life I was living, Doc, it's not uncommon."

"I know that, but that doesn't make it right."

"*Life* isn't right. So just let it go."

There was silence between them for a minute, thick and heavy, and then he said. "Talk to *me*, then, kid, before this shit eats you alive."

Kyler shook her head. "You don't want my baggage."

"I don't want you to snap and do something stupid either. So I'm here if you want to talk, and if you want to talk to somebody else I can get you in there pretty quick."

She lit another cigarette with the butt end of the first one and inhaled savagely, stomach churning. The rage was roaring through her, making her hands shake and she felt that old need rising up inside again. Kyler wanted to scream her fear and anger to the world, and actually found herself locking her throat against it.

"Drop it," she muttered, her eyes blazing. "Just fucking let it go, Doc."

Lamont took a deep breath and let it out slowly. The hurricane of emotions was tearing her apart, but he'd already seen the stubborn side of her and knew that right now there was no way she'd budge.

"All right," he said softly. "All right, Kyler."

She stared out across the water, trembling from the hatred racing through her veins, thinking she'd kill for a fix right then. Drawing deep on her smoke, she let it bite hard into her lungs, relishing in the pain.

"I'm sorry," Lamont's voice was quiet.

"Yeah," she dropped her head, giving a small exhausted nod.

The silence lasted longer this time, carrying an invisible weight of its own that pressed against them both. Somewhere across the wide horizon a seagull cried, and Kyler felt a hopelessness that ran bone deep, swamping her.

"Shit," she growled.

"Hold on," Lamont muttered beside her. "Just hold on."

She didn't answer as she got up and walked to the edge of the water. He watched her gaze out in the direction of the ocean, hidden behind the urban sprawl of the city, and wished he could find a way to help her talk out her pain, and to hopefully work through it.

"Emily and I . . ." he stopped and cleared his throat, seeing her shoulders tighten. "Emily and I might've come up with something to help you find a place to stay, but I gotta know . . . you really don't want to try another halfway house?"

"I told you I didn't," she mumbled.

"Even if it's not even close to Kennedy?"

"Doc . . ." Kyler sighed, and then stopped, swallowing heavily.

"They caught the guy, Kyler," Lamont said softly. "Emily told you that."

She dropped her head and stared at the ground. The good feeling was completely gone now, and she realized she would probably be forced into dealing with more bad shit here in the very near future.

Lamont sighed and gazed out over the water. "It's not a given just yet; Emily's still down at the courthouse working on it, but if they agree to it . . ." he stopped and took a deep breath.

"You need an address, Kyler; one that's viable and doesn't have a bad reputation. They want something concrete to put on your records to show that you're not still runnin' the streets looking to score."

"Anybody can put some kinda bullshit down, Doc," she stared at him, her eyes hard. "Anybody can fucking make up a lie and give an address just to keep the shit lookin' clean and legal."

His gaze bored into hers. "Would your old running buddies lie like that for you?" He asked quietly. "All those guys you fucked for dope, would they even think twice about you long enough to look and act credible enough to fool a judge into thinking you'd gone clean and sober and were trying to turn your life around?"

Kyler glared at him, shame and humiliation flooding through her, but in the back of her mind she knew he was right. The court system needed an address and knew if they got one it'd have to be a good one because nobody strung out would care enough about lying for somebody else when all they, themselves, were thinking about was when and where to score their next high.

"So what're you sayin'?" She said gruffly.

"You don't wanna go to a halfway house, ok. But you need an address, so if you're willing, you can use mine. But you'd have to stay there and not at the park or anywhere else."

He stared at her and shrugged. "It's up to you."

"Jesus," Kyler glared at him with fury in her eyes. "Tell me you're kidding, Doc."

A flash of anger rushed through him and he glared right back at her. "You don't have a whole lot of options, kid. Me and Emily, we're just trying to help you out, ok?"

She felt pummeled, pushed, and steered out of control. It took only a second for Kyler to realize her life wasn't her own anymore, and it hurt.

"Look," Lamont sighed, suddenly tired of everything, "it's my house or another halfway house, if you want to know the truth. Or jail."

The rage coursing through her seemed to spike and Kyler gritted her teeth. He saw it and held up his hands in surrender, eyes soft.

"I wish you'd trust me," he said quietly. "I know you can't, but I just wish you'd give it a shot." He paused and then added reluctantly, "I'll add a deadbolt to that bedroom door if you want me to. Give you all the keys."

Kyler shook her head, her eyes hard. "Don't, Doc. Don't go modifying your house just yet. Gimme some fuckin' time, ok? How long do I have to decide?"

He gave another shrug. "Day. Maybe two, I guess."

"All right," she started back towards the hospital. "I'll let you know in two days."

"Shit . . . Kyler . . ." he called half-heartedly, but she never even turned around. Lamont watched her walk in the doors before turning back around to gaze absently at the lake.

Kyler was aware of his eyes on her as she entered the hospital but never acknowledged him. Once the pneumatic doors closed behind her she kept on walking, down a hall and out a side door. Within minutes she was away from the hospital and putting more distance between it and her with each running footstep.

CHAPTER 22

"Jake, gimme 'bout ten minutes!" The words blared from the intercom and echoed out towards the Granger Mountains in the distance. Lamont was pulling into the parking lot at the skate park a day after Kyler walked out of the hospital, and he was relieved to hear her voice amplified through the loudspeakers.

Kyler was sorting through a shipment of new skate wheels when his shadow fell across the doorway; she glanced up but there was no anger this time . . . only exhaustion.

"Hey," Lamont stepped into the room.

"Hey," she muttered.

"I, uh . . ." he sat down in the chair across from the desk, watching her. "I wanted to apologize for yesterday."

She selected a four-pack of green and white wheels and tossed them next to the computer. He waited while she put the box back in the storage room and then came back to plop heavily down in her chair.

"I'm sorry, too," Kyler pulled a cigarette from her crumpled pack and lit it with a badly shaking hand. "I was letting too much shit get to me and you were the closest person to take it out on."

"Yeah, well …" Lamont shrugged, giving her a measuring look, noting the pale, haggard face and bloodshot eyes, "I can understand how you feel like you're being backed into a corner."

She exhaled a stream of smoke and reached for a wheel-less skateboard on the floor beside her. "Yeah, I *do* feel that way." He raised his eyebrows and waited as she typed the item number from the wheels into the computer and then tore open the package.

"But I also realize I'm the one to blame. I backed my ownself into this fucking corner by doin' all that shit to begin with."

She glanced at him before focusing back on the skateboard and the four wheels she was about to put on it. "Tired of blaming other people, Doc. I did it, and it's probably past time I own up to it."

Lamont was quiet for a minute, watching her. Each wheel fit perfectly, like it had been made for that specific skateboard. When she was done all four spun smoothly and easily; the ball-bearings and tiny mechanics on each formed to complete the skateboard, putting it into a whole new light.

"Nice job," he murmured.

Kyler shrugged and pressed the heel of a hand to her forehead. "Ain't nothin' but a couple screws."

He grunted and cocked an eyebrow. "Headache?"

She briefly met his gaze and then slid her eyes away. Without answering she reached for the telephone and hit the intercom button.

"Jake, you're ready!"

Leaning back in the chair, Kyler absently blew a couple smoke rings towards the ceiling. Lamont opened his mouth to say more but then a young kid came skidding to a halt at the doorway, grinning from ear to ear.

"You got it?"

"Yep," she handed him the board. "Lemme know how it handles."

"Thanks, Kyler. Um . . ." the kid shifted his weight to the other foot and lowered his eyes. "Um, how much? Mom gets paid on Friday and maybe she'll . . ."

Kyler flapped a hand at him. "I told you, don't worry about it. They're prototype wheels so there's no charge. Just give me some feedback on 'em when you get a chance."

"Ok," he offered a somewhat uncertain smile. "Um . . . ok, thanks." Without waiting for an answer, he was off again, headed out towards the ramps.

Kyler reached over and hit a key on the keyboard, studied the numbers for a second, and then reached into her pocket and withdrew a crumpled wad of bills. Separating a ten, a five, and two ones, she leaned back and dropped the money into the safe. Lamont had his eyebrows raised in question when she glanced back at him.

"I lied," she shrugged. "I know I told you I'm not really a liar—and I'm not—but sometimes it's a good lie." Jerking a thumb over her shoulder at the door she said quietly, "His family's on welfare. There's no way he could've afforded those wheels, but he shredded two yesterday and without new wheels he wouldn't be able to skate for a long time."

"So you paid for them."

"Yeah," she leaned towards the ashtray and crushed out her half-smoked cigarette. She rested her head on her hands for a moment, slowly massaging her pulsing temples, trying to will the bass drum in her head to go away.

"You ok?"

Kyler was quiet for a few long minutes and then forced herself to meet his eyes. "Hungover," she sighed. "Very hungover."

Silence for a beat and then Lamont said slowly, "Ok."

"But nothing else. I'm not high, I'm not crashing, and if you wanna test me we can go right now."

"No, I believe you. You, uh . . ." He trailed off, not quite knowing what to say, wondering how much of this was his fault by trying to force her to talk about the rape the day before. "How'd you get it? You're underage."

She opened a drawer and pulled out a green bottle, holding it up to Lamont. "Excedrin," she poured four into her hand. "You can check 'em out." She scooted the bottle over to him with a finger and dry-swallowed all four pills.

"Once again, I believe you," he said shortly. "But I think you just exceeded the recommended dosage, Kyler. Again." He scooted the bottle back towards her. "Too much of this shit will cause damage to your liver. Which brings me back to how the hell you got the booze?"

His eyes were angry, staring into hers, but she merely shrugged.

"I've been buying liquor for years, Doc. Hardly ever get carded."

He was silent, staring at her. She managed to meet his gaze for a few moments, but then pushed herself up from the desk, tearing her eyes away.

"Water?" Kyler asked, walking behind him to the little refrigerator.

"Yeah, sure."

She pulled a bottle out and started to hand it to him but he bypassed it and grasped her wrist instead, and not gently either.

"Jesus," Lamont said hoarsely. "Please tell me this is not what I think it is." He pointed a slightly shaking finger at the two band-aids that covered the inside of her left elbow.

"It's not what you think it is," she answered easily and gently peeled them off, revealing a blackish bruise and three or four small bumps.

"*Something* sure as fuck has been in your arm," he snapped. "If not heroin, then what?"

"Plasma," she set his bottle of water in front of him and pulled her arm away. "When I left the hospital yesterday I stopped by the plasma center down on Frankfort and donated."

He stared at her. "What? You donated plasma?"

"Yeah," Kyler plopped heavily back down in her chair and took a long drink of her water. "Don't worry, Doc . . . those people are as thorough as you guys are about testing for AIDS and stuff."

"Yeah . . . I know . . ." he flapped a hand vaguely, trying to get past the near-concrete surety he'd just had of her shooting up during the night. He gazed at her bruised elbow, then raised his eyes to hers.

"You let them stick a needle in you? And they found a good vein?"

She gestured to the small bumps. "It took them a time or two, and it wasn't easy on my part. I . . . well . . ." she gave a small shrug. "You know how I was when you tried it."

"You fucking puked," he said flatly. "And passed out."

"And I did it again—puked, anyway, but didn't pass out—right after I donated. If I'd've done it before they wouldn't've let me do it."

"Christ," he muttered. "Why, Kyler? What was the point?"

She lit another cigarette and ran a hand through her hair. "I needed money," she responded softly. "And I've only ever gotten money three ways, Doc. Two options didn't appeal to me, so I figured I'd try donating again."

"You needed money," he repeated. "Why?"

"I'm still on the city's time," she said patiently. "John won't be able to hire me for awhile."

"No, I mean *why* did you need the money?"

"I promised Jake new wheels." But something flickered deep in her eyes and he saw the underlying fear.

"You needed money because you wanted to get high, didn't you?"

Kyler took a deep breath and let it out slowly. Her cigarette trembled in her hand as she reached for the ashtray in silence.

"Talk to me, kid," Lamont said softly. "Please?"

She raised her hooded, bloodshot eyes to his and he saw the tight line of her jaw. She gave a barely perceptible nod as she flicked off her ash.

"When I left I was pissed off as hell, and thought this is just too much shit. Being forced to choose between staying with you and at another halfway house was . . ." she struggled for the right words. ". . . was crushing me, Doc. I'm not used to choosing between things like that. My whole life has been spent just choosing a place to crash for the night, or what store owner I could maybe convince to give me some leftover food so I wouldn't have to dig in a dumpster."

His eyes grew soft as he gazed at her.

"And, yeah, if I'd gotten the money another way, I probably would've got high. But donating plasma, you know . . . with that fucking needle in my arm . . . reminded me of the really low points of shooting heroin. Laying there, shaking on the bathroom floor, I knew that if I even survived that first hit it wouldn't be but just a matter of a day—if not hours—when I'd be puking and shaking again, probably in some alley somewhere.

"Then would come the convulsions and the seizures, and my body might not be able to pull out of it this time."

"I'd bet money it wouldn't, Kyler," Lamont's voice was surprisingly gentle compared to the way his stomach was churning, rolled up in barbed wire. "I already told you, you shoot up again it's probably gonna kill you."

"Yeah," she sighed. "But that don't stop me from wanting it, even now. But heroin withdrawal's the worst physical pain I've ever gone through, and, Jesus, I'm just so fucking tired of hurting."

He arched an eyebrow. "So it's all about willpower?"

Kyler slowly shook her head. "More like . . . like not wanting to hurt myself anymore, but really not wanting to hurt those around me either. People like you . . . and . . . and Emily . . . and . . ." she swallowed. "And I told you about Josh, right?"

"You've mentioned him," Lamont leaned back and crossed his arms over his chest. "Mainly when you're sleeping."

Kyler stared at him and gave a slow nod. She was silent for a few long minutes, thinking, reflecting back. Her eyes shined with the fierce light of regret as she gazed through the door and out across the expanse of the park.

"I loved him, Doc, a lot," her voice was very quiet. "And when he left, he took that part of me with him." She met his eyes. "All that I was left with was a desire to keep on using until it killed me."

"Kyler—" Lamont started, but she shook her head.

"He looked at me before he turned and walked away, and he had this look on his face that just shot right through me. It was like he'd completely given up on me—which I'm sure he had—and that I was the last person in the world he'd ever want to see again."

Kyler snagged another cigarette from her pack and lit it with a badly shaking hand. "That right there just about killed me, and he probably wasn't a mile away before I started on my suicidal trek."

Deep silence dropped down around them, and then Kyler abruptly got up and walked over to the door, her back to him. "That heroin kicked my ass," her voice was barely above a whisper, "and I lost so much because of it."

"But you didn't lose everything," Lamont responded softly.

"I know," she turned to look at him. "And that's another reason why I didn't score last night." She paused, sorting through her words. "You . . . uh . . . when I showed up at your door with a bloody nose and loaded up on coke . . . right before you picked me up off your porch I saw that same look on *your* face, Doc. And I . . . uh . . . ," Kyler swallowed heavily.

"If you give up on me, too, I won't last a day out here. And I don't want that to happen because . . . I love this park and I love working with these kids. I want to keep all that more than anything, but I'm scared shitless, knowing that monkey on my back's got the capability to take *everything* away."

She leaned against the door jamb, her exhausted eyes staring deep into his. He saw how lost she was, and the huge weight she carried that was dragging her down.

Wordlessly he got up and went to her, wrapping his arms gently around her. Kyler resisted at first, trembling from the fear inside her.

"It's gonna be all right, Kyler," Lamont said softly. "I told you before, you're stronger than all this, and you're gonna be ok. And I'm here, all right? I'm not giving up on you."

She took a deep breath and slowly let it out. He felt her arms circle his back as she gave in, surrendering as much as her pride would allow her to. Finally she pulled away and walked back to the desk.

"I appreciate that, Doc. You don't know how much," Kyler looked at him, her eyes boring into his. "It helps make this a little easier."

He nodded and stared out at the park. "I know," his voice was quiet. He waited a beat and then cocked an eyebrow at her. "How much did you get?"

"How much did I get where?"

"For your plasma. How much?"

"Oh, uh . . . twenty-five. If I go back again this week they'll give me another twenty-five."

Lamont grunted. "Are you goin' back?"

Kyler shrugged and gently ran a finger over the small holes where the needle had gone, her jaw clenched. "It was rough," she admitted slowly. "But the money's there, you know?"

He sighed and started to reach into his back pocket, but her sharp voice stopped him.

"Don't," Kyler held up a hand. "Don't, Doc, ok? Shit, I ain't hurtin', and it's not that big a deal."

"So why're you doing it? Why put yourself through that?"

"I don't know if I will again. I just . . . just did it this one time . . . mainly 'cause I *thought* I needed the money badly enough. I mean, I *did* promise Jake new wheels, but . . . you're right," her eyes just barely met his before sliding away, "I wanted to score some dope bad."

"But you didn't," his voice was soft.

"No," she pulled a cigarette from her pack and lit it. "I didn't."

Lamont walked back over and sat down across from her. "Can you answer a question for me?"

"If I can," she sighed.

He met her eyes directly, forcing her to look at him. "Where'd you sleep last night? Here?"

Kyler slowly shook her head. "No. I didn't wanna bring the booze here."

"Then where?" His eyes were hard, drilling into hers.

She cocked her head and gave a slight shrug. "You really wanna know?"

"Yeah," he answered, not knowing if he did or not.

"Under your deck."

Silence greeted her statement as he stared unbelievingly at her.

"What?"

"Under your deck," Kyler repeated. "In back. I crawled up under there sometime after midnight, I guess. Drank there 'til I passed out."

"You're kidding, right?" He stared at her and knew she wasn't. "Jesus, Kyler," Lamont shook his head. "Why didn't you just knock on the door?"

She was quiet for a minute, thinking, and then said softly, "I didn't wanna bring it to you, either. Plus, I was still pissed as hell and just wanted to be left alone."

He was silent for a long time, watching her. Finally he gave a heavy sigh and ran a hand through his hair. "All right, kid. I can understand that. But do me a favor, ok?"

Kyler met his gaze, not saying anything.

"Here," he reached for a piece of paper and wrote something on it. He handed it to her and she glanced at the four numbers with a raised eyebrow.

"The code to my garage. I usually leave the inside door unlocked so you can just go on in. Please tell me you'll do that tonight instead of sleeping under my deck or here or . . . out there . . ." he gestured over his shoulder in the general direction of the street.

Kyler shook her head and took a deep drag off her smoke. "I won't get off 'till late," she muttered.

"I won't even be there," Lamont countered. "I'm goin' to work at seven tonight."

She took a deep breath and let it out slowly. "Doc . . ." she started, and then stopped, defeated. Unbidden a memory came to her of Josh in an alley somewhere, his blue eyes staring into her own as he whispered, *You have a place to stay . . . no sense staying on the street.*

"Shit," she muttered and ran a hand through her hair. Lamont was quiet, waiting, praying she'd say yes. Finally she gave a tired nod and glanced at him.

"Ok. But I still haven't decided yet what I'm gonna do . . ."

"That's ok. One day at a time, Kyler. It would just make me feel better if I knew you weren't about ready to drown under my house with the high tide."

Kyler offered a distracted grin. "Tide wasn't that high last night."

"In my opinion, it was high enough," he stood up and stuck his hands in his pockets. "Call me if you need anything, all right?"

"Yeah," she slipped the paper with the code on it in her pocket. "Thanks, Doc."

Lamont nodded and headed towards the door. "I'll see you later."

Kyler watched him leave and then crushed out her cigarette and put her pounding head in her hands, wondering when she'd be able to feel something besides pain again.

When Lamont got home he walked around to his back yard and squatted down at the edge of his deck. Looking under it, far back to almost where the ground and wood formed a V, he saw what looked like that old army blanket Kyler had been using at the park. He gave a heavy sigh and shook his head, then headed on into his house.

CHAPTER 23

KYLER LEFT THE park sometime after nine that night and headed directly downtown to a certain street. Her heart was pounding with the raw nerve it took her to even get off the bus in this end of town, but she needed something specific to get her through the night, and this was the easiest place for the moment.

"Just as long as I can sleep," she muttered to herself, justifying her actions as much as she could. "Just enough to get me through a night without waking up wanting to scream."

And sleeping in Lamont's house wasn't making things easier. Her trust in him had grown just a little bit more, but it was still a far cry from wholeheartedly, and Kyler still felt the fear deep inside her.

Stopping on a street corner, she spotted a familiar figure half a block down and trotted down to meet him.

"Roger," she said, coming up to him, and he whirled with a glint of metal in the dim light that told her he had a gun and was pointing it at her. Kyler held up her hands, tasting cold copper in her mouth.

"It's me, man, take it easy."

The dealer grunted and kept the gun on her. "You alone?"

"As always," she muttered, and patted her own self down. "No wires, no weapons. I'm alone and I need some valiums."

"Valiums?" He smiled a crooked, ugly smile. "Kinda mild for you, ain't it? What happened to the smack?"

"Gave it up," Kyler dug in her pocket and pulled out what was left of her money. "Got any valiums or not?" She was in a hurry to get off this block and away from the demons that lived here. Lamont's house was looking pretty fucking welcoming right now.

"Sure," he slipped the gun in the waistband of his pants and pulled a bottle from his pocket. "How many you want?"

"Uh . . ." she was hoping to come up with more than three dollars. "Still two bucks each?"

"Yep."

"Take three for two?" She held up the bills.

"No," he sneered. "I'll take two for one. Your call. Want it or not?"

"Shit," she gritted her teeth, knowing one valium probably wouldn't do her any good, but was suddenly glad she'd refused the doc's money. Christ, no telling what she would've spent it on.

"Yeah," she gave in and shoved the two dollar bills in his hand. He grinned and passed her one valium, loving, Kyler knew, every minute of it.

She pocketed it and pushed past him down the street, not bothering to thank him, feeling old and used and abused. With her head hung low, Kyler started in the direction of Lamont's house, anticipating the feel of a real bed beneath her.

"Runnin' short on cash, honey?" The voice came off to her side and Kyler didn't even have time to react before a hand reached out and yanked her inside a recessed doorway.

"'Cause ya know I can cover it." Kyler felt the hand press rudely between her legs and hot, oily fear swamped her. "I always have, right?" The hand pressed harder as a sweaty, filthy body pinned her against the wall. "Just gimme what I want."

"Fuck off!" She shoved with all her strength and with the few inches of space she got she bolted out onto the sidewalk and into freedom. Running hard through the night, Kyler felt her heart pounding against her sternum and with each inhale there was a sharp pain across the upper left part of her chest, but she didn't stop until she was back on safer ground.

Within minutes she was up against the fence that surrounded the skate park and only then did she stop to look around her. Alone in the silence of the night, Kyler slid down to the ground and put her head in her hands. Her whole body was shaking convulsively, and the sheer terror she felt was enough to make her scream.

The ball of acid that was her stomach rolled over and exploded, and she lurched to the side, vomiting in the grass. It hurt, her stomach straining against the emptiness of having nothing in it for a day or two, and when she was done, Kyler fell on the cool ground, breathing raggedly.

"Jesus," she moaned, feeling the hand still pressed between her legs, blood and the copper taste of fear in her mouth. Reality, cold as an ice pick through her temple, washed over her and Kyler gritted her teeth against the insanity of it all pushing against her.

After a few miserable moments of lying in the grass, she managed to pull herself to her feet, hanging onto the fence.

"Get me through this," she whispered to nobody in particular. "Please just get me through this."

Stumbling, one arm lying protectively across her stomach, she made her painful way down the street and didn't stop until she was outside of Lamont's garage. Pulling the four numbers from memory, she punched them in with a wildly trembling hand. The door started slowly up and she was under it and pressing the down button from inside before it was even halfway up.

The door to the house was unlocked, just like the doc had said it'd be, and Kyler entered slowly; still feeling the suffocating terror; still waiting for that unseen threat to come crashing out at her.

Silently she crossed the living room and peeked into the kitchen before wearily climbing the stairs. The thought of a quick shower briefly crossed her mind, but her fear was overwhelming, and she couldn't bear having the noise of the water blot out any other sound.

Closing the door to the spare bedroom tightly behind her, she crawled up into bed fully clothed and curled up into a tight ball, begging for the one lone valium to hopefully work.

She walked down the hallway towards the bathroom in the dark, like so many times before. Her bladder wasn't really all that full, but sleep was next to impossible and the only way she knew to keep from wanting to crawl out of her skin was to move . . . to walk . . . to keep moving until these demons left her for another night.

She entered the bathroom and turned to flip on the light when two strong hands grabbed her and threw her into a stall. Her shoulder hit the toilet hard and her arm went numb instantly. She tried to roll, to scream, but the body was on her, pressing into her, hands locked on her throat.

Kyler looked up into dark, crazy eyes and this time the face had a name . . .

She bolted upright, and swept her eyes around the room, the scream locked in her throat only out of street-bred instincts.

For one panic-filled second she had no idea where she was, but then soft voices, seeming to come from the floor, filled her with the memory of coming to Lamont's house.

"Lewis," she moaned, and rolled out of bed, hitting the floor close to the air duct. She shut her eyes against the weight of his blows, so many times upon her body, and dug her fingers into the carpet.

For now—at least in her dreams—her attacker at the halfway house had a face, had a name. And it didn't matter that the real rapist was in the county lockup. What mattered was the sheer knowledge that she wasn't as far away from her past as she thought she was . . . as she hoped she was.

Kyler laid her ear on the register and relished in the cool air blowing against her sweat-soaked face. Distantly, she heard Lamont's voice and another softer, female voice coming from below her.

The words were barely audible and indistinct, and Kyler just closed her eyes and tried to quiet her pounding heart, slamming against her ribs. She lay there for a few moments, and then slowly got to her feet.

Quietly she slipped out of the room and down the hallway towards the stairs. The living room and kitchen were dark, but there was light coming from the basement, and she slowly started down the steps. At the bottom she peeked around the corner, but was only rewarded with a view of the basement stairs.

Lamont's finished basement, she knew, sported a soft leather couch, a fireplace, and a stereo and TV off to the right, on the other side of the wall. Stopping halfway down the steps, Kyler sat down and wrapped her arms around her knees, leaning her tired head against the wall.

The female voice belonged to Emily, and they talked back and forth softly from the direction of the couch. Kyler closed her eyes and tried to find some comfort somewhere inside her.

"She trusts you," Emily said quietly.

"No she doesn't," Lamont responded.

"Well, not completely. But more than anybody else. I mean, she's here, isn't she?"

Kyler heard Lamont sigh and behind her closed lids pictured him lying on the couch with Emily in his arms. The sound of his sigh squeezed her heart a little bit, and she didn't know why.

"She may not stay," he answered softly. "And then what?"

"She has to stay," and on the stairs Kyler heard the creak of leather, and her mind's eye saw Emily turning to stare at him. "She won't go back to another halfway house, and if she doesn't stay she'll lose her job and be arrested again." She paused, considering her words.

"If that happens, Keith, I won't be able to help her anymore. It'll be out of my hands."

"I know," he rubbed his eyes. "But what can I do? She won't talk to anybody—"

"Maybe she'll talk to you."

"I doubt it. Besides, I'm biased. I couldn't be objective."

Emily took a deep breath and let it out slowly. Kyler knew what was coming and felt the dull burn of anger low in her gut.

He's a fucking shrink, she thought. *Jesus.*

"Biased or not, I think you should still try. But don't analyze her, ok? Talk to her as a friend and not as a doctor."

Lamont was quiet, holding Emily against his chest. It amazed him that she could still function professionally with Curtis breathing off a respirator five hundred miles away. He thought of Kyler upstairs in bed, and wondered again at how close she'd come to ending up like him . . . or worse, ending up dead.

With the amount of poison that had flooded her body, and how she'd bullied herself through it, it amazed him how the will to live can push the human body to seemingly impossible limits even when the brain and heart are all too willing to give up the fight.

"I'll try," he muttered, and felt her nod against him before she rolled off the couch.

"C'mon," her voice was tired as she took him by the hand. "Love me, ok? Make me remember some good times when I'm flyin' back to San Fran tomorrow."

Kyler stood and quietly made her way back up the steps. She gently closed the door to the spare bedroom and crawled back in bed, her mind working. The anger was gone as quickly as it had come, leaving behind a weary respect for the doc for not prying into her brain all the times she was fucked up and vulnerable.

The sun wasn't even up yet when Kyler sensed rather than heard movement pass outside her closed door. Instantly awake, she picked up her smokes off the nightstand and waited a few moments before quietly getting out of bed and crossing the room. She slowly opened the door and eyed the hallway; the doc's bedroom door was shut but there was a shadow cast by the clock on the microwave moving in the kitchen.

She eased out of the room and made her way down the steps, fairly sure it was Emily getting ready to leave.

The shadow eased out of the kitchen, and in the dim light Kyler saw her cross the living room and quietly slip out the front door. She followed soundlessly on the thick carpet and stepped out on the porch as Emily was shutting her trunk.

"Hey," Kyler said softly. Emily glanced at her and nodded.

"Hey, yourself," she responded quietly. "Did I wake you up?"

"No. I've been awake for awhile."

Emily's exhausted eyes settled on hers, and in them Kyler saw her own sleepless night.

"I just . . . wanted to say thanks. For giving me this chance; for coming all the way out here and helping me."

Emily gave a small shrug and walked over to her. "It's my job," she said seriously, giving her a gentle hug. "Be good, ok?"

"Yeah," Kyler hugged her back hard. "Call us . . . if you need anything."

"'Us'," Emily pulled back and offered a small smile. "That mean you're stayin'?"

"Uh . . . maybe," Kyler muttered. "Probably."

"Good. Just remember, day at a time."

Kyler nodded and silently watched her as she got behind the wheel of her car. With a last wave, Emily pulled out of the drive and headed on down the street. She watched until she was out of sight and then plopped down on the step and lit a cigarette.

The sun was just barely peeking over the horizon and the air was cool around her, smelling like the ocean. When her cigarette was down to the filter, Kyler stood up and walked around back to the deck, sitting with her feet buried deep in the sand as the world slowly came to life around her.

CHAPTER 24

LAMONT SLIT HIS eyes and stared blearily at the clock. Ten-twenty in the a.m. The time was enough to tell him that he was alone in the house, as Emily's flight left at five-thirty and Kyler had to be at work at nine, but he still felt the absence of other human life besides his own in his house.

He rolled over to the other side of the bed and pulled the pillow that Emily had used close to him. On its fabric he could smell her, her perfume, her shampoo, even down to the faint smell of the love they'd made late last night.

His heart felt the ache of her being gone, and he squeezed the pillow tighter against him for a moment more before throwing the twisted bedclothes aside and stumbling to the bathroom.

Lamont gazed at himself in the mirror, and saw the emptiness of his eyes that pretty much matched the emptiness of his life right about then. Part of him wished he'd never asked her to come back, because it was a hell of a lot harder letting go this time.

He shook his head and gave a heavy sigh, reaching for his toothbrush.

Kyler was pounding in nails to the frame of the big ramp in the late afternoon sunlight when he walked up on her. He stood for a second, surveying her work, and was again surprised at her skill and agility to not only design this ramp, but to do most of the work on it herself.

It was coming along perfectly, and not even half-finished as it was, Lamont could see the enormity of its shape and mass beginning to take form.

"Hey, kid," he said. "Looking good."

Kyler glanced up at him and gave a little grin that, he noticed, didn't quite touch her eyes. In him she noticed a haggardness that had never been there before, and she began to understand the extent of his time spent with Emily, and how much he was hurting right now.

"Thanks," she moved to the edge and sat down with her legs dangling over. "I hope it comes out as good as I pictured it." She lit a cigarette and gave him a measuring look. "What's up?"

Lamont shrugged and sat down beside her. "Here," he gently placed something small and hard in her hand. "I want you to have this."

Kyler surveyed the key in her hand and offered him a sidelong glance. "Doc . . ."

"I'm not saying do it or don't, ok?" He raised his hands in surrender. "I'm not gonna force another ultimatum on you or harp on and on about you needing a credible address." He stopped and took a deep breath, slowly letting it out. He let his eyes roam over the park restlessly, searching for something more internal than external.

"You can't be serious," she muttered. "I pulled a gun on you for Christ's sakes."

"Yeah," he favored her with a wan smile. "But don't do it again, ok?"

Kyler shook her head and dragged deep on her smoke. "Really, Doc, this is just . . ."

"Just something to help me sleep better at night," he said easily. "Whether you're there or not is up to you, but at least I'll know I did what I could."

There was silence for a few minutes before she said quietly, "I'm a junkie . . . and a thief . . . and . . ." she swallowed, wondering just how the hell he could trust her enough to give her a key to his house.

"And you're tryin' to get better," he said softly.

"Yeah . . ."

The quiet of the evening settled down around them, easily and comfortably. Kyler could smell the salt in the air and relished the breeze coming in off the ocean, cool against her body. Lamont gazed out toward nowhere, lost in thought. Finally he stood up and looked at her with his weary eyes.

"Emily and I used to feed the ducks in the lake behind the hospital." He shrugged. "It's quiet, and you can think if you need to. I'm gonna go on over there and, you know . . . think about some stuff for awhile. You're welcome to the house, Kyler, as long as you need it, and you don't have to wait for me to be there, ok?"

She nodded wordlessly, her eyes on his.

Lamont swallowed heavily, then sighed, staring off towards the mountains in the distance. "I didn't think I'd miss her this much already."

"Yeah," she sighed. "I know, Doc." She stood up and gave him a gentle hug, still feeling a small amount of fear but glad to see it wasn't as controlling as before. "I'll see you later, all right?"

"Yeah," Lamont nodded and turned back towards the gate. Kyler watched him walk off and then picked up her hammer again with the weight of the key heavier in her mind than in her pocket.

The darkness had settled around her like a blanket, muting everything but the ocean, hurtling up against the packed sand just yards away from her. Kyler was sitting on the bottom step of Lamont's deck, her feet once again buried up to the ankles in sand, and drinking a cup of coffee. It was black and bitter, strong on her stomach, but it was good and filling. She had a feeling that even though it'd been yet another couple days since she'd eaten anything, her stomach wouldn't take to food as well as it was taking to the coffee.

The screen door squeaked open behind her as Lamont walked out with his own cup. He squeezed in beside her as she tried to extricate her feet enough to move over and give him room.

"Sorry," he gave a wry grin. "I didn't know you were burying yourself out here."

"Just the feet," Kyler answered with a smile of her own. "It's relaxing."

He grunted and sipped his coffee. "This is good," he said, then, "Been out here long?"

She shook her head. "No. Just got in not too long ago. Worked late on the ramp."

"John'll be surprised next time he sees it. How much longer, you think?"

"Maybe another week or two on the frame, and then after that it'll go pretty quick."

"Then what?"

"Then," she shrugged, "I'll probably start to work on some other ramps I've been thinking about building. None as big as that one, but they'll have more variety to 'em."

Lamont was quiet for a minute, and then he said gently, "So I guess that job's suiting you pretty good, huh?"

Kyler nodded and lit a cigarette. "Probably the best thing for me right now."

There was silence for a few long moments, as each was lost in their own thoughts. Then Lamont shot her a sidelong glance which she returned with raised eyebrows.

"How'd you meet him?" He asked quietly.

And Kyler, who knew exactly who the doc was talking about, looked at him and knew he needed to hear a part of her story so that he could hopefully better comprehend his own feelings for Emily leaving . . . and for losing such a huge part of his life.

"You need her," she responded softly. "But Curtis needs her more."

"I know," he muttered, staring down at his coffee cup. "But that doesn't stop it from hurting."

"Yeah," she agreed and drew deep on her cigarette.

Lamont looked at her. "So? Just tell me a story, ok?"

Kyler gazed at him, her eyes slightly narrowed. "You asking 'cause you really wanna know or because the therapist side of you is just curious?"

He arched an eyebrow in surprise, thinking surely to God Emily hadn't told her . . . had she?

Flapping a hand in an absent gesture, Kyler allowed a small smile. "I was bluffing, Doc, and you called it. Now I know."

Lamont sighed and shook his head. "I'm a physician, Kyler, first and foremost. Yeah, I studied both psychiatry and psychology in med school, but my main passion is the human body. I'm qualified but not certified to pick anyone's brain; not legally, anyway. Mostly I'm just curious for myself, ok?"

Her eyes bored into his, and then she glanced away, out over the ocean again. She still sensed he needed justification for the way he and Emily ended up, and that sense was stronger than her suspicion that he was trying to be a shrink and get inside her head.

Kyler nodded and dropped her cigarette in the sand, burying the coal. "All right, Doc." She paused for a second, collecting her words, and then took a deep breath and prepared herself to feel the pain of opening up barely-healed wounds.

"I met him when we were both twelve, up in L.A. I'd been on my own for a couple years; after I left the orphanage I learned quick how to survive and get by on the streets . . . but . . ." she swallowed and stared at the sand.

"I got by without driving my self-respect into the ground, you know? I didn't sleep with anybody. Mainly I just panhandled where I could, and I did ok, but more than a few times I'd break into places—stores, mostly; some houses—and walk out with stuff that I sold for cash."

She stopped and gave a heavy sigh. "I didn't like doing it back then, but the thing was, I was good at it, and I needed the money."

"For food?" Lamont asked quietly, but she shook her head.

"No. I got a lot of my food free from some people I knew who owned food joints, and I did a little for them sometimes on the side . . . cleaning up and stuff. Stuff that would humble me when I needed it to . . . when I had to stop breaking and entering for awhile 'cause my conscious was getting too loud."

She stopped and lit another cigarette and her voice was bitter as she muttered, "I didn't do any hard core illegal stuff until the heroin got to me. Before that, I was a halfway decent person."

Lamont laid a finger on her arm for a brief moment, silently offering comfort. He saw the sharp pull of mixed emotions deep in her eyes and thought about telling her it was ok, that she didn't have to tell him.

Kyler read this in his eyes and shook her head. "It's ok, Doc. Maybe it'll help me if I get it out."

He gave her a measuring look, and then gave a slow nod. "Yeah."

"Anyway," she sighed, "I was walking down the street one day and over behind this little store there were these two kids beating the shit out of another kid. The other kid was smaller, and two to one, it was a losing fight.

"I stopped for a minute across the street and watched them, and the more I watched the angrier I got. Bein' a street kid, Doc, it was usually better for me if I didn't get involved in stuff like that, you know? It was hard enough just surviving day to day without getting killed, but that day . . ." she stopped and gave a little shrug.

"It was just wrong . . . to me, that those two bigger kids could whale on this other kid, and even though I had no idea what the other kid had done to piss them off—hell he might not even had done anything but look at them wrong—I knew he was too small to've done anything too serious. He'd have to be nuts to try anything stupid on those bigger kids."

She crushed out her smoke and gazed over the ocean. "I got angrier as I watched them and then—not even knowing why I did it—ran over to help him." Kyler gave an absent smile, lost in long ago memories.

"We *both* got our asses kicked that day," she said, thinking back, reliving each moment in perfect clarity.

CHAPTER 25

SHE STOOD, NO more than twelve years old, against the brick side of an old building and watched a couple of boys advance upon another, slightly smaller boy. Though just a little more than a child, she had been living on the streets for the past four years, and had acquired a fair amount of sense in that time. She was smart and rough, and knew that if she got involved if she tried to help the smaller boy, she'd end up getting hurt.

But she possessed a rare quality to kids her age: compassion. And if it meant her spending the night in pain to help a strange kid who'd probably just steal from anyways . . . well, it just felt right.

The bigger kid of the three—thirteen or fourteen, she reckoned—grabbed the small boy by the collar and threw him against a fence, sending a fist crashing into his nose. Blood burst and the kid grunted, but didn't cry out. The second kid drove a powerful kick into his crotch and he went down, and the girl doubted if he could cry out now.

He curled into a ball on the pavement as they rained blows on him, and she felt a fierce anger deep in her gut. She clenched her jaw and stepped away from the building.

"I guess you guys are afraid of fighting fair, huh?" She said in a quiet voice.

They looked up, startled, and then the bigger one said savagely, "Back off, kid. You don't want none of this."

"Nope, not really," she said honestly. "But I'll take it if you're gonna try to dish it out."

They got through it—barely—somehow surviving it. After it was over, she had a deep cut along her right rib cage where the bigger kid had broken a discarded beer bottle over her. The cut probably would have required stitches if she was in a different life.

The small kid had two black eyes and a small laceration down his left jaw line; nothing too serious, and he recognized her unselfish attempt to help him. He took off his shirt and folded it up, then put it to her hurting side.

"Shit," he muttered. "We gotta get you to a hospital."

"Don't worry about it," she managed to grin through the pain. "I've been through worse."

"Yeah, well . . ." the kid paused, not sure how to go on, not even sure if he wanted to. "Is there someplace I can take you? I mean, well . . . like home, or something?"

"Listen," she looked at him, eyes hard. "I volunteered, ok? You can get outta here; I'll be all right."

The kid glanced away and took a deep breath. He looked back at her and said, "As much as I want to, sorry, I can't. You helped me out of a tough spot. Lemme give you a hand."

She stared at him for a long time, and then finally said softly, "Get lost, kid. It's the best thing you can do."

He looked at her. "Ok," he said in a quiet voice. "My name's Josh and I'm usually around Venice Beach. You ever need anything, look me up." He got up and walked away, not looking back.

She found some big butterfly bandages and taped the sides of the cut together. For the next week and a half she didn't move around much, and the wound slowly healed. She'd managed to score a bag of pills that helped to keep her mind off the pain. For the time being she was staying in the basement of a decrepit factory. It was dark and damp, and she caught a low-grade fever that made her head pound and her hands shake. She couldn't get better with no food and staying where she was, but somehow she did, and a week later she emerged weak and trembling, but nonetheless feeling good.

She stood in the predawn darkness, smelling the smoggy air, and listening to her body. There was a tension in her nerves and a tightness in her gut that she couldn't account for, and curiously she stood there listening, waiting. A streak of desire suddenly flashed through her, fierce and pure. She stood with her head down and opened up her mind, smelling sweet, salty air and feeling warm, dry sand. Without understanding or caring, she turned her hurting body in that direction and started walking.

Not long later she found what she was looking for: the small compact car sat parked at a meter and she glanced around, her sharp eyes noticing every little detail. Satisfied with the immediate surroundings, she walked in front of the car and casually ran her hand along the hood . . . it was cold. She made her way to the driver's side door and reached into her pocket as if for keys. Instead, she pulled out a wire-thin length of metal and inserted it into the lock by feel, her eyes looking over the roof of the car.

Three minutes later she was pulling the car sedately away from the curb. She turned the radio on and pulled a crumpled pack of cigarettes from her pocket, putting one in the corner of her mouth and pushing in the car's lighter. Signaling a right turn, she gave it a little gas and headed for the southbound ramp of the interstate.

The car's gas tank got her within five miles of the Venice Beach line, and she left it on the side of the road, footing it the rest of the way. Topping a small rise she saw the dark blue line of the ocean on the horizon and felt a moment of complete peace wash over her. It wasn't much different than the inner streets of L.A. in that she would still be sleeping on the streets that night, but with the sand beneath her feet things just felt right.

She walked the street, lost in the smell of the salty air, and would have passed right by the vacant lot on her left had she not heard a certain noise that stopped her in her tracks; a totally unfamiliar noise, but one that pierced her soul. It was the sound of rubber wheels on old boards, the sound of freedom in itself, and she turned to look, falling in love for the first time in her life.

The lot was vacant, littered with bottles and trash, except for an area towards the back that had been meticulously cleared of all debris. A wooden fence surrounded three sides of it, made of boards that had seen better days. And in the cleared area there was a u-shaped ramp that was maybe fifteen feet long and six feet tall. This was something new to her, and she leaned against a tree with a cigarette absently in the corner of her mouth, watching curiously. Her heart pounded.

A boy of about eleven or twelve stood on a battered skateboard on the edge of the ramp, and she recognized with sour amusement the same face she'd kept from getting beat in a little less than a month before. The kid leaned forward and rode the skateboard down the ramp and back up again, performing a little flip at the top. He came down and skated back across, doing another trick when he reached the top of the other side. He went back and forth, and her eyes watched him, studying his moves and body language as he maneuvered his skateboard across the ramp.

I want that, *she thought.* Jesus Christ, I really fucking want that.

One of the other boys noticed her and nudged his friend. She stared at them staring at her, and when the kid

(Josh?) came down off the ramp, he looked over at her, too. And smiled.

She watched as he made his way over to her, and the closer he got the more she realized that his eyes were the exact shade of blue as the ocean, coinciding perfectly with his shaggy blond hair.

"Hey," he said easily. "How's the side?"

She shrugged. "I've already forgotten about it."

Josh nodded, then inclined his head towards the ramp. "You skate?"

Over his shoulder, the ramp called to her. Josh saw it in her eyes and recognized it. "No . . . but if you guys don't mind . . . I'd like to try."

"Well, we're kinda workin' on something here—" one of the other boys said.

"Here," Josh said, cutting him off. "You can use my board. And these, too," he stripped off his knee pads and handed them to her. "I don't have a helmet, so if you start to feel yourself losing control, try to twist your body so you'll land on anything but your head."

"O . . . k . . ." she said slowly. She looked at the board and the pads, then up at the ramp. She was barely treading water here, far from any home ground she had ever known, but there was something about the feel of the board in her hand . . . and that ramp.

"C'mon, Josh, you really gonna let this girl do this? I mean—"

"Yep," he said, looking at her.

"You gotta be kidding me," the other one said angrily.

"You don't like it, get lost," Josh said absently. "Listen," he directed his voice to her, "If you think you can do it, ok. But I don't wanna hafta drag your ass to the hospital—"

"I think I can do it," she said quietly. Her gaze found the ramp again, and a faraway look came into her eyes.

Josh smiled softly. "Then do it."

"Christ, Josh, this is fucking ridiculous."

"Then leave," he snapped, favoring the kid with an angry look.

"Nope," the voice was hateful and menacing. "I wanna see her bust her head open first."

She climbed up on the ramp to those last few words, but when she stood on top and looked down into the bowl, all thought ceased. That peculiar flash of desire streaked through her again. She stood on the board like she'd seen Josh do, and let go.

The feeling was unlike anything she had ever known. Her small, lithe body opened up to the movement of the skateboard and the curvature of the ramp; she'd placed her feet perfectly, and the board was balanced and stable. Her mind raced and her heart pounded as she reached the top of the opposite side, but without hesitation she sailed up and over, holding on to the board with her hand. She came back down easily and in control, and continued on up the other side.

"Yeah, you're gonna tell me she's never skated before?" One of the boys said sarcastically, but Josh could only shake his head, his eyes never leaving her body.

"Fuck it," the boy said angrily. "I'm outta here, Josh." He picked up his board and stalked away.

"Shit," the other boy said regretfully. "I gotta split, too. He's got the money for the bus fare."

Josh just nodded absently, still lost in her graceful form, and then they were left alone as the setting sun cast long shadows across the lot.

At last she came down off the ramp, breathing rapidly, her eyes flashing. She handed the board and pads back to Josh.

"Where can I get me one of those?" She asked.

He looked at her. "You never skated before?"

"Nope."

"Ever?"

"No, I never stepped foot on a skateboard before today. Why, you writing a book?"

He smiled. "If that's true, then you got the biggest knack for this I've ever seen."

"It's true," she responded quietly. "It's true and I want to learn."

Josh stared deep into her eyes. There was something about her . . . something he'd felt a month before when she'd come to his aid . . . something that spoke out to him. He nodded decisively, coming to an inner decision.

"Ok," he held out his hand. "Josh Tomlin."

She surprised herself by feeling comfortable when she shook his hand; comfortable, and . . . when she glanced back at the ramp . . . strangely at peace.

"Kyler. Kyler Maddox."

CHAPTER 26

"HE SAID HE'D teach me if I was serious about learning," Kyler said softly, lighting another cigarette. "I told him I didn't think I'd ever been as serious about anything before in my life. It had me from the first, like the heroin, but unlike the heroin, skating never took anything away from me. I was connected to it from that very first time and I held on with everything I had."

"Don't fuck with me, ok?" Josh said quietly in that slowly darkening lot. "I saw you skate. You got the skill . . . the ability . . ." He paused, staring at her. "I ain't got much, and skating's most of it. You wanna learn, I'll teach you. But please don't make me waste my time. That's all I ask."

"Just show me. That's all I ask." Kyler met his gaze directly, staring at him as he stared at her. Josh was trying to find something in her eyes that would tell him to back off, to get lost . . . but there was nothing. Nothing at all. Kyler hid her emotions well, which was good because that run on the ramp had left her vulnerable.

For the first time in her life Kyler felt a hope that went beyond her everyday feeling, and it scared her a little bit. But it was already there now, deep inside, and without a doubt she knew she had to have more of it.

"Ok," he said slowly. "Uh . . . a good board'll cost you around a hundred . . ."

"You paid a hundred bucks for your board?"

"Yeah, but it's good quality and quality costs. It's already lasted me five years or so."

Kyler nodded, thinking. She didn't exactly have that kind of cash, but knew there'd be no trouble coming up with it . . . if she could get past her conscience.

"I wanna make sure I'm getting my money's worth, ok?"

"I'll help you," Josh assured her. "Meet me here tomorrow morning . . . say about nine-thirty?"

"Sure," she said and started to walk away, but his voice stopped her.

"Hey . . ."

Kyler glanced back at him, eyebrows raised.

"Where you staying tonight?"

Josh watched her eyes turn hard as she glared at him.

"What?"

He walked over to her. "I mean, well . . . if you don't have a permanent place . . . if, you know, you need somewhere—"

"I'm covered," she said abruptly. "I'll see you tomorrow."

He watched her as she walked away. He knew she'd spend the night somewhere on the street, because he did it every other week or so, but he didn't know how to call her back, or how to convince her to stay if he did.

Kyler found a spot under a pier down along the beach, away from the boardwalk and the people there. As twilight dimmed into dusk she thought about the skateboard . . . and the ramp . . . and the kid who said he'd teach her. She was smart and rough, and she *could survive in the streets. But this . . . this was something she didn't know anything about. It was like a web that she couldn't untangle, that she felt trapped in. And save for the unfamiliarity of the emotions, she felt quite comfortable inside. Comfortable and apprehensive at the same time. It was confusing and it gave her a headache.*

But just give me another chance on that board, on that ramp, *she thought.* Please just give me that.

It was morning, cold and damp, and Kyler sat against the wooden fence smoking a cigarette and waiting for Josh. She was feeling pretty rough; it's rained like hell for over half the night, and she was drenched within the first thirty seconds. She felt the fever coming back.

Josh walked into the vacant lot awkwardly carrying two skateboards and two steaming cups of coffee and Kyler cocked a questioning eyebrow at him.

"Morning, Kyler," he said with a small smile. "Figured you could use this," he handed her a cup. "I heard it raining pretty hard last night."

She grunted and took it with a slightly shaking hand. "What's with the board?"

"Well," he said, sitting down beside her, "I figured I at least owed you one for helping me out. It's not new but it's in good shape."

Kyler sipped her coffee, her eyes on his. "I'm not lookin' for handouts."

"Yeah, I know," Josh replied, his eyes soft on hers. "But it's yours if you want it, and I have a feeling you do."

She didn't know how to answer to that and shook her head, looking away. She ran her hands through her hair and sighed, a small seed of a headache starting to pound above her left eyebrow.

Josh ran his eyes over her body, noticing the dark bags under her eyes and hollowed cheeks, skin-and-bones body. "Flu's going around, you know."

"Yeah?" Kyler finished off her coffee and stood up.

"Yeah." He stood up with her and faced her. "How long's it been since you had a decent meal?"

She stared at him and smiled a cool smile. "Don't go playin' my father, all right? Now we gonna do this or not?"

"Sure," Josh said, his eyes a cold blue, "but we can't use the ramp today . . . too wet. We'll head over to the boulevard and I'll teach you a few tricks."

"Fine," Kyler slid past him, picked up her board, and walked off the lot. Josh stared at her for a moment, his brow creased in thought, then took a deep breath and grabbed his own board, jogging after her.

They didn't talk on the short walk to the boulevard, but Josh kept glancing sideways at her, measuring her with a calm gaze that was threaded with worry and curiosity.

He led the way to an abandoned parking lot behind a row of vacant buildings and showed her the three or four concrete curbings used for parking spaced that he and a few others had moved around according to their moods.

"People come here sometimes and use this lot as a kind of mini street course, you know . . . jumping the curbings and stuff 'cause they're not too high and if you fall you won't fall far."

Kyler walked over to one of them and squatted down next to it, looking it over. Finally she looked up at Josh. "Show me."

Without a word he picked up his skateboard and walked about twenty feet away. She watched as he gauged the distance, then skated forward, gaining speed quickly. About two feet away from the curbing he kicked down with his back foot and moved his front foot towards the middle of the board. The motion brought the skateboard *up and over the curbing, and he came down on the other side easily and gracefully.*

He walked back to her, board in hand. "See how I did that?"

She nodded slowly, walking around the curbing. "Show me again?" She glanced at him.

Josh jumped it six more times for her, going slow and easy, keeping it simple. After the sixth one Kyler said she'd like to give it a try. He nodded and backed away. She took her board and walked twenty feet away, feeling a tension throughout her body. Kyler held the board upright, one end on the ground, spinning it slowly. Her eyes were locked on the curbing, her gaze sharp and focused.

He watched her, seeing the ferocious desire in her eyes.

Kyler let her board drop and planted her right foot on the board, pushing off with her left. Her speed gained, and as she neared the curbing her left foot found its place on the on the tail of the board. Without slowing—and apparently without thinking, Josh thought—she executed the exact same motion and sailed cleanly over the curbing. She landed on the other side easily, without losing control. Josh smiled.

"That's called an ollie." He paused and arched an eyebrow, grinning. "Took me almost a month to learn that."

They spent the next hour and a half on the lot, with Josh showing her tricks that were more and more complicated . . . tricks she mastered quickly. He was impressed—amazed, really—at her incredible progress. She learned faster than anyone he'd ever met, and he began to realize that, although he was a pretty advanced skater, she would soon catch up with him, and finally surpass him.

Kyler had the ability and the skill, but more importantly, she had what he could only think of as outright fucking love for the sport, and God, did he admire her for that.

Josh would gladly have watched her skate all day, but by mid-afternoon Kyler had developed a hacking cough that wouldn't go away. She would've gone on had he not called a halt. He could tell she was faltering, getting weak, but she was still reluctant to quit.

"C'mon," he said, "let me buy you something to eat."

"Actually—" Kyler paused as another bout of coughing hit her. She cleared her throat and spit on the ground and started again. "I'm not really very hungry."

And she wasn't; her stomach seemed too small and full of acid, while her head seemed too heavy for her neck, and pounded like a fucking drum. Oh, yeah, she was getting sick, all right.

Josh looked at her, weighed the words in his mouth, and finally spit them out. "Come with me, Kyler. I'm staying with a friend right now and—"

Kyler was shaking her head. "No. I told you I don't need any fucking handouts."

"You can't sleep another night outside," he said matter-of-factly.

"Watch me," she said slowly, with an edge. "I've been out there a long time. I can deal with it."

"So is that a no?"

"Yeah," she picked up her board, glaring at him. "That's a fucking no."

"Ok," Josh said amiably. "Then I'll come with you."

Kyler stared at him, and he stared back. "You're staying with a friend? Where?"

"Over off Rose, in a two-room loft. It's just me and him and—"

"So why would you give up a night of that for a night on the street?"

Josh sighed. Christ, she was stubborn. "Because I'm out there nine times out of ten, just like you. I know what it's like. I just happened to get lucky this past month, but I'm smart enough to know it won't last."

"So, I repeat, why give it up for a night you'll most likely spend sleeping behind a dumpster?"

Josh looked at her, trying to see inside those dark eyes. "Got a cigarette?" He asked abruptly.

Wordlessly she handed him one and waited. He lit it and inhaled deeply, letting the smoke filter out his nose. He cocked his head, staring at her.

"You can't skate if you're dead," his voice was soft. "You keep this shit up, you'll die of pneumonia. Now, I don't know when you last had anything to eat, but I can pretty much tell that it's been awhile. You say you're not hungry now, fine," he stared deep into her eyes.

"But let me be there when you are. I'll try to get something that didn't come out of a garbage can, ok?"

Kyler was suddenly too tired to argue anymore. She stared and the ground and sighed. "Ok," she said quietly. "But if I don't like it, I'm leaving."

"It's just me there now," Josh said neutrally. "And I'll sleep in the next room. I know you can't trust me and that's fine. I'm not exactly sure I won't wake up tomorrow with the entire loft cleaned out, if you know what I mean." He offered a slightly hard smile.

"But I do know that you stepped in when I could've taken a hell of a beating, and I don't forget things like that. So please, let me at least give you a warm place to sleep for once."

Kyler glanced up at him, defeated. "All right."

CHAPTER 27

KYLER TOOK A deep breath and let it out slowly, feeling the sharp-edged pain course through her heart. She remembered all this like it was only yesterday, and longed with more emotion than seemed possible to feel Josh beside her again, keeping her together with his strength and his sanity.

The walk was short, but by the time they got there Kyler was burning up with fever and stumbling frequently. Josh slipped an arm around her waist and helped her up the two flights of stairs, feeling the heat emanating from her. He led her inside and back to the bedroom, where she sat heavily on the bed and put her pounding head in her hands.

"Listen," he squatted down in front of her, "I'm gonna run down to the store, see if I can find something to bring down your fever, ok? I'll only be gone a minute."

Kyler nodded without raising her head. "Can you pick me up some Excedrin?"

"Yeah," he said gently, and then he was gone.

She lay back on the bed, breathing shallowly, head thudding. A fit of shivers hit her and she clenched her teeth. It was hard to think, to keep her thoughts in order, but in a dim way she realized that she was too sick to move, and that she was basically at the mercy of this boy she didn't even know. The thought brought a confused sort of anger, a strong sense of pride, but there was really nothing she could do. Her body was done in.

Josh came back fifteen minutes later with an assortment of medication. He walked to the bedroom door and looked in on Kyler. She was sleeping, more or less soundly. He put a hand to her forehead, and even in sleep she pulled away, but not before he felt her fever . . . it felt no better, but it also felt no worse. He pulled up a chair and sat down beside the bed, watching her closely.

After a while he felt his eyes grow heavy and it wasn't too much longer before he drifted off himself.

Kyler woke with a start five hours later, confused, not sure where she was. She sat up in bed and groaned as a particular bad streak of pain shot through her head.

"What the fuck," she mumbled, and Josh stirred awake in the chair next to the bed.

"Hey," he said quietly. "You ok?"

She swallowed and scrubbed a hand across her face. "Yeah. What time's it?"

"Um . . . ," Josh reached for the clock on the table beside him and held it to his face. "A little after five."

"Jesus," Kyler muttered. "You didn't happen to get the Excedrin, did you?"

"Yeah. Got stuff for the fever, too. Your stomach up to taking 'em?"

Kyler looked around her and the room pulsed black and red in rhythm to her heartbeat. "Yeah."

"Ok," Josh said. "Watch your eyes." He turned on the overhead light and Kyler, caught off guard, moaned thickly.

"Here," Josh said, handing her a glass of water and two red and white pills. "These'll help cut the fever." Kyler took them with a shaking hand and swallowed them down.

"And the Excedrin," he handed her the green bottle. She shook two into her palm, contemplated, then shook two more and washed them down with water.

"Christ," she leaned back against the headboard.

Josh laid a hand gently on her forehead. Her fever, though still bad, seemed to be diminishing.

Kyler pulled away and rubbed her eyes. "I'll live," she said seriously. She sat there for a moment, and then made as if to get out of bed.

"Hey, where you goin'?" Josh asked.

She smiled a painful, beautiful smile, and it was then that Josh felt that he might be starting to fall in love with her.

"This is your bed," she said softly. "I'll sleep on the couch."

"Nope," he said. "You need your rest."

"No, you take it. I can't sleep knowing you're curled up on that chair like a fucking cat—"

"Kyler," his voice stopped her. She looked at him and he felt his heart lurch. He swallowed heavily and gave a small shake of his head. "Just go back to sleep. Please. If it bothers you so fucking much I'll sleep on the couch, ok?"

Kyler stared at him staring at her. She considered for a moment, watching him as he waited. Finally she said, "Take the couch. I'm not happy about it, but . . . I'll stay here."

"Good," Josh offered a small smile. "I'm right out there if you need anything."

She watched as he gently shut the door behind him, feeling a knot in her stomach. His deep sea-blue eyes burned in her mind, as glorious and tragic as the ocean itself.

She fell asleep thinking she wouldn't mind looking into those eyes for a while longer.

Kyler Maddox, raised on the rough streets of L.A., knew how to survive, how to be independent. She'd run away from an orphanage when she was eight, listening to the restless streak that constantly burned within her. By age ten she'd learned how to drive, and became very adept at breaking into and hotwiring cars.

Kyler would take them out for a spin, burning up the highways and byways of the city, and then ditch them whenever her gut instinct told her to. Along with the cars, she'd learned quickly how to slip through numerous locked doors and sensitive burglar alarms, and it was through this trade that she acquired a sort of roller-coaster income.

She was used to this life, used to being alone. It was rough and dangerous, but it was familiar to her. But this . . . her gaze settled lightly on her skateboard. Although this was new to her, she felt more at peace than she'd ever felt. And that scared her more than a little bit.

Kyler ran her hands through her hair and locked her fingers behind her neck. She stared down at the sand between her feet for a few long moments before finally raising her eyes to Lamont's, gazing gently back at her.

"He was just supposed to show me how to skate," she muttered. "I never meant to move in with him, or when he had to move on, move on with him. Even as sick as I was, without him I would've just scored some pills and holed up for a while, hoping to get better.

"But I stayed with them."

"Them?" Lamont asked with a raised eyebrow.

"He had a friend, Ryan, and whenever he wasn't off at some surfing competition somewhere, he was with us, and the three of us . . . well . . ."

"I loved those guys, Doc," she sighed and stared out over the ocean. "They were the only family I ever had, and there wasn't nothing I wouldn't do for either of them." She dropped her head and closed her eyes against the weight of reality.

"Except quit the smack," her voice was barely audible. "That was one thing I couldn't do." She stopped and took a deep, ragged breath. "I wanted to . . . more than anything, I wanted to quit because *they* wanted me to, and it broke my heart every time Josh begged me to, but I . . ." Kyler swallowed and ran a finger over the raised scar tissue on the inside of her right elbow, her jaw clenched, intentionally bringing the exposed nerve endings to life. It made her want to scream and she relished the feeling in a desperate masochistic way.

"I just couldn't," she growled softly. "It had too much of a hold on me."

Lamont reached out and put a hand gently on her shoulder, feeling her tense up.

"I think . . ." she stopped and cleared her throat. "I *know* it was Ryan who kept Josh sane when they left. There was nobody else and even if there were, nobody else would've been able to get past his shell. Shit," she dropped her head again and rubbed her eyes.

"I'm goin' inside," she murmured.

He nodded and stared out across the ocean. She got up and walked to the door, but paused and looked back.

"For what it's worth, Doc, I saw the way Emily looked at you. If it hadn't been for Curtis she woulda stayed."

Lamont gave a tired nod. "Thanks, Kyler."

She opened the screen door and slipped on into the house, feeling the weight of bittersweet emotions bearing down on her, wishing again, with insane need, to feel the calm serenity of Josh's arms around her.

Giving a heavy sigh, Kyler pulled herself up the steps, fighting the bone-deep weariness all the way until she fell gratefully onto the bed. Within minutes she was deeply asleep, lost in a coarse mixture of dreams and nightmares until the reigning image came back to her; haunting in its realism, sending sheer terror through her veins.

Bulging eyes, rank breath, sweat and fear making it near impossible for her to grip the hands that encircled her throat. The face familiar again and the name—Lewis—like vomit in her mouth. His weight was suffocating, crushing her to the floor, seeming to drill her right through the tile as he drilled himself into her.

Kyler pushed with everything she had but it wasn't enough. She caught an eyeball with a ragged thumb nail, but it was only the rough denim of his blue jean jacket. His hands clenched against her windpipe, his dick like a razor-edged mixer tearing her up from the inside out, and she was silently begging for death in an entirely hopeless way that was completely foreign to her.

No trace of the former fierce pride or hard-core stubbornness remained; she closed her eyes and willed death to come for her before any more pain could smash itself against her fragile body.

Kyler woke up gasping, bathed in sweat with the bed sheets in a tangled mess around her. Instantly she knew where she was, but Lewis's face still loomed surrealistically in front of her, and with a shaking hand she managed to snag her smokes off the nightstand and light one.

"Jesus," she moaned, drawing deep off the cigarette. Her hands were shaking, sending the smoke curling towards the ceiling in erratic half-lines. Giving herself just enough time to calm her pounding heart, Kyler rolled out of bed and reached for her clothes.

She glanced at the clock and noted the time: four-fifteen in the a.m. Dimly she realized that she had one hour and forty-five minutes before the plasma center opened, and why she was thinking about the plasma center was a mystery to her except she suddenly really extremely needed some valium in a way that went beyond just a need for sleep.

That part of her brain was starting to wake up . . . the part that in another hour or two would be begging for something—*anything*—to take it away.

Money was the key, Kyler knew, to solving a lot of her problems, but it was also just the key needed to open up doors better left closed.

"Just valium," she muttered shakily. "Just gonna donate enough plasma to get enough money for a few valiums just so I can sleep without having these fucking dreams."

And can you donate again? Her brain whispered. *Will your body allow you to even try?*

"Shit," she muttered, and then slipped quietly out into the hall. Doc's door was pulled to, leaving a space of about two inches between the door and the jamb. Kyler looked in and saw him in his own tangled bedclothes, stirring restlessly.

Silently she walked down the hallway and down the stairs, slipping out the front door and into the night.

CHAPTER 28

WITH HER BOARD balanced easily beneath her, Kyler skated hard and fast down the street. The wind coming off the ocean smelled strongly of salt and seawater, and it was deliciously cool against the sweat on her brow.

With the ease of long practice and natural ability, she used the asphalt and everything on it to help dispel the demons still lurking in her mind. When she was skating she always felt free of the heavy weight of too many regrets and way too many bad decisions. Josh's face could float in the front of her mind, and she was able to see his blue eyes again and look into them without the self-disgust that swamped her any other time.

It was the only time she could ever feel worthy of being alive, glad of having survived everything she'd put herself through and not have to wonder why the fuck she couldn't have just gone ahead and died.

Breathing hard, Kyler jumped the curb and purposefully landed hard on the grass. She lay there for a few minutes with her board beside her, staring up at the stars. Finally she got up and stumbled to the gate, unlocking it with a slightly shaking hand.

The skate park opened up before her, peaceful and calm in the early morning light, and Kyler was grateful again that she had this, that she'd been lucky enough—in spite of everything—to get this chance.

Still, though, even with the peaceful feeling just being inside the gates gave to her, she could feel the demons still there, and still fueling the fire.

In the office she checked the time again and saw that it was just a little past five. One hour until the plasma center opened; one hour until the needle was back in her vein, drawing plasma out on the promise of cash money in her pocket.

"It'd be great," she muttered, pulling a bottle of water out of the fridge, "if I can hold the puke down this time."

The thought of the needle scared her—petrified her, really—and drew her stomach into a tight ball. But it was necessary . . . *money* was necessary, and right now this was the only way she would allow herself to get it.

Kyler stared out the window across the dark expanse of the park, hopelessly wishing for years gone by. She gritted her teeth and lit another cigarette, trying to get her stomach to loosen up and checked the clock again.

Standing on a street corner at five-thirty, she felt the pressure building up in her. The closed shops and restaurants offered the temptation of money, which in turn promised dope in one form or another.

Kyler told herself again that she just wanted sleep, just wanted enough valium

(*or Xanax, Lortab, 'ludes, whatever,* her mind insisted on whispering) to let her body catch up on the sleep it so desperately needed. She just wanted sleep, nothing else. No more bloody noses from too much coke, no more of feeling like her entire body had been abraded with crushed glass from the withdrawal off the heroin.

"Just sleep," she mumbled, staring around her, the pressure mounting. "I just wanna fucking sleep and not have any more bad dreams."

The thought fleetingly occurred to her that she should turn around and go back, wake Doc from his own troubled dreams, sit him down at the kitchen table and tell him that she had a huge itch crawling up between her shoulder blades, in that place you can never quite reach, and that it wasn't far from hitting the base of her skull.

Once it did that it would slam into her central nerve center and cancel out all realism and rationale, demanding one thing and one thing only: that she do whatever needed to be done to put some kind of dope in her body; to feed the demon and to keep feeding it until her heart exploded.

Kyler dropped her head, hopeless and wanting to scream. Her strong, defiant pride forbade her to crawl back to Doc and open up her weaknesses to him, and she felt trapped again, crushed between her own conflicting emotions.

At six the plasma center opened its doors, and by six-ten she was reclined in a chair with the machine beeping beside her as the attendant prepared to insert the needle. Kyler closed her eyes and felt the sting; instantly revulsion and addiction rose up in her, battling her battered mind for precedence.

She intentionally bit down hard on her tongue, tasting blood and willing the pain to drive away the huge need raging inside her.

"You ok?" The attendant asked.

"Yeah," Kyler managed, her eyes still closed. "Just don't like needles."

"It's amazing how many people who donate say the same thing."

Kyler grunted in response, her stomach clenched. She was acutely aware of the length of the needle lying against her arm, the tip of it buried in her vein.

This could be heroin, her mind whispered. *The twenty-five bucks can get you a taste and in no time you can have a needle in your arm for real.*

Shut up!! The saner part of her brain bellowed. ***This is just for fucking valium!!***

And she knew it was, and had absolutely no intention of scoring any smack. But still . . . that monkey on her back was heavy and getting heavier with each passing second.

She took a deep breath and let it out slowly, thinking of the doc, her only friend right now, and how he'd turn his back on her in a heartbeat if she shot up again. Just like Josh and Ryan did, and she couldn't blame them, but it was highly realistic to her that if she lost Lamont she might as well get back to trying to die.

Her body was shaking from both cold and fear, and she prayed hard to whoever might be listening that she could just get through this one second at a time.

Just for valium, her mind whispered. *Just to keep from having these fucking dreams.*

"All right," the attendant was back and blessedly removed the needle from her vein. "Full bottle, again," he checked his chart and then ripped off a part from the perforated line at the bottom. "They'll take care of you at the counter."

He handed her the piece of paper and put a band aid on her arm. "Guess we'll see you in three days."

Kyler nodded and slid off the chair onto wobbly legs. She managed to hold onto her stomach while the clerk counted out the money and slid it across to her; managed to keep it in check until she was well away from the front doors of the building and halfway down the alley that ran beside it.

When she came to the back corner, she slipped around it and crumpled to her knees as her stomach opened up and sent its contents racing up her throat. Kyler braced herself against the brick wall and vomited again and again on the trash-littered ground around her.

After too many endless minutes, it finally trickled to a stop, and she leaned back against the building, taking one deep breath after another. When she felt she could, she pulled her cigarettes from her pocket and lit one with a wildly trembling hand, seeing for the first time the girl standing a few yards off, watching her with a look of mild disgust on her face.

Kyler stared at her, drawing deep on her smoke and willing her heart to stop its mad slamming against her rib cage. The girl gave a cautious nod and she nodded back.

"Think I can have one of those?" The girl gestured to her cigarettes.

"Sure," she tossed her the pack and watched as she lit one and walked over, handing it back.

"Thanks."

Kyler nodded and struggled to her feet, still hanging onto the wall for balance.

"Don't like donatin', I guess?" The girl inclined her head towards the puddle of vomit.

"Not really. You see me in there?"

"Yeah, I was in the chair just down from you." She paused and gave a grin. "You didn't look so hot in there."

"Yeah," Kyler grimaced. "I kinda figured."

They smoked in silence for a couple of minutes, and then the girl shot her a sidelong glance. "Whatcha doin' it for, the money?"

"Why else?" Kyler muttered, and ran a slightly shaking finger of the band aid on her elbow.

"Some people do it to see if they got anything; you know . . . AIDS and shit."

Kyler looked up at her with raised eyebrows. "Yeah?"

"Yeah, but not me," the girl said quickly. "I'm doin' it for the money; as much as I can get as quick as I can get it."

"Yeah . . . money's always good," Kyler thought about the twenty-five she had in her pocket and the anticipation of valium running through her system sent a calm streak through her. There was silence again around them, and then the girl dropped her butt to the ground and crushed it beneath her foot.

"Ok, thanks for the smoke. I gotta go, but I guess I'll see ya back here on Thursday, huh?"

"Probably," Kyler muttered, not even wanting to think about putting another needle in her vein. She watched the girl walk off in a way that reminiscent of her own self years ago, strong and wild but with a damaged look in her eye. Shaking her head, she crushed out her cigarette against the brick side of the building and then headed the opposite way.

Within a half an hour, she had located the dealer on a dim street corner, already open for business, and handed over twenty-four dollars in exchange for twelve small blue pills, tens, with the thin promise of small relief from the gouging points of her increasingly bad dreams.

Checking the time on a bank clock, Kyler saw she had a little over two hours before the park opened. She scrubbed a hand hard across her face and popped two of the valiums seemingly without thinking, and then headed uptown to hopefully sleep those two hours away in the back of the storage room.

She unlocked the gate and then locked it back behind her. Kyler felt the valium working its magic as she shuffled across the grass towards the office, already anticipating the feel of the carpeted floor beneath her weary body.

"Maybe one day I'll see about gettin' a couch in here," she muttered softly, stretching out on the floor along the back wall. She missed her army blanket, gone now to the pull of the ocean; sliding up against the wall as much as she could manage, Kyler pulled her knees to her chest and tucked her head down in an attempt to keep warm.

In no time the valium had her pulled down, and she was lost in the grip of induced sleep. It covered her like a warm, heavy blanket and for once it was dreamless and deep.

Kyler's internal alarm had always been somewhat reliable, and it was true again. She woke up at eight-thirty and stretched the stiffness out of her bones. She felt lighter, freer of the heaviness the nightmares had brought her, and she felt good for the first time in a very long time.

The big ramp was just about finished—probably would be today—and she resolved to spend much of her time that afternoon hammering down the last few boards and adjusting a last bolt or two. As twilight fell into dark and the gate was locked between her and the world, Kyler wanted to try it out for the first time.

Alone in the silence of the park, she wanted to be able to feel the pride at the project she'd completed, and to realize that she was still good and that maybe even just this little bit of the world still needed her.

She smiled and lit a cigarette, raked a hand through her hair, and then jogged across the grass to unlock the gate.

She sat on the lip of the ramp, nailing down the last little bit of wood when the thought came to her, harsh and jagged. It came on the hammer's downside arc and, missing the nail by a hair, hit mercilessly on the knuckle of her right thumb.

White-hot fire raced up her arm and she clenched her teeth against the howl of pain. The thumb throbbed in time to her erratic heartbeat, sending thousands of needles to settle in on her right biceps like it was a giant pincushion.

"Oh, Jesus," Kyler managed, and fell back against the platform. She cradled her thumb to her chest and closed her eyes, waiting, trying to keep breathing through the pain until the nerves had settled.

The valium! Her mind screamed frantically. *It's gonna show on the test!!* And then on the heels of that, *When did you take the one valium, the night Lewis pulled you into the doorway. WHEN WAS THAT??*

"Before or after the next test?" She asked the night, feeling the fire of her broken thumb literally take a back burner to this new problem. The drug test . . . she forgot about the fucking drug test.

"Christ," Kyler mumbled, and grasped the rail with her left hand, pulling herself to her feet. She stood swaying at the top of the ramp with her head down, trying to think past the panic and pain. "How could I forget? Shit. I've only been taking it once a week for the past month and a half."

Her stomach knotted up and she took a deep breath, trying to loosen it up. "Think," she growled. "Think, goddamn it. When did I take that fucking valium?"

But it was impossible; her battered brain couldn't keep up with the scattered time gone by. She stared around her, the panic more prominent now as the prospect of failing the drug test threw its reality on her. She'd lose her job and head back to jail. And Lamont? Lamont would . . .

"He'd turn his back on me," Kyler murmured, gripping the railing. Her body started shaking and she closed her eyes. In an intentional act of rage and semi-masochism, she brought her broken thumb down hard on the wood, and the instant fire that swamped her was both gratifying and deserving.

She shook her head and stepped down into the massive bowl, letting gravity pull her down. Kyler hit the wood hard enough to knock the wind out of her, and just lay there, staring up at the sky and wondering when she'd stop fucking up everything that was going good in her life.

Finally she found her feet and stumbled across the grass to the office. Pulling the first aid kit off the wall, she fumbled through it for a brief second and then her stomach knotted up again, harder this time, and wrapped in barbed wire.

Kyler turned to the bathroom and barely made it before her stomach unloaded its daily accumulation of acid and little else. She coughed and spit, staring down into the water, and then hit the flush. As the smell of fresh water rose around her, she laid her head exhaustively on the cool porcelain, feeling self-loathing wrap itself like a noose around her neck.

When Lamont's voice came from the doorway, she somehow wasn't surprised.

"Jesus," he said quietly. "I'm beginning to think you may have an ulcer or something." Kyler slit one eye open and looked at him, trying to drill his face into her memory because a memory was no doubt all he'd be in just three short days until she was tested again.

"I don't," she mumbled, hauling herself to her feet. "Just gotta weak stomach sometimes. And this," she held up her mangled thumb, "doesn't help it."

Lamont's eyes widened as he stared at the twisted shape and the blood seeping out from under the fingernail. "What happened?"

"I hit it with a hammer," she tried to slide past him but he caught her and led her to the chair. Kyler let him help her, her stomach again twisting with the massive hate she felt for herself at that moment.

"Lemme see," he took her thumb as gently as he could and held it to the light. She hissed in a breath of pain, feeling her body shaking. Lamont felt it too, and gave her a measuring look that she couldn't quite comprehend but managed to meet just the same.

"It's broken," he said quietly with a sigh.

"Yeah, I figured," Kyler gently took her hand back and lit a cigarette. She rubbed her eyes, feeling her mind still skittering around like a trapped rabbit, trying to find a way out of this hole.

"Hey."

She looked up at him, staring into his eyes. "What?"

"You ok?" Lamont's gaze was hard, trying to see past her wall. He strongly sensed something was wrong with her, and didn't believe it when she gave a tired nod.

"Yeah, Doc," she pulled herself to her feet. "I'm all right."

He was silent for a minute, gauging her face, and then gestured towards the door. "C'mon, I'll take you to the hospital and fix you up."

Kyler took a deep breath and let it out slowly, and then walked out to his car, holding her right hand gingerly to her chest. "I guess you just left there, huh?"

"Yeah," Lamont unlocked her door with a small smile. "Some days it seems like I live there."

"And I guess I don't help," she buckled her seatbelt and leaned her head back, staring out the window.

He watched her with his brow furrowed, then put the car in gear and pulled out of the lot. "Were you finishing up the ramp?"

Kyler closed her eyes, feeling the push/pull of the conflicting emotions inside her. One part of her wanted nothing more than to pop a few more valiums, wanting it, *needing it* like only a drug-addicted person could.

The other part, the part that still continually felt the sting of Josh's last words to her wondered what the fuck kind of person would keep going back to the drugs and the lifestyle that came with it.

And still another part—tiny, but there—told her that the valiums were nothing compared to the coke and the smack, and maybe, yeah, she liked her other pills too much, but the small blue ones were actually taken for a purpose other than getting high.

Valium eased her into sleep in a natural, completely non-addicted way, so what the hell did it matter if she took a couple more?

Because it'll show up on the drug test, the lone sane piece of her brain muttered. *And without a prescription, it'll be taken as unwarranted drug use—possibly illegal, depending on how my case reads.*

"Kyler?" Lamont asked gently. "Were you finishing up the ramp?"

"Yeah," she mumbled. "I was gonna skate it the minute that last nail went in."

"I can bring you back here after I wrap your thumb," he offered.

"No," she shook her head tiredly, feeling her stomach twist as her skin tightened against the air touching it.

Christ, I need a fix, the thought came unbidden, from out of nowhere, and she clenched her jaw.

"It'll be there tomorrow," her voice was barely audible. "I'll skate it then, and hopefully open it up to the public if it's safe enough."

Lamont grunted and swung into the parking lot on the side of the hospital. "It shouldn't take too long. I wanna x-ray it first, though, so I can see exactly how bad it is."

"All right," Kyler stepped out of the car. "Hopefully it ain't too bad."

He nodded and held the door open for her. Silently he climbed the three flights of stairs with her, still trying to figure out why he felt like she was trying to keep from exploding.

Sitting her down beside the table under the x-ray machine, he arranged her hand as gently as possible so to get the best picture of her thumb. Kyler's face paled as the pain shot mercilessly up her arm, but her jaw remained locked against the moan that wanted to slide out.

"Five seconds," Lamont said, stepping into the little room and turning the machine on. She shut her eyes and wondered again why the fuck she was still alive.

"Ok," he said, walking back to her and pulling up a seat, facing her. "Be about two-three minutes and we'll know."

Kyler nodded silently, scrubbing a hand hard across her face. Lamont gazed at her, his eyes narrowed.

"Listen . . ." he started, and she looked at him with exhausted eyes of her own.

"I'm ok," she said with a somewhat painful smile. "You don't have to worry about me."

"You'd tell me if you weren't?" The words were out before he could stop them, and he wondered at the stupidity of the question when it wasn't long ago at all when she was too afraid of him to be in the same room as him for more than a few minutes.

Kyler gazed at him, reading his genuine concern for her in his eyes, but all that did was serve to fuel her self-loathing.

Jesus, I really don't deserve to be living right now.

"Yeah," she said quietly. "I'd tell you, Doc."

And there goes another fucking lie, her brain spoke up sarcastically.

His eyes met hers directly, searchingly, and she stared back calmly enough given the hurricane her insides were in. A beep sounded in the little room and he glanced that way before looking at her again.

"All right," he said softly. He got up and went to check her x-rays, walking back to her as he flipped through them. "Yeah, it's broken pretty bad, but it's doable. I'll have it splinted in no time, and once the bone's back where it supposed to go it won't hurt as much."

Kyler nodded, glancing at the charts he laid in front of her.

"You're gonna lose the nail," He gently picked up her hand and pressed slightly along the knuckle. Kyler gritted her teeth but remained still.

"I'll wrap some gauze around it that'll protect it some, but you'll have to change it every night. Or I can, if you don't want to."

She nodded and took a deep breath, looking at him. "Go ahead and set the bone, Doc," and immediately there was a streak of white-hot pain as he pulled her thumb up and set the bone with his own thumb and forefinger. Kyler grunted and watched as the world shimmered around its edges before growing solid again.

"Stay with me, ok?" Lamont's voice was sharp and clear and she gave a slow, drunken nod.

"Yeah. I'm still here, Doc."

"Good," he expertly splinted the thumb with the quickness of long practice. "'Cause if you pass out I may be tempted to keep you here overnight."

She grimaced and shook her head. "I'm not gonna pass out, but just so you know, it's a miracle I didn't because that hurt like a motherfucker."

"Yeah," he agreed. "It does. But that should do you. Go easy on it for a while, and it'll heal quicker."

"I'll try," Kyler stood up slowly, anticipating the swoop and sway of the room, but this time there was none.

"Still ok?" He was closely watching her, ready to catch her if she started to pass out.

"Yeah," she carefully opened the door, still cradling her right hand. He held it open while she walked out, and then fell into step beside her as they headed back down the steps.

"You hungry?"

She walked down a full flight before answering, and then said reluctantly, "Sure . . . I guess so."

"No, you're not," Lamont said amicably.

"Yeah, you're right, I'm not," she stepped out into the cool purple haze of southern California dusk and breathed deep of the salty air coming in off the ocean. "But you're always tellin' me I gotta eat, right?"

He shrugged and hit the key fob on his key chain, unlocking the car doors. "You can't *not* eat." He slid behind the wheel and glanced over at her. "Right?"

Kyler gave a small nod. "I guess. Something light, though, ok? Like soup, maybe?"

Lamont smiled and shifted into drive. "I was just thinking that. Wanna try the Souplantation over on Canter? It's good."

"Ok," she said and gazed out the window. "How much is it?"

"Not enough for you to worry about. I got it."

He heard her take a deep breath and let it out slowly, but she didn't argue. His brow furrowed and he had to wonder again if there was something she wasn't telling him.

At the restaurant she managed to eat half a bowl of soup and a small piece of bread before her stomach started protesting. Lamont was satisfied, though, that she got even that much down.

"Sorry," Kyler muttered as they walked back out to the car after dinner. "My stomach ain't what it used to be."

"Even a little bit's good for you," Lamont offered a smile. "I just wish you'd give it a chance on a daily basis."

She shot him a look and got in the car. "I've never ate much, Doc, even before the dope."

He grunted and pulled out on the interstate. "All right," he responded easily. "I'll quit harping on it."

The road soared by them in flashes of light from the arc-sodiums down the middle. Kyler felt the throbbing of her thumb and wondered how good the medical attention was in prison.

She sighed heavily and stared out the window, silent as they rolled along towards home.

Home, her mind whispered wearily. *Is that what that is?*

"Hey, Doc?" She asked quietly, her eyes on the dark highway ahead of them.

"Yeah?"

"Um . . ." she pulled her words together, trying to form them into a question. "How soon do you want me out?"

"Huh?" Lamont shot her a sharp glance. "Out of what?"

"Your house," her voice showed patience she didn't feel. "When I can get off the city's time and actually start drawing a paycheck . . . maybe, you know . . . I can find something and get out of your hair."

He didn't answer for a long time and she stared out at the night, her stomach clenching.

"Kyler . . ." he finally started. "You're, uh . . . not bothering me at all. I mean, my house is yours for as long as you want it. Don't . . . be in a hurry to leave, ok? Thinking you're in my way, I mean. I . . . it's good having somebody else there since I never am. It at least makes the house look lived in."

She didn't answer as she mulled his words over in her mind.

"And I told you before, absolutely no fucking strings attached."

Kyler closed her eyes in shame again, as her previous job of earning money on her back slashed across her mind. Lewis's insane eyes stared back at her from the forefront of her brain for a brief second and then they were gone.

"Plus," he continued in a somewhat reluctant voice, "it's easy to fall back into old habits, you know? Maybe out of boredom or a sense of freedom of whatever." He met her gaze for a minute.

"I just . . . if you wanna go, I can't stop you, and I won't. I just want you to be sure those old demons don't—"

"I know," she murmured. "And I don't think I'm ready to go yet. Not quite . . . comfortable, thinking about long nights and . . . stuff. I just don't wanna be in your way."

"You're not," he assured her as they pulled into his driveway. "And if I was gonna kick you out this soon, I never would've told Emily I'd help you."

As if on cue, his cell phone rang as he pulled the keys from the ignition. "And speaking of her . . ." he said quietly, glancing at the caller ID.

Kyler opened the door and started out of the car as he hit the talk button.

"Hey," his voice was soft as he briefly touched Kyler's shoulder, handing her the keys when she turned back. She took them and shut the car door, giving him the privacy he needed and actually glad for the chance for him to be preoccupied for a minute.

She needed time to process the fact that apparently, yes, this was home. For the first time in her life, Kyler had a home.

And, Lord, how the bitter irony hit her hard. This was a home, a good home . . . and one that might be short-lived as she had only three days to figure a way out of this mess she'd gotten herself in.

CHAPTER 29

LAMONT FOUND HER outside on the back deck steps, feet buried in the sand, staring out at the ocean and smoking a cigarette. His heart was dimly aching from the sound of Emily's voice, still echoing in his ear. He missed her. A lot.

"Hey, kid," he sat down beside her. "You know you can make yourself at home, right?"

Kyler glanced at him with raised eyebrows. "Yeah . . ." she said slowly.

"Well, I mean, you're always out here. You wanna sprawl out on the couch and watch hours of TV, that's perfectly all right with me."

She offered a wan smile. "Never been much of a TV person, Doc."

"Music? There's the stereo downstairs. CD's and albums, mostly. Some cassette tapes."

"Good music?"

Lamont grinned. "I like to think so."

"Got any Eagles?"

"Yep. A couple on thirty-threes, but more on CD."

"Beatles?"

"Every song they ever sang."

Kyler nodded and stared back out over the dark water. "Yeah, that's good music."

"I don't play it as much as I used to," he said. "But four, five years ago Emily and I ran it almost non-stop."

There was silence around them, and then she looked at him. "How's she doing?"

He stared out over the ocean, contemplating the choppy waves crashing on the shore. Slowly he shook his head.

"Not too good. Curtis . . . he . . . well, there's no change. Emily doesn't want to keep him on the ventilator as a way of life, you know? Yet she's afraid to take him off if there's a chance he might get a donor heart."

"Is there a chance?" Kyler rested her eyes on his.

Lamont gazed back for a moment before answering, and when he did she could tell he was choosing his words carefully.

"Not . . . really. You see, donor organs are few and far between, reserved only for those in dire need and specifically for those who have a good chance of *continuing* to live a fulfilling life.

"Curtis never *lived* a fulfilling life to begin with, and the chances are slim to none he'd even try even if he did get a heart."

Kyler felt a dim rage low in her gut, and knew in the back of her head it probably wasn't warranted. But yet it was there, just the same.

"Because he's a drug addict and a thief?" She asked, hearing the edge in her voice.

He met her eyes directly and gave a short nod. "Pretty much, yeah. It ain't right, I know, but . . . that's how the system works."

She glared at the water for a few long moments, and then slowly shook her head. It was suffocating, her impending imprisonment, Curtis being stonewalled at a chance for life based on his past actions . . .

She sighed and rubbed her eyes.

"I didn't write this book, Kyler," Lamont said very quietly, sensing her anger. "If it was up to me, I'd give Curtis my own heart."

"For Emily," Kyler responded just as quietly.

"For Emily," he agreed. Running a hand through his hair, he shot her a glance. "I got some Stones down there, too, and Skynyrd . . . you ever listen to them?"

"Occasionally."

"When you get a chance, go down there and listen to *Simple Man* . . . it's on an album. Listen to the words, ok?"

Kyler gazed at him, and then shifted her eyes back to the water. "All right."

"I'm gonna take a shower and probably go to bed. I'll see you in the morning."

She felt the wood shift as he got up, heard the screen door close gently behind him. Pulling her smokes from her pocket, she lit another one and let the smoke filter through her nose, rising on the warm night air.

Later she slipped quietly into the darkened kitchen. The whole house was quiet, and glancing up the stairs she saw the space under Lamont's closed bedroom door was dark. Feeling her way confidently down the basement stairs, she walked over to the stereo and turned it on low. Skynyrd was already on the turntable, and reading the label upside-down in the dim light, she raised an eyebrow at the second song . . . *Simple Man*.

Switching over to phono and placing the needle gently on the record, Kyler settled back on the soft leather couch and let the music cover her.

The words themselves spoke of a serenity that she had rarely ever known, but it was familiar in a somewhat bitter, heart-wrenching way that reminded her too strongly of both Josh and Ryan, and the simple life the three of them had once led.

She closed her eyes and willingly let the memories wash over her, wishing with everything she had that she'd never picked up that fucking needle.

"Kyler," Lamont said softly, touching her shoulder lightly. He was standing by the couch holding the phone as she bolted upright, heart slamming painfully against her sternum.

"Sorry," he muttered. "Another bad dream?"

She didn't answer as she dropped her head in her hands and raked her fingers through her hair. Her body was shaking, covered in sweat, and she fought to free herself from the entangling snares of the phantom hand around her neck and the dangerous body pressed suffocating against her.

"Shit," she whispered. "What time is it?"

"Late," he answered. "Almost two. You got a phone call."

Kyler snapped her eyes up to his and he saw the sudden fear dancing just below the surface. "Phone calls this time of night are never any good," she mumbled.

He didn't answer as he held the cordless out to her. She took it in trembling hands and watched as he headed back up the stairs.

"Hello?"

"Kyler," Barb's voice floated across the line. "I'm sorry I woke you up, but I really need to talk to you."

"Are you ok?" Instantly awake now, Kyler fumbled her cigarettes off the floor and stuck one in her mouth.

"No. Well, I don't know. The baby had a seizure today . . . I felt it, and I . . . I'm scared. Jesus, I'm so fucking scared."

"How bad?"

"Bad, I guess," Barb sounded like she was crying. "Kyler, they shot methadone in my uterus to stop it, and it worked. *The baby responded to the fucking methadone.*"

Kyler took a deep, shuddering breath, feeling the impact of that single statement. *The baby responded to the methadone.*

"I knew she was addicted," Barb said, "but it just all hit home when the seizure stopped . . . and . . . *methadone*, Kyler. *They fucking shot me full of methadone!*"

Taking a deep draw off her cigarette, Kyler shut her eyes, remembering all too well the feel of methadone snaking up her veins, easing back the withdrawal of the heroin. It took her up to its own levels in its own sweet way, and weaning off of it was almost as painful as getting off the smack.

"Jesus," she growled softly.

Barb was quiet for a minute and then said, "Can you come up here? Tomorrow or the next day?"

"Yeah," Kyler scrubbed a hand across her face. "Tomorrow, ok?"

"Ok. Thanks, Kyler."

"I'll be there early." She hit the off button and tossed the phone beside her. Her eyes found the turntable and she wondered what had happened to her simple life.

Lamont was on his cell phone in the kitchen when she walked up the steps. His pager was lying on the table, still flashing an emergency page from the hospital.

"Ok," he said. "On my way."

He hung up and regarded her. "You're right; phones calls at this hour are never good. What's wrong?"

Kyler gave a small shake of her head. "My friend Barb's having trouble with her pregnancy. The baby's addicted to heroin. What's goin' on with you?"

"Bad accident on the Five. Family in a van crossed the median and hit another car head on. E.R.'s a madhouse right now."

She took a deep breath and fumbled another cigarette out of her pack.

"You gonna be ok?" He asked.

"Yeah."

Lamont started out of the room, but stopped and looked at her. "I'm sorry about your friend."

She nodded. "I'm sorry you had to get a call like this."

"It's my job," he said softly. Kyler watched as he grabbed his keys and went out the front door. Slowly she climbed the stairs and crawled into the bed in the spare room. Her mind was exhausted from the thoughts circling around in it, but it was too restless to even attempt to shut down. Over and over she heard the restless fear in Barb's voice; fear of using, restless because of the demon that spoke so sweetly in her ear.

She thought about the baby, seizing in its mother's belly, feeling the same insane need and rage she herself felt, only . . .

"Only the baby doesn't know why it feels that way," Kyler mumbled. "Jesus."

She glanced over at the clock and then out the window. It was pushing three-thirty in the a.m., and suddenly she threw back the covers and reached for her clothes on the floor.

With a sharp pang of guilt and a shouting consciousness, she crept into Lamont's room and glanced around, her eyes settling on the dresser. In amongst a pile of change there was a wad of crumpled-up bills. Kyler separated them and counted out almost twenty dollars in ones and fives.

She shook her head and closed her eyes briefly, feeling the self-hatred build up. With a small groan she stuffed the money in her pocket and reached for a pen and the back of a receipt tossed towards the edge of the dresser.

> *Doc,* she wrote, *I went to see Barb early this morning after you left. They gave her and the baby methadone when the baby had a seizure in the womb, and she's really upset about it. The methadone's almost as hard to get off of as the smack, and I think she's afraid the baby will like it too much. I took the bus and I owe you twenty I took off your dresser. I'll be back probably tonite.*
>
> Kyler.

She took a deep breath and set the pen down. Grabbing her board, she headed downstairs and out the door, skating hard and fast towards the bus station.

CHAPTER 30

KYLER STAYED LOW and quiet as she snuck around the building to her old room. She thought back to the nights when she'd wake up to find Barb gone, and wondered why she'd never realized the convenience of having a bottom floor window.

Not that I ever had a reason to sneak out, she thought. *But this made it easier for Barb and Jimmy to get together.*

Poised beneath the window, she hesitated a brief moment, hoping Barb was still in this room and that they hadn't moved her. She wondered fleetingly what she'd do if she wasn't, and then tapped softly on the glass.

A shadow crossed the room and then Barb's face was inches from hers. She grinned and unlocked the window, helping her friend over the pane.

"I guess you were expecting Jimmy," Kyler said in a low voice.

Barb shrugged, giving her a hard hug. "I figured he had to be the only one outside my window this time of night. I didn't mean for you to come this early."

"Yeah, sorry," Kyler sat down on the empty bed she used to sleep in. "I figured you needed to talk now and not at nine when they'd let me in the front door. Did I wake you up?"

"You kidding?" Barb's eyes turned hard. "I couldn't sleep if you paid me."

Kyler gave a slow nod, her eyes assessing her friend, gauging the amount of fear and anger she saw in her gaze. Dropping her eyes, she gave a grin at the hugeness of her belly. She reached across and laid a gentle hand across her abdomen, feeling soft movement.

"You're what, seven months already?"

Barb nodded, giving a small smile of her own. "Almost eight."

A vague memory tugged gently at Kyler's brain, and she smiled. "A girl, you said?"

"Yeah," Barb sat down on her own bed and passed Kyler the ashtray. "You can smoke if you want to. It doesn't bother me."

"You give it up?" Kyler arched an eyebrow as she pulled her smokes from her pocket.

"Yeah. For the baby, you know. Didn't wanna put her in anymore harm than I already have.

Kyler nodded and lit a cigarette. "You name her yet?"

Barb finally gave a genuine grin. "Bailey. Whatcha think?"

"Bailey," she said reflectively. "I like it, Barb. I really do."

"Thanks. Jimmy does, too." She paused a minute, staring at the floor. "I hope he stays, Kyler," she said quietly. "But sometimes I think he won't."

Kyler drew deep on her cigarette and let the smoke filter out of her nose. There was silence between them for a moment, and then she said softly, "He'll stay, Barb. And if he won't, I'll be here, ok?"

Briefly, unbidden like always, a dim memory tickled the back of her mind . . . almost the exact words she'd just spoken . . .

He won't run. But if he did, I'd *still be here.*

Ryan's voice, coming to her across the years, promising to stay if Josh bolted when he found out he may become a father . . . at just thirteen years old.

Kyler scrubbed a hand hard across her face, thinking Barb's eyes were the same green as Ryan's, wondering where Ryan was right now, and if he'd been able to hold Josh together after they'd left her fixing from dirty works in the back of some filthy alley.

"You ok?" Barb asked quietly.

Kyler grimaced and offered a wry grin. "Yeah, but please don't worry about me, ok? I'm supposed to be the one here worrying about you."

She sighed and stared out the window. "I'll be ok, Kyler. Whatever happens, I'll be ok."

Kyler reflected on the strength her friend possessed, strength to keep her head up and to keep one foot in front of the other with a heroin-addicted baby just two months form being born, and both of them with methadone still in their veins.

"I know," she answered. "Just know that I'm here for you, ok? Anytime . . . two in the morning, you need to talk, I'll be here."

Barb regarded her, giving a slow nod. "I know, Kyler. I appreciate that."

There was silence between them for a few minutes, and then Kyler gestured towards the empty bed she was sitting on with raised eyebrows.

"They didn't fill this up after I left?"

"Nah," Barb shook her head. "Said it'd probably be better since I'm pregnant. Besides, I only got a few more weeks and then I'm gone, too. Thought I'd head down by you."

"San Diego?" Kyler grinned.

"Yeah. I've been doing some checking, and I can get into a program that will help me get some skills I need to get a job or maybe even try to go to school. I can get into a halfway house for about six months that will help with daycare if I need it to."

"Damn," Kyler said, "I think you'd be stupid to turn that deal down. But . . ." she paused, trying to keep the tremor out of her voice, "where's the halfway house?"

Please not on Kennedy, her mind whispered.

"Over on uh . . ." Barb reached over and snagged a notebook off her nightstand and flipped through it. "Over on Merriam Avenue. You know where that's at?"

"Yeah," Kyler flicked an ash from her cigarette. "Just a block or two from where I work."

"Still working at that skatepark?"

"Yeah. Well, I'm still on the city's time, but the guy who runs it said he'll hire me full time once I pay off the community service."

Barb nodded and looked at her for a moment before saying quietly, "When you gave me your . . . uh . . . doctor's phone number, I figured he'd be able to get in touch with you . . . let you know I called. I wasn't expecting him to just hand the phone to you."

Kyler gave a slow shake of her head and took a deep drag off her smoke. "I'm . . . staying with him. The halfway house didn't . . . didn't work out for me."

Barb met her eyes, and Kyler read what she was thinking.

"It's not that," she said quickly. "He . . ." she took a deep breath and let it out slowly, thinking back to that horrible night at the halfway house.

"He's letting you stay with him," Barb muttered, and a spark of anger flashed in her eyes. "Jesus, Kyler."

"I told you, it's not what you think."

"Yeah," she flapped a hand and glanced away. "Ok."

Kyler angrily crushed out her cigarette and ran a hand through her hair. "I was raped, Barb, at the house. A guy was in the bathroom when I went in one night to take a piss, and he . . ." she swallowed heavily. "Fuck, I never saw him coming."

Barb stared at her with wide eyes, incredulity shooting from her gaze. "Oh, God."

"I told Doc I couldn't go back to that house, and . . . I didn't wanna go to another one. They caught the guy, but . . ." she gritted her teeth, still—*still*—feeling that hand around her throat. "I was pretty messed up, but I needed to go *somewhere* or else they'd put me back in jail.

"Doc pulled some strings and got it to where I could stay with him until I complete the community service. But he's got a spare room," her eyes were angry, staring at Barb. "And I'm *not* sleeping with him, for Christ's sakes."

"Ok," and now her voice was softer. "Fuck, I'm sorry, Kyler."

"Yeah," Kyler pulled another cigarette from her pack and lit it with a trembling hand.

"No, really, I am. I—" She stopped and gazed at her, comprehension slowly dawning in her eyes. "They wouldn't lock you up for getting raped. But they *would* if you used again. You used, didn't you?"

Giving a heavy sigh, Kyler stared out at the dark night. "I told you I was pretty messed up. I was out runnin' the streets for two days before I even went to the doc. Yeah," her eyes met those of her friend's, defiant and fearful at the same time. "Yeah, I got high. I did a few lines of coke—I don't know how many—but that's all I did, and I know that for a fact 'cause Doc tested me."

Barb took a deep breath and let it out slowly. There was silence in the room for what seemed like a long time to Kyler, but she didn't say a word. Finally Barb cleared her throat and looked at her.

"Why didn't you call me? After the, uh . . . rape? Before the coke? Or after, I don't care. But why didn't you?"

Kyler shrugged. "You have your own problems; why would you want mine laid on you, too?"

"Because we're friends."

"Besides, I didn't wanna feel like I was letting you down, even though I know I was. I'm clean now, but that doesn't mean anything. I still fell into the clichéd category they told us about here."

"Yeah, but I think you had a good excuse."

Kyler grimaced and crushed out her cigarette. "It doesn't matter now."

"I think—" Barb broke off as a huge bolt of pain ripped across her lower belly. She gasped and leaned forward, cradling her abdomen.

"Oh, shit," she said breathlessly. Another slash of fire, stronger and hotter than the first, tried to rip her in two as she struggled to control the pain. The baby kicked once, hard, and then again as if in extreme agitation or duress.

"Kyler . . ." she reached for her friend, but Kyler was already there beside her. "Help me. It's too early for her, it's too . . . early . . ." she let out a shriek as ripples of razor-edged pain centered around her womb. "Oh . . . fuck . . ."

"Hang on," Kyler said frantically, panic trying to numb rational reasoning. "I'm goin' for help." Without waiting for an answer, she bolted out into the hallway and hurtled towards the front desk.

The night receptionist glanced up, alarmed, as she skidded to a halt in front of her. "Call nine-one-one," she snapped, pointing back down the hall. "Barb Taylor's goin' into labor."

"What?"

"Now!!"

The woman snatched up the phone and Kyler watched as she hit the three vital buttons. "Tell 'em to hurry, ok? It's too early for the baby so they gotta hurry."

Kyler ran back to Barb's room and found her on the floor, curled up in a ball, fingers digging into the carpet. Her lips were pulled back from her teeth from the pain as she laid terrified eyes on Kyler's.

"You . . . gotta tell . . ."

"Shh, they're coming, all right? Just hold on, Barb, just stay with me."

"Tell Jimmy," she snarled. "Tell Jimmy, you gotta tell Jimmy."

"I will," Kyler cradled her head on her lap, feeling the shaking in her body. "I will, ok? I'll go tell him as soon as EMS gets here."

"I'll tell him," a voice came from the doorway. Kyler looked up and saw a young girl standing indecisively just outside. "I'm kinda seeing his roommate; I'll tell him, ok, Barb? You go with her," she glanced at Kyler.

"All right," she nodded and shot a look towards the window and the sounds of sirens coming down the treatment center drive. "They're here, so just hold on, ok?"

Barb shut her eyes and gritted her teeth against the pain. Her heart was breaking as her whole being felt the baby's feeble movement.

"Don't let her die," she whispered. "Please, God, don't let her die."

Kyler shut her eyes and waited, trying to say a prayer of her own in amidst the chaos of the room.

She watched as they wheeled Barb through into the maternity ward, prepping her for an emergency caesarean section. Her whole body was drained, exhausted, and she sighed heavily as she walked over to the phone in the corner.

"Doc," she muttered into his answering machine. In her mind's eye she pictured the machine on the table in the living room, with its reliable red blinking light. "I'm still up here in Leitner. Barb went into labor and . . . well, she's, you know . . . only seven months along, and they got her in surgery for a c-section."

She stopped and took a deep breath, rubbing her forehead. *A drink would be good right now,* she thought randomly, and then more specifically, *or a fix.*

"I might be here for another day or two, but . . . what day is it? Tuesday? I got a piss test Thursday at nine in the morning, and I have to be there for that, so maybe tonight but I'll try to head on back tomorrow sometime.

"I just . . . you know . . ." she sighed and glanced up as Jimmy came barging into the room. "I wanna be here just till I find out something. I'm at the Eastbrook Center in south Leitner. Uh . . . I'll try to give you a call back later, ok?"

She hung up and faced him, snagging his jacket to stop him from going through the double doors. "She's in there, Jim, ok, and they're doing what they can for her and the baby."

"Shit," he hung his head. "They said anything yet?"

"No, they just took her back there."

He sighed and glared at the receptionist glaring back at him. Kyler took him gently by the arm and led him to a chair.

"Relax," she growled softly, "and don't go ballistic."

"I'm not," he mumbled. "Yet. But Kyler, she doesn't have insurance. Most times people don't have insurance, they don't keep them."

"There's the baby," she responded. "They have to keep her here for the baby's sake."

"How is she, the baby?" He gave her a sharp look. "Still . . ."

"Yeah, alive. They're doing a c-section."

Jimmy gazed at her for a long moment, then glanced at the TV. His mind was far from the show that was on, and the minute the doors opened almost two hours later, he was up and striding towards the doctor before Kyler could stop him.

"Well?" He asked gruffly. *"Well?"*

The doctor stopped and shot the receptionist a look that Kyler understood completely. "Wait," she said sharply. "We're just worried, ok? We're the only family she's got, so cut us a little slack. Don't call the cops just yet."

"What?" Jimmy looked at her, the confusion on his face quickly turning into a murderous rage. "You gonna call the *cops* on me?"

"I won't," the doctor crossed his arms over his chest and stood his ground, "if you're halfway sensible and stop yelling."

"I'm not . . . yelling," he dropped his voice a notch. "How is she?"

The doctor gazed at him. "Barbara is doing as well as can be expected, considering. She's resting right now and she'll be sore when she wakes up. The baby . . ." he paused, choosing his words.

"The baby had a seizure as we were pulling her out. A shot of methadone stopped it quickly, but I'm . . . almost certain the seizure affected some part of her. I won't know for a while . . . at least a day or two. It may have damaged a part of her brain that controls motor skills, taste, sight, whatever, but . . ." he shrugged. "I think it did some damage somewhere."

Jimmy stared at him and beside him Kyler could sense the tension running through his body.

"Because she's two months early, she'll be in an incubator for a length of time while her lungs continue developing."

"How long?" Kyler asked quietly.

The doctor shrugged. "I can't say for sure. She's definitely a heroin baby . . ." she saw his eyes drop to the tracks her arm and felt the jagged edges of anger start to tear into her stomach.

"And I'll tell you right now that if that baby had died, by law I could have the mother arrested for murder."

Stunned silence dropped like a ton of rocks between them, and Kyler felt Jimmy's anger peak and surpass her own.

"You motherfucker . . ." he growled, and started forward. Kyler reached for him and felt her hands slide harmlessly down his back. In the time it took to take a single breath, all hell broke loose.

CHAPTER 31

TWO HOURS EARLIER Lamont stood in his living room and replayed Kyler's message. He shook his head, feeling the frustration start to build up, then grabbed his keys and headed back out the door. It would be a little while longer before he would be able to feel the soft warmth of his bed again.

He stepped out of the elevator to a huge commotion down the hallway on his right. A young man was struggling with two security officers, fighting hard and mean . . . with Kyler beside him, holding her own against the mass of moving bodies.

"You think she did this on purpose?" The young man screamed as he lunged towards the doctor standing off to one side. *"She ain't had a fix in almost eight months!"*

One of the security officers finally managed to put handcuffs on the man's wrists as Kyler stepped between him and the doctor.

"Wait, goddamn it, just wait a second." She had one hand on the young man's chest and the other held out to the doctor. "Don't call the cops."

"Why not?" The doctor snapped, glaring at her. "He just about damn-near assaulted me."

Oh, Jesus, Lamont thought, instinct keeping him almost hidden by the elevator.

"Listen," she implored him, "this isn't good, I know, for any of us, but look at him, ok? He's just worried, I'm worried. That's my friend in there, his girlfriend, and his daughter."

"Still, that doesn't—"

"Please," Kyler looked at him. "Lemme talk to him. Give us two minutes, ok?"

"Fuck, Kyler, come on—"

"Shut up!" She whirled on him, eyes blazing. From where he stood, Lamont didn't think he'd seen such rage in her before.

"Two minutes, please," she turned back to the doctor. "I'll calm him down, and if I can't go ahead and call the cops."

The doctor gave her a long, measuring look, considering. Finally he nodded to the security officer. "Two minutes. He comes after me again, he's going to jail."

Kyler nodded, relief shooting through her, then grabbed the young man as soon as the cuffs were off and shoved him towards the stairway. Behind Lamont the elevator doors opened and he quickly stepped back in, almost falling over a couple coming out.

"Sorry," he muttered, not looking at them, and jabbed the button for the floor directly below. In seconds he was down and out, taking quick strides halfway down the hall to the stairs.

Gently he opened the door and slipped through, easing the door quietly shut behind him. One floor above him Kyler's voice came hissing down, quiet and full of anger.

"*Jesus*, Jimmy, you gotta fuckin' stop."

"Murder," he growled. "That asshole said he'd've booked her on murder, Kyler. *Barb ain't had nothin' stronger than a fucking cigarette in eight months.* She gave it all up the minute she found out she was pregnant, so *how the fuck can he say that? And you know what?*" Jimmy's voice was rising, threaded through with an insane anger that chilled Lamont's blood.

"*I think that motherfucker wanted Bailey to die, just so he could charge her.*"

"*Jimmy, I don't know!*" Kyler snarled. "*I don't know what the fuck he wants or doesn't want, but I do know that you're not helping anything by acting fucking crazy. What, you think they're not serious about calling the cops? Or you think so what if you go back to jail, huh?*"

"Christ, Kyler," Jimmy's voice lost a little of its edge. "That ain't what I think, you know that."

"Shit," she snapped, and Lamont heard the flick of a lighter. There was silence for a minute, and then she muttered, "What you got, Jim, two, three years on the shelf? We're not talking jail here . . . we're talking *prison* for you. Is that what you're after?"

"Fuck you, Kyler. You don't know shit."

"I know you just had a daughter who's addicted to heroin because her mother's addicted. What's gonna happen to them if you're locked up? Or . . ." she paused, watching him. "Maybe that *is* what you're after?"

Jimmy stared at her, rage shooting from his eyes. "You better watch what you're saying," he said softly. "This ain't been a good day for me."

"Yeah? Well, me neither," Kyler shot back. "You just tell me right now, Jimmy . . . you lookin' for a way outta this? Thinking maybe you got a lot more than you bargained for?"

Dead silence covered them. One floor below, Lamont was straining to hear, expecting an explosion.

"I love her, Kyler. You know that," Jimmy's voice was now almost a whisper. "Or at least I thought you knew that."

Kyler took a deep breath, trying to collar the rage coursing through her veins. "Then stop this stupid shit."

"No," he shook his head. "Anybody else, Kyler, and they'd be treated with even a little respect. She don't have insurance, she's a smackhead, and when she gets out of treatment she'll be one step above homeless. That fucking doctor knows all that."

"Yeah, I know," she hissed, feeling the old frustration building up. Somehow it always came around to this . . . being treated like dog shit on the bottom of a shoe because of the way they looked: the addicted, the homeless, and the perpetually tormented.

Kyler thought back to the night before, sitting out on Doc's back deck and listening him tell her Curtis wouldn't get a heart because of the lifestyle he'd led, the drugs he did, the crimes he'd committed. She shook her head, feeling the frustration feeding the rage.

"Fuck," she growled and lit a cigarette. She let the smoke bite hard into her lungs before exhaling.

"Shit ain't gonna change, Kyler. I know it and you know it. And fuck this motherfucker," Jimmy gave the closed door behind him the finger. "He'll release her soon, I bet, 'cause she ain't got no insurance. I just hope he lets the baby stay."

"Jesus, Jimmy," she sighed and ran her hands through her hair. "And what if he doesn't?"

Jimmy shot her a look that was both fierce and raging. "He'll wish he did," his voice was very quiet, betraying the tension coursing through him.

"Stop it!" She snapped. "Get a grip, Jimmy, shit."

"Forget it, Kyler," he muttered. "Just fucking forget everything."

He turned and started down the steps. Lamont just had time to duck back out into the hallway before he heard Jimmy pass by the door. He got back in the elevator and hit the button for the next floor up, and when he stepped out he saw Kyler sitting in a chair outside the doors to the maternity ward with her head in her hands.

Quietly he walked up to her, and when she glanced up at him he saw an uneasy mix of rage and sorrow in her eyes.

"So," she said shortly, "here you are again. I'm beginning to think you're stalking me."

Wordlessly he sat down in the chair next to her, meeting her gaze. He took a deep breath and let it out slowly, and then said, "No, I'm not stalking you."

"So then why're you here? Unless . . ." she arched an eyebrow at him, her gaze narrowed. "Unless I'm not allowed to leave the county?"

Lamont merely looked at her.

"Jesus Christ," she growled. "Every fucking time I turn around there's a new stipulation on this whole court thing."

"Well, no offense, Kyler, but nobody did this to you, you know?"

"Yeah, no shit, Doc," she snapped. "Every day I wake up and realize how much I fucked up."

"Take it easy, all right? I'm not the one you're mad at," he responded coldly.

"Right now I'm mad at the whole fucking world," she said savagely. "You come here to bring me back?"

He glared at her and then glanced towards the maternity ward. "No. I came to see how you're doing. You didn't sound too good on my machine."

"Wonder fucking why," her voice was heavily laden with sarcasm.

Lamont sat where he was for a minute more and then stood up. "Here," he pulled his cell phone from his pocket. "You keep this while you're here, ok? At least then I'll know you got a way to call me if you need to." His eyes were hard, staring into hers.

Kyler felt the anger slowly melting away, leaving exhaustion in its place. She reached up and gently took the phone from him.

"All right," she murmured.

"And you're gonna be back Thursday, right?"

"Maybe tomorrow; I don't know."

Lamont nodded. "Call me, ok, if you need me."

She nodded, feeling drained. "Yeah."

He glared at her for a moment and then headed back down the hall. She watched him get on the elevator, wondering if this long, long day would ever end.

"Hey," a voice said in her ear. "Hey, wake up."

Kyler felt a hand shake her shoulder, and reluctantly she opened her eyes. "What?"

Her neck and shoulders were stiff and sore from the position she'd been sleeping in, awkwardly curled up in the chair. Glancing around the room, she saw she was alone for the moment, and just how long she'd been asleep or where Jimmy had gone she had no idea.

"She's awake and wants to see you. I'll give you five minutes, all right?" It was the doctor who'd woken her, and in his eyes she could still read the contempt he felt for her and Jimmy . . . and probably Barb, too.

We're all low-life criminals in his eyes, she thought bitterly, shooting him a thin glare and standing up.

"Make it ten," she muttered, and walked into the room without waiting for an answer.

Barb was lying on her side when she walked in, and her eyes were filled with pain and exhaustion. Kyler walked over and sat down in the chair, offering her her hand. Barb took it and squeezed hard as a tear slipped from the corner of one eye.

"She's alive."

"Yeah," Kyler nodded, glad Barb was squeezing her broken thumb. She needed the pain like a drug, willing it to clear her mind of everything but this moment with her friend.

"Did you see her?"

"Yeah," Kyler smiled. "She's tiny but she's strong. She has your eyes."

Barb offered a wan smile of her own. "They said she'd have to be in the incubator for probably a month, if not more. You think . . . you think she'll be ok?"

"I know she will. I told you, she's strong."

There was silence for a minute or two, and the Barb said quietly, "And blind. Half-blind anyway. The doctor told me he tested her sight and the seizure caused her to lose sight in one eye."

Kyler scrubbed a hand across her face, feeling the pounding of her heart against her sternum and the closeness of the walls.

"I'm scared, Kyler. How'm I gonna do this?" Barb stared at her, looking small and frail in the middle of the bed.

Kyler leaned over and hugged her hard, resting her head on her shoulder. "You're gonna do this with me right here with ya, ok? And Jimmy. And we're gonna do the best we can."

She closed her eyes and wondered where the fuck Jimmy was at that moment, and if she'd just lied to Barb in what could possibly be the most vulnerable time of her life.

"Yeah," Barb sighed. "I know. That's all I've ever done. Maybe this time, though, I can do it without fucking up too bad."

Giving a small, bitter laugh, Kyler wiped her own tears out of her eyes and sat up. "Maybe we all can, but I gotta tell ya, I tend to fuck up a lot."

"Great," Barb grinned. "This kid's gonna get raised by three fuckups."

"Yeah, probably," she grinned back. "But …" she shrugged, "we'll do what we can. And speaking of fuckups . . ." she managed to hide her worry for Jimmy, "Where's your better half?"

Not halfway across the country by now, I hope, her mind whispered uneasily.

"He told me he got a room at a motel down the road. Room two-nineteen at the Dover Hotel. Check on him, will ya? He was pretty pissed off earlier but he wouldn't tell me why."

"Sure," Kyler said. "Look, I got a drug test on Thursday at nine, and I have to take it. But I'll be here 'till then, ok?"

"Drug test for what?" Even after just having given birth, Kyler felt the sharpness of Barb's gaze as, from one addict to another, she searched for the lie, maybe hidden somewhere.

"For the deal I made with the courts. I get piss-tested once a week for three months, and I have to take it or else I'm headed back to jail, no questions asked. But that's Thursday, and I'll be here till then."

"Ok," Barb nodded and stared out the window a moment before turning back to Kyler. "She's really ok?"

"Yeah, all ten fingers, ten toes. And so what if she's only got one good eye? She's *your* baby . . . you did this; you made her. She's perfect, Barb."

Barb looked at her, the tears shining from her eyes betraying her fragile emotions. "Thanks, Kyler."

Kyler leaned her forehead against the glass and stared at Bailey in the incubator. All fingers, sure, and all toes, but she was small enough that Kyler could cup her in the palms of her hands. The wires and tubes running in and out of her diminished what little size she had, and she looked too small and pale and helpless.

"Be ok," Kyler whispered. "Just be ok." She stared at her a moment more before turning away.

Standing outside room two-nineteen at the Dover Hotel, Kyler knocked loudly for the third time, and still received no answer. Glancing around her, she dug in her pockets to see if she had anything she could pick the lock with and finally came up with a paper clip and a pen.

"This'll work," she muttered, and went to work utilizing the skills learned on the streets and honed from years of various B and E's. Within seconds she felt the lock slide back and slowly opened the door.

The room was dark, the one bed rumpled, and seemingly empty. She stepped inside and closed the door, focusing on the pale light shining out from under the closed bathroom door. A vivid image of Jimmy hanging from the shower fixture invaded her mind, and Kyler felt the breath hitch in her throat.

It was a realistic thought, she knew, because for people like her and Jimmy, demons came before family. Even though the woman he loved was lying in the hospital after just giving birth to the child he would raise as his own, his own personal hell was raging strong inside him.

How many times have I held a gun to my own head? She thought wearily. *Even now, with a chance at finally getting straight, I still think too much about what a shitty person I really am, and how more times than not this world would be a better place without me.*

Kyler took a deep breath and slowly opened the door. What she saw was only one step above what she thought she'd find.

Jimmy was crouched down on the floor next to the toilet, hunched over a small mirror lying on its closed lid. The fine white powder, laid out in neat lines on the glass shot both a rush of adrenaline and a deep loathing through her. She watched as he snorted up a line through a hollowed-out pen, and then leaned back against the tub, eyes watering.

"The best thing you can do, Kyler, is turn around and walk out the door. I know it ain't no excuse, but I've had a really shitty day."

Kyler closed her eyes, praying for strength, asking for forgiveness, begging for just a little bit of redemption because here she was once again, kneeling before her god, her demon, reaching for the pen.

The coke hit her brain like a freight train, making her stomach clench up and her heart start an erratic pounding in her chest, eager to break free and fly away. She leaned against the wall and felt the live current as it rushed through her veins.

Lamont was gone from her mind, as was the drug test, the rapist with Lewis's face, Skynyrd and *Simple Man*, and yes, even Josh was gone. There was nothing left but the rush, the high, and the never-ending chase to keep it coming.

Kyler took another long snort, inhaling deeply, willing—*needing*—the coke to hit her hard, *harder*, slamming into every fiber of her being over and over until there was nothing left.

She reluctantly handed the pen back, thinking, *The monster's loose. God help me, I woke the fucker up and now he's loose.*

Jimmy snorted a line and closed his eyes against the fire racing up his nose. When he looked back at her, his eyes were bloodshot and full of bottomless despair.

"Seems like I'm still chasing the devil," he muttered. "I get caught with this shit and I don't pass go or collect two hundred dollars. And like you said, then where'll Barb and Bailey be?"

Kyler nodded and ran her hands through her hair. "I'm with you, Jimmy. I gotta piss in a cup in two days . . . you don't think this is gonna show up in neon?"

"Jesus, you gotta take a drug test?" He stared at her with wide eyes. "And here I thought I was really fucked up just by tempting them."

"Yeah, well, I'm not sure I woulda passed it anyway. I've been popping valium for a couple weeks now, and without a script to show it's legit, it's still drug use in their eyes."

He shook his head and shot her a thin glare before snorting up half of the last line. "Still, Kyler, valium's legal. There mighta been a way around that for you. Now you're really fucked."

"Thanks for the optimism," she said sarcastically, and reached for the pen he was holding out to her. She snorted up the last of it and felt it snaking through her body, wondering why she felt this high was worth everything she stood to lose.

"And yeah, I guess I really am just fucked up all around." She met his eyes and he saw his own terror and despair mirrored in her gaze. "You got any more or was this just to piss me off?"

"Yeah," he sighed, thinking all this shit had to end sometime. This fucking vicious circle was enough to drive anybody completely and totally fucking insane. Rolling down his sock, he pulled out a small baggie and poured its contents on the mirror. Kyler watched as he took a razor blade and started making those neat white lines. Her mouth was watering and her heart was breaking, and she just wished she had the inner strength to snatch it up and flush it all down the toilet.

"We're both fucked up," Jimmy muttered, and reached for the pen.

Two hours later every speck of the coke was gone, and an hour after that they ran out of cigarettes. Fifteen minutes later Kyler's nose started gushing blood in huge amounts that made her ravaged stomach roll over in sheer terror. Jimmy, acting quickly, sat her on the bathroom floor with her head laid back over the tub and used wads of toilet paper to soak it up.

"Fuck," she murmured, throwing one wad of tissue in the toilet after another. After a very long time, it finally began to slack up, and then stopped completely. Jimmy's face was pale as he looked at her.

"What the fuck, Kyler? You can't die right here, ok? I mean, I'll take you to the hospital and I'll go to prison for having the shit, but you're not gonna die here."

"Relax," she said gruffly, sounding far braver than she felt. "I'm not gonna die. This always happens when I do coke . . . which would be a good reason to quit, ya think?"

"Yeah, you'd think," he snapped, feeling weak at the sight of all that blood. "You stay here, all right? I'm gonna run and get some ice."

"No, I'm all right now," she pulled her self up and sat on the toilet, hoping he couldn't see how dizzy she was. "The coke's gone, the blood's done . . ." she shrugged. "Now all we gotta do is make sure we don't OD and things'll be cool, ok?"

"Jesus," he sank down to the floor and put his head in his hands. She could see him shaking from all the cocaine coursing through him, and knew he felt like ripping and tearing and slashing and crushing everything around him . . . just like she did.

"You got an extra shirt?" Kyler asked quietly. "This one's pretty much shot."

"Yeah," he got up and went into the bedroom, returning with a t-shirt. "Might be a little big for you."

"That's ok," she mumbled. "It's better than wearing this one covered in blood."

The endless night finally came to an end, and Kyler stood at the window, watching the sun peak over the roof of the hotel. She hadn't slept at all, and neither had Jimmy. Both were ravaged with grief, hopelessness, and cocaine, and while she restlessly paced the floor for hours, he'd obsessively flipped through the channels on the TV, over and over and over.

"Barb's gonna know," he said softly. "She'll see it in my eyes."

Kyler glanced at him and then back out the window. Holding a hand up in front of her, she grimaced at how badly it was shaking. "I know," she sighed.

"You think she'll leave me?"

She shoved her hands in her pockets and hung her head, feeling that monkey on her back still screaming for more. "She might leave both of us, Jim. I don't know."

CHAPTER 32

BARB LOOKED UP when they entered her room, and immediately her eyes went hard. Jimmy hung his head, the weight of the world on his shoulders, and slipped into the chair beside the bed. Kyler managed to meet her friend's cold stare, but wished the floor would open up and pull her down.

The silence in the room was thick and oppressive, and she felt the walls quickly closing in.

"Baby," Jimmy said softly, reaching for her. Barb pulled away and glared at him.

"Fuck both of you," she growled. Kyler felt her stomach clench at the rage in her voice, and walked over to the window, searching for the ocean. She put her palms and forehead against the glass, wishing she could go back and change everything.

"What was it, Jimmy, coke?" Barb snapped. "Who had it?" The shift in her voice told Kyler she was now looking at her, and she felt the blame centered between her shoulder blades.

"Barb—" he started, but she cut him off.

"No, I don't wanna know. But I'm guessing it was a lot for you to be wearing his shirt. How much does it take for your nose to bleed so much that you ruin a shirt, Kyler?"

She finally turned around and looked at her. "A lot, Barb," she admitted quietly. "A lotta coke and a lotta blood."

"Don't you gotta take a drug test tomorrow?" Barb's voice was full of venom and rage.

Kyler nodded, wishing she had a chance to change everything, wishing she had more coke, wishing she had a needle full of smack laid out in front of her. Wishing she had a gun so she could blow her brains out right now.

Barb glared at her, and then turned her angry gaze to Jimmy. For a few long minutes there was complete silence between them, empty of words but full of accusations and betrayal. Finally she shook her head and said quietly,

"Let me tell you something . . . both of you. This is the last time. You do this shit again and you will not *ever* come around me or my baby. I'll write you guys off and I'll disappear because I've got something to live for now, and I'd rather it be us two fighting through this world by ourselves than be around a fucking bunch of drug addicts who ain't no good to nobody."

Jimmy laid his head on her bed and she felt him shaking.

"I'm sorry," he whispered. "Please, Barb, please don't leave. I swear that's the last time, and I'm gonna do everything I can for you and Bailey."

Barb looked at him and felt her world trying to tear in half. Grudgingly but tenderly, she reached out and ran a hand through his hair, feeling her love for him counter the near-hatred she felt for him at this moment.

"Barb, I'm trying," Kyler said quietly. "I swear I am. And I'm still high and I should be feeling it, but all I feel is I just wanna crawl into a hole and die. I fucked up bad, I know, but . . . but I told you yesterday I'm a fuckup, right?"

"Admitting it, Kyler, doesn't grant you permission," her voice was softer now, but the words were still like a spear through Kyler's heart.

"I know," she mumbled. "Jesus, don't I know it."

Silence again for a minute, and then Barb pulled herself up into a sitting position, grunting a little from the pain.

"Ok," she said. "We're clear, right? No more of this shit?" She stared at both of them, her eyes drilling holes in each of their souls.

"I'll admit everything," Jimmy murmured. "I'll tell 'em, and I'll pay the consequences, ok? I'll get help and then . . . then maybe . . ."

"Don't say anything," Barb said reflectively. "I'm asking you, honey, ok? Do you think you can let go of it this time? Be there for me and Bailey and not go out runnin' the streets night after night, coming home wired to feed her and change her while I'm sleeping in the next room?"

Jimmy was quiet for a long time, thinking carefully. "I'm gonna try, Barb," he said finally. "But I will promise you that if I even think about doing that, I'll check myself into an outpatient program first. I'll go to meetings, I'll get a sponsor."

Barb closed her eyes against the frustration of too many lies over the years, some told to her, some told *by* her . . . these exact same lies, and maybe he really meant it this time, like she'd done so many other times. But addiction was addiction, and sometimes it didn't matter how hard you tried or how many meetings or sponsors you had . . .

"I'll try," he said again, his brown eyes staring into hers. "I'm tired, honey, ok? I'm just really, really tired." His head dropped back down to the bed and against her will her heart was aching to pull him into her arms.

She put a hand on the side of his head, torn, and turned her eyes to Kyler.

"What about you?" She asked.

Kyler gazed back at her, her own heart aching from all the different emotions racing through it.

"I think I'm pretty much fucked," she said softly. "I can be like Jimmy, Barb, and promise it won't happen again, and I'd probably be telling the truth 'cause I think I'm headed to prison real soon, myself."

Barb gave her a long measuring look. "Once, a long time ago, I got locked up for a GTA in another county, then used the car to commit a robbery in this one. I tested positive for smack, but was offered a deal and got off with community service. They tested me once a week like they're doing you, Kyler, and you know how it goes . . ."

Her eyes were hard, staring into hers.

"I didn't stay clean, even though I knew I'd be headed to jail when the test showed positive. So you know what I did?"

Kyler looked at her, eyes narrowed, mind working. She gave a slow shake of her head.

"I found this girl who said she'd sell me her piss. She was straight, no drugs, not pregnant. I bought it, used it for the test, and I passed."

Stunned silence filled the room, and Kyler found herself allowing a little bit of hope to enter her otherwise scrambled mind.

"You find somebody like that and you might be ok. Short notice, I know, but . . ." Barb shrugged. "It's worth a shot. Probably the only shot you got right now."

Kyler dropped her head and closed her eyes. Now, slowly coming down, Lamont entered her mind again, and the helplessness coursed through her again with the idiocy of her actions.

"Go get on the bus, Kyler," Barb muttered softly, "and call me, ok? No matter what happens, call me and let me know something."

"Yeah," she responded quietly. "Ok." She reached down and gave her friend a gentle hug and then turned and wrapped her arms around Jimmy's neck. "We gotta keep the faith, Jim, all right?"

"Yeah," he agreed, hugging her back hard. "Just keep on holdin' on."

Kyler nodded against his shoulder and then gently pulled away. She left the room without looking at either of them, her mind working feverishly against the obstacles in front of her.

Kyler laid her head against the window and stared out at the passing scenery. The bus was only about half full and quiet as it rumbled down the interstate, and she knew she'd be back on familiar ground in a little under an hour. Slowly coming down, she was only just now beginning to feel the effects of almost thirty-six hours with no sleep, and once again felt overwhelmed with the frustration of having to keep moving even though her body cried out for rest.

No sleep, she thought, watching the road slip by beside the bus, *until I can track this girl down and convince her to sell me her piss.*

Kyler shook her head and sighed at how ludicrous it all was, and knew the chances were pretty good that even if she could find this girl, she'd probably only look at her like she was crazy and walk away.

"And who could blame her?" She glanced up as the bus slowed down. "Anymore *I* think I'm crazy." She sighed again and picked up her skateboard as she slid out of the seat. Stumbling down the steps and standing in the bright sunlight of the day, Kyler felt the cocaine still weaving through her system, even as her brain groaned under the heavy weight of sleeplessness.

She reluctantly started down the street, her stomach clenching up with every step, thinking how quick Barb knew; how she only had to look into their eyes to see they were wired to the max. Now, five hours later, would the doc see what she saw? Or would he only see the bloodshot of exhaustion?

Kyler sincerely hoped it was the latter. For the sake of her own soul and the little bit of redemption she'd found with the doc—the little bit she'd so willingly given up just hours before to the monkey that rode her back with her neck in a chokehold—she prayed he wouldn't see how badly she'd fucked up . . . again.

Lamont glanced up at the hesitant knock on his office door and from the doorway Kyler saw his eyes narrow. After a brief second he nodded and waved her in.

"Hey," he said quietly.

"Hey," she answered, stepping in and meeting his gaze.

"I figured you wouldn't be back until tomorrow," Lamont leaned back and laced his fingers behind his head. "Everything all right?"

Kyler gave a small shrug and dug in her pockets for his phone and the rest of his money. "Bailey's blind in one eye from the seizure, but . . ." she shrugged and laid the stuff on his desk. "I guess she's ok, otherwise. They won't know for sure until later, though."

He gave a slow nod and watched as she fell heavily into the chair on the other side of the desk. Exhaustion hung off her like a cape, making her face drawn and pale. And he was positive she'd lost another couple of pounds.

She can't lose much more before she winds up in the hospital with subconscious anorexia. Jesus, is *there such a thing?* He shook his head and gave a heavy sigh, looking at her. Kyler stared back with her bloodshot eyes.

"Look, Doc . . ." she started slowly, "I'm . . . sorry about yesterday. I was trying to take my bad day out on you, and it, uh . . . it wasn't right."

Lamont nodded and rolled his head on his neck, feeling it pop in half a dozen places. "That's all right, Kyler. It was a bad day for all you guys, I guess, and . . . I just probably showed up at the wrong time. I know I wasn't the person you wanted to see right then."

She shrugged and rubbed the back of her neck. "I just felt like . . . you know, that you were checkin' up on me, and I'm not used to that. But, I know where you're coming from, and I swear I didn't know I wasn't supposed to leave the county," her eyes met his. "I didn't know, and uh . . . that pissed me off, and then you being there pissed me off. My friend, Jimmy, pissed me off . . . that doctor pissed me off . . ."

"So you weren't kidding when you said you were mad at the world," he said softly.

Kyler offered a somewhat pained smile. "I just got a bad temper sometimes. Not often, but it's there."

Lamont nodded. "Yeah, I know. I'm the same way. Here," he scooped up the money and handed it back to her across the desk. "You keep this, ok? Get something to eat and then get some sleep. You look like you really need it."

She stared at him for a long moment, and then reluctantly reached out and took the bills from him. "I'd rather—"

"I know," he said gruffly. "But it's no big deal, Kyler, ok? Please, just take it and quit arguing about it."

Kyler sighed and stuffed the money in her pocket. She pressed the heels of her hands hard against her eyes, feeling weighed down.

"Get some sleep," he repeated softly. "I called John and told him you'd be back tomorrow, so you got all day to do nothin' but relax."

She was quiet for a minute, and then pulled herself out of the chair. "All right, Doc. I'll talk to you later, ok?"

"Yeah," he responded and watched her walk out without another word.

Kyler shuffled down the hall to the stairs, trying not to think beyond the next ten minutes. Her brain was still buzzing, wired up on coke, even as her body wanted nothing more than to shut down. Doc's spare bed was calling out to her, but the fear she felt about failing the drug test and her stubborn pride were driving her on, forcing her to fix what she'd broken while she still had a few hours left, anyway.

Too tired even to skate, she walked to the nearest plasma center, a few blocks down from the hospital. It wasn't the same one where she'd met that girl, but that was ok because the girl probably wouldn't be at that same one until tomorrow. They kept records, and unless one knew how to get around those records, it was really hard to donate at the same place more than twice a week.

Kyler knew that, and she figured the girl did, too. And she also figured that if the girl needed money as badly as she said she did, she'd already figured out ways to slip in and out of those records in order to donate more, and hence, get more cash.

With her stomach churning, she entered the plasma center and told the woman behind the counter she wanted to donate.

"Is this your first time?" The woman asked.

"At this center," Kyler responded, and the woman handed her a clipboard and a pen, instructing her to fill out the forms attached. Finding a seat off to one side, she filled out the paperwork, routine by now, with a fake name, fake address, fake phone number, fake everything. She kept one eye on the door, constantly searching (and fervently hoping) for the girl to show up.

Handing over the paperwork, Kyler was told it would be about a half hour, and then the woman explained the financial aspect. Her eyebrows shot up at the prospect of thirty-five dollars this time, instead of the twenty-five she was used to, and the woman explained that the majority of the money was handed out on the first visit to hopefully lure donors back the second time.

"A lot of 'em see all that money and tend to spend it quick, so they're really hurting by the time the second donation comes around," the woman shrugged.

"Yeah," Kyler muttered. "Makes sense, I guess."

"But, yeah, give 'em about a half hour and we'll get you back there, all right?"

She nodded and returned to her seat, wondering how the hell she'd be able to handle that needle again.

Not very easily, as it turned out. Her stomach rose up into her throat as the needle was inserted into her vein, and she felt the old familiar hate/love cover her in the form of sweat and goose bumps. Struggling to breathe and to maintain normalcy, Kyler closed her eyes and forced herself to count off seconds; willing herself to make it through them one at a time.

Jesus, her mind moaned, *I can't keep doing this.*

Gritting her teeth, she bore down with every inch of her will, *demanding* her body to be still just a few more minutes. Her brain screamed for a fix even as her sanity struggled to hold on.

After an endless five more minutes later, she felt the blessed removal of the steel from her vein, and let her breath out in a trembling, moaning sigh.

"Just about a full bottle," the attendant ripped a sheet of paper off his clipboard and handed it to her. "Just take it up to the counter."

Kyler rolled off the chair and stood on shaky legs, her stomach clamped in a vise. For a brief moment, the world tilted, and she leaned back against the bed and waited, her eyes closed. When it righted itself, she forced her feet to carry her across the room to the counter where she pocketed her money wordlessly and stumbled out the door.

Around back, once more kneeling on the ground next to the building, she let her stomach go, flinching from the pain as it threw up acid again and again. Focusing her gaze on the ground in front of her, Kyler drilled the pieces of trash, broken glass, old cigarette butts, and discarded fast food bags deep into her brain in an effort to pull her mind away from the thought of that needle in her vein.

"Jesus, you gotta be fuckin' crazy to keep doin' this to yourself." The familiar voice came from slightly behind her, and despite her inner turmoil, Kyler smiled in relief.

"Yeah," she muttered, and faced the girl, absently wiping her mouth on her sleeve. "I guess I am."

"Guess you need money as much as I do to slide up in here a day early." The girl's sharp gaze bored into hers. "Either that or you're just crazy, like I said."

"Probably a little bit of both," Kyler leaned back against the building and scrubbed a hand hard across her face. She lit a cigarette and then offered up the pack. The girl nodded and caught it when she tossed it to her, and pulled one out before tossing it back.

Taking a deep draw and letting the smoke bite hard into her lungs, Kyler waited a moment before forcing herself to meet the young girl's eyes.

"You really need money that bad to do this shit more than twice a week?" She asked.

"Apparently no more than you," she answered neutrally.

Kyler looked at her and gave a slow shake of her head. "I don't really need the money," she started slowly, "except to buy favors. And I really need one from you right now."

The girl merely looked at her, but Kyler sensed the flight plan she was contemplating.

"I'm in a lot of trouble."

The girl arched an eyebrow, conveying a look of absolute agreement, yet she remained silent.

"Look," Kyler let her cigarette dangle out of the corner of her mouth while she dug in her pockets for the money. "On me right now I've got . . ." she counted, adding Lamont's cash to what she'd just gotten for her plasma, "forty-three dollars. Tomorrow I'll head over to the center on Frankfort and give more for another twenty-five. It's all yours, ok? For just—"

"Just what?" The girl's eyes were narrowed and suspicious.

Kyler felt desperation rising up in her; the prospect of her last chance at staying out of prison dwindling, slipping through her fingers. But even more than that, as she gazed deep into the girl's eyes, she again thought of her as slightly damaged; forced to grow up long before her time due to the circumstances in which she was living.

Jesus, she could be me, she thought, and briefly closed her eyes at the thought of the girl she once was, and of the girl standing before her now, sliding a needle effortlessly into her vein with the conceit and confidence of the first-time user.

"I need your piss," she finally muttered. "I have to take a drug test tomorrow morning, and unless I can turn this shit around I'm gonna fail it."

There was complete silence between them for a few long minutes. Kyler dropped her cigarette butt on the ground and crushed it beneath her shoe, and then pulled another one from her pack. The girl was staring at her, eyes hard and mean, but Kyler could see the load of having all that money weighing on her.

"What makes you think I'm straight?" The girl finally asked.

"Just a hunch."

"You trust your hunches that much?"

"Usually," Kyler looked at her.

The girl gave a small nod, then took a deep breath and shifted her gaze to the vacant lot around her. Kyler waited, giving her the time she needed.

"That's a lot of money," she finally mumbled. "You'd go through all that," she gestured at the congealing puddle of vomit on the ground, "just to pass a drug test?"

"To pass the test and to stay out of prison," Kyler answered. "I fucked up, yeah, but . . ." she shrugged. "I'm an addict," she admitted slowly, "and that's what addicts do . . . we fuck up."

The girl looked at her for a long time, weighing her options, Kyler knew; wanting to forget about the money and just leave and Kyler knew that, too. But whatever the girl was running from was gaining ground, and that was too much money to pass up.

Finally she gave a short nod. "Ok."

Relief washed over her as she handed over the money, even as a huge part of her brain insisted that this girl would just take the cash she now held in her hand and run, forgetting about Kyler and the promise of another twenty-five the minute she was around the corner.

"What time's your test tomorrow?"

"Nine a.m."

"And you're gonna donate at Frankfort before that?"

"I'll be there at six, when they open the doors."

"Ok," the girl said again, stuffing the money in her pocket. "I'll be there then or shortly after. I'm gonna donate, too, and then I guess . . . what, find a bathroom somewhere? What're you gonna put it in?"

"I'll think of something," Kyler said.

"Sure," she shrugged. "All right, I guess I'll see you tomorrow."

Kyler nodded and watched as she started down an alley. "Hey," she called, and the girl turned back, eyebrows raised in question.

"You're not pregnant, are you?"

For a brief moment the girl's eyes turned a murderous black and Kyler saw an insane hatred in them. Again she thought of the girl's life and reflected back on her own living on the streets.

"No."

"All right," Kyler gave a shrug. "I'll see you tomorrow."

Without answering, the girl turned away and slipped around the side of a building. Kyler closed her eyes and leaned back against the building, praying hard that the girl would hold true to her word and show up in the morning.

It was a huge gamble, placing all her faith on the shoulders of this wayward young kid, especially one who'd just gotten over forty bucks in cash. But what choice did she have at this point? None, really. All other options were nonnegotiable, null and void.

She took a deep breath and let it out, then slowly started down the opposite way; the thought of Lamont's spare bed looming up large and comfortable in her otherwise battered mind.

CHAPTER 33

"KYLER," LAMONT GENTLY shook her awake. She snapped her eyes open and looked at him in the dim light coming through the window. He held the phone in his hand and she felt her stomach drop.

"What time is it?" She muttered.

"Not late. 'Bout nine-thirty." He handed her the phone and walked out of the room. Kyler took a deep breath and sat up, reluctantly pressing it to her ear.

"Hello?"

"She's deaf in one ear, too," Barb's voice was quiet across the wire. "I just . . . thought you might wanna know."

Kyler closed her eyes, both at the shame that swamped her and the sorrow and accusation she heard in her voice.

"It was the seizure," she muttered.

"Yes," Barb answered. "But I'm sure all the smack I shot up didn't help none."

"You've been clean since you found out you were pregnant," Kyler said gently. "You did what you could for her, Barb."

There was silence for a long moment, and then Barb said softly, "Anyway, I gotta get off here. I just wanted to call and tell you."

"Barb," Kyler's voice came out hoarse and she stopped to clear her throat. "Let me be there, ok? For you and for her. Please don't shut me out."

"Kyler," Barb sighed. "Listen, Jimmy's checking into an outpatient program in the morning. I didn't ask him to; he offered. He said it was as much for him and his life as it was for mine and Bailey's. Maybe . . . maybe you should think about that. Not for me, ok? Or Jim or Bailey. But you're so close to finally getting on the right track, and I know losing that job would tear you apart. Don't fuck it up this time."

Kyler took a deep breath and reached for her cigarettes on the nightstand. Barb's words cut through her like a knife, saturated with truth and honesty. She thought of Josh, now long gone, and felt the old familiar pain bloom inside. And then she thought of the doc, downstairs, still willing to give her a place to stay and a chance to get it right.

She felt torn between her emotions, what she wanted most and what her body needed most.

"Kyler . . ."

"Yeah," she mumbled. "You're right. I need to stop it now before it gets out of control again."

"I'm still planning on moving down there. I'd like to have a friend when I get there."

"You will."

Another moment of silence passed between them, and then Barb said gently, "Ok. But look, I gotta get off here. Take care, and call me when you can, all right?"

"Yeah," Kyler said. The phone clicked softly in her ear and she was left with dead silence before the dial tone kicked in. Giving a heavy sigh, she scrubbed a hand hard across her face, and then reached for her clothes on the floor.

Lamont was at the kitchen table when she walked in, absently flipping through the channels on his little countertop

TV. The sound was turned down low, and Kyler got the feeling he was only watching just to be doing something.

He looked up at her and nodded. "Hey."

She nodded back. "Hey."

"You ok?"

She gazed at him, wondering if he knew how much of a mess she was; how her emotions were on the familiar rollercoaster ride of coming down from the coke; how she was swaying between the insane need that was clawing at the back of her skull, screaming for more, and the bottomless pit of self-loathing and despair that threatened to eat her alive.

"Doc . . ." she started, only just barely managing to look into his eyes. He waited, eyebrows raised. "I'm goin' skating," she gestured vaguely with her board. "I . . . it calms me."

He glanced at the clock, then out at the dark night. "It's dark. You goin' to the park?"

Kyler gave a half-shrug, and then slowly shook her head. "No. I'll probably just skate the streets for awhile."

Lamont looked at her, trying to see past the barrier she always put up. He saw the tension in her body, and tried to determine what it was from, and how much it was tearing her up inside.

Finally he gave a slow nod and stood up. "Be careful, all right?"

She watched as he put his coffee cup in the sink and walked past her, putting a hand lightly on her shoulder.

"I don't wanna have to patch you up again. I'm tired."

"I will," she promised, realizing only after he was halfway up the steps that she didn't flinch this time from his touch. Slowly her distrust for him was fading, and that made her feel all the more guilty about doing all the stupid shit she'd been doing.

Kyler gave a weary sigh and quietly slipped out the back door.

She hit the streets hard and fast, using everything in her path to add variety to her reckless skating. The streetlights came and went in flashes from the arc-sodiums, giving her bright light one minute, followed a split second later by almost complete darkness. This only fueled her insatiable need to skate as hard as she could to work everything out of her system.

Skating through the streets of downtown San Diego, she began to feel the calming effect the board beneath her feet always gave her, and although it didn't completely alleviate her turmoil, it did a real good job of pushing it firmly to the back burner.

After only a few minutes of the rubber wheels grinding across the concrete, the thought of passing or failing the drug test began to fade back and Bailey's disabilities seemed to lose their sharp edges of addiction and accusation. Josh's face flashed across her mind as benches and garbage cans flashed by beside her, and this time it didn't hurt as much.

When she was skating as good and as pure as she could skate, it always seemed like he was right there beside her, like he once was, and there was no hurt in his eyes and no despair in her heart. These were the few good times she was given, and even though she probably didn't have many of them left—*because* she probably didn't have many of them left—she didn't allow any negative thoughts or emotions force her to waste a single minute.

Finally, almost two hours later, sweating and breathing hard, Kyler collapsed on a bench. Her body was shaking from exertion but her heart was lighter, free of the burden of worry and self-hatred that had plagued it for far too long.

She leaned her head back and stared up at the stars, smelling the salt on the cool breeze that wrapped itself around her.

"Help me not to fuck it up this time," she muttered. "Please just help me finally get it straight."

After a few more minutes, she stood up and wearily began to make her way back to Lamont's house. She was quiet as she slipped back in the back door and silently made her way by familiarity up the steps to the spare bedroom. The bed called to her, welcoming her into a deep sleep, free, for once, of nightmares and bad memories.

In his room, Lamont heard her as she got into bed, and his own heart was able to let go of the worry he'd had of her hitting a bad spot on the asphalt and skidding headfirst into the path of an oncoming car . . . or any other mishap that could happen to a young girl running the streets at this time of night.

In the secret part of his heart, it wasn't the thought of her breaking a bone or hitting something in her way as she skated down the street that worried him so much. Rather, it was something more sinister, more addicting, more her style of getting into trouble.

Just the fact that she was here was enough to let him know she hadn't gone to score any dope, and he closed his eyes in vast relief.

CHAPTER 34

KYLER WAS OUT on Lamont's back deck early the next morning, exhausted, having gotten barely any sleep the night before despite her body's desperate need for it. Her stomach churning, she stared out at the slowly brightening ocean, trying to retrieve her calm feeling of the night before.

But it was gone, lost in the depths of depression and despair that covered her along with the goose bumps in the early morning air. She shivered and wondered if the girl would show, and if she did, would this last-minute attempt at fixing her fuckups work and keep her sorry ass out of prison.

The back door opened and Lamont walked out on the deck, carrying two cups of coffee. He handed her one wordlessly and squeezed in beside her on the steps.

"Thanks," she said.

"Sure," he gazed out over the ocean and took a sip. Kyler wrapped her hands around the mug, trying to work the warmth into her hands, up her arms, and into her heart. The coffee was hot and bitter, nicely paralleling the bitterness she felt for her past mistakes, and more so for her continuing to make those or similar mistakes.

"Up early, aren't you?" He asked casually, shooting her sidelong glance.

"Yeah," she stared into her cup, feeling his eyes on her.

Lamont shook his head and gave a heavy sigh. She swallowed and stared out over the ocean.

"I never figured you'd be one to put that much emphasis on money, kid," he said very quietly. "I mean, I know you need some for little things . . . like maybe a burger or something, but . . ." His eyes on hers were hard. "Enough to do this?"

He reached across her and gently took her left arm, running his thumb lightly over the marks and purplish bruising from donating plasma.

She shuddered and bit back a moan as the nerves came alive kicking and screaming. Swallowing hard, she pulled her arm away and ran a hand through her hair.

"I know you're not shooting up," Lamont said matter-of-factly, gazing at her. "The only thing I can figure is you're donating, what, three, four times a week now?"

Kyler stared out over the ocean, needing its peacefulness to calm the turmoil raging inside her, and didn't answer.

"Talk to me, Kyler," he said softly.

"Doc . . . it . . . uh . . ." she faltered, trying to find a viable excuse and hating herself for feeling like she had to lie to this man. "It's plasma, yeah. The center on Frankfort's got all the paperwork if you wanna see it."

"I believe you, Kyler, and this is not me checking up on you, ok?"

"Then what is it?" She asked, feeling tendrils of anger. She felt it more for herself, but Lamont was close and it was hard not to turn it on him.

"It's me starting to worry about you," he shot back. "It's me wondering why the hell you need money so goddamned much to do this to yourself, and what it's taking for you to hold it all together just long enough to collect that cash."

Kyler gritted her teeth and didn't answer.

"You need money that bad, all you gotta do is ask me. It ain't a loan, it ain't . . . nothin, kid, just take it, all right? 'Cause I'm tired of seeing you tear yourself up like this."

She took a deep breath and let it out slowly, struggling to rein in her anger. "Let it go, Doc," her voice was very quiet.

"No," he snapped. "You think I don't hear you when you're in there sleeping? *You cry, Kyler.* You cry in your sleep, and sometimes you scream like somebody's ripping your heart out. You—"

She abruptly got up and started back across the deck, feeling her anger spike into near rage. This was not what she wanted this morning, or needed, and the fact that she was *this close* to saying something she'd horribly regret while sitting in a jail cell later on this evening because of a failed drug test was like a spike digging into her brain.

"I don't need this shit right now, Doc, ok? *Leave it alone.*"

He got up and came after her, catching her before she got in the door. Her eyes were blazing, glaring into his, and he could read the depth of her anger.

"Wait a minute," his voice was softer now. "Just stop for a second."

Kyler walked a couple steps away and stared at the ocean, taking one ragged breath after another. The rage circled her, wrapping her in a constricting web that made it hard to breathe. She ran her hands through her hair and locked her fingers together at the back of her neck. Behind her, Lamont saw her body shaking.

"Look," he sighed, "I'm sorry. It . . . ah, shit . . . Kyler . . ." he plopped down in a chair and watched her. "I wish I could help you . . . and I'm really tryin' but it's hard when I got nothin' to go on."

She dropped her head. "You can't fix me, Doc, so please don't waste your time trying."

"I'm not trying to fix you," he muttered. "I'm just trying to figure out a way to help you. You need money, ok. I'm not gonna ask you what for and . . . well, it ain't none of my business anyway." She turned to look at him and he said gruffly, "Long as it ain't nothin' illegal.

"I just hate to see you like this. You know, you're losing weight, you're not eating . . . and donating the plasma's dropping the pounds off you like there's no tomorrow. And I gotta ask you, Kyler . . ." his eyes drilled into hers. "How the fuck do you do that without getting sick or passing out? Or going ballistic when they put that needle in your arm?"

She looked at him a long time and then finally gave a slow shake of her head. "I puke, Doc," she mumbled. "Every time. But I manage to hold it down long enough to do it around back of the building. They wouldn't let me do it again if they saw it."

"Jesus," he growled.

"It . . . uh . . ." Kyler swallowed and pulled her pack of cigarettes from her pocket. "If there was any other way to donate plasma, I'd do it 'cause . . . I . . ." she scrubbed a hand hard across her face. "I don't like needles, you know? It's too much like shooting up."

"Yeah," he said sarcastically. "So why're you doing it?"

She glanced away and lifted one shoulder in a half-hearted shrug. "I need the money."

"Goddamn it," he sighed. "Here," standing up, he pulled his wallet from his back pocket.

"No," she shook her head. "I'm not a freeloader, Doc. I'm not taking your money on top of everything else you've given me."

"Fuck, Kyler, you're not making sense."

"Look," she met his gaze, "would it make you feel better if I said today's the last time I'm doing it?"

"No," he admitted. "'Cause then I'd have to wonder why all of a sudden you're quitting."

"'Cause I can't take it anymore," she responded. "Just like you said."

"So why go today?" He asked, feeling frustrated.

Again, that slow aggravating shake of her head. "I just need to, Doc, ok?"

"That's not enough for me, Kyler."

Her burning gaze bored into his. "It's gonna have to be, at least for right now. I can't . . ." she trailed off, faltering, wondering how much better all this stupid shit would be if she just broke down and told him.

But Kyler couldn't bear to see the disappointment in his eyes, couldn't stand the thought of him losing whatever faith in her he might have.

She looked at him a long time, feeling the weight of everything laying hard on her. Lamont saw her eyes turn sad and her shoulders slump. She turned away and sighed, unable to say any more.

Against his inner voice's warnings, he went to her and gently folded his arms around her. Kyler resisted for a moment, battling a wild panic that conflicted with a comforting feeling that was somehow familiar, and very calm. She closed her eyes and leaned against him, defeated.

"It's all right," he said softly. "It's ok, kid. I won't push you anymore."

She didn't answer, but she didn't pull away, either. He considered this a positive step, and held her for as long as she let him. Finally she did pull away and looked at him.

"I gotta go, ok? I'll talk to you later on tonight."

He glanced at his watch and saw it was pushing six o'clock. "It opens up at six?"

"Yeah," she opened the door. He followed her in and watched as she rinsed her cup out and put it in the dishwasher.

"Lemme give you a ride."

Kyler glanced at him, hesitating, and then gave a small shrug. "Sure, if you don't mind."

"I wouldn't have asked if I minded."

"Yeah," she responded quietly. "Ok."

He walked with her to the front door, the silence heavy between them. Kyler slumped in the front seat of his car, battling a new panic this time, one that dug at her sanity and put her stomach in a razor-sharp vise.

I can't do it this time, her mind moaned. *Jesus, I just can't.* And then on the heels of that, *Last time . . . just do it this one last time.* She shut her eyes and leaned her head back, feeling the acid start to build in her stomach.

It won't be the last time, she thought wearily. *What, you think the coke's gonna be out of your system by this time next week? You'll have to find another way to pass it, and if this girl agrees to another buy, how're you gonna pay her except by donating plasma? Shit, even you gotta admit it's a helluva lot better than letting some guy fuck you for it.*

Kyler gave a heavy, shaky sigh, and lit a cigarette with trembling hands. Lamont glanced over at her, his brow furrowed.

"I wish you'd let me help you," he muttered quietly.

"You said you wouldn't push me anymore," she responded. "Left at the light."

"I know, and I'm not. I won't. It's just . . ." he turned left at the stoplight and the plasma center came into view up ahead, still dark. A glance at the dashboard clock told him he had maybe ten minutes to try to talk her out of it.

"You don't wanna do this," he pulled into a spot. "I know you don't, kid; I can tell just by looking at you."

Kyler rolled down the window and relished the cool breeze blowing against her face. She smelled the salt and seaweed in it, and wished with everything she had that she could be walking along the beach right now, waves cold against her ankles, water splashing up to soak the bottoms of her jeans, rolled up to her calves.

"This's the last time," she mumbled, not even sounding halfway convincing.

The acid was building in her stomach, and for the first time she wondered if she'd puke *before* they stuck the needle in her arm. Her steel will rose up and she gritted her teeth, trying to pull out of this negative way of thinking before it affected her fragile mindset any more.

The outside lights came on, followed by row after row of fluorescents on the inside. Kyler shot a glance at the clock and noted the time at two till.

"I gotta go, Doc. Thanks for the ride." She pushed open the door but stopped when his hand touched her shoulder. Glancing back at him, her face was drawn and haggard in the dim glow of the dome light.

"Want me to wait for you? Give you a ride back?"

"No," she shook her head. "Thanks anyway. I'll see ya." She got out and shut the door, and Lamont's stomach sank as he watched her walk reluctantly in the door.

"Fuck," he muttered, and then glanced across the street at an all-night diner. Without thinking about why he was doing it or how mad she'd be if she saw him, he pulled across and parked in a spot that was hidden somewhat in semi-darkness.

He walked in and found a booth that faced the front of the plasma center, ordered coffee, and watched from a distance as Kyler was led to a back room. Even from this far away, he saw how much she was shaking.

The nurses' aid or whatever the guy was who took her blood pressure was young and halfway attractive. His eyes were a deep blue that pierced her heart and Kyler clenched her jaw against the wave of emotions that washed over her.

With his gloved fingers, he gently began to probe the bruised area on her left arm, searching once more for a usable vein.

"Let me try the other arm," he said. "This one's pretty torn up."

Instant alarm flashed across her brain, and the acid was halfway up her throat before she was able to swallow it back down. Heart pounding, Kyler willed herself to stay calm and not lose it entirely.

Last time last time last time . . . her brain screamed repeatedly. *Just hold on for one last time.*

"You can try," Kyler's voice was barely audible. "But you won't catch a vein in it."

The young man apparently didn't believe her, but then his eyebrows shot up at the thick, corded skin, shot through with the charred tattoos of too many home-sterilized needles that covered most of the inside of her right elbow, dipping a little towards her wrist and slipping up higher towards her biceps.

"No," he said slowly. "I guess I won't." For a brief moment his eyes met hers, but then he went back to her left arm. "I can maybe find one, but after today you might want to take a week or two off, let this heal some."

"Yeah," she agreed. She felt him probe some more, looking for a usable vein, wanting to scream, needing to puke, wishing all of this was over, even if that meant death for her.

When the steel of the needle slipped somewhat jerkily into her arm, she felt the edges of her sanity start to crumble. Willing herself to just hold on

(hold on hold on hold on, Jesus God just please hold on)

Kyler counted off her breaths, in and out, one at a time, and fought hard to keep the acid from shooting up her throat. Her stomach was a ball of barbed wire, twisted and burning, raging with a need to unload its entire contents *right now, right fucking now.*

Not yet, Kyler thought. *Not yet, just hold on.*

Finally, after an endless amount of time that could've lasted years, the man withdrew the needle and taped a cotton ball over the puncture mark.

"You're done," he said gruffly. "But remember what I said, ok? You only gave half a bottle, and we'll pay you for the full amount this time, but if it happens again we can only pay for what you give us. Let that arm heal some and you'll be back up to a full one in no time."

Kyler nodded weakly and took the paper he handed to her with a severely shaking hand. Stumbling up to the counter, she passed over the paper and waited in agony as the woman counted out twenty-five dollars in mostly fives and ones. Stuffing the money in her pocket, she clenched her jaw shut against the nearly-overwhelming urge to vomit and pushed open the door.

Across the street Lamont felt his stomach drop at the sight of her staggering out into the early morning light. Kyler was more haggard and beaten than she'd been just a mere twenty minutes ago, and for the first time he had to wonder about her mental state.

Who would keep doing this to themselves? He wondered. *What the fuck is wrong with her that she's gotta do this again and again?*

He watched as Kyler made it around the side of the building to a narrow alley that ran between it and the building next door. From this angle, he could still see fairly well . . . almost too well, in fact, as her legs gave out and she fell to her knees, vomiting violently.

For what seemed like too, too long, she heaved again and again, until finally it was over, and she leaned against the rough brick and scrubbed a shaking hand across her face.

"Jesus," she muttered, and pulled her legs up to her chest. Draping her arms across her knees, she dropped her head on her forearms, trembling all over. Lamont's jaw tightened as his heart gave a squeeze. Shaking his head, he narrowed his eyes and watched as another young girl walked up to her.

"Hey," the familiar voice brought a rush of relief over her otherwise shattered mind. "You gotta still be fuckin' nuts, huh?"

"Apparently," Kyler managed a small, shaky smile. "Didn't think you'd show."

The girl shrugged. "Told you I would." She paused and reached into her back pocket. "A friend of mine works over at the chem. lab at the university, and he gave me this." She held out a thin beaker, topped with a cork.

"Wasn't sure if you'd be able to find anything, so I asked him if I could have it. It's clean, never been used, so it won't fuck up anything."

Kyler looked up at her, and then slowly stood up, taking the beaker from her. "Yeah," she nodded. "Yeah, this should work." Cocking an eyebrow, she asked quietly, "You didn't—"

"I didn't tell him what I needed it for," the girl responded. "He gives me things from time to time, you know . . . to help me out."

Kyler stared at her, connecting chemistry with whatever this girl needed to get "helped out," but the girl, reading her mind, gave a slow shake of her head.

"No drugs, I told you that. You're safe there. He just knows more about me and my life than you do, and, well . . ." she shrugged. "Sometimes it's food, sometimes cash, whatever, you know?"

"Yeah," Kyler sighed, and handed the beaker back to her. "I know. C'mon, let's go around back. Too close to the street here."

They headed around back, Kyler running a hand along the brick wall to hold the world steady. It kept wanting to slide off kilter, and she briefly shut her eyes, willing it to right itself.

"You all right?" The girl asked, watching her carefully.

"Yeah," Kyler stopped around back and pulled her smokes from her pocket. She pulled one out and then passed the pack over. The smoke and nicotine, flooding her lungs, felt like heaven and she began to feel herself steadying.

"Here," she pulled the money out of her pocket and handed it to the girl.

The girl nodded and put the money away without looking at it. "Ok, I guess I'll step behind this dumpster, here. Watch my back, all right?"

Kyler nodded and glanced up and down the vacant lot. "I won't need much."

"Ok," the girl slipped back behind the dumpster. Kyler took a deep breath, feeling the hard knot that was her stomach. Again she wished for the solace of the ocean and prayed with what little faith she had left to just please get her through today.

"I brought along some napkins just in case," the girl came out wiping the beaker. "Good thing I did. It's hard to piss in that little hole."

Kyler nodded and flicked an ash from her cigarette. "You're a lot better prepared than I am," she reflected softly. "You'd think I'd've thought all this through."

The girl shrugged. "Better to have it and not need it, you know?"

"Yeah. And we needed it, so it's a good thing you got it."

"Also got this," she pulled a roll of masking tape from her back pocket. "My friend at the chem. lab? I didn't tell him but he kinda guessed, and he said it's best if you keep it warm. The armpits and high up inside the thighs are the warmest places on the body, and it kinda makes sense, you know? You don't wanna pour this into a test cup when it's no longer warm."

Kyler stared at her, contemplating, slightly ashamed that this girl had to basically lead her through the steps of faking her own drug test. The girl mistook her expression and slowly shook her head.

"I'm not gonna fuck you on this, all right? You don't trust me, fine, but I saw how much trouble you went through to get the money, and . . ."

"But you're not gonna give it back to me," Kyler responded with a smirk.

"No," she answered truthfully. "But I am gonna help you out as much as I can."

"Why?"

The girl looked at her. "'Cause I don't think you're crazy. I just think you're desperate, and since I know what that feels like, I'm gonna try to do what I can to help you pass that test. Now," she gestured with the roll of masking tape. "Under the arm or on the inside of your thigh?"

Dropping her cigarette to the ground, Kyler crushed it beneath her foot and started pulling an arm through the sleeve of her shirt. Having had enough of phallic-like objects near her vagina to last her a lifetime, she opted for the armpit.

The girl nodded. "Good choice. It won't be quite as warm as the thigh would, but it's less likely to spill on your way over there. Hold still and I'll tape it up."

Holding her arm high above her head, Kyler looked down as the girl tore off a long strip of tape and secured the beaker to her skin along her right rib cage. She taped it two or three more times before stepping back.

"Ok. That should hold you if you're careful. Try to keep that arm down over it, too, ok? Keep it warmer."

Sliding her arm carefully back into her shirt, Kyler offered a small smile. "You're pretty good at this."

"Been doin' shit like this for awhile now," the girl muttered. "All right. Looks like you're all set."

"Yeah. Thanks again, all right?"

"Yeah. Maybe I'll see ya around."

Kyler watched her walk off without a look back, seeing herself all over again, and hoping the girl got out before she ended up like herself.

Locating a bank sign on a street corner, Kyler saw it was getting close to seven o'clock. Even though her test wasn't scheduled until nine, she started in the general direction of the outpatient hospital, fairly certain they would let her in early. They were usually pretty flexible, especially when one had a job to go to at nine.

The beaker holding the valued piss was snug against her side, and Kyler once again found herself praying she could make this work.

CHAPTER 35

As DUSK FELL across the city, Lamont slipped quietly into the front gate at the skate park, noting the arc-sodiums bright over the huge ramp. It still amazed him to believe that Kyler'd built it from the ground up, and kept building on it until it towered high above the rest of the park.

That's where she was now, he knew, and skating hard by the sound of it. The rubber wheels almost sounded angry against the smooth wood, and he hoped that whatever was bothering her would work itself out in one of the few places she sought solace . . . her skating.

Climbing the bleachers (another one of her contributions) he stopped midway up and sat down to watch her, cringing one minute and elated the next. His heart seemed to stop every half second as he was absolutely positive she'd miscalculate and fall the fifty feet to the hard wood below. But then in the next breath he felt the freedom she instilled on the world around her, just by being able to be so free herself . . . at least during this short period of time.

Her friend from the skate shop was right: watching her, Lamont had definitely changed the way he thought about skateboarding.

Using every inch of the ramp and soaring seemingly higher with each pass along the wood, Kyler pulled every trick, flip, and grind from her repertoire, aggressively skating with reckless abandon.

Lamont watched her and noted that she was more at ease than she'd been in a long time, and from that he began to finally realize just how much she loved it and how much a part of her it was.

An endless, heart pounding fifteen minutes later, she slid down into the bowl and hopped off into the grass. He wasn't sure she'd seen him, but then she veered off in his direction, limping slightly and looking still haggard but not quite as beaten as she had earlier that morning.

He waited as she climbed up the steps and nodded to her as she plopped down beside him.

"Who knew a piece of board with four wheels nailed to it could do all that?" He reflected easily.

Kyler offered a rare smile. "Screws and bolts nowadays, Doc, and it's fiberglass instead of rough, heavy wood. All that was back in the early days."

"Still," he shrugged, "you really are good on that thing. How come you never went pro?"

She lit a cigarette and stared out over the park. "I could never skate for money. It commercializes it, takes away the heart of it."

"Even if you're getting paid for doing what you love?"

"*Especially* if you're getting paid for doing what you love," Kyler muttered. With her fingertips she gently turned over his left wrist so that the light reflected off the face of his watch. Lamont glanced down and noted the time at quarter past nine.

"Got somewhere you need to be?" He asked casually.

"No," she stared down at her skateboard, lying across her knees, and sighed. "Checking the date. Josh's birthday's today."

Lamont stared at her, surprised; noting that Josh's name continually came up at odd times, when one would think her mind was a million miles in the other direction.

He really had a hold on her, he thought.

"How old is he?"

"Nineteen," she murmured. "I hope he's doing ok." Her eyes rested on the far horizon as yet another piece of her heart broke off.

Lamont swallowed and wished he knew the right words to ease her deep-seated grief and regret. "You wanna try to find him? I'll help you."

Kyler was quiet for a moment and then stood up, pitching her half-smoked cigarette over the side railing. "C'mon, Doc. I'm tired. Wanna give me a lift?"

"That's why I'm here," he followed her down the metal stairs. "How 'bout it, kid?"

"No," she shot him a sidelong glance as they started across the grass towards the office.

"Why not?"

She gave another heavy sigh. "He wanted to disappear and that's what he probably did. Kids like him . . . and me . . . Doc, it's not that hard to just fade back, you know? Soak into the city and just disappear."

"Kyler . . ."

"I haven't been straight that long," she said patiently, thinking, *Christ, not even a week*. "I owe him that much to just leave him alone. It . . . it's better this way. Maybe not forever, but for right now it is."

He walked beside her in silence, reflecting on her words. "You love him. You just gonna let that go?"

She was silent as she opened the breaker box in the office and killed the lights over the park, and Lamont waited patiently as she locked the gate and walked to the parking lot.

"He was your only family . . ." He tried again.

Kyler opened the car door and slid into the passenger seat, not answering, wishing she'd never said anything. A mental picture of Josh crouching in some alley somewhere, hungry and cold . . . and deeply heartbroken . . . tore at her, and with everything she had she wished she could reach through time and space to touch him and pull him into her arms once more.

Lamont shook his head and turned the ignition.

"Doc," her voice was quiet beside him, and he glanced at her.

"You love Emily, but you had to let her go. Sometimes you just have to let them go; you know that."

"Yeah," he sighed. "You're right, I do know that. Still, if you ever just, you know, want to at least *try* to find him, I'll help you if you want me to."

"Thanks," she looked at him. "And maybe someday, but not right now, ok?"

He nodded and pulled out of the lot. Kyler stared out the window at the dark night, feeling the deep, deep loss. She closed her eyes and pictured his blue eyes and shaggy, blond hair, lying in his arms, warm against his body, and far away from needles, drugs, and piss tests.

"How'd it go today?" Lamont asked quietly. "At the plasma center?"

And speaking of piss tests . . .

"Rough," she answered. "The guy had a hard time picking up a vein, and when he finally did, it went in hard."

He briefly glanced down at her arm, lying across her skateboard but hidden in the dark.

"I can imagine," he said gruffly. "That arm's not lookin' too good, kid."

"I know," she sighed. "Looks like I'm shooting up again." She paused and muttered, "I could only give half a bottle today. That right there tells me I need to lay off for a while."

He shot her a look before turning down his street. "That mean they only paid you half?"

Kyler shook her head. "No, but if it happens again they will."

"So then what's the point?" He pulled into his garage and shut off the engine, staring at her.

"Doc," she growled softly, "I'm beginning to think there's not a point in anything, anymore." Before he could answer she opened the door and stepped out. He unlocked the door in silence and let her walk in ahead of him. At the head of the basement stairs she stopped and looked back at him.

"Would you mind if I went downstairs and listened to some music?"

"Oh, shit," his eyebrows shot up and he gave her a smile. "I almost forgot. No, go ahead, I'll be right back." He walked back out to the garage and Kyler heard him open the trunk of his car.

She headed downstairs, already anticipating the feel of the music surrounding her, soothing her, relieving all the stress and exhaustion, heartache and despair that were covering her.

"At least I passed the test," she mumbled in a low voice. At least she was fairly certain she did. Within minutes of testing her cup of piss the results would have been known, and if she'd failed she wouldn't have been allowed to roam free outside of a jail cell for the past eleven hours.

She glanced up at Lamont's footsteps on the stairs and waited as he came down with a plastic bag in his hand.

"Here," he handed it to her. "I picked these up for you today."

Kyler peeked in the bag and smiled a genuine smile at the two albums in it. Pulling them out, she noticed the slight wear on the edges and corners of each, and the faded but still legible covers.

It was like she held a piece of history in her hands; history that had the power to reach into her soul and pull out all the fear and hatred and replace them with everything good, sweet, calm, and serene.

"You've used my stereo more than I have lately, so I thought you might want to start a collection of your own," Lamont said quietly. "Music is something to hold onto, Kyler, even if you gotta let everything else go." He paused and then said gently, "Including love."

She gazed at him, knowing he was right, and having absolutely no idea how to repay him back.

"How much . . ." her voice croaked and she cleared her throat. "How much were these? How much do I owe you?"

"First of all," he pushed the power button on the stereo and gestured for one of the albums. Kyler looked at both of them and handed one over. "It's a gift, which means it's given, no strings attached." His eyes sharp on hers, again tried to drill into her the message he'd been trying to convey since he'd met her.

"Secondly," he gently dropped the needle on the record, "with the age of digital music and downloads and everything else like it, you wouldn't believe how cheap LP's have gotten."

"Twenty?" Kyler ventured a guess, hardly daring to believe she was even close, but having been raised on the streets, really had no experience with albums or CD's or cassettes or anything like that.

Lamont shook his head, smiling. "These were less than a quarter apiece. Sometimes certain albums may range up near a dollar or more. I saw one for fifteen once, but it was a rare one. Mostly though, depending on the artist or the condition of the album, usually under a dollar.

"These are in good condition so I'm surprised they were so cheap." He shrugged. "Or maybe the people I got 'em from just didn't like the Eagles, who knows?" Grinning as the first tendrils of music drifted from the speakers, he said, "Their loss. Enjoy, kid."

He slipped behind her and started up the steps, but turned back when she called to him.

"Where'd you get 'em from?"

"Passed by a yard sale earlier today. That's the place to get albums. You go to a store you're likely to pay three, four times as much."

Kyler nodded. "Thanks, Doc."

"No problem."

She watched him walk up the stairs and then she stretched out on one end of the sofa, feeling the leather ease into her body the way the music was easing into her heart. Picking up the albums, she looked at them as the music surrounded her. Both Eagles, one had a picture on the cover that reminded her strongly of Santa Monica; the other, the one currently on the turntable, began playing a song that struck her to the center of her being.

Fuck, I could've written this song, she thought, and closed her eyes against the razor-sharp whirlwind of emotions racing through her.

She lay curled up against him, his warm and familiar shape molded against hers. Wrapping her arms around his waist, she burrowed her face into his neck and relished his nearness, skin against skin, heart to heart.

"Don't leave," Josh mumbled, deep asleep. "Don't leave this time."

"I won't," Kyler promised, but it was a lie. It was always a lie because here she was again, standing on a street corner and looking fervently around her for the shadow that would provide her with the drugs she needed so badly.

"Comin' back for more, huh?" He suddenly appeared beside her, only this time it was Lewis, grinning his psychotic smile and twirling a long needle between his fingers.

"Always comin' back for more."

She tried to run but he grabbed her and slammed her against the wall. Grunting, he rammed against her, driving his erection painfully into her lower belly.

"Still you're comin' back," he snarled, stabbing her in the neck with the needle, "runnin' back," depressed the plunger, and she felt the hot liquid shoot into her jugular.

"Comin' back for more," he ripped her shirt off and scraped long, ragged, filthy nails across her breasts, drawing blood and a deep scream that ripped from her throat.

"Take it to the limit, bitch," he laughed and slapped her. "One more time."

Kyler felt the bottomless pit of utter hopelessness loom in front of her, and longing for Josh more than she ever thought possible, passed over the edge and fell swiftly down.

Hearing a scream, Lamont bolted up in bed and stared wildly around the room. The moonlight shining through the window threw shadows on the wall, and he reached out a shaky hand to grasp the bedside clock, holding it close to his face.

Three a.m.

His heart pounded, making it hard to hear, but down on the floor, through the register, he heard a low moan and then a whimper that ripped right through his heart.

Throwing back the covers, he got up and padded swiftly across the room to the hallway. He bypassed the spare bedroom, already knowing it was empty, and made his way down the stairs to the living room and then down to the basement.

Kyler was curled up on the couch, head buried in her arms, shaking. The tears running from her closed eyes were like a fist to his stomach and he swallowed hard. He started to reach out a hand to wake her, but then decided against it. Brow furrowed, he hit the power button on the stereo and pulled a blanket off the chair behind him, draping it lightly over her.

With a soft hand he gently wiped a tear from one cheek, wondering if maybe he really should wake her from this nightmare. Instead, he just gazed down at her for a moment, and then retreated softly back upstairs, but it was a long time before he was able to fall back asleep.

CHAPTER 36

KYLER GASPED AND twisted as claustrophobia covered her. She rolled off onto the floor, feeling the blanket finally slide off, and then she just lay there, shaking. The stereo was off and the basement was cold, but the dim light coming through the window told her that dawn wasn't far off.

"Jesus," she mumbled and reached for the blanket, pulling it around her once more. She sat for a long time, bundled up; smoking one cigarette after another until her nerves quieted and her heart slowed its erratic pounding.

Finally she took a deep breath and stood up on slightly trembling legs. The nightmare still surrounded her, and the shadows in the basement were unfamiliar and frightening. Giving careful looks around her, she made her way to the stairs and took them two at a time until she stood in the kitchen, grasping the countertop in a near-panic and wondering how close she was to going crazy.

Dawn slowly brightened outside the window, and the sound of the waves pounding on the sand served to lend her some calm. Kyler slipped out the back door in bare feet, goose bumps from the cool air rising on her body, and walked down the steps to stand in the water. Taking a deep breath of the salty air, she willed it to enter every part of her body, giving her the peace it always gave her.

She started off down the beach, running hard along the edge of the water with her feet in the cold, wet sand. Not thinking, trying not to feel, she went on until she felt sanity start to return to her nearly-fractured mind.

Lamont was sitting on his deck drinking a cup of coffee when Kyler appeared on the horizon, way down the beach. He took a deep, relieved breath and waited until she was almost to his deck before going in and fixing another cup of coffee. He was liberal with the sugar and cream, knowing she needed it, and stopped to grab a thick towel out of the laundry room before stepping back out on the deck.

Kyler pulled herself up the three little steps, clearly exhausted, and soaked to the bone. In the cold, early morning hour goose bumps covered every inch of her skin and she was shivering so much her teeth were chattering.

Wordlessly he draped the towel around her and led her over to a lawn chair. She sat down and pulled the towel up close under her chin and as far over her knees and legs as it would reach.

"Here's some coffee," he set the cup on the deck beside her and sat down on the other lawn chair.

"Th-thanks," she stuttered, and reached out a shaking hand to grasp it. The heat was heaven, working its magic from the cup to her fingertips, and the first sip went down hot; an instant ball of fire that quickly began to warm her from the inside out.

Lamont regarded her over the rim of his own coffee cup. "You go swimming?"

Kyler stared down into her cup as the steam rose around her. "Kinda." She waited a beat and then looked at him. "Did you put the blanket over me?"

He arched an eyebrow and gave a slow nod. "Nobody else in the house, kid."

She nodded, meeting his eyes. "You heard me?"

He gave a small shrug. "At three this morning. You screamed and woke me up. The, uh . . . acoustics in my house are kinda weird. The registers are like open phone lines connecting each room and it's really clear coming from the basement."

Kyler grunted, remembering the night she heard him and Emily down in the basement. "Was it bad?" She asked. "I mean, was I . . ."

"You were crying," he responded neutrally. "I thought about waking you up, but I know you needed the sleep, even if . . . you know . . . even if the dream was pretty bad." He paused a moment and then said softly, "Which I'm guessing it was."

She stared down into her coffee cup again for a few minutes, and then took another long, luxurious sip. It burned all the way down, driving back the bone-chilling cold.

"I figured you'd be out skating," he commented. "Trying to work it out."

"I thought about it. But you're right . . . it was really bad. I just . . . started running, trying to work it out that way. Ran until I thought my lungs would explode, and then I jumped in the water."

A heavy silence descended between them at her last words. Lamont stared at her, an uneasy mixture of sorrow and anger mixing in his eyes.

"Jesus Christ," he muttered.

"Not to drown myself," Kyler said quietly. "Just . . . sometimes, Doc, I gotta keep going. There's something in me that drives me, you know? Makes me shoot up again and again to see how low I can get the smack to take me, or snort up line after line of coke to keep going higher and higher.

"Without the drugs . . . and no booze around . . . I just ran. Sometimes I skate, yeah, because it eases this ache . . . this . . ." she gestured helplessly, "this fucking *need* to keep going. And today . . . today I just ran because I wanted to be by the ocean."

His eyes bored into hers, hard and furious. "But it would've saved you a whole helluva lotta trouble if you'd drowned, right?"

She met his gaze calmly and he saw the truth in her dark eyes. "Sometimes I think it's the only way out of this for me."

Lamont shook his head and opened his mouth to speak, but then closed it back. He sat where he was for a minute longer, trying to calm his shocked nerves, and then deliberately got up and sat down beside her.

With an arm around her shoulders he pulled her towards him, feeling rock-hard resistance at first. Finally, reluctantly, he felt her give a little as her weight leaned against him.

"Don't," he said softly. "Don't think that way, ok? Let me try to help you first. Let me do what I can."

"There ain't really nothing you can do," Kyler mumbled, and he felt the absence of her body as she leaned back away from him.

"Just talk to me; let me in a little."

She shook her head and stood up, her eyes on the ocean. The towel wrapped around her shoulders made her look small and innocent, like a child bundled in a beach towel staring out at the crashing waves for the first time.

"I'm tryin' to do what's right," she said hoarsely. "But you've already done more for me than anybody, Doc. What I got goin' on, it . . . it's better if I don't lay it on you."

"I'm asking you to, Kyler."

"Doc . . ."

"And not as your shrink," he muttered gruffly. "Not as your doctor, either, but as your friend."

Kyler hung her head and sighed, aching for something—*anything*—to get her through this. "You got too much to lose," her voice was quiet. "You got too much to give to people, whereas I—"

"Don't?" His voice was carefully even. "Whereas you *don't* have anything to give to people?"

She was silent for a minute and then turned to face him. "Look at me, Doc. This is all I am, and I'm pretty fucked up. What the hell can I give to people that's not gonna send them into the nearest mental hospital?"

"Now that's pretty fucking dramatic, don't you think?" He growled. "What about those friends of yours? Barb and Jimmy? And their new baby? I think there's a lot of you that's holding them together, kid, whether you think so or not."

"And a lot more of me tearing them apart," she shot back.

Lamont took a deep breath and let it out slowly, trying to rein in his anger. "C'mon," he gestured. "Let's go inside before you catch pneumonia."

Kyler regarded him, her eyes resting easily on his angry ones. "I'm not giving up, Doc," she said softly. "I know you think I am . . ."

"That's the way it sounds, Kyler."

"I just . . ." she sighed heavily. "I'm tired, Doc, and I don't see the shit gettin' no better."

"C'mon, let's go," he put a hand lightly on her shoulder. Kyler allowed him to lead her into the kitchen, where the air was warm compared to outside on the deck. She was aware she was still shivering in her soaked clothes, and as if reading her mind Lamont pointed towards the stairs.

"Go on up and take a hot bath, ok? I'll throw your clothes in the washer."

For a second she hung back, watching him. Lamont glanced at her, eyebrows raised.

"This is what I'm talking about," she muttered quietly. "All this shit you're doin' for me? This just shows you've got a lot to give. Me . . . me, I ain't nothin' but a junkie, Doc, and I don't see how I can turn that around. When I sleep, I just have nightmares about all the stupid shit I've done and every time I remember that I just realize that I can't—"

"What about the park?" He snapped. "You don't think you did any good by turning that place around?"

For that Kyler had no answer and she dropped her eyes. She couldn't quite believe she'd actually made a positive impact on something that huge.

"Those kids, Kyler? They got someplace to go now, someplace that's gonna keep 'em outta trouble, off the streets, and away from drugs and gangs, *and you don't think you had anything to do with that?*"

"First one that came up to me and offered to sell me dope I'd probably take it," she snapped. *"Because I can't let it go."*

Lamont glared at her, then shook his head. "Go take a bath, Kyler, and then when you come down I wanna show you something, ok?"

Instantly suspicious, she hung back, staring at him with hooded eyes. "What?"

"Something that might make you change your way of thinking," he responded, pouring himself another cup of coffee. She was silent, standing behind him, and when he turned to look at her he read something far more real in her eyes: fear.

"What?" She asked again, feeling the knot tighten in her stomach.

Oh, Jesus, her mind moaned. *Maybe I really did fail the drug test. Or maybe . . . maybe . . . did my blood test come back showing positive for something?*

Her stomach rolled over as the acid started to build.

"Nothing bad," he said quickly, seeing her face pale slightly.

"What about the test?" She asked. "The blood test? You never told me if . . . if maybe . . ."

"Oh, shit," he stared at her. "I'm sorry, Kyler, I forgot. You're good; you're ok. Negative for hep, AIDS, STD's, you name it, and I tested for just about everything. I'm sorry," he repeated. "I've been meaning to tell you for a couple days now."

Kyler looked at him, trying to comprehend what he'd said. She'd been so sure she had *something* that with him telling her she was clean—for now anyway—it was hard to focus on what that meant.

"But you know," his eyes were serious, drilling into hers, "AIDS takes at least six months, kid, and . . ."

"I know," she muttered. "But right now I'm ok."

"Yeah."

She shook her head, shaking now more from relief than from the cold.

"Go on," he said softly. "Go take a hot bath and then we'll go for a ride."

She took a deep breath and glanced at the clock. "I gotta be at work at nine."

Lamont nodded. "We've got plenty of time. Try to trust me on this, ok, Kyler?"

Swallowing hard, Kyler slid her gaze away and turned towards the stairs, not answering. Only when she sank down into the tub full of hot water, feeling it soak into her cold skin, was she able to relax somewhat. Tired—exhausted, really—worn down to the bone, the day already seemed a million years long, and it was only pushing seven in the morning.

CHAPTER 37

LAMONT PULLED INTO the hospital parking lot and Kyler felt her stomach clench up again. He glanced at her as he maneuvered into a parking space.

"Nothin' bad, I told you."

"Doc," she scrubbed a hand hard across her face, "I can't see anything good about why we're here."

"That's because every time you've been here it's been for something bad. Believe it or not, kid, but some good things actually do happen here." He shut off the engine and looked at her. "Trust me, ok?"

Kyler sighed and opened her door. "You keep saying that."

"I know," he pushed his own door open and stood, looking at her over the roof of the car. "And I know you probably can't, at least right now . . . and that's ok. But just know that I'm not gonna lie to you."

His eyes were open and honest, staring into hers, and Kyler, who was usually very good at reading people, once again had no problem reading him. And she couldn't detect any lie, whatsoever.

Finally she nodded and slipped around the car towards him. As they walked in the front doors, she followed, all too aware of the bank of elevators off to her left. Lamont, though, walked on past them and entered the stairwell.

"Just up to the third floor."

Kyler nodded, keeping pace with him as they walked up the three flights. When he opened the door for her and she walked through, she had to stop in surprise at the huge sign hanging from the ceiling halfway down the hall.

"The pediatric unit?" She turned and looked at him. "What—"

"C'mon," he pointed to one long window down on the right. "I want you to see something."

"Doc . . ." she started, but he was already walking away. Walking fast to catch up with him, Kyler almost ran into him when he suddenly stopped and looked through the window. She looked, too, and felt her heart melt.

Lamont heard the breath whoosh out of her and offered a small smile. "Here, put this on." He was holding a blue gown and Kyler had no idea where he'd gotten it.

"What—?" She started, but then he was sliding the gown over her arms and tying it in back.

"This, too," he placed a mask over her mouth and nose, hooking the elastic straps behind her ears. "Now you can go in and see her."

Kyler's eyes were big above the mask, full of questions, but he just shook his head and gestured towards the door.

"Something good, Kyler, like I said. And something that's easy for you to hold on to."

Somewhat numb, Kyler stepped slowly through the door and took smalls steps over to the tiny metal crib. Bailey was lying on her back with an oxygen tube in her nose and an

IV in one foot, but her one good eye was on Kyler's; focused and intent.

"Oh my God," she murmured, and at the sound of her voice, Bailey grinned an absolute beautiful baby grin. Holding out a finger, Kyler felt her heart melt even more as Bailey's small hand wrapped around it.

"Hey, baby girl," Kyler whispered. "Boy, am I glad to see you."

Her eyes were as blue as Barb's, as blue as the ocean, and even though one drifted off to the side, the another one pinned Kyler's eyes with a look of innocence mixed with a fair amount of intelligence.

Intelligence? Her mind whispered. *She's not even a week old.*

Still, it was there. Small and almost hidden by the girl's tiny, underweight body, but Kyler saw it. Suddenly she felt a fierce urge to protect this baby at all costs; to gather her up in her arms and shield her from the horrors and dangers of the world.

"Wanna hold her?" Lamont was beside her now, dressed in his own gown and mask.

Kyler looked at him. "Yeah."

Lamont gently slid his hands under Bailey's body and lifted her up, passing her carefully over to Kyler. The baby's weight—barely nothing—in her arms only intensified her desire to fight and kill and maim and destroy anything that threatened to do her harm.

"Is she ok?"

"Yeah," he answered. "Lungs are progressing normally. Heart and brain functions seem to be normal, but it'll take some time to be really sure on those. Right now the only physical signs are the deafness in one ear and her blind eye."

Kyler stared down at Bailey, staring up at her for a long time. Finally Bailey gave a huge yawn and her eyes closed, opened briefly, then closed again. Gently Kyler laid her back down in the crib and pulled the small, thin blanket up over her belly.

Humbled and ashamed by the reckless way she'd jumped into the ocean just a mere hour ago, she stroked the baby's cheek one time and then turned and walked out of the room. Lamont was behind her and stripped off his mask as she collapsed into a chair.

"Are *you* ok?" He asked, sitting down next to her.

"Yeah," Kyler said absently, staring at the floor.

"Sure?"

"If she's ok, then why's she here?" Kyler raised her eyes to his. "How long's she been here?"

"Two days. Your friend, Barb, called me the other day and said she was moving down here to a halfway house. She wanted to know if I could help her with Bailey, if I could give her some options or advice."

"Seriously?" Kyler's eyebrows shot up. "What else did she say?" *Please nothing about me and Jimmy loaded up on coke.*

Lamont shrugged. "That's it. I know some people up at that hospital they were staying in and I called in a favor or two. Bailey's only gonna have to be here maybe another week or two, just to be on the safe side, and Barb's probably moving into the house as we speak."

"*She* called you?"

Lamont nodded.

"Asking *you* for advice?"

He shrugged. "Legally, I couldn't help her, but she knew that. She just asked for some advice on . . . well, starting from scratch on becoming a mother, and one who'll probably need help down the line because Bailey's handicapped." He paused and looked at her. "Why?"

Kyler slowly shook her head and got up, walking over to the window again. "I kinda got the feeling she didn't trust you."

"What makes you think that?" His voice was neutral behind her. She looked at Bailey was sleeping, one thumb stuck in her mouth, her tiny chest rising and falling with each breath.

"Because she thought I was . . ." Kyler closed her eyes and leaned her forehead against the cool glass, "sleeping with you. In return for letting me stay with you."

Lamont felt sucker punched, his chest wrapped up in razor wire. He took a deep breath and the feeling lessened somewhat, but thin betrayal and disappointment took its place.

"Jesus," he growled. "Another one."

Kyler heard the underlying pain in his voice and gave a heavy sigh. Pushing away from the window, she turned and faced him. His eyes were hard as they stared into hers, but she could see the hurt in them, too, and her own stomach gave a brief squeeze.

Lamont shook his head and shifted his gaze away to stare absently down the hall. "I woulda married her, Kyler, if she'd stayed."

"I know," she responded softly.

"And I don't blame her a bit for leaving. If it'd been my kid up there in San Fran hooked up to a ventilator, I'd have had to go, too."

"Yeah," she walked back to him and sat down in the chair, leaning her head back against the wall.

"And just 'cause Emily left don't mean I'm gonna jump in the sack with the next available prospect," now his voice held an edge, and she sensed the deep underlying anger.

Kyler took a long, slow breath and leaned forward with her elbows on her knees. Raking her hands through her hair, she locked her fingers at the base of her neck and stared at the floor.

"I'm sorry," she said quietly.

Lamont didn't answer; his eyes still focused on a spot far down the hall.

"Her and I, Doc . . ." she started, and then trailed off, trying to choose her words carefully. "We got along on the streets the only way we could and . . . and it . . . at first it was hard for *me* to believe that maybe you *didn't* want anything in return, you know? Let alone sex."

There was thick silence between them for what seemed like a long time. Finally Lamont stood up and shoved his hands in his pockets.

"I'm gonna get me a cup of coffee down in the cafeteria. Take your time and I'll, uh, give you a ride to the park when you're done."

Kyler gave a brief nod, still staring at the floor. "All right."

She sighed and watched him walk down the hall to the elevators, knowing he was hurt and angry, but still feeling all too real all the times that she'd *had* to pay for something in return. Gritting her teeth, Kyler shook her head in frustration. After a few minutes she got up and headed towards the stairs.

She found Lamont in a far corner of the cafeteria with a cup of coffee in front of him. Sitting down opposite him, she pulled her cigarettes from her pocket and lit one, catching his eye.

"Doc . . ." she started, "I'm sorry. About everything. And about . . . about you getting accused of something you haven't even done." She took a deep breath and let it out slowly, running a hand through her hair.

He gave a short nod and took a sip of coffee. "It's ok, Kyler. I just . . . it gets old, everybody thinking . . . this . . ."

"I know," she sighed.

"But," he continued, "I kinda understand why you would think that. You and Barb have been through shit that's hard for me to even comprehend, and, uh, it'd be a goddamned miracle if you could ever trust anybody again."

"There's a wall," Kyler responded softly. "In me. You know, that makes it real hard. I can't speak for Barb, but . . ." she reached across and snagged the ashtray, crushing out her barely-smoked cigarette.

"Guys scare me, Doc," her voice was barely audible, but her eyes on his were tough and angry. "Men, I mean. Some of 'em . . ." she swallowed hard, her face working. "Some of 'em were, um, pretty violent, and . . . well, most of them were, and . . ."

"It's all right, Kyler," Lamont muttered.

She shot him a dull look. "No it ain't."

He gazed at her for a long time, trying to see past that barrier. "It will be," he said finally. "Just keep on holding on, and I promise it will be."

Kyler arched an eyebrow. "You keep saying that."

"I know," he stood up. "C'mon, before you're late."

She glanced up at the clock and saw it was pushing nine a.m. Pulling herself to her feet, she fell into step beside him as they walked out to the lot. When she got in the car she glanced at him.

"Thanks for bringing me to see Bailey."

"No problem. Thought you might need an uplift."

"Yeah."

The ride to the park was long and silent, but it was a comfortable silence. In the back of her mind, Kyler again briefly wondered how she was going to pass the drug test the following Thursday, but then thought of Bailey's frail body, and that fierce sense of protection swamped her again.

"She's really gonna be ok?"

"Yeah," Lamont pulled into the lot. "So far."

Kyler opened the door but looked back at him. "Can I see her again?"

He smiled. "Anytime, kid."

Nodding, she gave a small smile in return. "Thanks, Doc. See ya later on tonite."

"All right." He waited until she was inside the gate before pulling back out onto the street, trying hard not to think just how much violence Kyler had had to endure in that one short year she was out on the streets.

"Jesus," he muttered, and then the pager on his belt went off and he focused on dialing his cell phone as he raced down the highway back towards the hospital.

CHAPTER 38

KYLER WAS SITTING in the deep end of the pool, applying instant concrete to a few cracks when the cordless phone in her back pocket rang. She glanced up at the blameless blue sky, giving herself a brief moment of pleasure as the warm southern California breeze cooled the sweat on her forehead.

"Beaumont Skate Park," she said, cradling the phone between her ear and shoulder.

"Congrats are in order, Kyler," John's voice sounded thin and far away as it traveled over three-thousand miles of phone line. "Feel free to celebrate as long as it's drug-free."

"What'm I celebrating?" She climbed up the sharp incline and plopped down on the rim, her legs dangling over the edge. Lighting a cigarette, she surveyed her work from this new height, looking for any chips or cracks that she might've missed.

"You're off the city's time," he sounded amused. "You're done with the community service."

"What?" Kyler felt her heart speed up. "Are you sure? I've really been here that long?"

"Right at three months," John answered. "The court called me today. Tomorrow I'll put you on the payroll, ok?"

"Yeah," she said slowly, somewhat numb. "Yeah, ok, thanks."

"You sound shocked."

"Well, I kinda am," the nicotine in her blood added to her pounding heart. "So . . . I'm gonna get a paycheck?"

"Yeah, once a week."

"Excellent," she said, grinning. "Thanks, John."

"You're the one who needs thanking. If you hadn't come along when you did, I'm pretty sure that place'd be under five feet of weeds by now, if not bulldozed completely, awaiting the city's next big project."

"Ah," she stood up and walked around the edge of the pool to where her skateboard lay near the shallow end. "I was just trying to occupy my time."

"Well, you definitely turned that place around. But anyway, look, I gotta get off here. I just wanted to call and tell ya."

"Thanks again."

"No problem." The phone clicked in her ear, and Kyler slowly lowered it, absently hitting the off button and staring into the pool. Her heart was still pounding and, with a small smile, she scooped up her board and in one smooth, fluid motion glided onto the smooth concrete.

She raced across the surface and up the near ninety-degree incline of the wall, soaring high into the air above the tiled lip. Deliberately, she ran her board across the repairs she'd just made, searching for the slightest flaw that could cause a potentially bad accident.

Around the sides, up to the shallow end and back into the bowl of the twelve-foot deep end, Kyler used every bit of concrete, feeling the freedom overtake her in the wake of finally—*finally*—being able to have herself enough together to actually draw an honest paycheck.

Feel free to celebrate, long as it's drug-free, John's words repeated themselves in her mind. Kyler flew up one side and snagged her board effortlessly out of the air, landing perfectly on her feet. Breathing hard, she stared at the pool, her mind a million miles away.

Long as it's drug-free.

"Well . . . yeah . . ." the hesitation in her voice made her flinch. Already her mind was working, trying to find ways around pissing clean on the test and still getting high. Trying to find justification, as well; some viable excuse to do what she was pretty sure she was getting ready to do.

"Fuck," Kyler scrubbed a hand hard across her face. "What the hell'm I doing?"

She glanced around her; the good feeling that skating the pool had given her quickly dissipating in the wake of the itch that suddenly appeared near the base of her skull. The prospect of not having to go through the hell of donating plasma again—and of having a guaranteed certain amount of money each week—had awakened a part of her better off asleep.

Feeling the anticipation start through her, she dug in hard, deliberately asking herself just how the fuck she expected to pass a drug test in less than a week if she went out and got high.

"Well . . . shit, I probably wouldn't've passed it anyway," she said softly, aware of her voice shaking. "There's still coke in my system."

So what's it matter? That demon voice spoke up, egging her on. Kyler clenched her jaw, knowing she wasn't strong enough to deny it.

One last time. You deserve it, right? Getting this far, being able to draw a paycheck?

"I ain't drawn one yet," she mumbled and closed her eyes.

Maybe just a pill or two . . . don't have to be coke. Just something so maybe I can sleep tonight. Something mild, something that maybe won't raise too many questions on the drug test.

Completely aware that all she was doing was standing on the edge of the pool, making excuses, trying to justify everything, Kyler gave a sigh that was almost a moan and turned towards the office.

The phone rang at just past nine that night. Kyler had been sitting in the chair for the last hour, watching the clock and gauging her strength, her ability to bypass her sudden, violent need for drugs; just lock the gate and head directly to the doc's house, drug-free.

She glanced at the clock again and sighed, reaching for the phone. Lamont's voice on the other end didn't surprise her, and in the back of her head she willed him to ask if she needed a ride home.

"Hey," he said. "Just wanted to call and say congratulations. John called me earlier and told me the news, but it's been a helluva day and I just now got a chance to call you."

"Thanks," she responded, her heart sinking. He wasn't coming, she knew. For the first time since she'd known him, he wasn't coming, wouldn't be able to be there for her. "Be a new experience cashing that first check."

He gave a quiet laugh. "Yeah, I'll bet."

"Busy day, huh?" She asked quietly.

"Yeah. Too damn busy. Dropped you off earlier, and it ain't stopped. Car accidents, shootings, overdoses, you name it. I've been runnin' all day."

"And you're still there, I take it?" Kyler lit a cigarette, inhaling deeply. The nicotine bit hard into her lungs, burning.

"Yeah," his voice sounded tired. "Hopefully I won't be too much longer, but with the way this day's been going, who knows?"

"True. Well, ok, then, I guess I'll see you later, maybe?"

"Sure. I don't have much to eat, but I know there's gotta be at least one can of soup in the cabinet if you're hungry. And milk and Cokes in the fridge."

"I'll be all right, Doc, thanks. Don't work too hard, ok?"

"Tryin' not to, Kyler. But I just wanted to say congratulations."

"Thanks. I'll talk to you later."

"All right. Be careful, all right?"

"I will," she said, her heart giving a painful squeeze. Hitting the off button, Kyler gently laid the phone on the desk as her mind raced in back and forth in different directions.

Finally she took a deep breath and pulled herself to her feet. Locking the office door, and then the gate behind her, she turned and faced the world. Two steps later the rat that lived inside her skull and survived on dope came alive with a vengeance, tearing its way around her fragile brain, *screaming*, like it always did, for more and more and more.

Kyler clenched her teeth and raked her hands through her hair. She stood for a few long moments on the curb, her skateboard at her feet, and then deliberately turned and headed off south, towards the city and the insane calling raging within her.

She studied the street corners and alleys as she walked, searching for the dealer who had the ability to ease the twisted hurricane of her thoughts, racing madly inside her skull. Almost to familiar ground and comforting drugs, she suddenly stopped, thinking, *Jesus, I ain't got no money. How the fuck did I expect to pay for this shit?*

An image popped up in her tortured brain of a young girl, stoned and looking to get more so, lying on her back, paying with her body for the drugs she needed so much.

"Oh my God," Kyler moaned. She leaned against the brick side of a building and pressed the heels of her hands against her eyes. "What the fuck am I doing?"

There was silence for a minute, and then a soft voice growled from just around the corner, "Gettin' ready to get fucked."

She whirled and was greeted with an explosion against the side of her head. It seemed to come out of nowhere, a sharp blow that left her reeling. She dimly felt the slivers of glass fall off her shoulders, some sliding down the back of her shirt. Kyler grappled with the wall beside her, desperate to remain upright, but her knees buckled and she crashed to the ground.

"Now, bitch," the familiar voice came from above her, blowing rank breath down into her face. "Now you gonna tell me no, huh? Now you gonna tell me to fuck off?"

Rising panic fought through the numbing fog in her brain, and Kyler felt the terror, real and intense, as it wrapped around her.

"How 'bout I fuck you with this first?"

She tried to scream as something sharp was shoved down her pants, digging mercilessly into the unprotected hollow of her pelvis.

"Nope," a fist crashed into her nose and she heard the crunch of it deep in her head. She had time to draw half a breath before the hand then clamped hard over her mouth and nose, cutting off ninety-percent of her air flow. "Not screaming 'till I get what I want. First with this," the sharp object down her pants moved violently, gouging into her flesh.

"And then with this," his hips bucked against her hard; she felt his erection digging into her as the knife or whatever it was moved again, opening more flesh and getting dangerously close to her vagina.

Fuck! Her mind shrieked. ***Jesus Christ, somebody help me!***

Blood rolled down her forehead, stinging her eyes, and she felt her jeans becoming saturated with it. Struggling, desperate to just live through the next few seconds, Kyler felt wildly around her. When her hand closed upon a long shard of glass, she didn't hesitate.

Swinging it in a long arc, she felt clothes and skin part as she buried it deep in his side. With strength she didn't know she had, she pulled upward on it, feeling the palm of her hand cut wide open on the sharp edge, but even more aware as the shard slipped under his rib cage, buried deep in his flesh.

Giving a breathless howl, Lewis rolled off her, trying frantically to pull it out. In half a second Kyler forced herself to her feet and stumbled down the alley, leaving big drops of blood behind her from God only knew how many deep cuts and gashes.

She didn't allow her brain to think as she staggered towards Lamont's house. She didn't know how badly she'd been cut or even if she would be able to make it before bleeding to death in the street. The world swung around her, fading in and out, and when she finally collapsed on his front porch it was blurred, dark gray retreating swiftly to black.

All sense of focus was lost, and by feel alone Kyler pulled her keys from her pocket, located the right one, and slipped it into the lock. Her knees buckled again, but she caught herself before she fell, fighting grimly for consciousness as she followed a weaving path across the living room and up the stairs.

Falling by the side of his bed, she managed to steady herself by grabbing the corner of the nightstand and reached out a badly shaking hand to touch his arm.

"Doc," her voice came out a croak.

Lamont bolted awake, instantly alarmed. "Kyler," he muttered, and in one smooth motion sat up and reached for the lamp. "You ok—?"

The bright light showed her battered body in front of him in stark gruesome detail.

"Oh my God," he managed, feeling the panic automatically rise, and somehow managing to squash it under his medical training. Without a word he gently took hold of her and carried most of her weight into his bathroom. Sitting her on the closed toilet, he acted on impulse, pulling the towel off the rack and putting it over the deep gash on the side of her head.

"Don't move," he commanded, surveying the blood coming out of her from all sides of her body, trying to determine which was the worst and not really knowing where to start. Running a washcloth under cold water, he began to carefully mop up the blood, revealing shattered eyes that stared back at him through a numbing fog.

"What happened?" he asked quietly, working his way around her broken nose.

"I . . . got in a fight," she mumbled.

"I didn't know you were a fighter," his voice was carefully neutral; his hands steady as he gently cleaned the deep gash on her head. It needed stitches, and needed them as quickly as he could get her to the hospital.

"I got jumped."

"Jesus. By a gang?"

"No," she said in a trembling voice. "One guy. He …" But she broke off and her whole body started shaking. Lamont gently put a hand on the side of her face and met her eyes. Her skin was cold against his palm, and he read the telltale signs of shock on her face.

"Stay with me, Kyler, ok? You're gonna be all right, I promise."

"I feel like I'm gonna puke," she said faintly.

"Here," he slid an arm around her and helped her to the floor. "Easy," he muttered as he flipped up the lid on the toilet. "Just hang on."

Kyler laid her head on the cool porcelain, sending more shivers through her body. Lamont put a hand on her back and wiped the sweat and blood off her forehead. "Who was it?" He asked, and then stopped as he noticed the blood pooled around the waistline of her jeans.

"Where else are you bleeding?" He asked, facing her. She didn't answer as she leaned back against the tub. "Kyler, talk to me."

She swallowed heavily and closed her eyes. "Just don't lemme die, Doc."

"You're not gonna die—" he broke off and stared at the front of her blood-soaked jeans. Reaching for the button, he undid it, but stopped when her hand lightly touched his. Much like a new father, the emotion of her fingertips barely resting on his skin sent his paternal instinct into a highly-protective mode, almost like what Kyler had experienced earlier that day holding Bailey.

He was surprised at the sharpness of the pain that pierced his heart at the sight of the lone tear rolling down her cheek.

"Don't," she whispered.

"Kyler, I have to," he responded quietly.

She opened her eyes and looked at him, defeat and resignation prominent in her gaze.

"I promise," he muttered gruffly. "I promise I won't do more than I have to, but I have to look. You're not gonna bleed to death on my bathroom floor."

She didn't answer, and he took a deep breath and slowly peeled back the front of her jeans.

Her underwear was shredded, and so was, it seemed at first sight, her entire abdomen. Looking at it, Lamont savagely willed the cold blanket of professionalism to drop down over him, to keep his hands steady, his eyes sharp, and his mind clear as he searched for sliced organs or severed arteries in the lower belly of the girl he was becoming very fond of, considering her as close to the daughter he would never have.

He reached behind him and opened the cabinet under the sink, pulling out another towel. As gently as he could he folded it over her ravaged pelvis and put one of her hands on it.

"Hold it right there. I gotta throw on some clothes."

"It's bad," she murmured, and though he knew it wasn't a question, answered it anyway.

"Yeah, kid. It's bad. I'll be right back."

Kyler felt the pain as it washed over her. In her mind she saw herself skating the pool, feeling the itch, needing to get high so fucking bad it hurt. Another tear slipped out from beneath her closed eyelids and she took a deep, ragged breath, wondering why she still wanted to get high.

"All right," Lamont said softly. "Let's go. Lean on me, ok? Let me take most of your weight."

She felt his arms gently circle her body and pull her to her feet. She would have fallen if the doc hadn't been there, but true to his word, he held on, carrying almost all of her weight. Closing her eyes, Kyler leaned into him, putting her full trust in this man for the first time, and praying to God she wasn't wrong.

Slowly he guided her down the stairs and out the front door, putting her in the back seat of his car. Feeling the soft fabric beneath her, she was suddenly completely and totally exhausted, barely able to keep her eyes open.

"Talk to me, kid," he backed out of the drive and headed fast down the street. "Let me know you're still with me." With one hand he dialed his cell phone, reaching the hospital and instructing a gurney to be ready when he pulled up.

"I'm still with you," her voice was slightly slurred.

"Wanna tell me what happened?" He glanced at her in the mirror, feeling his heart pounding in aggravation at the slow traffic on the highway.

"Doc . . ." Kyler said quietly, "it . . . doesn't matter."

"Who cut you?" He swerved off the ramp and headed down a side street, now within minutes of the hospital.

"I heard a Meatloaf song on the radio today," her voice was fading fast. "You got any of him?"

"I think so," he answered, screeching to a stop in front of the ER. "But if I don't I'll buy you every album he ever put out as long as you're still alive to hear 'em. Hold on, Kyler."

She felt arms on her, carefully pulling her out of the car. Even though the night was warm, her entire body was covered in goose bumps, mixing uneasily with the sweat that slicked her skin, pouring from her forehead, back, and sides, burning in the cuts and gashes that seemed to cover her.

Above her she faintly heard Lamont's voice but couldn't make out his words. At the edge of that familiar black pit, she took a step forward, over the rim, and fell hard into unconsciousness.

CHAPTER 39

Kyler was aware, faintly at first, of the solid black that covered her slowly taking on the lighter hues of gray. Edges and lines began to appear, and reluctantly she found herself returning to consciousness.

She hurt, everywhere, and remembering the events of that night sent her body trembling and her heart racing. Moaning, she turned her head into the pillow, willing her brain to just shut down, forget everything.

"It's all right," the doc's familiar voice said softly, and he placed a soothing hand on her forehead. "You're all right, Kyler."

"Doc," she croaked. "I think I mighta killed him."

"Killed who, kid?" Lamont glanced at the monitor beside the bed, watching her vitals as the IV dripped fluid into her veins.

"Lewis . . . the guy who did this to me. I think I mighta killed him."

Kyler hitched in a deep breath, feeling an unsettling *pulling* sensation from her lower belly. Her stomach twisted, and she carefully took another breath, trying to calm it.

"Why?" He asked, watching her. Her eyes were closed against the jagged edges of that night, her brow furrowed. Her body shaking, she shook her head as the fear of going to jail—this time for murder—swamped her.

"I didn't mean to," her voice was barely audible. "I don't wanna go to jail, Doc."

"You won't," he responded quietly. "You didn't kill him, Kyler."

Her eyes flew open and she struggled to sit upright, grimacing from the pain.

"Whoa," he grabbed her shoulders and pushed her back down. "You're gonna tear your stitches, kid."

"I didn't kill him? How do you know I didn't kill him?"

"Because he was brought in here. The piece of glass stuck in his lung came from the same industrial-sized jar that nearly cut your head wide open. I put two and two together." He stared at her, ready to stop her if she tried to sit up again.

"You punctured his lung, but you didn't kill him. He'll be all right and ready to stand trial before not too much longer." He paused, gazing at her. "How do you know him, Kyler?"

She was silent for a few long minutes, trying to gather her thoughts. Lewis was the worst of the men who'd fucked her; he enjoyed violence more than most, and loved to hurt her. If she told doc how she knew him, all this and more would come out, and somehow she didn't want him knowing every sexually perverted detail.

Lamont sensed this somewhat and leaned back, his eyes on hers. "It's all right, Kyler. Get some rest, ok? I'll be back later to check on you."

She nodded. "How bad did he cut me?"

"Pretty bad. You've got fifteen stitches in your head and close to sixty in your abdomen. I'm guessing he cut you with some of that same glass, but since your jeans were in the way, it was more like . . ." he paused, then said reluctantly, "more like he *gouged* you. The gashes aren't uniform, you know? Like he took a sharpened spoon to you."

Kyler swallowed back acid, her stomach churning.

"But a friend of mine, he's real good at stitching up stuff like this. It won't scar much, if at all."

She flapped a hand vaguely. "I'm not worried about scarring. I'm just . . . did he cut anything permanent? Something I need?"

"No," Lamont shook his head. "To be honest, Kyler, I don't know how he didn't, but you're all right there. The cuts were deep, most of them, but none of them penetrated any organs. Your uterus and bladder are fine; colon, lower intestine, the same."

He clenched his jaw and took a deep breath, his eyes boring into hers. "You got really lucky, kid. Something like that—and the way you looked in my bathroom—I would've sworn he'd hit something fatal."

Kyler put a gentle hand on the thick padding that covered her stitches, picturing in her mind the shard of glass digging into her vulnerable flesh. With little meat on her bones, there wasn't much stopping power, so how the hell couldn't he have hit anything?

She closed her eyes. "Jesus Christ."

"Get some sleep," Lamont put his hand back on her forehead, smoothing back her hair. "I'll be back around later to check on you."

Kyler didn't answer and he silently left the room, shutting the door quietly behind him. Once in the hall, away from her sharp eyes, Lamont shook his head and gritted his teeth. It had taken him hours and multiple cups of coffee to get his body over the physical aspects of the adrenaline dump once he'd gotten her in and out of surgery.

This was the first time he'd assisted in putting back together the body of someone he knew, and the personalization of it all, coupled with the intense stark images of all the blood pouring from her in his bathroom that his mind kept insisting on repeating to him had sent his body into adrenaline overload. It was only later, after the surgery, that Lamont started shaking, feeling the emotional pull that girl had on him.

Kyler held her left hand up to her face, noting the thick gauze bandage that covered her palm. She dimly remembered it slicing open on the sharp edge of the glass she was digging into Lewis's side, and it was only now that she felt the dull sting of the pain.

With trembling hands she pulled the sheet off her body and slowly lifted her gown away from the front of her body. White gauze seemed to cover almost every inch of her torso, with the one across her abdomen slightly bloodstained. She swallowed back hot bile and closed her eyes against the weight of all that white, suddenly needing to vomit.

Through a sheer act of will she managed to hold it back, thinking that doing so would pull the stitches out of her tender skin. Quickly she covered herself back up and pulled the blankets back around her, shaking violently.

I should be at work right now, her mind moaned. *Jesus, I wish I was at work.*

The picture of Lewis coming at her penetrated her thoughts again, and Kyler gave a quiet moan, burrowing her face deep into the pillow.

When Lamont came back by, three hours later, she was still awake and still shaking. Her wild eyes stared into his, bruised a deep purple from her broken nose, and he recognized the terror running through her body.

As gently as he could, and without saying a word, he wrapped his arms around her, hugging her to him. Kyler let her guard down enough to let him, knowing she probably owed her life to him.

And knowing something else as well: that if ever the doc had a chance to pull any of that bullshit on her that she was used to men doing, his chance was the night before, when she was about out of her mind with pain and fear.

She remembered him gently peeling back the waistband of her blood-soaked jeans; remembered her own terror escalating as she anticipated him trying to make a move, and when he didn't the relief she felt was overwhelming.

In that instant, leaning against him with blood gushing from a dozen different gashes on her body, Kyler felt her first real trust of the man come to the surface. And now, stitched up physically but still mentally falling apart, his arms around her felt safe and sane, giving her a sense of stability she'd been lacking for far too long.

Lamont felt her relax against him as she was finally able to drift off. Carefully he pulled his arms away and stood up, willing her to get the sleep she desperately needed. As he exited the room, closing the door quietly behind him, he felt again that sense of protectiveness, and marveled once more that the girl was still alive after that horrible, vicious attack.

When he ducked to check on her right before dawn, however, he somehow was not surprised to find the bed empty. He briefly closed his eyes in frustration, and then, giving a low, guttural growl, turned and headed for the elevators.

Kyler sat on top of the big ramp, backed into the corner of the rail, and smoking a much-needed cigarette. She'd managed to last the entire day at work without doing one single thing, and guilt over getting paid for not working was top on her list of emotions. Under that—a close second—was the guilt she felt for leaving the hospital, and when footsteps started to climb up the stairs as dusk settled over the park, she had no doubt they belonged to Lamont, and that he was most likely highly pissed off.

Her pain-filled eyes met his angry ones as his head popped up above the platform. She waited in silence as he walked over and sat heavily down across from her. His measuring gaze noticed the sheen of sweat across her pale forehead and drawn cheeks, and his anger diminished somewhat.

Gesturing vaguely, Kyler pitched her cigarette over the side and looked at him. "The walls were closing in on me there, Doc. Plus, you know I can't stand IVs in me."

"IVs that were giving you a liquid form of food that you don't seem to eat otherwise, and also antibiotics to fight off infections that may want to enter through your ripped up stomach."

She sighed and scrubbed a hand across her face. "I couldn't stay there, knowing Lewis's in the same place," she reluctantly admitted. "He'll kill me if he gets the chance."

"Which he won't," Lamont assured her. "He's handcuffed to the bed with a twenty-four hour watch outside the door. The minute he's well enough, he's headed to jail." He paused, gazing at her. "Please tell me you didn't do anything stupid today."

"Like what?"

"Like trying to repair a ramp or skating that concrete thing over there," he jerked a thumb over his shoulder towards the flatland.

Kyler grimaced. "I barely made it up these stairs, Doc, and I only did that 'cause I needed some peace. Besides, it makes me sick when it, you know, kinda *pulls* on me. Like when it, uh . . . I don't know . . . kinda feels like my intestines are stretching."

He grunted. "You throw up?"

"No," she shook her head. "But not because I didn't need to. I managed to hold it back 'cause I was afraid I'd tear something."

Lamont took a deep breath and let it out slowly. "You need antibiotics, Kyler, more than anything. Let me take you back to the hospital."

She looked at him and he saw the fear again in her eyes. It brought back his protective instinct and he shook his head, aggravated.

"All right," he sighed. "I'll write you a script for some Keflex, but promise me you'll take them, ok?"

Kyler nodded and leaned her head back against the railing, staring up at the first few stars. "I promise."

There was silence for a couple minutes, and then Kyler spoke quietly, "He was the worst, out of all of them. He . . . he liked to hurt people . . . me . . . when he knew he could do what he wanted and get away with it because I needed the smack so fucking bad. All I wanted was to get high, and a lot of times I managed to do that by paying a high price."

Lamont looked at her, trying to read behind the barrier. "What'd he do, kid?" His voice was quietly gentle even as his mind burned with mental images.

"Everything," she muttered, her voice trembling. "Everything he could." She stopped and swallowed heavily. "He . . . especially liked to hurt me physically. He'd hit, punch, bite, kick, whatever. It was like the sight of my blood . . .

um . . ." she struggled for the words. "Excited him even more, and the more I bled, the worse he got."

Staring at her, Lamont found it hard to breathe around the weight of the hatred he heard in her words. The pictures in his head grew more graphic, and he swallowed back rage of his own. He started to slide over next to her, but stopped when she flinched away, reverting back to her real terror of men in general.

The sudden movement sliced a jagged bolt of pain across her abdomen, and a small groan escaped her.

Holding up his hands, he met her tortured eyes. "It's just me, Kyler, ok? And you know I'm not him."

Kyler stared at him for a few long seconds, and then reluctantly nodded. "Yeah. I know, Doc. It's just real hard to forget . . . all that."

"Yeah," he agreed, and slowly sat beside her with his back against the railing. Kyler ran a hand through her hair and sighed. He watched as she lit another cigarette with shaking hands, and then inhaled hard to drive the smoke deep into her lungs.

"He, uh . . ." and now her voice was so soft he had to strain to hear, "used things on me." Her hand gestured vaguely to her pelvic area, giving Lamont a specific, horrible, idea of what she was trying to convey to him.

"Bottles and stuff. Anything, really that was . . . usable." She took a deep, shaky breath and looked out over the park. "It was all part of his twisted lifestyle, and the only reason I got involved was 'cause I had no other way to get the money I needed to buy dope."

She pinched the bridge of her nose, shutting her eyes. He gently put a hand on the back of her neck but she pulled away, more out of shame and self-loathing than of any real fear.

"Anyway," Kyler mumbled, "that's how I know him." She forced herself to meet his eyes. "And I'm gonna tell you something now, Doc, and you can do with it want you want, ok?"

Lamont gave a slow nod, watching her and knowing he probably did not want to hear what she had to say.

"I can't sleep, you know that. I have these bad dreams and then I wake up shaking, and they never really go away. For awhile there it got so bad that I didn't want to go to sleep, but short of doing speed

(*Or coke, her mind whispered.*)

I had to sleep sometime, right? So I . . . found this dealer I know and I bought some valiums off of him. I did it a couple times, just trying to sleep for a few hours."

She watched him, her sharp eyes gauging his reaction.

Lamont stared back steadily enough, but on the inside he had no idea how to respond. She may as well have gone back to the heroin, with the way the court would look at it. But then he thought again of all the nights he'd find her crying in her sleep and shaking from fear. From that angle he could see how the valiums might have helped.

"Did you, uh . . ." he paused, considering, "ever buy anything else?"

"No."

"Ever?"

"No. Just valiums."

Kyler waited, giving him the time he needed to consider his—and her—options. Finally he shook his head, staring at her.

"How'd you pass the drug test?"

"I met this girl who needed money real bad, and I bought her piss."

His eyebrows shot up. "Kyler . . ." he sighed.

"She was clean," she muttered. "And she needed the money."

"You needed money, too, if I recall," he responded. "Or was that just to pay her?"

"To pay her . . . and to buy the valiums. That's why I was donating plasma."

"And that's how you happened to run into that guy last night," it wasn't a question, but Kyler nodded anyway.

"I was on my way down there and he came out of this alley."

But you weren't gonna buy valiums last night, were you?

Pitching the butt of her cigarette over the railing, she scrubbed her hands across her face, wishing she could just scour away all the bad shit she'd done.

After a seemingly endless amount of silence, Lamont finally took a deep breath, letting it out slowly.

"All right," his voice was very quiet. "This stays between you and me, ok?" His eyes bored into hers.

Kyler nodded, a mixture of gratitude and pain in her eyes. "Thanks, Doc."

"Yeah," he said gruffly. "Just . . . even if you can't talk to me, don't throw away everything you've got now on this stupid shit, kid. There's always ways out of things, and . . . I mean, Jesus, he coulda killed you last night."

"I know," she murmured. She took a ragged breath and shivered slightly. The wind coming off the ocean had a chill to it, but it was the chill inside her that was the coldest. Laying a hand over her stomach, Kyler felt the itch and heat through the thick pad.

Lamont said quietly, "C'mon, kid, lemme take you home before you get sick." He carefully wrapped his arms around her and she allowed him to help her to her feet. He was as careful as he could, but she still felt the huge pain flare up, tearing at her tender abdomen. Gasping, she held onto the railing and hung her head.

"Wait a minute," her voice came out a low moan.

"Ok," he said, easily holding most of her little weight. "How the hell'd you get up here?"

"Very carefully."

"Why again?"

But she just shook her head and gestured vaguely towards the stairs. "All right. Let's go."

Slowly, walking with her and carrying most of her weight, Lamont led her to the steps. Kyler gritted her teeth and held on, knowing with stark reality how she'd probably tear in half if she fell. The thought made her stomach twist up, and the acid was already coming up her throat before she was able to swallow it back.

His arm around her waist, he felt the sweat on her back as it slowly soaked through her shirt. Halfway down they had to stop as wave after wave of monstrous pain ripped across her midsection. Kyler locked her throat against the scream that wanted to burst out, but he felt the violent trembling in her body.

Tightening his jaw, Lamont again wondered why the fuck she'd gone up the steps to begin with, and just had to hope to God she hadn't done any damage then.

"Easy," he murmured. "Almost there."

Kyler didn't answer, but by the time she was able to climb into his back seat, she was racked with exhaustion and couldn't stop the tears of pain from slipping beneath her closed eyelids.

"Sorry, Doc," she croaked. "I didn't think I'd have to keep getting saved like this."

He didn't answer as he started the car. In the back of his mind he didn't think he'd ever be the one doing the saving, and at last began to realize how Emily must have felt.

On the whole, it wasn't that bad, knowing that sometimes you receive more than you give, even if you give everything you've got. As much as he'd already pulled Kyler again and again from that edge, she'd given him more of a sense of purpose than most people he'd saved on the operating table.

CHAPTER 40

"I'LL BE RIGHT back," Lamont glanced over the seat at her. "You all right?"

"Yeah," Kyler answered, lying as still as she could. The pain had gotten so bad that even the slightest movement caused a wave of agony to rip through her stomach. Her eyes were closed against the bright lights of the hospital parking lot, and Lamont could see the frailty of her body alongside the huge back seat.

He opened his door and got out, striding quickly into the main entrance. Kyler took a deep breath and wondered if she had it in her to try to score some painkillers. She moved her leg a little bit and the white-hot pain that tore across her abdomen shot that idea instantly out the window.

She gave a small moan that was almost a whimper and gritted her teeth, digging her fingers into the seat cushion.

Christ, just get me through this, her brain whispered. *Just please get me through this.*

Within minutes Lamont was back at the car and opening his door. She heard the rattle of a small sack as he dug through it, and then the distinct pop of the top off a medicine bottle.

"Here," he handed her a somewhat large pill over the seat. "Shit," he stopped, looking around his car. "I don't have anything to drink it down with."

"That's all right," she took the pill and swallowed it effortlessly. "I can take 'em without anything." Taking deep breaths, trying to sneak minutes at a time around the monstrous pain, she asked wearily, "What was it?"

"Keflex," he started the car and pulled out of the parking lot.

She'd hoped for a painkiller, but there was no way she could ask him. Not now; probably not ever. Telling him that stuff up there on the ramp had taken a lot out of her, and like sneaking the minutes past the pain, she hoped she could sneak by him in the weeks and months to come without having to see that disgust and contempt she was sure he felt for her in his eyes.

Another tear slipped down her cheek, thinking about it. To her, right now, having the doc look at her like that would be the one thing that would send her on a self-destructive path from which this time there'd be no saving her.

The ride back to his house was long and quiet. In the backseat Kyler tried to hold on just a little bit longer . . . past the shame, past the pain.

Hold on, she willed herself. *Please just fucking hold on.*

"Don't move," Lamont pulled in his garage. "Let me help you." He killed the engine and put the sack in his pocket. Kyler waited with the unstoppable, hated tears still rolling down her face until he opened the back door and gently helped her out.

The pain was enormous, sending jagged streaks of pain across her belly. She gasped and fell against him; he caught her easily and held her stable until she was able to get her feet under her. The tears on her cheeks tore at his heart, and he strongly suspected that, although the pain was real and extreme, there was more going on with her.

"Easy," he said softly. "I've got you."

Slowly they entered his house and he guided her towards the upstairs.

"Wait," Kyler stopped, her shaking body like live wire in his arms. "Can I go downstairs and listen to some music?"

"Yeah," he changed course. "But don't try to climb up the stairs by yourself, ok? When you're ready to go to bed, lemme help you." He stopped as they started down the first couple of steps. "Or you can sleep down here; it's up to you."

"Ok," she said shakily. "I might do that 'cause I don't know if I can get up back up tonight, even with your help."

He didn't answer as he carefully led her to the couch. Kyler crawled up on it, trembling, her jaw tight. Her eyes were shut against the pain, and he saw the tenseness of her muscles.

"Hang on, I'll get you a blanket."

Kyler nodded and took a ragged breath, and then a warm down comforter was draped over her, staving off the chills that were working their way through her body.

"I got you something," Lamont said, and she opened her eyes to regard him. Reaching back behind the stereo, he pulled out two albums and a CD . . . all Meatloaf.

"I told you I'd buy all his albums," he said with a small smile. "These two were at the thrift store on Market, but this one," he indicated the CD, "is too new to be on LP. I'll look for more tomorrow."

Kyler managed a grin and held out her hand. He handed them to her and turned to the stereo. "I thought I dreamed telling you that."

"No, you really told me," he hit the power and switched to phono. "Got one in particular you want to listen to?"

She handed him *Bat Out of Hell*, reading the back of the album cover. "Were they hard to find?"

He shrugged as he put the record on the turntable, gently dropping the needle on it. "No harder than any other. Different stores have different ones. It's just all a matter of looking in the right place."

The music poured out of the speakers, dropping her slowly into relaxation. As always, it seemed to run through her as smooth and cool as the ocean easing up on a beach. Closing her eyes, Kyler laid her cheek against the soft leather of the couch, allowing herself to relish in this rare moment of pure peace.

"Thanks, Doc," she murmured, slitting one eye to look at him. He stared back, trying to read her gaze.

"You're welcome, kid," he said, and then watched as she shook her head slightly, sending a lone tear sliding down her face. She absently wiped it off, shifting her eyes away.

"I'm gonna fix some coffee," he said quietly. "You want some?"

Kyler thought about it and then shook her head. "No, thanks. My stomach ain't too good right now."

He nodded. "Ok. I'll be right back."

She was left alone in the basement as he climbed back up the stairs, listening to the gruff voice of Meatloaf, willing it to wash away all the fear and hatred that surrounded her.

She heard the stairs creak as Lamont came back down, and also the crackle of a paper bag. Looking at him, Kyler saw he held a small white sack; the kind that came from a pharmacy.

"Sure you don't want any coffee?"

"Yeah, I'm sure," she muttered.

He grunted and sat down in the chair across from the couch. "You ok?"

"I will be, I guess," she sighed. "Can't expect to feel topnotch only a day after just about being cut in half."

"True," he responded. He waited a beat and then asked quietly, "Can I ask you something?" She heard the hesitation in his voice and her stomach clenched up even more.

"Yeah."

He leaned forward and met her eyes. "If you were able to, would you get up right now and go find your dealer to try to get something for the pain?"

Jesus, it's like he's reading my fucking mind.

Kyler gazed at him. "Probably. But only because it's all I've ever done."

"Even though you're an addict?"

She considered, trying to gather the right words. "I'm a *heroin* addict, Doc. That doesn't mean I'm gonna go chasing every other drug on the planet trying to get high."

As soon as the words were out of her mouth, the weight of the falsehood crashed down on her. It was probably the biggest lie she'd ever told anyone, and the fact that she was lying here, telling it to the doc with a straight face, cut through her like a knife to the heart.

Fuck, her mind moaned. *I think I just opened up something I shouldn't have.*

Lamont's eyes on hers were sharp and measuring, gauging the depth of the truth.

Kyler sighed and struggled to sit up, despite the lightening bolt of pain that slashed across her.

"Shit, kid, lay still," he started to get up, but she waved him back.

"Listen, Doc," she managed, "I chased heroin all day, everyday. It was all I thought about. Painkillers were a form of variety, sure, but I didn't need them like I did the smack. They were secondary."

She pulled the blanket tight around her, her eyes hard and blazing on his. "You coulda showed me every pill in the world, and then showed me just one needle full of heroin and I'd take the smack in a heartbeat, every time.

"Would I go now and try to get something if I could? Shit, yeah, I would, but only because I'm in so much fucking pain." She clenched her teeth against the heated torture inside her belly, but her eyes were clear and rational as they glared into his.

He gazed back at her and asked directly, "Would you go even if I asked you not to?"

The question was so unexpected that her eyebrows shot up in confusion and indecision.

"If I said next time you probably wouldn't be so lucky and you actually *might* get killed?"

Kyler stared at him for a long moment and then reached carefully into her pocket, pulling out her battered pack of smokes. Lamont waited patiently as she lit one with a badly shaking hand, and then exhaled a long stream of smoke.

She thought her response over carefully, and he let her take her time, needing a completely honest answer out of her, even if it wasn't the one he wanted.

"I . . . don't know. Honestly, Doc. I mean, knowing me I'd have to say yeah, I'd still go. But . . . but if it was *you* that asked me not to . . ." she shrugged, looking halfway ashamed. "I really don't know."

Her brow furrowed as she looked at him. "Why?"

Lamont gave a slow shake of his head, and then got up and walked over to her, handing her the bag. "I don't want to be an enabler, Kyler. I'm a pretty easygoing guy, and I'll do just about anything you ask me to, but not if it's illegal or if I'm enabling your addiction."

She stared at him for a long minute, then carefully peeked in the bag. It contained two bottles and she pulled both of them out, reading the labels. One was the Keflex, and the other was Percocet.

Instantly the rat that lived in her skull, feeding off her addictions, came alive. She fought back an insane urge to rip off the top and pour half a dozen down her throat, suddenly needing the painkiller for more than just the physical pain. And actually, the jagged rip in her stomach had pretty much taken a back seat in light of the drug—*an actual, honest-to-God* **drug**—that she now held in her hand.

I don't want to be an enabler, his words came back to her, and Kyler, swallowing heavily, gazed at the doc.

"I'm in a lot of pain," she muttered, and feverishly hoped he couldn't read her need in her eyes.

"I know," he responded quietly. "Which is why I had them fill that for you. But don't let me be the one to send you running back out there, kid."

"You won't be," she promised, and popped the top, pouring one into the palm of her hand. She held it up to him and then swallowed it easily, already anticipating whatever high it could give her.

"I'm not gonna keep track of 'em, Kyler," Lamont sighed. "But just know that . . . I had to think long and hard about this, and . . . I still have some reservations."

Kyler dropped her eyes, shame washing over her. "You keep them," she held out the bottle. "Just give me one when I need it, and then I won't be tempted and you won't have to feel guilty."

He gazed at her, making no move to take it. "*Would* you feel tempted?"

"No," she answered immediately, and there again was another fucking blatant lie.

Shit, she thought, somewhat wearily, *didn't take long for the lies to start coming again once I had access to more drugs.*

The shame turned into contempt for her selfish weakness, and Kyler found herself torn between an unfamiliar but strong loyalty to Lamont, and her own old easy and understandable way of life.

Her eyes were conflicting with various emotions when she finally looked back at him, and Lamont felt that squeeze on his heart again.

"I just . . ." she started, but he held up his hand and got up, gently taking the bottle from her.

"It's ok, Kyler," he said softly. "They're here when you need them, ok?"

Kyler nodded and the pain of giving up the pills almost paralleled her real pain deep in her abdomen . . . making her realize she'd done the right thing. The Percocet might not have been the heroin with its unique way of hitting that certain spot at the base of her skull, but it had a high of its own it could give her. And knowing that was enough to send her in a rare panic, both because she wanted it so fucking much and also because chasing that dragon again—or *any* dragon—was the one thing that she hated more than anything right now . . . including Lewis.

"Thanks," she murmured, lying back down. The pills were gone now, allowing her to focus back on her shredded belly, and the pain that had jumped back to the front of the line again. She wondered how long it would take the Percocet to kick in . . . and how long it would be before she had to swallow her pride and ask Lamont for another.

Neither spoke for quite some time as Meatloaf, with his emotionally realistic lyrics, poured from the speakers, filling the air around them. Kyler finally began to feel numbness first at that spot at the base of her skull, and then slowly throughout her body. The rat was satisfied for the moment, and she was able to sink down inside herself, away from it all.

Lamont drank the last of his coffee and stood up, watching her. Her heavy eyes slit open, regarding him.

"I'm going to bed," he said quietly. "You gonna be ok down here or do you want me to help you back up?"

"I'll be ok," she answered. "Percocet's kicking in."

"I can tell," he grabbed the afghan off the back of a rocking chair and draped it over top of the comforter. "It's gets kinda cold down here, so I'm gonna leave this on the table, ok?" Holding up his cell phone, he made sure she saw it as he dropped it beside the ashtray. "Call the home phone if you wanna come back up. I'll have it right by my bed. Don't be a hero and try to climb the stairs by yourself."

"I won't," her eyes slipped closed again, and then struggled back open. "Hey, Doc?"

"Yeah?" He looked back at her.

The Percocet was weaving its slow, steady way through her body, and the world was as comfortably numb around her as she was within it. The words were out before she knew they were coming, and if the pill hadn't kicked in one last little notch right then, Kyler would have felt the shame and humiliation all over again.

"He was tryin' to fuck me with that piece of glass," she gestured towards her lower belly. "Which is why I'm all cut up."

Lamont stared at her, horror and rage making an uneasy mixture in his clenched stomach. He walked back over to her and put a cool hand on her forehead.

"It's ok, now, kid," he said softly. "He's in jail and you're safe here, I promise."

"I know," she sighed, giving up the fight to stay awake. One lone tear slipped out from beneath a closed eyelid, leaving a trail down her cheek.

Jaw tight with rage, Lamont turned and headed up the stairs.

CHAPTER 41

THE CRY WAS what woke him, coming up through the vent. A kind of whimper that was just loud enough to pull him from sleep, sending a spike of raw emotion through his heart and enhancing that protective sentiment he'd come to feel for her.

Shit, he thought, throwing back the covers. Making his way downstairs, he found her curled up in a ball on the couch, covers thrown back, shaking and breathing heavily. She was awake and her fear-filled eyes bored into his as he came around the corner.

"Sorry," Kyler croaked. "I didn't mean to wake you."

"It's ok," he crouched by the couch, surprised when she reached for him. Gently he wrapped his arms around her, feeling the trembling in her body. "Bad dream?"

"Yeah."

Lamont held her in silence for a long time and then carefully pulled away. "It's cold down here. You want me to help you back up?"

Looking around the darkened room, Kyler felt the shadows moving in on her. The nightmare, in all its stark reality, had followed her back to wakening, and Lewis's demented eyes were all around her.

"Yeah, if you don't mind."

"C'mon,"

He slid his arms around her and eased her gently off the couch. Kyler shut her eyes briefly and clenched her teeth together against the pain blasting across her mutilated stomach.

"Almost there," Lamont murmured as they reached the living room landing. He felt the sweat again as it seeped through her shirt, and had to wonder how she was even holding on through the pain.

Something like this, he thought, *should have kept her in bed at least a week.*

At last they were in the spare bedroom and she slid gratefully down on the bed, shaking. Lamont pulled the covers over her as she burrowed her face in the pillow, still trying to dispel the horrible images of her nightmare.

The pain in her belly pounded out an erratic rhythm with her heartbeat, and Kyler focused on that as the lesser of the two evils. Still, though, in the back of her mind, Lewis had succeeded in penetrating her with the shard of glass, and was happily shredding her internal organs as he played this insane sexual game on her.

She laid in the bed with Lamont's soothing presence beside her, and remembered the raw fear she'd felt, along with the surety that she'd be dead by the time he got around to actually placating his own sexual desires on her.

Lamont stared down at her, wondering what kind of strength and knowledge he possessed in his own currently rattled mind to help lead her through this. The tears slipped again from beneath her closed lids, and he crouched down beside her with a hand gently on her shoulder.

Kyler gave a ragged breath and looked at him, lost in her own tortured fear. "Jesus, I wish this shit would just stop," she said softly.

"It will, kid," he responded quietly. "Just hold on, ok?"

Her eyes slipped closed again and she curled up into as much of a ball as her stitched and padded stomach would allow. "What time is it?" She mumbled.

"Just after two."

"Shit," she sighed. "I'm sorry I woke you up."

"That's all right." He hesitated, and then asked reluctantly, "You want another Percocet?"

Kyler was silent for a long time, and then, swallowing heavily, gave a slow nod. She felt him leave and gave a soft growl, hating herself more than ever, but still not able to ignore the raging need within her. Facing the truth, she realized that if he'd leave the whole bottle with her, it might be significantly diminished by the time the sun rose . . . if not completely empty.

Lamont came back and she watched as he handed her one pill. The bottle was nowhere in sight, and she gave an internal sigh of relief even as that psychotic part of her screamed in frustration.

Swallowing it down, she silently instructed her ravaged stomach to break it down quick, needing the numbing relief it would bring.

"I called John and told him what happened," Lamont said. "He said to give you as much time as you need, ok? No rush to get back to work."

Kyler grimaced. "He's gonna fire me before I can even draw my first paycheck."

"No, he won't."

She took a deep, haggard breath and let it out slowly. "I'm tryin, Doc. I really am."

He looked at her surprised. "Hey . . . Kyler, don't worry, I know you are. None of this shit was your fault."

She looked at him, and he saw the depth of her despair and helplessness in her eyes. "I shoulda come here instead of chasing valium. Six fucking months of rehab and I swear I'm only reverting back to my old idiotic ways instead of going forward."

"Kyler," he sighed, "nobody's asking you to just forget about all you've been through and go on like it never happened. I know you can't do that, just like I know that you're probably gonna always think about getting high. The thing is . . ." he stopped, thinking. "The thing is to learn from it, and take everything—the good and the bad—of using to help keep you clean."

There was silence for a couple long minutes. Kyler gratefully began to feel the first few numbing tendrils of the Percocet working, and silently wished for the full, head-on effect to hurry up and overtake her.

"How do you know all that?" She asked.

"Narcotics Anonymous," he responded. "I went to some meetings with Emily awhile back. I went to support her and her son, but I ended up learning a few things myself." He waited a beat and then said quietly, "Are you still going to meetings?"

"Yeah," she said. "I have to, you know that. I mean, I guess I have to. Nobody told me different, and I'm still getting those papers that need to be signed."

Lamont was quiet, watching her. The painkiller was starting to work, he could tell, and it wouldn't be too much longer before she would fall into the sleep her body desperately needed.

"Just keep going," he muttered softly. "Ok? Trust me, kid, it *does* help."

The doubt he saw in her eyes was massive and deep, but she offered a tired nod.

For you, she thought wearily. *I'll go for you and your faith in it but, Jesus, Doc, if you could only see what I see there.*

"I'll keep going," she said, her voice fading as her eyes slipped closed. "Just tell John not to fire me, yet. I'll be back at work as soon as I can."

"No hurry," he said, somewhat sternly. "Those were his words, Kyler, but I'm adding to them. It ain't gonna be a good thing if you rip open your stitches."

"I know," she said. "I'll try not to."

She was fading fast, he saw. Quietly he stood up and left the room, shutting the door partway behind him. Crawling back in his own bed, Lamont felt the weariness coursing through his body, but it was a long time before he was able to sleep again.

CHAPTER 42

FOUR DAYS LATER, Kyler was sitting out on Lamont's deck, smoking a cigarette and watching the waves crash on the shore. Her abdomen was a little better, though not as much as it should have been. All her running around, climbing stairs and yes, even sneaking off to work, slowed the healing process quite a bit.

Lamont was doing a good job of taking care of her, but he had to go to work as well, and that's when she got restless. The park alleviated some of that restlessness, even though she couldn't do much more than enter the inventory invoices into the computer. Just being there helped lift her spirits in ways that any amount of physical healing couldn't.

The itching in her lower belly told her that it was healing, but sometimes it was almost enough to drive her crazy. On this day, with boredom and restlessness competing for the primary emotion inside her, and with the constant aggravating itch always there to demand her attention, Kyler was slowly counting upwards, relying on her steel will and long patience to slowly work her way though, second by second.

"Christ," a familiar voice came floating over the railing of the deck at her, "your doctor says you're getting better, but you look like hell to me."

Grinning, she looked through the wooden slats at Jimmy and Barb, standing on the edge of the driveway. Barb was holding a small bundle that could only be Bailey, wrapped in blankets. Between them was a wheelchair.

"Shoulda seen me a week ago," struggling to stand, Kyler looked at them.

Barb's sharp eyes stared into hers. "He said you about got cut in half. That true?"

Kyler pitched her cigarette over the railing and gave a half-shrug. "I guess. It wasn't pretty."

Jimmy's eyes were hard as he walked around to her. He gave her a very careful hug and then stepped back, looking at her abdomen. "I'll kill him, Kyler, if I ever see him."

"He's in jail now," she responded. "On attempted rape and murder. He'll get his justice, Jim." She looked over at Barb, looking back at her. In her friend's eyes she could still read the betrayal she felt over her and Jimmy relapsing, but above it was a deep concern, and the empathy she felt for a fellow streetwalker junkie.

"Can we see it?" Barb asked quietly, walking over beside Jimmy. "Or would you rather we didn't?"

Kyler hesitated, glancing at Jimmy. Her friend, true, but still one with the ability and hormonal instinct to be like every other guy.

"Hey," he said quietly, reading her eyes, "that's ok, Kyler. I don't have to see it. Barb's the one with the morbid sense of interest."

"No," she shook her head and unbuckled her belt. "That's all right. Can't really see much anyway 'cause it's still got a patch over it. But I've been sneaking peaks so I could get an idea . . ." she peeled back the front of her jeans to reveal a large piece of gauze that covered her entire abdomen. With slightly shaking hands, she lifted up one side, and, wincing from the pull of the tape, slowly pulled away the patch.

"Oh, God," Barb muttered. The wound, criss-crossed with heavy black stitches was raw and a deep red. Dried blood was flaked around the random edges, giving the whole thing the look of a gruesome, Frankenstein-ish, week-old murder scene.

"Kyler, I swear to God if I ever see him . . ." Jimmy started in a hoarse voice, but she cut in.

"You won't do a thing, Jim." Slowly sticking the patch back over it, Kyler felt the familiar churning of her stomach; the image of her shredded belly making her halfway sick. "You got Barb and Bailey. Don't blow it on something stupid." Buttoning up her jeans, she looked into Barb's shocked eyes.

"Can I hold her?"

"Absolutely," she handed over the sleeping baby, feeling sick herself over the ragged wound. Jimmy felt her lean against him and he wrapped his arm around her, both of them stunned and trying not to show it.

Kyler slowly sat back down on the steps, cradling little Bailey to her chest. The baby's blue eyes opened and looked at her, and once again she felt her heart melt.

I'd kill for this kid, the thought was random but she recognized the hard-core truth in it.

"What're you guys doing here?" She looked up at them.

"Well," Barb sat down on the step below her, "we got an apartment, me and Jim. I convinced my PO and the court that with Bailey, I needed somewhere where I could have the space I needed to care for her. I got put in this program that helps with financial assistance and job training, and Jimmy's goin' to work for his cousin in the stockyards."

"And the only way I could come was if I got into an outpatient program down here that would help me finish my treatment," Jimmy added. "We just got here yesterday."

"How'd you find me?" Kyler asked, staring at Bailey staring back at her.

"I called your doctor," Barb said. "And then he said he was just getting ready to take a lunch break if we wanted to come join him. So we did and that's when he told us what happened to you and told us how to get here."

Doc willingly gave out his address to these people, she thought, *based only on the fact that they're friends of mine.* Putting that much faith in something was a concept that was foreign to her, but slowly Lamont was teaching her to how to do it.

"He said you should be here, but if not you'd probably be at the park." Barb met her eyes. "He hoped you'd be *here* because you're too tore up to be going anywhere. I can completely agree with him now."

"Yeah," Kyler nodded. "Me, too. But I get restless sometimes, and being at the park helps it."

There was only the sound of the ocean for a minute, and then Jimmy said quietly, "Well, we kinda thought you'd wanna help us move."

Kyler offered a wry grin. "I'll do what I can," she made to stand up, and as one both Barb and Jimmy moved forward, with Barb taking Bailey and Jimmy easing her up with an arm around her waist.

"Thanks," she muttered.

"Yeah," he said, and then gestured towards the wheelchair. "No physical help from you, but would you mind watching Bailey?"

Kyler grinned as she limped slowly towards the chair. "Not at all. But just so you know, any other time I'd be lifting that heavy shit with you. I hate being halfway helpless like this."

"Yeah, yeah," Barb handed her the baby as Jimmy slowly pushed her back around front. "Still fucking stubborn, I see."

"Always," Kyler responded. "Where'd you get the chair?"

"Your doc. He told us you'd probably rip open the stitches if you tried to walk."

"Good ol' Doc," she murmured. "Thinkin' ahead. Where we goin', anyway?"

"It's over on Fontaine, just right around the corner from your skate park."

"Yeah, I know where it's at. There's only one apartment building on that street, isn't there?"

"Yep," Jimmy said from behind her. "Nice little place, good neighborhood."

Kyler looked down as Bailey stretched a little arm up, yawning. The child in her arms soothed the restless ache that was so much a part of her, and she was reminded of simpler times in her life. When the world consisted of nothing but Josh and Ryan and the ocean and miles of asphalt she could skate.

This kid should know times like those, she thought, and vowed with all the inner strength she had that she would help her friends give this baby just that.

"What all you got to move?" She asked.

"Not much, really," Barb admitted. "But his cousin gave us a TV and a couch, and we managed to get some money for a bed and a crib. Right now it's all in storage at that place right across the street from our apartment, so at least we don't have to move it far."

Kyler nodded and settled back in the chair. Jimmy pushed her easily with Barb beside him as they walked the six blocks to their new home. She was happy for them, that they'd pulled themselves together this much, and that they would be close to her. With the thought of safety in numbers, she figured that if things got too bad, her friends could hopefully pull her back before she stepped over that fatal edge.

Jimmy stopped in front of the small apartment building and offered her a hand as she eased out of the chair. "No elevator, but if you let me help you, it shouldn't be that bad. It's up top, third floor, but the flights are only about six steps each."

Kyler threw an arm across his back and gripped his shoulder as they started up the two porch steps. "No elevator's cool with me. I hate those things."

With Barb behind them cradling Bailey and dragging the wheelchair, they slowly made their way up the stairs. It wasn't really all that bad, but Kyler was sweat-soaked and pale by the time they stood outside the apartment door. The strain on her stitches had turned the itch to a screaming pain that slashed across her stomach, and she tightened her jaw against the throbbing ache.

"You ok?" Barb stared at her. "Didn't tear your stitches, did you?"

"Nah," Kyler managed a sarcastic grin, not knowing if she did or not. "Just the usual pain."

Jimmy unlocked the door and motioned Kyler in ahead of him. Barb followed with Bailey while he grabbed the wheelchair. Standing in the bare living room, Kyler's eyes roamed the place, empty yet of furniture, but still so full of dreams to come. She nodded approval and took the bundled baby when Barb handed her to her.

"Not bad, guys. Movin' up in the world." She paused and lifted her shoulder in a half-shrug. "Wish I had a house-warming gift for ya."

Jimmy slung an arm around her shoulders and offered a wry grin. "Just stay alive, ok?" His voice was amicable, but his eyes were hard as they stared into hers, and Kyler could read the unspoken message.

I'll kill him, Kyler. I swear to God.

Before she could open her mouth to snap a protest, he glanced at Barb. "Think you girls can behave yourself? I'm gonna go on down and start pulling things out."

She nodded. "Yeah, babe. I'll be right behind you. I'm gonna change her first and get 'em settled." She glanced at Kyler. "Your doctor says you ain't been sleeping good, and it shows. You wanna crash here for a little bit, you're more than welcome. We already got the bed up back there," she jerked a thumb over her shoulder.

Kyler shrugged. "Maybe. I don't know." She watched as Jimmy shut the door behind him and pulled her smokes from her pocket. "Kinda feel bad sleeping in your guys' place while you're workin' to move in it."

"Please," Barb shot her a sarcastic look. "We won't work that hard, trust me." She spread a blanket on the floor and pulled a clean diaper from the bag under the window. Kyler sat with her back to the wall, watching as she changed Bailey.

"He got you on anything? Your doctor?" Barb shot her a glance, her voice casual.

She hesitated, using the excuse of lighting a cigarette to pull her words together. "Percocet," she admitted reluctantly. "And Keflex."

Barb grunted, pulling Bailey's dress back down. "Antibiotic and painkillers, huh?"

"Yeah, but I told him to keep the painkillers and just give me one when I ask for it. So far it ain't been a problem."

Gesturing for her pack of cigarettes, Barb's eyes bored into hers. Kyler slid the pack over to her, not looking away.

"So you are taking them, but not many?"

"Yeah. He . . . wasn't sure whether to give 'em to me or not, and to get rid of both our fears, I asked him to stash them for me." Kyler paused, and then said quietly, "I've managed to not ask for that many. Only when the pain's real bad."

"And even then, sometimes you don't ask." It wasn't a question and Kyler didn't comment either way, knowing Barb could see past her wall because she'd been there and done all that.

"No offense, but you look like shit," she commented softly. "I know you're scared, Kyler, but there's gotta be another way. You can't keep living in pain like this."

"It's slowly getting better," she responded quietly. "It ain't gonna last forever."

There was silence for a few minutes. Kyler felt the nicotine riding mellow through her veins and felt her eyes growing heavy. She gave them a brisk, hard rub and took a deep breath and stood up. She gazed out the window, watching as Jimmy and another guy pulled the couch out of the storage unit.

"Who's the other guy down there?"

"His cousin," Barb answered, standing up to look out the window beside her. "Look, the bed's all yours, ok? C'mon, Kyler, I know you're dead on your feet."

She shook her head and offered a tired smile. "Can't. Promised I'd watch Bailey, remember?"

"She's sleeping. Take her in the bed with you; at least try to get a good half hour in."

Kyler glanced towards the back bedroom, hesitating. Exhaustion was pulling at her from all angles, and she knew it showed on her face and in her eyes. At the moment she couldn't think of anything better than to just relax for even a few minutes; to forget about the monstrous pain in her abdomen and to allow the demons to fade back for awhile.

"Go on," Barb gave her a gentle push. "Trust me, you need it."

Kyler looked at her and then gave a slow nod. "All right. But wake me up in a half hour, ok?"

"I will," she smiled and opened the door. "We'll be in and out but I'll try to keep the guys quiet."

Shaking her head, Kyler sighed. "Don't worry about it. You're right; I'm tired. I feel like I could sleep through an earthquake."

Barb gave a slight nod and then stepped out the door. Looking down at the sleeping baby at her feet, Kyler tried to derive some solace from her small body, still breathing, still alive, despite the seizures, half-blindness, and deafness. Gathering her up gently, she walked them both back to the bedroom.

The queen-sized bed was set in the middle of the room, already made. Pulling back the covers, Kyler laid Bailey down and then slid in next to her. The baby's warmth against her side helped to ease the jagged pain in both her stomach and her heart, and with each inhale and exhale of Bailey's small lungs, she felt her eyes grow heavier until she was deep down, letting the darkness swallow her whole.

The same old nightmare had her surrounded, drowning her with its terror and pain. The hatred bored into her with sharp teeth, demanding that she take the piece of glass and shove it into one of Lewis's eyes as far as she could.

Her jeans ripped, giving him free access to her vaginal area, and in a single breath she felt her insides slashed apart by his rough, cruel hand. The blood poured from her as he steadily pushed the shard deeper and deeper into her. Uterus, bladder, intestines . . . organ after organ was shredded until there was nothing left but blood and darkness.

And unbelievably, now Lewis was beginning to rape her with his own engorged penis; driving himself into her harder and harder, both of them covered in blood and gore as she quickly bled to death on the trash-littered alley that was the hub of all her nightmares.

Beside her on the cracked and pitted concrete was a syringe full of pure heroin, and with the last of her strength, Kyler scooped it up off the ground and drove it into her own neck, depressing the plunger with all the hope of the hopeless suicidal street-freak junkie.

Bolting upright in the bed, Kyler tried to gasp in air around the tightness of her throat. Shaking violently, she stared fearfully around the room, not at first sure of where she was. Finally her eyes settled on the small, wrapped bundle in the crib at the foot of the bed. Sliding out from under the covers on weak and trembling legs, she made her way over and gazed down at Bailey's perfect face, eyes closed and mind far away in the sweet dreams that are exclusive for babies and the innocent.

Feeling the sweat snake down her back and sides, Kyler continued to drag in deep breaths, trying to calm her erratically pounding heart. After a few long minutes, she drew away and staggered out into the hallway.

Both Lamont and Barb stared at her as she came into the living room, alarm at her shell-shocked face apparent on their faces.

"Jesus," Barb muttered. "You ok?"

She nodded weakly. "Shaking off these fuckin' nightmares." Scrubbing a hand hard across her face, she asked quietly, "What time's it?"

"Little after eight," Barb answered.

"At night?"

"Yeah," Lamont said softly. "At night." His eyes drilled into hers. "Jesus, kid . . ."

She shook her head and ran her hands through her hair. "What happened to the half hour wake up call?" She asked Barb.

"I lied," she said seriously, giving a small shrug. "I figured you needed your sleep."

Kyler was quiet for a brief second and then turned her eyes towards Lamont. "What're you doin' here, Doc?"

"I called him, Kyler," Barb said. "I thought he might be worried about you."

"Worried, yeah, but not checking up on you," Lamont pitched in. "I know you probably think—"

He cut off as Kyler's dark eyes looked at him. The depth of her exhaustion tore at his heart, and he fought off an urge to walk over and wrap his arms around her.

"Not tonight," she said quietly. "Maybe you were and maybe you weren't, but tonight I don't care. It hurts too much to care about stupid shit like that."

His eyes softened as he saw the pain in her eyes surface just below her fatigue. "All right," he said quietly. "Barb said you can stay here, but I'll give you a ride back to my place if you want."

Kyler glanced at Barb, a somewhat beautiful smile on her otherwise tired face. "Thanks, but I think you and Jimmy should spend this first night in your new place alone. Looks like you got everything moved in all right."

Her eyes roamed the little living room, taking in the couch, coffee table, and few other pieces of furniture. "See you even got the crib up," she gestured back towards the bedroom where Bailey was still fast asleep.

"Yeah. I tried not to wake you up when I put her in it."

"You didn't," she said. She pressed the heels of her hands hard against her eyes. "Wouldn't've bothered me none, though, if you had. I coulda done without that dream."

"I know," Barb said quietly. "I heard you back there." She didn't say exactly what she'd heard, and Kyler didn't want to know anyway. When Barb handed her a pack of cigarettes, her hand was shaking as she shook one out.

"Seriously, though, you can stay. Jimmy's working right now, and he won't be in 'till late."

Kyler looked at her, and then shot Lamont a sidelong glance. "Thanks, Barb, but I might not go back to sleep tonight, and you know . . . bein' near the ocean at his house kinda helps me to . . . not feel like I'm going totally nuts."

Barb nodded, complete understanding in her eyes. "Ok. We should have a phone by next week. I'll give you the number."

Kyler hugged her friend hard and then pulled away. "All right. You know where to find me if you need me."

"That goes both ways," her eyes were serious, staring into hers. "And here," she handed her the pack of cigarettes. "These're yours. I swiped a couple."

Waving an absent hand, Kyler shook her head. "Keep 'em. I can get more."

"Sure?" Barb raised her eyebrows.

"Yeah. I'll see you later, all right?"

Nodding, Barb walked them to the door. Lamont gave her a brief hug before stepping into the hall.

"Take care of that baby," he said with a small smile. "Call if you guys need anything."

"I will," she watched as he slid an arm around Kyler's waist and eased her down the first step. Only after they turned the corner down the next flight and out of her sight did she step back in the apartment, shutting the door behind her.

Kyler gripped Lamont's lower back and gritted her teeth as bolt after bolt of white-hot pain shot across her abdomen. He felt the tightness of her muscles and murmured softly, "Almost there, kid."

She didn't answer as they slowly and carefully made their way down the final flight. In silence he guided her to his car and unlocked the passenger side, lowering her gently down in the seat. When he sat down behind the wheel he glanced at her, slumped down with her eyes closed.

"You ok?"

"I will be, I guess," she muttered.

Her face was pale against the darkness of the night, and after a moment's hesitation he reached into his pocket and pulled out the bottle of Percocet.

"Here," he poured one out and pressed it into her palm. "'Cause I know you're not gonna ask for it."

Although her eyes remained closed, he saw the tightness of her jaw against her own indecision. After barely a moment's pause, she placed the pill in her mouth and swallowed it.

"Thanks."

Lamont grunted and threw the car into drive. "Wanna talk about it?"

Kyler opened her eyes and stared out the window. "'Bout what?"

"That dream you had."

She sighed and turned her head to look at him, shrugging slightly. "Just the same old shit, Doc. Nothin' new."

He glanced at her but remained silent. She leaned her head back and stared at the passing roadside, caught in flashes of light from the passing arc-sodiums. Exhaustion roared through her, but so did a massive fear of sleeping again. It seemed every time was worse than the time before, and without turning from the window she said it.

"It gets worse every time, Doc," her voice was barely audible. "It went from Lewis not being able . . . to get to me 'cause of my jeans to him tearin' 'em off and . . . and then . . . you know . . ." Kyler trailed off, swallowing hard. "Every time. Every time I go to sleep it's the same fucking thing."

Lamont was quiet beside her as he steered through the streets. He waited with experienced patience, but she said nothing more. Finally he pulled into his driveway and shut off the car, letting the silence fall down around them. Kyler reached into her pocket for her pack of cigarettes, forgetting she'd given them to Barb. Coming up empty, she gave a heavy sigh and pushed open the door.

"We can go back out and pick some up," Lamont said from behind her.

"Nah, that's ok," she responded. "I'll get some in the morning."

He pushed open his own door and stepped out of the car, following her into the house.

"Mind if I use your shower?"

"I told you, you don't have to ask," he answered quietly.

Kyler nodded and made her weary way up the stairs. He watched her go and when he heard the faucet turn on he walked into the kitchen and picked up the phone.

After about an hour, when she didn't come back downstairs, Lamont went up to check on her. The door to the spare bedroom was partially shut, and sliding up next to it he heard the sound of her regular breathing, letting him know that she was sleeping.

But who knows for how long? He thought as he turned and headed back downstairs.

CHAPTER 43

LAMONT BOLTED AWAKE in the dead of the night, heart pounding. He glanced towards the hallway, ears straining for any sound that might have woken him up. Hearing nothing, he leaned over and put his ear close to the register, thinking she might have gone back downstairs to listen to the stereo and fallen asleep on the couch.

Nothing from there, either.

Throwing back the covers he got out of bed to go check on her. The moon was full and bright and movement outside caught his eye. He leaned close to the window, staring intently at the object out in the water, and in a panicky instant he recognized Kyler. She was standing waist deep, swaying as the waves crashed around her, staring out towards the horizon, invisible now in the darkness of water against the darkness of sky.

Not even bothering to put on a shirt, Lamont raced downstairs and out the back door, barely pausing as the breathtakingly cold water engulfed him.

"Kyler," he said sharply, getting nearer to her and completely prepared to grab her if she decided to dive under.

But the closer he got the more he could see she barely had the strength to stand against the pulling waves, let alone aggressively meet the ocean head-on. At the sound of his voice, her head dropped as if the weight she was carrying was suddenly too heavy to hold any longer.

"Easy," he pulled her into his arms, feeling the tightness of her body. She was shaking from a chill that he knew went much deeper than the cold wind blowing across her wet skin. He felt the violence of her tremors deep within his own bones as he held her.

"Tell me I'm not goin' crazy, Doc," Kyler's voice was low, nearly muffled against the pounding of the surf.

"You're not going crazy," he responded firmly, almost angrily, and Kyler appreciated that. It told her that at least *he* still believed she was somewhat halfway sane.

"C'mon," she felt his arm around her waist press gently against her, guiding her back to the beach. "Before you catch pneumonia."

Lamont led her onto the steps of his deck where he left her to rest for a minute while he ran inside and grabbed a towel. Wrapping it around her shoulders, he sat beside her in silence.

Kyler continued to shiver violently, her eyes on the never-ending waves. Her face was drawn and haggard in the moonlight, bearing the weight of too many undead demons.

"There's a song for every mood, kid," he said softly. "You're never alone in anything you do because at least one person has been through it, too . . . the songwriter.

"Find the song, Kyler, and it'll help you get through this."

She didn't answer, but her eyes staring into his said she couldn't quite dare hope.

"Just gotta keep the faith," he said, gazing back. "And just keep on holding on."

"I know," she sighed. She was quiet for a moment and then murmured, "I just wish I could skate right now. I could get it all out of my system if I could get back on my board." She dropped her head, muttering, "At least I hope I could."

Lamont remained silent for a few minutes beside her. Finally he looked at her, eyebrows raised. "Want some coffee?"

"It's late," she answered. "Don't you need some sleep?"

"I'll be all right," he replied. "And I can probably use some."

Kyler shot him a brief glance before staring out at the ocean again. Giving a slow nod, she grasped the rail and pulled herself shakily to her feet.

"All right," she agreed. "I can use some, too."

Lamont stood up with her and helped her into the house. "You wanna take a hot bath while I'm brewing this?" He asked, pulling the coffee out of the fridge.

"Nah, I'm ok," Kyler sat down at the table, pulling the towel tighter around her still-shivering body.

He nodded and filled the carafe with water. "Up in that cabinet by the microwave are the Percocets," he kept his back to her, not turning around.

Behind him Kyler felt her heart speed up. The dream she'd just had had been the worst of all, and the fear it instilled had driven her nearly to the brink of insanity. The thought of drugs—*any drugs*—in her system once more brought her a step back from that brink, giving her something to hold onto even as the shame filled her.

But the need for relief quickly overcame the shame, and with her mind filling with anticipation, she stood on shaky legs and walked across the kitchen.

Lamont heard her open the cabinet and briefly closed his eyes, wondering if he'd done the right thing.

"Hide 'em again, will you?" Kyler's voice was soft. "I don't need to know where they're at."

"Yeah," he said quietly, turning to look at her. She quickly popped the three she'd taken from the bottle, feeling the familiar mixture of self-loathing, shame, and impending relief. Scrubbing a hand hard across her face, she shifted her eyes away and walked back over to the table.

Wordlessly he set a cup of coffee down in front of her and she wrapped her hands around it, relishing the warmth. Lamont watched her, his brow furrowed.

"It ain't gettin' no better," he muttered. "Right?"

She looked at him but didn't answer.

"You remember a while back when I said that maybe talking to someone might help?"

"Yeah." Her eyes were hard staring into his, but there was no anger in her voice.

"Wanna give it a try?"

Kyler stared at him, trying to feel angry and only feeling scared and tired.

"It's just an outpatient program, Kyler, and completely anonymous. Nobody'll know what you guys talk about. Including me."

She was silent, thinking. Each time she tried to sleep she felt the shifting of her mental stability and the blurring of the edges of her sanity. This was already way past way too much, and it was tearing her apart and eating her alive. In the back of her mind she knew it was past due, and the only part of her that needed convincing was her pride.

But that would be a difficult task, she knew.

"I . . . I don't know, Doc."

Lamont gazed at her, surprised there was no vehement anger this time, and that gave him hope.

"You don't have to answer right now, kid," he said. "I just thought I'd offer you that option again. I think . . . I think this time you might need it even more."

She stared out the window for a long time, reluctantly admitting to herself that the doc was right. This shit was just getting to be too much.

"I'll think about it."

He gave a slight nod and got up to pour another cup of coffee. "I'm gonna run upstairs and change out of these wet clothes. Want me to grab you some?"

Kyler was still thinking about talking to somebody, wondering if she had it in her to let down her defenses long enough to do so, and still feeling so much of that street-bred instinct that had to wonder if shit like that even worked. She gave an absent nod at his question and reached for the pack of cigarettes that wasn't there.

"Shit," she muttered, glancing at him. "How much do they cost?"

"How much do what cost?"

"The, uh . . . sessions? With the . . . therapist."

Lamont gave a slow shake of his head from the doorway. "Nothin' with your insurance. Well, that and the rehab deal you got. If it'll help you stay clean, the state'll probably foot the bill."

"And . . . if it doesn't?" She looked at him.

He offered a slight smile. "It will, Kyler. Don't let that sway your decision, ok?"

Without waiting for an answer he slipped out of the kitchen and up the stairs. Kyler reached again for her cigarettes and gave an aggravated growl, her jaw tight. Taking a deep breath, she tried to focus beyond that, to think about how talking to a complete stranger would help her not feel utterly terrified every time she tried to sleep.

"Here," Lamont stepped back into the room with his dirty clothes in one hand and some clean clothes for her the other.

"Thanks," she muttered. Reaching behind her she grasped the top of her soaked T-shirt and pulled it over her head. Her eyes met the doc's and she stared deep into them, reading his emotions and thoughts as if they were printed in a book.

She'd seen the various degrees of hunger—whether raging, insane, or desperate—in many pairs of eyes, both male and female, as they looked into hers and tried to stare her down . . . or at least into submission. But there was none of that in Lamont's eyes; just shock and nothing more. Not even pity and she admired him for that. Kyler knew it was hard for someone to look at her naked body and not feel pity.

But Lamont just gazed at her with the shock in his eyes and deep down she felt the wall she'd built up start to weaken.

In his own heart he was again wondering how she could still be alive, having gone through the wars and come out battered and as massively scarred as she was. As if reading his mind, Kyler let the baggy shirt drop down over her skinny torso and stared at him.

"They don't hurt, and most of 'em I don't even remember."

He was quiet for a long moment and then said softly, "So I guess this means you trust me?"

Kyler gazed at him, hesitating. "As much as I can. I figured if you were gonna try anything it woulda been that night this . . ." she gestured at her abdomen, "happened."

"You were bleeding everywhere, kid," he said gruffly. "That would made me pretty fucking sick, don't you think?"

She shrugged as if to say that was irrelevant. "Lotta sick fuckers out there, Doc."

He stared at her for a moment and then gave a slight nod. He waited while she changed into the sweat pants, gingerly letting the loose waistband rest gently against the gauze pad across her abdomen.

Reaching for her wet clothes, he said quietly, "I'm gonna throw these in the washer. Wanna come down and listen to the stereo? See if you can find that song?"

Feeling the comfort of the warm, dry clothes and the Percocets starting to work through her, Kyler nodded. She took the wet stuff from him and he kept the dry ones, slipping an arm around her waist to help her down the stairs. The act was familiar enough to him by now that he was no longer thrown into shock by the protrusion of her bones, but the image of her emaciated and scarred body stayed in his mind.

Easing her down on the couch, he went into the laundry room and started the washer. Kyler gazed at the extensive collection of albums, CDs and cassettes, wondering where the song might be that would alleviate the pain she had digging into her.

Lamont came back out and stood in the doorway, watching her. His own mind wandered over his collection, reaching out here and there for the artist that would sing the song. Finally his brain settled on it.

"I got it," he murmured. "Hang on, that one's not in there." He went back up the stairs and Kyler leaned back against the couch, feeling the soaked pad across her stomach.

"Fuck," she muttered. "I need to change this." She pulled herself painfully to her feet, now feeling her heartbeat deep within her belly, in the core of the ragged wound. She was at the bottom of the steps when he appeared at the top.

"What's up?" He asked, stopping her before she could come up.

"Lookin' for that," she grimaced from the pain, pointing at the gauze pad and surgical tape he held along with a CD.

"Yeah," Lamont gently guided her back to the couch. "I know. The one you got on is soaked and that ain't good for the wound."

She waited as he turned on the stereo and put in the CD. "Who is it?"

Lamont adjusted the balance of the speakers as the first few notes began to emanate around the room. "Keith Whitley. Country singer. Emily always said my taste in music is as diversified as this city, and she's right, I guess." He paused and looked over the collection. "I really need to organize all this. I got Roy Clark's Christmas next to Zeppelin, and Creedence alongside Tammy Wynette. It's hard to find a song that pinpoints a mood when this shit is all mixed up, you know?"

And Kyler, who had no idea who Roy Clark or Tammy Wynette were, but had heard of Led Zeppelin and CCR, just gave a slow nod. Lamont saw the confusion on her face and offered a small smile.

"You listen to every one of these and you'll see the difference. Every piece of music I own is good, but it's hard to focus on the theme of a song if it's followed by a completely different genre."

She arched an eyebrow, still confused and not knowing what the word "genre" meant, but getting the meaning anyway. From the sound of the music coming out of the speakers, slow and mellow, with a somewhat painful country twang, she could already hear the difference from the Meatloaf and Skynyrd she was accustomed to.

Lamont handed her the gauze pad and the tape. "I'm not gonna press my luck and ask you to trust me more than you can, ok?" His eyes were serious now, staring hard into hers. "That's a . . . sensitive area . . . and I'll help you if you want me to, but . . ."

"That's ok, Doc," Kyler replied. "I can do it." Yeah, she trusted him, but still the thought of him taping another piece of gauze across her lower stomach was almost more than she could handle. It was too close for comfort and she didn't want to feel that fear again.

He nodded as if that was what he expected. "Ok. You can use the bathroom," he pointed to a half-bath by the stairs. "I'll be here if you need me."

Pushing off the couch, Kyler slipped by him and went in the bathroom, shutting the door behind her. The pain was steadily increasing and she knew it was only because the wound was wet. Once the dry pad was on it, it would ease up some and the Percocets would swamp over what was left of the throbbing.

Looking forward to the calming relief of the drugs, she dropped her sweatpants and stood before the mirror, staring at her body from the waist down. It was still covered in bruises, now fading to yellow, and she closed her eyes, feeling the terror all over again.

Gritting her teeth and clenching her jaw tight, she slowly removed the old bandage. Even as wet as it was, it still clung to the wound in places, making her want to scream as it pulled not only on her skin but on the flesh beneath it. Tears leaked from her eyes and she was glad Lamont wasn't there to see her like that.

In a final, harsh gesture, she yanked it all the way off, swaying on her feet as the pain notched up even higher.

"Christ," she whispered hoarsely and tossed the soiled pad in the trash without even looking at it. With her stomach roiling, she managed to survey her abdomen, noting the slowness of the time it was taking to heal. Luckily, though, it didn't seem to be quite as infected as it was just a day before, and she put a little bit more faith in the Keflex.

With trembling hands she laid the fresh piece of gauze over her stomach and ripped off tape with her teeth, taping it securely to her skin. When she was finished, she pulled her sweats back up and collapsed on the closed toilet, wondering if she was going to throw up.

"Kyler?" Lamont's voice was hesitant through the door. "You ok?"

"Yeah," she muttered. "It just . . . you know . . ." her stomach turned over and she swallowed back bile.

"Can I come in?"

"Yeah."

He opened the door and saw her sitting on the toilet with her head in her hands, elbows on her knees. The sweat was again rolling across skin covered in goose bumps, and he squatted down next to her, staring into her eyes.

"I'm all right," she said shakily. "I just felt sick there for a minute. It . . . it kinda turned my stomach, lookin' at it."

"I know," he said quietly. "Give it time; it'll heal."

"Yeah," she sighed and forced herself to her feet. Without the soaked gauze lying heavily on her torn stomach, the pain had almost entirely abated. Now the Percocets were kicking in again with a vengeance, and she anticipated the relief it would bring.

"C'mon, lemme help you back upstairs," he said. "Or would you rather sleep down here?'

"I don't wanna *sleep* anywhere, Doc," she said honestly. "But, yeah, I'll stay down here."

He didn't reply as he led her back to the couch. She lay down gratefully, wrapping the blanket tight around her trembling body. Lamont watched her for a minute, contemplating. He adjusted the volume as the current song grew louder, and then said quietly, "I'll be right back, ok?"

"Yeah," she murmured, laying loosely on her side to prevent pressure or stretching on her torn stomach. The music surrounded her smoothly and she let it, needing the release of the pain and fear.

Lamont went back upstairs to his office, relying on both his profession and his heart to guide him in his decision. He took a deep breath and pulled his personal prescription pad out of the drawer above the kneehole in his desk.

Kyler was listening to the pain-filled song drifting from the stereo, wondering how the hell somebody could sing with so much exhaustion and desperation and still manage to not put a gun to their head. Then she wondered how this song could drive a stake right through her heart, echoing her own pain to the exact shade, like she had written it herself in her lowest and most desperate times.

Finally, the question crossed her mind of how Lamont knew the song she needed was on this CD. Did he know it would be this song, or was this just a really good guess?

She figured it didn't matter. Nothing mattered except the raw and utter pain she heard in this man's voice. It cut her deeply, completely overriding her own physical pain.

"Hey," Lamont's voice came from the direction of the stairs. "Still ok?"

"Sometimes it's the singer, too, Doc," she mumbled. "You know, the one that sings about the pain I feel."

He paused next to her and cocked an ear towards the stereo. "Yeah," he said slowly. "This one always got me right here," he tapped his chest. "You can hear it in his voice."

She nodded. "Who's he singing about?"

"Lori Morgan, his wife. She was the only one who kept him hanging on."

"He's dead?" Kyler glanced at him.

"Yeah," he replied, somewhat gently. "OD'd on booze and pills."

There was silence for a few long minutes as she soaked in his words. Finally she said quietly, "That doesn't surprise me. He's in a lot of pain."

Lamont didn't answer as he sat on the edge of the couch in front of her. Kyler scooted back to give him more room as the song ended and went onto the next one. He dropped his eyes to the piece of paper he held in his hand and then shot her a glance.

"Just because *he* died doesn't mean *you* have to give up the fight," he said brusquely. "Ok?"

Kyler met his hard eyes and didn't answer.

"Kyler . . ."

"Yeah, ok. I know that, Doc," she responded.

His gaze remained locked on hers for a long moment, and then he finally gave a slight nod, apparently satisfied by what he read on her face.

He stared down at the paper again, and then held it out to her. "Here."

"What's that?" Kyler looked at it but didn't take it.

"A script for valium. You need it, I know. I, uh, wasn't sure at first—I'm still not—but if it's the only way you'll be able to sleep then . . ." he trailed off, shrugging. "They're only fives, though," he said, somewhat apologetically. "If they don't work, I'll bump you up to tens, but—"

Kyler nodded, her eyes on his. He saw the dull shame in them and felt that squeeze on his heart again.

"Thanks, Doc," she said quietly, finally taking the paper from him. "It . . . it'll help, I know."

"Sure," he muttered. "And it's legal now. You know, for when it shows up on the test." He paused and then said softly, "Just . . . just promise me something?" His eyes drilled into hers, uncertain and questioning.

"If I can."

"Don't . . . uh . . . don't take them with the Percocets. And don't take 'em all at once, ok? I mean . . . don't kill yourself with them. That . . ." he stopped, swallowing. "That wouldn't be something I could live with very easily, you know?"

Kyler stared at him, seeing past the transparent wall he tried to put up. He meant it, she knew, just like she also knew she'd never do that to him. Committing suicide was a private matter, with the act of doing it on one's own, with no strings attached to any other person. No need to throw more guilt on them than they would already feel.

"I won't," she answered. "I mean, I'm not gonna kill myself and if I was I wouldn't do it with these."

Lamont gazed at her for a long time without answering. Finally he gave a slight, tired nod and stood up.

"All right. I'm goin' up to bed. You sure you're gonna be all right?"

"Yeah," she burrowed deeper into the couch, nearly lost in the thick blanket.

"Ok," he said softly. He left the light on as he passed the switch on the wall, figuring it would help solidify her surroundings if she awoke from another nightmare.

"Hey, Doc?" Kyler's voice was quite behind him. He stopped and turned around, eyebrows raised.

"Thanks for doing that. For coming out in the water to get me. I wasn't gonna go under, but it helped that you were there."

"I know," he responded. "And you're welcome, kid. Anytime."

She watched as he headed up the stairs, and then closed her eyes, the fatigue heavy on her. Keith's voice was soothing, the pain in it paralleling her own, allowing her to see she wasn't alone. And the doc was right . . . she was never alone as long as she had music like this. Though long gone, his words, his pain, and his exhaustion still had the power to carry her down into a somewhat dreamless sleep; one that for once was free of the terror that had followed her for so long.

CHAPTER 44

SLOWLY THE DAYS passed, and with each passing hour Kyler's slashed abdomen got a little better. She was able to head back to work and actually do a few small of the many repairs that were quickly backing up. The valiums were a Godsend, easing her into dreamless sleep each night. The nightmares were held at bay and she could feel the difference immediately.

The fear wasn't as suffocating against her, and even Lamont finally grudgingly admitted they were a good idea.

She was in the work shed sawing on some wood late one afternoon and feeling better than she had in a long time. The sun was warm against her skin with the breeze coming off the ocean smelling like it did when she was younger . . . freer.

Not for the first time, Kyler wondered at the drastic turn her life had taken in just a little less than nine months. Lamont, against all her boundaries and walls, had managed to get inside her circle of trust, and she now relied on him for his friendship and stability more than she ever thought possible.

With the last of the wood cut and stacked in the wheelbarrow, she stepped back for a breather, finally starting to feel a dull ache deep in her belly. She lit a cigarette and sat gently on the edge of the table, staring absently out the window.

With the sun sinking behind the Granger mountain range, she allowed her thoughts to settle lightly on the thought of Josh and Ryan, feeling that same old twinge of regret. Her small family at one time, Kyler felt the bond between them still strong within her; stretched thin, perhaps, but still holding.

"Be ok, guys," she said softly. "Just be ok."

The cigarette burned her lungs and she took another deep drag, forcing the nicotine further into her body. She shut her eyes briefly against the force of emotions, and when she opened them she noticed the room was considerably darker.

Turning her eyes to the door, she raised her eyebrows at the figure of a young kid leaning against the jamb. He was holding a skateboard and she immediately saw that one truck was swinging back and forth by just one bolt.

"Hey," she said.

"Hey," he answered, taking a step into the room. "I, uh, was wondering . . . if maybe you've got an extra set of trucks I can buy? Kinda fucked this one up."

Kyler regarded him, her eyes settling first on the skateboard and then on the four-inch long scrape along his left forearm.

"Fucked up your arm, too, huh?" She carefully slid off the table and limped towards him. The ache in her stomach kicked up a notch and she swallowed hard.

"Yeah," he admitted. "Crashed in the pool."

She grunted and pitched her smoke across the grass. "Sure, I got some. C'mon, over to the office."

He hesitantly followed her as she started towards the office. Kyler felt his presence beside her, but he was silent both in words and movement. She glanced at him as they walked in the door, and motioned towards the chair.

"Have a seat, I'll grab some. You gonna need something for that arm? I got a first-aid kit on the wall there."

The kid glanced behind him at the wall and then looked back at her with a small shake of his head.

"Nah. I'm all right, thanks."

She nodded and slipped into the storage room, picking up a box heavy with spare new and used trucks. Staggering a little as the pain spiked, she gritted her teeth and managed to carry it back out into the office.

"Shit," the kid stood up, walking towards her. "Lemme get that."

"S'ok," she mumbled as she set it on the desk. "It's not really heavy; I just got a . . ." she gestured vaguely towards her stomach. "I've got stitches and, well . . ." she trailed off, shrugging.

The kid nodded, his eyes on hers. Kyler looked at him, seeing the kid had a barrier of his own. She drilled her gaze into his, trying to see past it. The main emotion was pain, seemingly bottomless and shining unabashed from deep inside him.

"I'm Kyler, by the way," she extended her hand. "Kyler Maddox."

"Max Anderson," the kid shook her hand.

She nodded and offered a small smile, despite the steadily increasing pain in her abdomen. "Sure you don't want that first-aid kit? Maybe at least throw some peroxide on that arm?"

"I'm ok," he replied, looking into the box.

"Ok," Kyler plopped down in the chair and opened the lower desk drawer. "Take your time; I'm in no hurry." She pulled an Excedrin bottle from the mess of invoices and spare tools and poured two small white pills into the palm of her hand. Popping them almost absently into her mouth, she regarded the kid as he handed her a set of trucks.

"I think these'll work."

She nodded and reached for his board. "These're good ones. I got a set on my own board."

Max watched in silence as she took off his old trucks and screwed on the new ones. It took less than ten minutes and then she handed it back to him.

"Try it out, lemme know how they are."

"Thanks," he reached into his pocket and pulled out a fold of money. "How much do I owe ya?"

Kyler looked at him for a few long moments, thinking. Finally she shook her head and pulled herself to her feet. "Tell you what, kid, if you can do me a quick favor, they're yours."

Max's eyes narrowed in suspicion and she almost laughed because it was more or less the way she would have responded. Holding up her hands in mock surrender, she gave him a relaxed smile.

"Nothin' too strenuous or illegal. I just . . ." her smile faded a little as she jerked a thumb over her shoulder towards the work shed. "My stitches are really starting to hurt and I was wondering if you'd wanna help me take that wood across to the ramps on the other side of the park."

Max was silent for a minute or two, staring at her. He looked down at his board than at the money in his hand. Finally he put the money back in his pocket and nodded.

"Ok."

Kyler offered a brief nod of her own. "Won't take too long."

Max shrugged and waited for her at the door. "That's all right. I'm not in any hurry."

"Not even to try those new trucks out?" She slipped by him with raised eyebrows, getting rewarded by a small, reluctant smile.

"Well . . . yeah . . . kinda in a hurry to try those out, I guess," he admitted.

"Yeah," she offered a somewhat painful grin as they started back across the grass. "I don't blame ya. Cause of this," again she gestured towards her stomach, "I haven't been able to skate for awhile. Really missing it."

Max grunted but remained silent. She led the way into the shed and pointed to the wheelbarrow.

"I don't think it's that heavy, but . . . just in case, with both of us . . ." she stepped on one side and grasped the handle. Max shook his head and gently moved in front of her, taking both handles.

"I'll get it," he said. "Just lead the way."

"Sure?" Kyler stepped back, looking at him.

"Yeah."

"Ok," she limped out of the shed, one hand protectively across her now-pounding belly. "Just across there," she pointed with a slightly shaking finger to the ramps near the far fence.

The walk across was quiet. Kyler was beginning to wish she'd asked the doc for some Percocets before coming to work. She could feel the sweat starting to gather in her temples and armpits, sliding down her back and sides. Gritting her teeth, she forced the pain to the back burner as they stopped beside the first ramp.

"This is good," she mumbled. "Thanks."

"Yeah," Max said. He stepped back and looked at her. "Um . . . you, uh . . . you maybe gonna need some help or anything?" He faltered, hesitant again.

"Nah," she said. "I'm just gonna leave it here till tomorrow." She glanced at the now nearly-dark sky. The last of the sun was just disappearing behind the mountains and the first of the stars were bright above them. "Almost closing time."

Max nodded and ran a hand through his hair. "All right. Guess I'll see you tomorrow."

"No, I didn't mean you had to leave," she flapped a hand vaguely. "That was just me giving myself an excuse to hold this shit off till tomorrow. No, you go ahead, check out those trucks."

He looked at her uncertainly. "Well, I mean, I don't wanna hold you up . . ."

Kyler shook her head. "You're not holdin' me up," she said, lighting a cigarette.

Max shifted from one foot to the other and looked back towards the pool. Kyler caught the faraway look in his eye and felt his vague ache deep in her own gut. She found herself wishing fervently for the day when she could get back on her own board.

"Go on," she said softly. "Crashed and burned once already. You gonna let that pool get the best of ya?"

He gave her a sharp look, reading his thoughts in her eyes. Kyler waited patiently, gazing steadily back at him.

"All right," he gave in. "But I'm just gonna try 'em out. I won't be too long."

She shrugged. "No problem. I'll be in the office, ok?"

Max nodded and watched as she limped back across the grass. He grabbed his board off the wheelbarrow and trotted in the opposite direction, headed towards the pool.

Kyler finished putting the final invoices in the computer and then shut it down. She glanced behind her out the door and saw Max still skating hard in the pool. She rubbed her stomach gently and lit another cigarette, waited a minute, and then pulled herself out of the chair.

Walking slowly across the grass, she sat down on a low concrete wall that ran along the edge of the pool and watched as he went back and forth on the smooth surface. He used every inch and pulled a variety of tricks, some of which Kyler didn't even know. Watching him, she found the kindred spirit of a fellow skater in him; one that lived for even just the mere feel of the board beneath his feet.

After a few minutes he flew up the side and landed easily, catching his board nimbly in one hand. He was grinning slightly as he walked towards her, and Kyler was happy to see that the painful look in his eye had been banished for the moment.

"Seeing you skate like that, it's hard to believe you went down earlier," she responded with a smile of her own.

"Yeah, I know," he stopped a few feet from her. "Lost my groove, I guess."

Kyler nodded. "Been there a time or two myself. Be skatin' along, in the zone, and then think about something; next thing I know I'm headfirst in the concrete."

Max looked at her, his smile fading a bit. She saw the light in his eyes dull somewhat, replaced by the pain again. He shifted his gaze away and gave a small shrug.

"You know that guy?" He nodded towards the office.

Kyler glanced over her shoulder and saw the silhouette of the doc, backlit by the light above the desk.

"Yeah," she stood up painfully. "He's my ride."

"You ok?" He looked at her as they started back across the grass.

"Yeah."

"Guess I'll see you tomorrow, then, huh?" Max slid by the doc, nodding at him, and then walked out the door to the parking lot without waiting for an answer. Lamont looked at him and then turned to Kyler.

"Hurting again?"

Managing a painful smile, she opened the breaker box and killed the lights out over the park. "Damn, I hate being that obvious."

He allowed a small smile and handed her the pill she was craving. As they walked out to his car he gestured towards Max, now on the far side of the street, heading towards the bus stop on the corner.

"You know him?"

Kyler shrugged and pulled her smokes from her pocket. "Just another skater, I guess. I've seen him around here."

Lamont grunted and hit the unlock button on his key fob. "Looks kinda familiar to me."

She looked towards the corner where the kid was sitting on the bench, skateboard at his feet. Her eyes were narrowed against the dark of night and she absently took a draw off her smoke.

"He's damaged," her voice was quiet. Lamont shot her a look, eyebrows raised, but she didn't take her eyes off the kid.

"How?" Lamont asked quietly.

She shook her head. "I didn't ask and he didn't say. But I can see it in his eyes."

"So are you," the words were out before he could stop them, and he instantly regretted it. Now it was Kyler who shot him a look, unreadable in the darkness.

"Yeah," she agreed neutrally. "Probably why I can read him so good," she nodded towards Max as they pulled out of the lot.

"Hey . . . Kyler . . ." Lamont started. "I'm sorry. I . . ."

"Pull over, Doc. Lemme see if he needs a ride."

Lamont pulled over to the curb in front of the bus stop and Kyler rolled down the window.

"Hey. You want a ride somewhere?"

Max looked first at her and then at Lamont. That uncertainty was back in his eyes again.

"Nah," he answered. "Bus'll be here in about ten minutes."

"You sure?" Kyler said, glancing around. "This ain't a bad neighborhood, but . . ." she offered a small shrug. "You never know."

"I'll be all right," he responded quietly. Kyler nodded as if that was what she expected.

"Ok," she said. "See ya tomorrow, all right?"

Max nodded and watched as Lamont pulled slowly away from the curb. As the taillights disappeared around the corner he again felt that deep, sharp pain in his heart . . . still too fresh for as old as the wound was.

In the dark he felt the tears start down his cheeks again, and because he was by himself he didn't bother to wipe them away.

CHAPTER 45

KYLER WAS LYING under the ramp early the next morning, slowly ratcheting bolts to the underside of the boards she had just laid. Fighting off the ragged claws of claustrophobia, she took one deep breath after another, working her way through the task second by second. With sweat stinging her eyes, she grimly tightened bolt after bolt, thinking only of not letting the small space get the best of her.

Max walked towards her in the bright light of the early morning, seeing her legs sticking out from beneath the ramp from twenty feet away. As he got closer, though, he noticed something strange around her waist. Her shirt had pulled up enough so that he was able to see part of the huge white bandage peeking above the waistline of her jeans, and his eyes widened as he saw the pinkish trickle of blood around the edge.

Without thinking he bent down and lightly touched the part of the gauze right above her protruding hip bone.

"Christ, Kyler, you're bleed—" his words were cut off as she shot out from underneath the ramp and backed against the ramp away from him. Her eyes were wild, shot through with a deep fear, staring at him with seemingly no comprehension whatsoever.

Max held up his hands and stayed where he was, his eyes on hers. Kyler gave a quick shake of her head and gulped in air, shaking violently.

"Fuck . . ." she moaned thickly. "Don't . . . Jesus, Max, don't do that."

"I'm sorry," he said quietly. "I didn't . . ."

She squatted down and hung her head, not sure if she was about to pass out or puke. With her heart pounding painfully against her sternum, Kyler waited, hoping, that the fear would pass. He watched as she grasped the edge of the ramp, searching for either mental or physical stability; he wasn't sure which.

Probably both, he thought, somewhat numbly. Squatting down slowly in front of her, Max waited for Kyler to look at him again. The fear in her eyes was powerful, driving him down with her.

Lost in her own hell, Kyler felt the trembling in her body as well as her sanity. Max's light touch on her stomach had sent her right back into Lewis's twisted nightmare, and combined with the closing walls underneath the ramp, she'd completely lost it. In an instant she relived that night again, and the terror ran through her veins like the heroin once did.

Minute after minute went by until her heart began to slow its erratic pounding. With a shaking hand she managed to pull her smokes from her pocket and lit one, inhaling deeply. The nicotine helped to push the fear back a bit, and after a few more moments she was able to somewhat function again.

Max saw her pulling herself together with an almost physical effort on sheer will alone. He had no idea how barely touching the bloodstained pad could have sent her so close to the edge like that, but he understood fear and pain, and so he waited with a patience that only a damaged person can know.

Finally she stood up, still trembling, but able to look at him again. Shaking her head slightly, Kyler took a last draw off her smoke and then used the butt end to immediately light another.

"Sorry," she muttered. "You . . . uh . . . kinda caught me by surprise."

"More like I scared the shit outta ya," he responded easily. "Sorry, I didn't mean to."

She shrugged, trying to dismiss it but that fear was still sharp in her eyes. "Just . . . carrying a lot of baggage, and when this happened," she gestured towards her lower belly, "it wasn't . . . it wasn't a good night, you know?"

Max nodded, not really understanding but not pushing it, either. He, too, was struggling with a huge weight, and like her, he didn't want to talk about it.

He swallowed and pointed towards her abdomen. "You're bleeding."

Kyler glanced down as she pulled her shirt up a little. Her jeans hung low on her skinny hips and she noticed the blood along one edge of the white gauze. "Fuck," she muttered. Taking another deep breath, she ran a hand through her hair and sat down on the edge of the ramp, her stomach churning.

Max sat beside her, keeping space between them, and let the silence drift down undisturbed. After a few minutes Kyler shot him a glance.

"What's up?"

He gave a slight shake of his head. "Nothing. I just . . . you know, I looked up those trucks online last night, and they're worth a lot more than me just hauling some wood for you. I thought you might need some help with this," he waved absently at the ramp, "to help pay you back a little more."

She was quiet for a moment, looking at him. "I told you, don't worry about it," she finally said. "It's not a big deal."

"Except you said you have stitches, and I think you mighta tore one or two," he replied casually. "It's not a big deal for me, either, Kyler, but I don't like to take handouts."

Kyler stared out over the park, still feeling that solid fear. The thought of going back under the ramp multiplied that fear and she felt her stomach roll over once more. Finally she sighed and gave a small nod.

"You know how to work a ratchet set?"

Max just looked at her, slight annoyance in his eyes. She offered a grin and shrugged.

"Had to ask." She stopped and took another deep breath, and then said, "Ok, lemme show you what I goin' on here." Gritting her teeth, she slid back under the wood with Max beside her. It was extremely tight quarters, with the both of them shoulder to shoulder in the dim light.

"The bolts go along the edges here," she said, and he heard the slight trembling in her voice. "I had a flashlight somewhere . . ." she felt along the sides, finally finding it at the edge of her reach. "Here," she laid it on his chest. "I gotta get outta here, all right? Just for a minute."

Before he could answer she was back out in the warm sunlight, shaking again, feeling the claustrophobia digging into her. Sliding out to look at her, Max met her eyes again. Kyler shook her head and shrugged.

"Sorry."

"It's no big deal, Kyler. I got this if you wanna take a breather, all right?"

She gave him a long, level look, and then finally nodded. "Ok. I need to make a phone call, anyway. But I'll be just right over here," she gestured vaguely. "Holler if you need help."

He nodded and slipped back under the ramp. She pulled the cordless phone from her back pocket and dialed from memory with a shaking hand. She waited as it went into the doc's voicemail, her eyes closed against the fear still raging hard within her.

"Doc," she muttered at the beep, "call me, ok? Just whenever you get a chance." She hit the off button and was about to slide the phone back in her pocket when it rang in her hand.

"Beaumont Skate Park," she answered, her eyes on Max's legs poking out from underneath the wood.

"What's up?" Lamont's voice came across the wire.

"Sorry," she said. "I know you're at work."

"That's ok," he answered, his brow furrowed. Through the phone he could tell her voice was shaking. "What's wrong?"

Kyler was quiet for a beat, feeling torn again. Finally, because of the deep fear she still felt, she managed to bypass her pride.

"You remember . . . you said maybe you could find me somebody to talk to?"

A pause. "Yeah."

She gave a heavy sigh and closed her eyes. "I think I might wanna do that."

Lamont heard something in her voice but couldn't identify it through the phone. "Ok," his voice was quiet. "When?"

"I . . . I don't know. I just . . ." she swallowed. "Shit."

"It's ok, Kyler," he said quietly. "Trust me."

"Yeah," she conceded reluctantly.

"What happened?"

She was silent, watching as Max switched out one size of the ratchet for another.

"Kyler . . ." Lamont paused, then continued softly, "you don't have to tell me, all right? Not now, not ever. But just let me know when you wanna come in here. I know you're schedule's long, but we got people who can work around that, either early before you go in or after you get off."

She didn't answer, pressing a hand hard against her forehead. There was silence on the line for a minute before she muttered reluctantly, "I think I tore some stitches."

He was quiet for a beat, and then asked softly, "How many, you think?"

"I don't know. I didn't look. It's bleeding, though."

"Ok," Lamont said, thinking. "Pain bad?"

"No," she answered honestly, as the pain was nowhere near as complete or controlling as the fear.

"How bad's it bleeding?"

"Doc . . ." she sighed, feeling her stomach roll over. "I don't know. Right now I think I'll probably throw up if I have to look."

He forced back an aggravated sigh and didn't answer for a moment. "All right," he finally said. "Do this, ok? Stop whatever you're doing, working on a ramp or whatever. You don't have to look at your stomach right now 'cause, yeah, you're right, you'll probably puke. But take it easy the rest of the day; don't put any more strain on it."

Kyler took a deep breath and let it out slowly. She lit another cigarette, feeling the headache start to really pound inside her skull.

"I'll be there after work," he said quietly. "And I'll bring you back here and get somebody to look at it."

She shut her eyes and sank down alongside the edge of the ramp. "No," she replied. "Look, Doc, give me a minute, ok? My stomach'll be all right and I'll look at it and tell you how it is."

He was silent for a few long moments, and then repeated softly, "What happened?"

She glanced up as Max slid out from beneath the ramp and looked at her. His eyes were unreadable as they stared into hers, and then he dropped his gaze down to the tool bag and reached for an adjustable wrench. Raising his eyebrows he held it up and then gestured towards the ramp. Kyler nodded and covered the mouthpiece of the phone. "Use the other one. That one's got a quirky mechanism."

Max nodded and pulled out a slightly smaller one and then crawled back under the ramp. She rubbed her eyes and turned her attention back to Lamont.

"I'm no shrink, Doc, ok, but . . ."

"Listen," he said calmly, "this isn't about trying to analyze shit, ok? I'm never gonna analyze you and whoever you talk to won't either. It's even worse if you try to do it on yourself because you're too biased and you're carrying too much weight. Don't think, Kyler. Just talk to me."

She gave a heavy sigh and rolled her head on her neck, feeling it pop in numerous places. The fear was still raging strong inside her, despite the reality that had finally come back.

"Hang on," struggling to her feet she finally began to feel the first tendrils of pain, throbbing in time with her heartbeat. Glancing around, she saw that besides Max, who was back under the ramp, she was alone for the moment, as most of the skaters were clustered around the flatland across the park.

She unbuckled her belt and jeans, folding the material gingerly back away from the gauze pad.

"Don't do it if you don't think you can," Lamont said softly. "Ok?"

Kyler didn't answer as she took one edge of the pad and pulled it back in small, trembling jerks. The tape pulled on her skin and the partially-dried blood, sending the pain spiking. She gritted her teeth against the scream that wanted to come out, but wasn't able to stop the moan.

"Shit, kid," the doc's voice was somewhat weary and resigned. "Why do you do this?"

Her legs gave out and she fell to her knees, holding the blood-stained pad in one shaking hand. She had to swallow back bile for a full minute before she was sure it was going to stay down.

"Kyler . . ."

"Hang on a sec," she muttered, eyes closed. "Gimme a minute, Doc."

He was silent, waiting a lifetime in a few mere seconds. He'd heard the agony in her voice even though she'd tried to hide it, and it was tearing him up inside.

Taking a deep, shuddering breath, Kyler finally opened her eyes and looked first at the soiled pad. It was covered in dried blood and something that looked like small pieces of her stitches. Her stomach turned over again and she quickly looked away.

"All right," she muttered, finally forcing herself to look down at her mostly-healed belly. The side where the stitches had torn was bloody and raw, the new skin ragged and shredded. Looking at it was too much for her stomach, and in an instant the vomit was racing up her throat. Turning her head, Kyler let it come, praying silently to anybody listening for just a little relief.

Lamont shut his eyes and shook his head, hating her stupid pride. "Jesus," he growled.

She spit on the ground and took a deep, shuddering breath. "All right, Doc," she grasped the edge of the ramp and pulled herself up, moving away from the puddle of puke on the grass, not looking back. "I'm all right. But I don't know about these stitches."

"Still doesn't hurt?"

"No, it hurts. A lot now."

He sighed. "Give me a half hour, ok? I'll come get you and—"

"No," Kyler mumbled. "It's not that bad. I can't leave anyway."

"Kyler, look—"

"How 'bout if I put peroxide on it? Keep it clean until later?"

"Then what?" He asked gruffly. "You'll fight me about it when I say let's go back to the hospital to get it looked at?"

She sighed and stumbled over to the side of the ramp, leaving her pants undone and her underwear rolled down enough to keep the material away from her sliced-up stomach. "I won't fight you," she said in a tired voice. "I promise, ok?"

Lamont was quiet for a long moment, and then took a deep breath. "At least . . . at least stop whatever you're doing. Do that for me."

Kyler dropped her head into the palm of one hand, still feeling the shaking in her body. She felt like she'd kill for a fix right about then, and hated herself for it. She felt pulled again in so many different directions, with fucking Lewis and his demonic ways at the steering wheel. Staring out over the park, she felt her heart crying for a little redemption, a little sun on her skin, the sand between her toes . . . and the death grip of all her past shitty deeds loosened just a bit from around her neck.

"I'll talk to you," her voice was very quiet. "Ok? I can't open up to a stranger, Doc, but . . . I'll talk to you."

The silence coated the wire like oil, thick and cloying. She put a tentative hand across her stomach and it came away smeared with partially-dried blood.

"You don't have to, Kyler. You know that. But I'll listen, and I won't judge you."

"Or try to fix me?"

"I never said you needed fixing," he replied seriously. "Just a lightening of the weight of all that guilt you're carrying."

She dropped her head and closed her eyes. "All right," she sighed.

"I'll pick you up tonight, all right?"

"Yeah."

"Hold on."

"I'm tryin." She hit the off button before he could reply and ran her hands through her hair, locking her fingers at the base of her neck. Behind her she heard Max crawling out from underneath the boards and stood up, buttoning her jeans against her mangled flesh. His eyes met hers again as he stepped up on the smooth wood, walking across to her.

"I got it," he said. "You ok?"

Kyler nodded and stuck the phone back in her pocket, feeling every move she made reflected in the pulling of wet, raw skin against the rough fabric. "Thanks."

He nodded. "Sure. I'm not doin' nothin' if you want me to work on anything else."

She shook her head and walked over to get the tools. "Nah, that's about it."

Slipping into step beside her, he was silent as they walked across to the tool shed. She tried not to show her pain, but was still limping by the time she put the tool bag back on the shelf and locked the door.

Lighting a cigarette, she gazed out over the park and sighed. Max looked at her, easily seeing past the battered wall of her pride. Feeling the jagged edges of his own pain and guilt, he sensed their torture shared some of the same qualities.

She glanced at him, eyebrows raised. "I know you're not done skating, right?"

Max shook his head. "Hell, no. It's not even noon yet."

Starting in the direction of the office, Kyler grunted, limping badly. "So why you following me around instead of hittin' the ramps?"

He was quiet for a few steps, watching as she walked in the door and pulled the first aid kit off the wall with shaking hands. She put it on the desk and opened it, glancing at its contents before looking back at him. The cigarette dangled from one corner of her mouth and she had one eye squinted against the smoke. She waited, watching him.

"Uh . . ." he shifted, looking away. "Can I use the bathroom?"

Kyler stared at him and then gestured towards the storage room. "There's one in there."

Max nodded and slipped inside the door, away from her penetrating gaze. She watched him go and then heard the bathroom door shut. Her brow furrowed as the suspicion rose in her.

"What's he want?" She muttered to herself, searching through the first aid kit again. Her hand fell on some medium gauze pads and she pulled them out, looking at them. Figuring they'd do until she got back to Lamont's house, she started to unbuckle her belt again, and then hesitated as she contemplated the still-closed bathroom door.

Hoping Max would give her a few more minutes before coming back out, she quickly unbuttoned her jeans and, grimacing from the spiking pain, folded back the rough material. It was already sticking to the dried blood, and as it pulled against her flesh she felt the room shift.

"Hold on," she murmured, grasping the edge of the desk. "Don't fucking pass out now."

She closed her eyes and took a deep breath, trying to steady her pounding heart and shaking hands. Fumbling a roll of surgical tape out of the kit, she tore off a ragged piece and, placing one pad over the worst of the torn stitches, managed to get a corner taped down.

Her stomach was a churning ball of acid, caught in a sharp-toothed vise, and she clenched her jaw, holding back the trembling moan.

"Here," from far away she heard Max's quiet voice and felt him take the roll of tape from her. Instinct alone made her reach for the button on her jeans, but his hands on her shoulders stopped her. There was no panic this time, though, because reality had reasserted itself, and Max carried nowhere near the violence that Lewis did. She knew this for a fact, and how she knew it didn't matter as long as she *did* know it, and as long as she really did believe it.

She still resisted, though, but only out of street-bred pride and shame rather than fear.

"Fuck off, Max," her voice was more weary than angry, and she felt the vomit try to rise up again.

"Just hold on, ok? Here, lean against the desk before you fall," Kyler felt him as he pressed her gently against the heavy wood. "Your jeans'll just stick to the blood again, and it'll be even worse the next time you try to take them off."

She took a deep, shuddering breath and tried to pull away. "Don't. Just don't. It ain't your problem."

"I know," and the resigned tone in his voice made him more real to her, sharing her exhaustion. Kyler savagely bit her own tongue, forcing the room to stop moving. Ironically as the blood filled her mouth she felt the pain in her stomach shoot up to a new level, full of white-hot agony.

"Shit," she gasped, and leaned forward, sure the vomit was coming this time.

"Easy," Max said softly. "Just take deep breaths, all right?" His eyes were sharp and focused on hers, and she saw his genuine concern.

"Why do you care?"

"Look," he tore off a piece of tape, "I'll give you these and you do the taping. I'm not gonna touch you, but if you faint I'll probably have to try to catch you."

Kyler looked at him, and then wordlessly took the tape from him. She got another corner secured with a badly shaking hand, and then another as he handed her more pieces. Her abdomen was a ball of rapidly increasing fire, and when the gauze pads were finally secured, she stumbled around to the chair and fell heavily into it, feeling the sweat on her sides and back.

"Fuck," she leaned over and rested her elbows on her knees, staring at the floor. "Thanks," her voice was quiet.

"Sure," Max dropped the roll of tape back in the first aid kit and met her gaze. "Um . . ." that uncertainty was back in his eyes again, and he swallowed, shifting from one foot to the other. "Can I ask you something?"

Oh, Jesus, Kyler thought. *Please, God, don't let him start asking me stupid questions about what the fuck happened to me.* She stared at him, eyes narrowed, waiting in silence.

Max saw the suspicion in her eyes and took a deep breath, shoving his hands in his pockets. "You hiring?"

"What?" The suspicion was replaced by surprise as her eyebrows shot up. "For what?"

"For . . . whatever," he waved a hand absently. "For repairs, or . . . uh . . . I don't know," he shrugged. "I . . . I mean, you know . . ." he shrugged but didn't look away.

Kyler looked at him for a long time, weighing his words. Finally she shook her head and gave a slight shrug of her own. "To tell you the truth, kid, I have no idea. I just work here; I don't run the place."

Now it was his turn to look surprised. "What?"

"The guy who runs it lives in Kentucky. I just work here," she repeated patiently.

"Oh . . ." he responded quietly. "Ok, well . . . I was just wondering . . ." He bit his lip, contemplating, and then gave an easy shrug. "If you're ok, uh . . ." he jerked a thumb back over his shoulder, "I guess I'm gonna go skate."

Kyler nodded and watched him walk out the door. She ran a careful hand across her stomach and wondered why she'd let him help her. Even on the verge of passing out like she was, she still bore the weight of her strong will and pride, and she'd managed to take care of herself in worse situations.

The answer was in her heart, though, and she knew it without even trying to deny it.

"Because he needed to help me," she mumbled. "As much as I needed him to help me."

She hadn't lied to the doc when she'd told him Max had a damaged look in his eye, and it was only her rare compassion—rare for someone born and raised on the streets, anyway—that reached out to that torn place in his heart with the sympathy of one who'd been through similar wars.

Reaching in the desk drawer by her knee, she dug through the extra invoices and spare pens until her hand closed around the familiar bottle. Despite her promise to

Lamont—or maybe in spite of it—she'd gone back to the street, collecting here and there a pill or two until she'd acquired a variety.

She poured the contents out on the desk and poked through them until she encountered one last Percoset. Popping it without a second thought—much less one that leaned towards guilt over her broken promise—she willed it to do what it was supposed to do and ease the fireball her stomach had become.

Kyler leaned back in the chair and stared at the ceiling, thinking about the long days and hard work it took to keep the park up, and then about Max and that lost look in his eyes.

"I don't think he needs money all that bad," her voice was soft in the empty room. "I think he might wanna work here for more than just a paycheck."

She didn't know how she knew this, but she'd relied on her instincts for far too long to start doubting them now, and that was the truth she felt in her gut.

His eyes told a story that his voice didn't, and the emptiness and borderline despair she saw in them matched her own all too well. It went farther than just the commonality of the love they both shared for the sport held so close to their hearts; for Kyler, it was the familiar look of devastation he carried on him like a physical weight, and for that alone if nothing else, she felt a closeness to that kid that paralleled her old love for her once two best friends, Josh and Ryan.

Glancing towards the open door out into the park, she saw his profile high up on the ramp, standing on the edge and staring down into the bowl. Her heart gave a surprisingly painful twist, and she shook her head. After a brief moment she pushed herself up out of the chair and walked out the door.

Lamont came into the office at just a little before closing time and walked over to the door, looking out over the park. In the distance he spotted Kyler climbing the stairs to the big ramp that stood like a huge, white elephant amongst the smaller wood and concrete ramps. One hand was laid protectively over her lower belly, and he clenched his jaw in frustration.

"Fuck that damn pride of hers," he muttered.

He watched as she limped across the platform, and then with the ease of a gymnast with the balls of a suicidal person standing on the edge of a building thirteen stories off the ground, she pulled herself up on the railing, watching the kid as he skated back and forth. With his own heart in his throat, picturing her falling backward into that deep space, Lamont was dumbfounded when she casually lit a cigarette and hooked her heels on the support bar below her.

Completely at ease, Kyler relaxed against the emptiness behind and below her, and waited patiently while Max ran over every inch of the ramp, unaware that back in the office Lamont was silently and fervently praying over and over that she wouldn't fall.

"Jesus," he muttered shakily, and started out the door. Just then the kid flew up on her side of the ramp and landed smoothly on his feet, catching his board out of the air. Kyler slipped down off the railing and Lamont was flooded with relief.

"Fuck her pride, give her some fucking sense, please," he growled softly in the empty office. He watched as Kyler said something to him, and then they both sat down on the edge of the bowl, legs dangling over the side. Running a hand across his forehead, he wasn't surprised when it came away wet with sweat.

"That kid's liable to give me a heart attack," he said, and leaned exhaustively against the doorjamb.

"Hey," Kyler watched as he snagged his board out of the air. Max just nodded, watching her. She slid down off the railing and offered a small smile. "Every time I watch you skate you got something new."

Max lifted one shoulder in a shrug. "I read a lot of magazines. Watch a lot of the X-Games. I'm always tryin' new shit."

She nodded and took a draw off her cigarette. "Wanna sit for a minute? My stomach's killing me."

He hesitated, and then gave a reluctant nod. "All right. But it's just about closing time, ain't it?"

"I don't know," she shrugged. "Probably."

Sitting along the edge of the coping with her legs dangling down into the bowl, she longed more than ever to be able to get back on her board again. For a split second she was more than half-tempted, but then she shifted and the pain flared up raw and hot in her stomach. She grimaced and gently rubbed it with a trembling hand.

"Still hurtin', huh?" Max looked at her.

"Yeah," she waved a hand. "But it ain't a big deal."

He grunted and looked towards the mountains in the distance, and she knew he didn't believe her.

"I, uh . . . wanted to say sorry about freaking out before," she mumbled. "You kinda snuck up on me."

He gave a slow nod and looked at her. "Everybody's got demons, Kyler. It's just that some people's have more teeth than others. You . . . I think yours might have a lot."

Kyler stared at him, her eyes drilling into his, wondering if she was seeing as far into him as he was apparently seeing into her. She thought she was, because his own demons were raging fierce inside his gaze, with their multiple rows of teeth bared and sharp.

Finally she nodded and looked away. There was silence for a long time as they were both lost deep in their own thoughts. The sun slowly sank below the horizon as the air dropped a few degrees in temperature.

She stuck another cigarette in her mouth and offered him the pack, but Max shook his head.

"No thanks. I don't smoke."

Nodding, Kyler cupped her hand around the flame of the lighter and relished the nicotine burning her lungs.

"What *do* you do?" She asked. "Besides skate, I mean."

"What, you mean, like drugs?" Max looked at her, eyes narrowed in the dusky twilight.

"No," she offered a wry smile. "Like can you do more than just ratchet in a few bolts on a ramp? Maybe saw some wood or help me cut all this grass?" She made a sweeping gesture with her arm, vaguely encompassing the great expanse spread out around them.

He stared at her, brow furrowed. "What're you saying?"

Kyler hesitated. "I don't know. I don't even know if we're hiring, but if we are, I guess you want the job?"

"I wouldn't have asked if I didn't."

She nodded and took a deep draw off her smoke. "How old are you?"

"I'll be sixteen next month," he replied.

Again silence dropped down around them, and then she shot him a look. "You're dependable? You'll show up?"

"Yeah," Max stood up and offered her his hand. "I will."

Reluctantly Kyler grasped his hand and allowed him to pull her to her feet. She grimaced at the bolt of pain that shot across her abdomen, and waited until it subsided.

"All right," she said quietly. "I'll call him and see what's what."

Making her way carefully back down the stairs with Max behind her, she stepped off into the grass and started back towards the office. Glimpsing Lamont standing in the doorway, she gestured with her head.

"That's my doctor, there. He's here to give me a ride, I guess. And probably wants to get something to eat, too," she sighed. "Wanna come along?"

She glanced at Max, and then stopped when she saw he wasn't beside her. She turned and saw him standing a few feet back, staring towards the office.

"What?"

"He's a doctor," Max said, and it wasn't a question. "I thought he looked familiar."

Kyler walked back to him and shrugged. "Yeah. Why?"

There was a deep sorrow in his eyes now that squeezed her heart, along with a resignation that ran bone deep. He shook his head and shifted his eyes away.

"Nothing. I'll see you tomorrow, ok?"

She watched as he bypassed the office and headed out the big front gate. Shaking her head she headed on back towards the office and nodded to Lamont.

"Hey, Doc."

"Hey," his eyes rested on hers. "You ok?"

"Yeah," she sighed. Walking over to the refrigerator, she pulled out two bottles of water, handing him one.

"That the same kid from last night?"

Kyler nodded and took a long drink. It was blessedly cool against her throat, and half the bottle was gone in three gulps. "Yeah . . . Max. He recognized you, too."

"Really? Huh," he said. He walked over to the door and watched as Max headed towards the bus stop on the corner.

"He got a funny look on his face when I told him you're a doctor, like it hit him where he knew you from."

"It's gotta be from the hospital, but I can't think of when." In the back of his mind a quiet memory edged forward, and as he looked towards Max sitting on the bench, it was almost close enough to grasp. When he tried to coax it forward, though, it retreated back, still not ready to be known. Or remembered.

Lamont shook his head and turned to look at her, eyebrows raised.

"Well? How is it?"

Kyler gazed at him and shook her head. "I don't know. Hurts, still, but . . . I can't . . . I haven't looked at it."

He regarded her for a long moment, and then took a deep breath. "Kyler, I'll look at it, if you want. But I'll be more than happy to take you back to the hospital. Doctor Jericho'll be there for another hour, or I can find somebody—"

"No," she muttered. "Will you . . . just look at it? Just to see?"

Lamont met her eyes, gauging her emotions. "You're sure?"

Kyler nodded, swallowing heavily. "I'd rather just . . . not go back to the hospital, ok? I mean, if it's bad enough, I will, but if I don't have to go . . ."

He was silent for a moment, and then said quietly, "All right, kid." He held up his hands, palms outward in surrender. "Remember, it's just me, right? Not Lewis or anybody else."

She gritted her teeth as the humiliation rose up again. She dropped her gaze and set her bottle of water on the desk with exaggerated carefulness. As she reached to unbuckle her belt, Lamont took the first-aid kit off the wall and opened it. He pulled out a pair of latex gloves, a bottle of rubbing alcohol, and a few cotton swabs.

Meeting her eyes briefly, he put the gloves on and opened up the alcohol. "Ready?"

Kyler took a deep breath and slowly pulled the waistband of her jeans and underwear down below the white of the patch across her stomach. Lamont pulled up a chair and sat down in front of her, reaching for the tape stuck to her skin.

She pulled back out of reflex, and then forced herself to hold still as he gently began to pull the gauze pad off the tender wound. Shutting her eyes, Kyler felt her stomach roll over and gritted her teeth, begging it to be calm.

"Easy," Lamont said softly. "I'm trying not to hurt you."

She didn't answer, and he pulled it the rest of the way off. With hip bones that protruded way too much, her emaciated lower belly was a mess in itself, without the raw, bloody pieces of partially-healed flesh. With his brow furrowed, he ran a gloved finger lightly over the torn stitches. Kyler hissed in a breath and pulled slightly away.

"All right," he said softly.

"All right, what?" She asked in a shaky voice.

"Um . . . lemme clean it up some so I can see it better." He poured alcohol on a cotton swab and looked up at her. "This is gonna hurt." No sooner were the words out of his mouth than he placed the swab over the torn stitches. Kyler yelped and jerked back but she was stopped as the edge of the desk bit cruelly into the backs of her thighs. Sweat gathered in her temples and slid down her sides as she struggled not to scream. Lamont put a calming hand on her arm and felt it shaking violently.

"Hold on, ok? Just breathe."

Kyler clenched her teeth and forced herself to stand still despite the swarm of angry wasps that had suddenly invaded her lower stomach. As gently as he could, Lamont used the alcohol to clean the mostly-dried blood from around the fresh wound.

"Shit," she whispered, eyes still closed.

"I know. Just hold on."

As more of the blood was wiped away, he could see that minimal damage had been done by the tearing of the stitches, helped out by the fact that the whole wound itself was almost completely healed. He inspected the tear with gentle fingers, probing the skin and looking for the telltale signs of infection. There were none, and satisfied that it wasn't too serious, he sat back and looked at her pale face.

"It's not that bad, Kyler. The whole thing is almost healed and you just tore a couple stitches. I doubt it'll even scar."

She looked at him through exhausted eyes. "Really?"

"Yeah. I mean, I know it hurts like it should be cut wide open, and it looks like jagged glass but, yeah, really, it's not that bad."

"Do I need more stitches?"

Lamont looked at it for a brief second and then shrugged. "Nah, I wouldn't think so."

Kyler shut her eyes again, but in relief this time. He reached over and snagged the first-aid kit and dug through it until he managed to find two more medium-sized gauze pads and a tube of Neosporin.

Gently, he dabbed a generous amount of the ointment across her whole abdomen, and then taped the fresh pads on. Finally he stood up and stripped off the gloves, guiding her to the chair.

"Sit for a minute before you fall down."

She eased into the seat and he handed over her water. Taking another long drink, Kyler met his eyes. "Thanks."

Lamont nodded and took a drink of his own. "Sure. Can I tell you something, though?"

Kyler sighed and gave a reluctant nod.

"You put some meat on those bones it might not hurt so much."

"Shit," she offered a sardonic grin. "I don't think that matters one way or the other, but I'm guessing you want me to eat something, right?"

He shrugged, eyes hard on hers. "Won't do no good if you're just gonna puke it back up."

She shook her head and pushed out of the chair, buttoning her jeans gingerly across the gauze pads. "I can try to keep something down, Doc, but I can't promise anything."

"That's all I'm asking," he said quietly.

She nodded wearily and walked around the desk to shut down the computer. "Lemme kill the lights and then we can go."

Lamont walked back over to the door and looked out, squinting through the darkness at the bus stop down the street. He made out Max's form on the bench, sitting with his knees drawn up and his arms around his legs. Shooting a look back at Kyler, he cocked his head.

"Want to see if he wants to come?"

She shrugged. "I already asked him but I think he got spooked when I told him what you do. We can try again, though."

He waited a beat as she opened the circuit box and flipped the switches that shut off the lights to the park, and then fell into step behind her as she walked out the door. That memory slipped forward again, and he caught a quick glimpse of a Max who was a couple years younger. Like working a splinter out of a thumb, he gently worked the memory back and forth until he had a good grip on it.

As they pulled up to the bus stop, he suddenly remembered Max, two years younger, and staring at him with his hazel eyes full of an overwhelming grief.

Shit, his mind moaned as Kyler once again rolled down the window and leaned out, locking eyes with the still-grief-stricken kid sitting on the bench.

"Thought I'd ask you again," she said easily. "I told you Doc here," she inclined her head back to the car, "wanted me to eat something, so . . ." she shrugged. "How 'bout it? Wanna come along?"

Max stared at her and then glanced at Lamont, looking back at him from across the front seat. "I, uh . . ." he started, and then trailed off as the bus rolled around the far corner. Kyler waited, not breaking her gaze from his face.

"Sure," he sighed and got up, grabbing his skateboard off the bench beside him. "Can you bring me back here, though?"

"Yeah," Lamont replied as he opened the back door and slid in. "But I don't mind dropping you at home. You live anywhere around here?"

Max hesitated and watched as the bus drove on by the now-empty stop, vaguely wishing he was on it. "Over on Wexler," he mumbled.

"Four blocks over," Kyler responded, pointing.

"You know where I live?" Max leaned forward, staring at her.

"No," she glanced back at him. "But I know where the street is. Doc, this is Max. Max, Keith Lamont."

Max nodded as he leaned back. Reaching into his front pockets, he pulled out a crumpled wad of bills, sorting through them.

"I got it," Lamont's eyes met his in the rearview mirror. "Don't worry about it, all right?"

Max held his gaze for a moment and then quietly said, "Thanks."

"Sure. You two in the mood for anything in particular?"

Kyler shot him a sarcastic glance. "Just something light for me."

"Um . . . yeah, me, too, I guess. Anywhere's fine."

"Souplantation?"

"Ok," Max said and Kyler gave a small nod.

Silence filled the car for a few miles before Kyler turned in her seat again and regarded Max in the back.

"The guy's name's John, who runs the place. You still want me to call him?"

He nodded. "If you don't mind."

She shrugged. "I can use the help. I'll call him tomorrow."

Lamont shot her a glance with raised eyebrows but remained silent. Pulling into an empty spot, he shut off the engine and got out of the car. Kyler and Max followed suit and the trio entered the restaurant, with her holding back by him as she sensed his reluctance and uncertainty.

"Doc's always tryin' to feed me," she said casually. "Tryin' to turn me into a pig, I guess."

"Just trying to get some meat on your bones," Lamont said in a mock gruff voice. He put a light hand on the back of her neck and she was surprised she didn't feel the need to pull away. "You're too damn skinny, you know that."

"Yeah, yeah," she offered a wry grin and rolled her eyes at Max. "He's always saying that."

"It's true," Lamont said seriously, leading the way to the drink machine. He handed them both a glass and waited while they each poured a drink. Max took a sip of his Mountain Dew and glanced from one to the other, wondering if they were father and daughter, despite the fact that Kyler called him Doc.

And then that thought, the thought of having a father, put such a harsh squeeze on his heart that he had to turn away, blinking back the tears, using the time as an excuse to find a table.

Even now, two years later, that sharp pain still had the ability to sneak up on him and rip his heart out.

He set his glass on the table and walked over to the huge pasta buffet to get some food he didn't really want. Behind him Lamont hung back by Kyler and looked at her questioningly.

"He asked me if we were hiring at the park," she said quietly. "Like I told him, I can use the help."

"Yeah," he agreed slowly. "That you can."

"I'll tell you more about it later, ok?" She caught Max in her peripheral vision, heading towards them. "And for right now, don't get mad if I can't eat a whole lot, ok?"

"Do I ever?" He offered a pained grin and gestured towards the food. "I'm down to settling for *anything*, Kyler, that you can get down and keep down."

"Yeah," she sighed. "I know."

Lamont nodded to Max as he slid into the booth, watching the uncertainty in his eyes. "Go ahead and eat, all right? You don't have to wait on us."

He gave a small nod and reluctantly picked up his fork. Kyler looked at him for a moment before following to get her own plate of unwanted food.

CHAPTER 46

DINNER WAS MAINLY silent as conversation lagged. Kyler managed to get one plate down and then leaned back, lighting a cigarette. She shot Lamont an apologetic look that he returned with a nod. Max ate a little bit more, but then he, too, pushed his plate way.

"Thanks," he looked at Lamont. "That was good."

"No problem," he responded easily. "You looked like you might be hungry."

"Yeah, I was, a little bit."

Kyler slid out of the booth and gestured towards the front of the store. "I'm gonna take a piss. I'll be right back."

Max watched as she slipped between the tables and headed towards the restroom. When he looked back Lamont was staring at him. He stared right back and for a brief moment his eyes went hard.

"I know you," he said softly.

Lamont nodded slowly. "Yeah."

"You're the one who came out and told me my dad died."

Brief pain flared up in Lamont's eyes as he remembered that night. "I'm sorry, kid. We did everything we could to save him."

Max shook his head and dragged the heel of his hand across his eyes. "It was more like he didn't do enough to save himself."

Lamont hesitated, thinking of Kyler and the demon whose grip she still had around her neck. "Sometimes . . . sometimes people try, Max. They try as hard as they can but . . . it's just not enough."

He watched Max's eyes grow hard, glaring into his. He started to say something, but then Kyler was back to the table. She gazed at them and felt the weight of the emotion between them.

"Shit," she sighed. "Don't tell me you two are fighting already?"

Max shook his head. "No. But I gotta get going. I told my mom I'd be home early."

"Ok," she waited while he slid out of the booth. Over his shoulder she met Lamont's eyes but he just gave a slight shake of his head.

The ride to Max's house was silent until he began to point Lamont down various roads. Kyler sat quiet in the front seat, staring out the window. The passing houses were middle-class and well-kept, and she recognized guiltily that these were the types of houses she once burglarized, stealing for cash or dope. These were the kinds of people who either couldn't afford an expensive alarm system or never thought they'd need one, and that alone made it all the more easier for her to do what she needed to do.

"Turn here," Max instructed. "It's the one on the corner."

Lamont pulled into the drive and put the car in park.

"Thanks," Max grabbed his board and stepped out. "I'll see you tomorrow, Kyler."

"Sure," she said. "I'll call him first thing."

He nodded and they waited while he walked up to the front door, unlocked it, and walked in the house. Lamont dropped into reverse and backed out of the driveway, headed towards the interstate.

"You all right?" He asked.

"Yeah. You?"

"Yep."

"Thanks for dinner."

"No problem."

Kyler stared out the window at the passing scenery, caught in flashes of the arc-sodiums. Her mind settled on the friction she'd felt between the doc and Max, and wondered about their connection. Though her pride would never allow her to voice it out loud, she'd hoped that because Lamont had been able to save her

(and yes, that's what it boiled down to. He'd saved her again and again from the weight of her past deeds, and still, even today, continued to do it.) that he would be able to do the same for Max. In those hazel eyes of that fifteen-year-old kid she read a pain that ran deep, possibly deeper than hers, and had hoped that Lamont could lift some of it away.

She glanced at him and inclined her head back the way they'd just come. "Is *he* ok?"

He shot her an unreadable look. "You tell me, kid. You're better at reading people than I am."

"No, I mean . . ." she trailed off, faltering, battling her pride. "You know him, right? From another time?"

She waited while Lamont gave a small, reluctant nod.

"I'm guessing it wasn't a good time."

He paused, gathering his words together. "No, it . . . it wasn't." He stopped, not sure if he should tell her any more. True to his earlier statement, though, Kyler picked up on it and shook her head.

"You don't have to give me any details, Doc. I just wanted your input on the kid. He wants a job." She shrugged and lit a cigarette. "I barely know him, but there's something about him that . . . uh . . ." she struggled for the right words. "That maybe I can relate to."

"Well," he turned into his own driveway and pulled into the garage. Shutting off the engine he just sat there, thinking, then looked at her. "If you want my honest opinion, kid, I think you need help there. It's a lot of work, I know, and that," he gestured towards her lower stomach, "ain't never gonna heal right if you don't take it easy. Yeah, it's doing ok and almost healed . . . but it won't heal *right*, and you may always have problems with it if you don't give it some time."

Kyler was quiet, processing his words. "So . . . you're saying I should just hire anybody."

"No," he opened his door and got out. She followed and waited while he opened the door to the house. "I think you should hire *him*. You said you can relate to that kid and I think that's important."

He walked into the kitchen with her trailing behind. She walked over to the back door and looked out, staring at the ocean, thinking.

"Here," he said, handing her a Percoset. She nodded her thanks and swallowed it dry, turning back to the waves crashing on the shore.

"I don't even know if I *can* hire him, Doc. John would have to make that call, don't you think?"

"I think he'd agree to whatever you think is best," he put a pot of coffee on and leaned against the counter, arms crossed over his chest. "He knows how hard it is, working just to keep the place up, let alone dealing with the inventory and everything."

Kyler took a deep breath, feeling the dull pain in her abdomen. Finally she shook her head and pulled open the door, walking out on the deck. "He may not even be old enough, Doc. He's only fifteen. What's the legal hiring age here?"

"Fifteen, for part-time," he followed her and sat beside her on the steps.

She grunted and ran her hands through her hair. "Either real convenient or he just got lucky."

"*You* got lucky," he commented, and she had to agree with that.

"Yeah. I did."

"So? You gonna hire him?"

Kyler shot him a slightly aggravated look. "I should probably still call John first, you think? I mean, since he'll be the one signing the paychecks?"

Lamont offered a smile and briefly leaned against her. "Relax, kid. You're trying to carry too much again. This shit'll wait 'till tomorrow."

"I know," she sighed. "It's just that . . ." she trailed of, shrugging.

"Yeah," he said quietly. "I know."

There was silence between them for a few long minutes, and then Kyler dropped her head in exhaustion and defeat. "You want me to tell you? What happened that made me call you today?"

"Only if you want to," Lamont responded quietly. "I won't push you, you know that."

She was silent, battling her pride.

"Tell you what," he said. "I'm gonna get us cups of coffee. We can drink 'em out here and if you wanna talk, I'll listen. If you don't, we can just sit out here and relax, ok?"

Kyler nodded and looked out across the ocean, trying to derive some peace from it. "Ok."

He walked in the house and poured two cups of coffee, black, and then stepped back out on the deck. Handing her hers, he sat down and took a sip, silently watching the waves as they pounded the beach.

"I was under one of the ramps today," she said finally, "bolting some boards down. I'm . . ." she gestured vaguely. "My pants don't really fit anymore, you know . . ." she waited, but he didn't say anything. Relieved, she went on.

"I guess the waistband slipped below my hips, moving around under there, and . . . I was kinda lost in my own thoughts. I didn't even know I'd torn the stitches until . . ." she stopped and took a drink of the coffee, liking the way it burned her throat and chest.

Lamont took a sip of his own and waited patiently, not saying anything.

"Max came up and I don't know if it scared him or what, seeing that blood, but he touched it . . . right around here . . ." Kyler drew a light circle in the air around her hip bone, "and it just sent me right back to that night Lewis was . . . uh . . . when I was trying to fight him off."

He looked at her for a long moment and then asked gently, "You think it was sexual?"

"What?"

"Max. You think it was something sexual, him touching you like that?"

"Oh, uh . . ." Kyler stopped, thinking. At fifteen, he was certainly right at that age, but then she pictured the deep pain in those hazel eyes, and her gut told her there was no sexual intent on his part.

"No," she replied seriously. "No, I really don't think so, Doc. I think he was just concerned. He said something like,

'Shit, you're bleeding,' and reached out out of impulse, I think. But for me, I just felt like it was Lewis again, ready to tear me open."

She took a shaky breath and took another long drink of her coffee. "It . . ." swallowing hard, she managed to meet his eyes. "The reason I called you, Doc, is that, yeah, the valiums are working and I don't have any more bad dreams at night, but . . . but like today, sometimes it just comes outta nowhere, and it's more than just a bad memory, you know? It's like I'm *actually there* again, and it takes a minute before I can get reality to come back. Today, I mean, I saw Max and I knew it was him and that he didn't mean to scare the shit outta me, but then in the back of my head I kept expecting Lewis to grab me and . . ." she looked away, trembling, "start doing his crazy shit to me again."

Dropping her head, Kyler ran her hands through her hair and locked her fingers together at the base of her neck. Lamont felt her shaking beside him and put a gentle hand in the middle of her back. She tensed for a brief second and then relaxed.

"And this isn't the first time it's happened?" He asked quietly.

She hesitated and then shook her head. "It's happened once or twice before, but I've always been by myself. Like last week I was in the storage room at the park and I reached in the closet for something and I just pictured him back there, in the corner, reaching for me. It hit me all at once and I freaked out. I ran out of the room and I couldn't go back to that closet for two days. And it's just that today, when Max touched me, I swear to God I thought it was him again, Doc. It's bad enough when it happens when there's nobody around, but you know . . . today was the pushing point for me.

"It's like I crossed over this line and can't uncross it. And I guess maybe doin' this shit by myself ain't really working. So I thought that maybe if I got it out, maybe talked to somebody . . ."

Lamont nodded thoughtfully, staring into his coffee cup. She let the silence cover her as she got up and walked into the ocean up to her knees. He watched as she let the waves crash around her, a faraway look in her eyes as she stared across all that open water.

"You scare me when you do that, kid."

The roar of the surf was loud but she heard his words just the same. Moreover, she heard the truth and the fear in them and her stomach clenched. Walking back out on the beach, Kyler sat down beside him again and looked at him. "Sorry, Doc. I didn't know. I . . . I guess I didn't really think about it."

He shook his head and drank the last of his coffee. "I trust you, Kyler, and I think you wanna live, but . . . the way you just walk out there like that, like you could keep on walking until it takes you, without a second thought or a look back . . ." he trailed off and shrugged.

She dropped her eyes and stared at the sand.

"But you're carrying a lot of weight here," he gently tapped her forehead, "and in your heart. And you're carrying it like it's the heaviest burden in the world, and I know to you it is."

Kyler crossed her arms over her knees and laid her forehead on them. "I know," she muttered.

Lamont wrapped an arm around her and pulled her close. She let him hug her, trying to derive some comfort from his presence beside her.

"If they'd given me some magic words in school to just throw out there to make everything all right, I'd say 'em in a heartbeat, kid," he said softly. "But there's no magic to it. It's about acceptance, and forgiveness, even if the person you have to forgive is yourself."

She took a deep, shaky breath and didn't answer. In her heart she heard the fierce call of the ocean again and had to wonder what it would be like to let it take her. No more heartache or pain; she could let go of all the regrets that were weighing her down and never have to wake up with the feel of Lewis's hands around her neck or of Josh's blue eyes staring into her own ever again.

Lamont held her and felt his heart squeeze from the pain and remorse she had weighted on her like an anvil.

"I know you can't see it, Kyler, but you've come a long way from when I first saw you, physically maybe, if not emotionally. And you *were* healing emotionally, right? Up until you were raped at the halfway house . . ."

Kyler pulled away and looked out across the ocean wordlessly, the line of her jaw tight.

"And then it was Lewis who pushed you further back," he said quietly.

She shook her head and pulled her smokes out of her pocket. "None of that matters, Doc."

He took a deep breath and let it out slowly. She sensed his frustration and met his eyes.

"*All* of that matters," his voice was bitter. "I love my job, Kyler, and I'm good at it, but when I saw you convulsing on the floor in the ER that night I was ready bet everything I have that I couldn't save you. And then when your heart stopped—"

"My heart stopped?" She stared at him, surprised.

Lamont nodded. "I tried CPR and when that didn't work we brought out the paddles."

"But you got it beating again."

He shrugged. "Only after a while. At first you didn't respond to the paddles, either."

Kyler thought about this for a minute, letting his words sink into her mind.

Lamont sighed. "You're a fighter, kid," he said quietly. "I knew it that first day when you shoulda been dead but weren't. Your body kept going even when your heart and your brain shut down. You don't wanna die. Hell, if anything you got too much fucking pride to quit."

Now there was anger in his voice as well, and she welcomed it with a relieved smile. He was right, and now her pride was telling her to keep going if only for the sake of keeping going.

"Lewis and that asshole at the house?" His eyes were hard. "You walk out into that ocean, or OD on pills, or put a gun to your head . . . you know they won, don't you? People like that only exist to break other people, and if what you told me about Lewis and how he used you is true—"

"It's true," she muttered.

"—then even *you* gotta know deep down that he didn't break you. He may have tried like hell and he may have come close, but you fought him off that night, Kyler, and you were willing to kill him if you had to."

"I didn't want to end up back in jail," her voice was soft. "Or prison."

Lamont shrugged as if to say that wasn't possible. "It was self-defense. You woulda got off."

"Maybe, maybe not."

He glanced at her. "You would've."

Kyler shifted her gaze away and took a long draw off her cigarette.

"Anyway," he continued, "my point is that you keep looking at that ocean like you want it to take you . . . like that'll solve all your problems."

"Won't it?"

"You'd be quitting," he said flatly. "And they'd win."

She was silent for a long time, feeling a dull anger that stemmed more from the meaning of the words rather than the fact that it was he who said them. Finally she took a deep breath and ran a hand through her hair, relenting.

"All right," her voice was quiet. "You're right, Doc."

"Am I? Or are you just saying that so I'll quit hounding you?"

"No . . ." Kyler shook her head. "No, you're right. I don't want to die. I've got more now than I've ever had. That park and those kids give me lots of reasons to keep hanging on, and I guess maybe I'm not ready to call it quits yet." She paused, thinking. "Especially if I managed to get past . . ." she flapped her hand vaguely, still not ready to say it outright, "that stuff at the house, and then Lewis . . ."

Lamont was silent as her words died off, and the only sound between them was the pounding of the surf. Kyler took a final draw off her smoke and then pitched the butt over the railing of the deck. Her eyes were once again on the ocean, but they'd lost that vacant, longing stare.

Finally she gave a heavy sigh and stood up. "All right, Doc. I'm goin' to bed."

He stood up beside her and offered her a measuring look. "You all right?"

"Yeah. Percocet's kickin' in."

He nodded and walked with her back into the house. Kyler paused in the doorway to the living room and looked back at him.

"Thanks."

"Sure," Lamont gazed at her. "Anytime, ok?"

She gave a small nod and slipped out of the room, and he was left with the creak of the stairs as she headed up to bed.

CHAPTER 47

KYLER CAUGHT THE early bus the next morning—wishing as usual that she was skating to the park instead of relying on public transport—and unlocked the gate an hour before her usual time. After she'd booted up the computer and lit a cigarette, she reached over and snagged the phone off the charger, now able to dial the number from memory.

"S'John," his voice was its usual gruffness, making him sound perpetually angry.

"John, it's Kyler," she glanced at the clock on the wall and saw it was a little past eight in the morning, which meant it was after eleven in Kentucky. "I know I didn't wake you up."

"Horse trainers hardly ever sleep, Kyler," he responded mildly. "I've almost already put in my first eight for the day."

She grunted and took a drag off her smoke. "Listen, I was wondering . . . what would think about me hiring somebody?"

He was silent for a minute, and then said slowly, "Work's gettin' to ya, huh?"

"Not even close," she said with a small smile. "But you know, since I got hurt—"

"Oh, shit, I forgot about that. Sorry, I never thought—"

"No, it's not a big deal, really. It's just that . . . well, actually it never would've occurred to me if this kid hadn't come lookin' for a job, and then you couple that with the fact that I can't even do many repairs since I got these stitches . . ."

"Yeah. Ok. I mean, whatever you feel you gotta do, Kyler. I trust you. But I feel bad 'cause I guess I shoulda realized all this before, you know?"

"Don't worry about it. But I just wanted to check with you to see if it's ok if I get this kid on here."

"Yeah, absolutely. Um . . ." across the wire, he paused, thinking. "I'm at work right now, but I'll sneak home about four or so . . . that's what, one your time? Ok, when I get home I'll get the paperwork together and fax it to you. Just have him fill it out and then fax it back, ok?"

"Yeah, ok," she responded. "But he's only fifteen, John. Doc says that only qualifies for part-time."

There was another pause as he did more thinking. "Yeah, that's right, I think. I always forget what the hiring age is in what state, but, yeah, that sounds right. Ok, he won't have to fill out that much then. Be lookin' for it and then just fax it back when it's ready."

"When can he start?"

"Soon's I get the paperwork back from ya."

"All right. Thanks."

"Sure. Call me if you need anything else." He clicked off before she could respond and she was left with a dead line.

Pulling the phone book from a drawer, Kyler flipped through to the A's, scanning down the list to see if anything stood out. But the Anderson's took up two and a half pages and none were on Wexler.

She slammed the phone book shut and blew out a breath. In an instant of absolute decision, based on what her heart suddenly demanded rather than what her brain was telling her, Kyler reached behind her and pulled her skateboard off the shelf. It hadn't been used in a while and felt good and familiar in her hand. Pushing out of the chair, she walked through the door and out into the park, anticipation already filling her as she headed towards the flatland.

Max watched her as he walked across the grass, his eyes following her every move as she skated hard across the concrete. It was still early and besides her he was the only one there. Stepping lightly up on the low concrete wall, he walked around the width of the flatland until he came to the start of the long iron rail. There he sat down with his own board at his feet and just watched her as she worked the entire conglomeration of concrete, iron, and wood.

As she skated hard around the flatland, Kyler finally began to feel the loosening of the vise around her heart, and even though it was at the expense of her vulnerable abdomen, it was more than well worth it. After nearly a half an hour, she jumped hard up on the low wall and skated towards Max with the ease and confidence that had finally come back to her.

He stood up, reaching out a hand to catch her as she stepped off her board.

"Thanks," she said, managing a small smile around the suddenly monstrous pain streaking across her stomach. Plopping down on the concrete, she leaned forward and laid her head on the end of her upright board. From Max's spot beside her, it looked like she was deriving both support and release from the worn fiberglass deck.

"You ok?"

Kyler nodded but the tight line of her jaw betrayed the amount of pain she was in.

"Is it bleeding again?" His voice was quiet.

"Probably," she muttered.

He nodded and stared across the flatland. "That thing you did at the end . . . you think you can show me that some time?"

She turned her head and gazed at him without lifting her head off her board. "Yeah. Soon's my stomach heals. Think you can teach me that thing you did yesterday on the ramp? That little twist-flip?"

He nodded and offered a small grin. "Sure."

She grinned back and then using her board, pushed herself up. "Wanna walk with me? I'm expecting a fax sometime soon, I think."

Max stood up beside her and looked at her. He wanted to ask again about the job, whether or not she'd talked to John yet, but he didn't. Briefly his mind settled on her doctor—his father's doctor from a mere three years before—and he tried not to feel the animosity he'd felt the previous night.

"Sure," he muttered, answering her question. Kyler shot a quick glance back at the inviting concrete and then took a step in the grass. Pain slashed across her abdomen and she stumbled. Max reached for her and then just as quickly stepped back.

Battling the pain, she met his eyes and gave a slow shake of her head. "It's ok, Max," she muttered grimly. "It's not that I don't like to be touched, it's just that . . . I don't like not knowing it's coming. And this . . ." she gestured vaguely, "you know, it's still kinda fresh . . ."

He slid a cautious arm around her waist and took on some of her weight. "Both the wound and the memory, right?"

Kyler didn't answer as he carefully guided them towards the office. He felt her protruding bones pressing into his palm and forearm, but unlike Lamont, he wasn't shocked or surprised. It was what it was, and it was easy for him to accept that. In the past three years Max had grown familiar with acceptance and he knew that it was the ghosts she carried that made her who she was.

He supported her as they walked in the door to the office, and then let her down gently in the chair behind the desk.

"Thanks," she said quietly. Pulling the bottom drawer open she took out the Excedrin bottle and poured two pills out, swallowing them. "There's water in the fridge if you're thirsty."

Max walked around to the refrigerator and opened it. He paused a moment, and then pulled out two bottles of water. Handing her one, he gestured to the bottle she was tossing back in the drawer.

"Can I have a couple of those? I've had a killer headache all morning."

Kyler hesitated, then pulled open the drawer above the kneehole. She pulled out a larger Excedrin bottle and reached across the desk, handing it to him.

"Those're actual Excedrin."

"And those . . . ?" He pointed.

"Aren't," she finished for him. He held the green bottle in his hands, but made no move to open it. His hazel eyes narrowed as they stared deep into hers, questioning silently.

"Percoset," she said gruffly. "My doctor prescribes them for the pain."

Max arched an eyebrow and gestured absently towards the desk, indicating the drawer. "If he prescribes them," he started slowly, "then why are they in an Excedrin bottle?"

Kyler grunted and lit a cigarette, thinking he was quick with that one. She didn't answer for a minute, and felt his eyes still on her. Finally she gave him a somewhat irritated glance and muttered,

"Because he didn't prescribe *these*. The ones he *did* are in a bottle at his house. *These* I got from a friend so I could keep them here." She paused and took a drink of her water. "In case the pain got too bad, which . . ." now her eyes bored into his, "it has."

For a long moment Max just looked at her. Finally he dropped his eyes to the bottle he held in his hand and in one quick movement, twisted off the top. She watched as he poured two of the pills into his hand and turned them over, looking for the familiar "E."

"Trust me, Max," Kyler flicked an ash from her cigarette into the overflowing ashtray. He watched as it missed completely and settled on the worn wood of the desk. "Those actually are Excedrin."

He looked at her sharply and gave a small shake of his head. "No offense, Kyler, but I haven't trusted anybody for three years, let alone a—"

Max cut off abruptly and looked away. Deep down Kyler felt a dull anger start to burn and fought to control it.

"A what?" She asked quietly.

He gazed at her with his own anger shooting from his eyes and gave a slow shake of his head. He started to say something, but just then a low ringing came from the fax machine behind him.

"Saved by the bell," he growled softly.

"Who, you or me?" Kyler pulled herself out of the chair and walked around the desk. She slid by him, eyes locked on his, and then turned to the fax machine. Behind her Max took a deep breath and let it out slowly. Raking his hands through his hair, he turned around and walked away a couple of feet, trying to rein in the course anger running through him.

"Shit," he muttered. "Look, I'm sorry, ok?"

"Yeah," her voice was facing him again and he turned to look at her. "Me, too." Kyler stood, leaning against the counter, holding a few papers in her hand. When she glanced up at him, he saw the anger had diminished and the exhaustion was back.

"You still want that job?"

Max arched his eyebrows and gave a slow nod.

"Just fill these out, ok? Soon's I fax 'em back to John he can get the ball rolling." Kyler paused and rubbed an eyebrow where a headache was forming. "I, uh . . . he didn't say what he'd start you out at, but, I mean . . ." she shrugged. "I can call him back and talk to him or you can talk to him . . ."

Max took the papers and gave a slow shake of his head. "No, that's ok. I'll just wait and see."

Kyler looked at him and nodded. "Ok. Just leave them on the desk when you're done. I'm gonna get back to work."

"Ok."

He watched her walk a couple of steps and then pause at the door, looking back at him. There was a small smile playing around the corners of her mouth that was somewhat bitter and came nowhere near close to touching her eyes.

"Not trusting me is one thing, ok? I can understand that. But don't judge me." Now here eyes were even darker with the anger shining from them. "Not yet. Get to know me first."

Max just stared at her, offering neither agreement nor disagreement. A flicker of regret flared up in his gaze for a brief instant and then he finally gave a short nod. She looked at him for a moment longer and then slipped out the door.

CHAPTER 48

MAX SKATED HARD all day long, using his board in much the same way Kyler did. It helped to ease the anger he'd felt earlier, and then the shame and regret when he knew he was wrong. That anger had come up irrationally and sudden from out of nowhere, and it only served to remind him again of how much the death of his father was still with him, almost three years later.

Sitting on the edge of the pool as the sun started its western descent, Max chanced a look over his shoulder and saw her putting the tools away in the storage shed. She locked the door and then made her weary way across the grass to the steps of the huge ramp on the edge of the park. He hesitated a minute, and then made a decision. He hopped off the concrete and followed behind her.

Kyler was sitting along the coping, staring down into the bowl, when he popped his head up above the platform. He stared at her uncertainly for a brief second, and then cautiously climbed the rest of the way up.

"Hey . . ." he said quietly, sitting slowly beside her.

She nodded without looking at him, her mind focused elsewhere.

"I'm, uh . . ." he ran a hand along the back of his neck, "I'm sorry about earlier."

"Yeah," she sighed. Taking a deep breath, she let it out slowly and raised her head, staring into the sun. She lit a cigarette and let the smoke filter out of her nose. Her profile caught the sunset, and Max couldn't help but notice the gaunt and weary expression on her face.

Dark circles were prominent beneath her eyes, and he thought she looked more than exhausted, like she could easily curl up on the platform and fall into a much-needed sleep.

"You ok?"

Kyler dropped her head and took another deep drag off her smoke. She was quiet for a long moment and then gave a slight nod. "Yeah."

"Sure? 'Cause ya really don't look it," he said softly.

She shook her head and favored him with a slightly sarcastic smile. "How *do* I look?"

His hazel eyes stared hard into hers for a minute. "You really wanna know?"

She swallowed and slid her gaze away. "Nah," she muttered. There was silence for a few seconds and then she gave another heavy sigh and scrubbed her hand hard across her face.

"I faxed your paperwork over. John'll probably call me tomorrow. If not, I'll call him."

Max nodded and looked down into the bowl. He put his hand on the deck of his skateboard, deriving unconscious comfort from it. Kyler glanced down at the board, feeling her stomach twist in a knot of want and need.

Gently she took it from him and ran her fingers along the worn grip tape. He watched her and knew she wanted to skate—*needed to*—as much as she needed her next breath.

"Go on," he said, gesturing towards the bowl. "Take it out there."

Kyler was quiet, feeling the familiar edges of the board. Her heart cried out for the freedom it would bring . . . even as her ripped-up abdomen quietly cried out in horror of becoming more shredded. She closed her eyes and gritted her teeth, fighting again that never-ending battle within her.

"This . . ." she ran a hand lightly across her lower belly, her fingertips barely touching the fabric of her baggy shorts. "When this happened, it like . . . it's like it zapped me. Took all my energy, and anymore I'm just so fucking tired . . ." She ran her hands through her hair and locked her fingers at the base of her neck. "Like . . . it took everything I had and I got nothin' but pain left."

There was silence between them for a moment, and then she brought her eyes to his. "That's what those pills're for, Max. For this fuckin' pain. And, no, Doc didn't prescribe those exact pills, ok? But he *did* write me a script for Percosets that I keep at his house."

"You don't have to explain it to me, Kyler," Max muttered. "I just . . . let my anger jump up too quick, I guess."

"I know," she responded. "But I just wanted you to know. I, uh . . ." she paused, considering. "I don't do drugs. Not anymore. I'm actually . . . on probation, and I gotta take a piss test once a month. Doc prescribes Valium and Percosets, and anything else in my system is in violation of my probation."

Max looked at her, eyebrows raised.

"Which means, if anything else shows up on the test, I'm headed to jail, no questions asked."

He gave her a measuring look and Kyler waited for the questions that she was sure he was going to ask. But he just gave a slight nod and glanced away, his eyes once more on the bowl in front of them.

The silence was heavy between them for what seemed to Kyler like a very long time, and she had to wonder if he was reconsidering taking the job. Finally, he took a deep breath and let it out slowly.

"You know . . ." he started, and then paused, gathering his words. "Once, a long time ago, something happened to me that . . . that zapped me, too. It wasn't physical, but it was something that . . . that broke my heart. And it took everything out of me. My energy, my . . . drive, everything, I guess. I couldn't even get out of bed and, like you, I was so tired all the time."

Max raised his head and it was her turn to study his profile in the westering sun. In his eyes she read sorrow and anger mixing uneasily, noticeable along the tight line of his jaw.

"It went away," he murmured softly. "Finally. Took a long time but one day I was able to crawl out of bed and the first thing I reached for was my board. It . . ." he paused and ran a hand down the worn deck. "It kept me sane until I could get myself together again."

She remained silent and lit another cigarette with the butt end of the first one. Like her, Max waited for the questions but wasn't all that surprised when she didn't ask them.

"It'll go away," he said finally. "Eventually. And you'll be back to skating everyday like you were this morning."

"I know," she said quietly. "Doc tells me to just keep on holdin' on, and I keep trying."

Beside her Max nodded. He gazed at the sun as it sank behind the mountains and heard the train whistle from the other side of them. The air was warm, playing soft against his skin, and for the first time in a very long time he felt ok, like a huge weight had rolled off his heart.

"'Bout closing time, isn't it?" He asked.

Kyler shrugged. "Probably. But you don't have to rush. I gotta finish up some stuff in the office."

He glanced at her. "Mind if I come with you?"

Offering a slight smile, she gazed at him. "Sure."

"Think you can show me some stuff?" He stood up and held out a hand, pulling her gently to her feet. He held onto her as she grimaced and placed a hand across her lower belly.

"You ok?"

"Yeah," she responded. "And, yeah, if you want I'll show you some stuff." She paused and shot him an unreadable look. "So I take it you still want the job?"

"Yeah. Why wouldn't I?"

Kyler shrugged and started carefully down the stairs. "I don't know. Just asking."

"I got school, but I can come afterwards. Like about four-thirty or so 'till close."

She nodded and led the way across the grass to the office. "I can't give you more than fifteen, twenty hours a week 'till you turn sixteen, ok?"

"That's fine. It's only another month, anyway."

She smiled a genuine smile this time and gestured towards the chair in front of the computer. "Then what? Gonna get a license and tear up the town?"

"Nah," he offered a somewhat absent smile in return. "Just take it easy. I think I'm still halfway insane, ya know?"

Kyler matched his intense stare with one of her own and gave a slow nod. "Yeah, I know." Pulling up the other chair, she sat beside him and pointed towards the stack of invoices shoved haphazardly in a plastic file slot nailed to the wall.

"These," she laid them out on the desk when he handed them to her, "are invoices from the different trucks we get in, like the supplies for boards I keep in there . . ." her hand flapped vaguely towards the storage room, "and the Pepsi truck that refills the soda machines out front, and this one here that brings us stuff like T-shirts and hats that we sell.

"Also this one . . ." she pointed, "Harbor Lumber, brings all the wood I use to do the repairs, as well as the Quik-rete for patching up cracks in the pool and on the flat, and the rolls of coping. You gotta sign every invoice and then they leave a copy. All this shit's gotta be entered into the computer and then at the end of the month I fax it all over to John."

"How often do they come?"

"Once a week, but more if I need an extra delivery. Now," she pointed to the computer, "exit out of all that."

Max hit the escape a couple times until he came to the background. It was a picture of a skater flying up the side of a graffiti-covered concrete culvert with the purple haze of dusk behind him.

"That's a good one," he said. "You take that?"

"No," Kyler shook her head and lit a cigarette. "Found it online. Click on that icon."

Max did so and a chart popped up.

"See how the vendors are already in there?" When he nodded she went on. "Just type in the invoice number—found here . . ." she tapped the upper left-hand corner of one, "and the amount and the date. Usually I'm pretty good at keeping up with them, but . . ." she shrugged and gave a lopsided grin.

"Lotta shit for just one person," he said.

"Yeah," she got up and walked over to the fridge, pulling out two bottles of water. "You came along at a good time." She paused and looked down at the bottles for a minute, then handed him one. "Um . . ."

He glanced up at her, eyebrows raised.

"I skate a lot . . . here, but . . . it's also a lotta work, and I, uh . . ."

"You don't want me to think it's cake job where I just skate all day, right?"

Kyler gave a shrug and gazed at him. "I know it can look like that, but—"

"I've been thinking about this for a while now," he said seriously, "and I've been watching you do all this work. You only skate late at night after everyone's gone, right? Or early in the morning?"

Her eyebrows shot up and suspicion crowded her eyes.

"No, I haven't been stalking you," he replied. "I'm just saying I know it's a lot of work. And I'm not here to just skate, ok? So don't think that *I* think that that's what I'm gonna get paid for."

She was silent for a moment, watching him, and then gave an easy shrug. "Ok. Just so you know."

"I know," Max turned back to the computer, but then shot her a somewhat irritated glance. "I'm not gonna fuck you over on this, Kyler."

She didn't answer as she sat down next to him again and he knew she didn't believe him. It'd been a mistake, he now realized, mentioning the specific times she skated. He hadn't lied when he said he hadn't been stalking her, but that didn't mean he hadn't been hanging around unseen before and after hours off and on.

Something about the park called out to him, and he'd been watching her to see how it was run, what she did, and how she worked it all. It was soothing to see her skate at night, easing an ache that had been deeply rooted in his gut since his father passed away. And he also hadn't lied when he said he was still halfway insane from grief and rage, but it all seemed to disappear when he was at the park.

The idea to ask for a job was merely an act of intense self-preservation; Kyler was correct in her assumption that he really didn't need the money. Anymore he really didn't need much of anything, including sanity, but his pride-driven will refused to allow him to give up, and in the center of all this turmoil was Kyler . . . skating . . . with the purple haze of the southern California dusk reflected behind her.

In those moments, watching from outside the fence, Max was able to find a peace of mind and soul that had been missing for far too long.

CHAPTER 49

KYLER AND MAX quickly found a rhythm together, easing into one another's habits and attitudes slowly but comfortably. The schedule became routine, with Max working four nights a week after school, giving Kyler more time to skate. She stayed with him on those nights, but it was a huge relief to know the work was getting done while she was free to become comfortable with her own board again.

In the moments she was racing up the side of fifty-two, feeling the wood fall away beneath her and nothing but air around her, Kyler was able herself to let go of all the fear and insanity that had followed her for far too long.

Oftentimes, after they'd locked the gate at closing time, they'd hit the ramps or flatland together, forming a comfortable team that coincided with each other's talents and abilities as they worked every inch of smooth skate-able surface.

Kyler found it surprising how fast she began to rely on Max, not only for helping her at the park, but also for being there merely as a friend. It'd been too long since she'd had one of those; someone to skate with, laugh with, to comfort and be comforted by. His damaged nature paralleled hers, and they gave and took what they needed from each other.

Max found himself feeling the same way; becoming more comfortable with her as time went on. While there was no sexual attraction between them, there was a sense of a fierce protectiveness on both their parts, and it wasn't very long before Kyler began to realize there wasn't a whole lot she wouldn't do for him.

Aside from Lamont, there wasn't anybody else in her life that she could say that about, and it made her feel both vulnerable and strong at the same time.

They sat in IHOP one night after closing. Kyler had ordered a small salad that she'd barely touched, but it was still more than enough to relieve Lamont had he been there. Max had eaten all of his breakfast, and now they sat, relaxed in the booth, both silent and lost in their own thoughts.

Max sneaked a glance at her right arm again, feeling the question rise up and out before he could stop it.

"Can I ask you something?"

Kyler glanced at him and nodded. She struck a match and applied the flame to the tip of the cigarette dangling from one corner of her mouth. She went to drop the spent match in the overflowing ashtray, but then froze when the words slipped from his mouth.

"Where'd you get those scars? On your arm?" Max reached out a finger to touch the tracks but she dropped the match and pulled her arm back before he could.

Taking a deep draw off the cigarette, she let the smoke filter slowly out of her nose, her dark eyes hard on his. There was thick, heavy silence between them and Max began to feel apprehensive.

"I'm sorry . . ." he started. "I didn't—"

"No, it's ok," Kyler gave a slow shake of her head. She paused and took another deep drag before saying quietly, "About a year ago, Max, I was . . . really hooked on smack. Heroin. This . . ." she gestured vaguely without touching the scar, "came from shooting up."

Max stared at her, feeling the apprehension grow. She arched an eyebrow and met his gaze, her eyes serious. "That bothers you." It wasn't a question.

He was quiet for a long moment, thinking, knowing now at least some of what her demons were. Her dark eyes were intense and patient, waiting. Finally he shook his head once and offered a small shrug.

"Just don't do it around me," he muttered.

Kyler's smile was somewhat bitter. "I don't do it at all anymore, kid. Doc says next time I fix it'll probably kill me." She slid out of the booth, snagging the bill on the way.

"Wait, I got that," Max reached for it but she pulled it away.

"I asked *you* out, remember?" She grinned. "When that happens, the person who gets invited doesn't have to pay. It's like a known fact or something. Besides, I owe you for the tacos yesterday."

"Of which you only had one," he said pointedly.

She shrugged. "Whatever, it doesn't matter." She paid the bill and they walked out into the dusk of early evening. The air played soft and warm around them, and the smell of the ocean was heavy as they walked along.

"Doc helped you off of it?"

"Yeah . . ." Kyler said slowly. "He got my heart started when I OD'd and from there it's like he's saving me around every turn. He . . . uh . . ." she paused, trying to form the right words. "He's held on when he didn't have to, you know?"

Max nodded, watching her, marveling at how the same man who couldn't save his father was the one who saved her; wondering who made those kind of chips fall where they did.

"You don't like to talk about it," Max's voice was soft and it wasn't a question.

She shook her head and favored him with a glance. "Not really. But maybe one day I'll tell you about it."

He nodded and the silence dropped again between them, easy and comfortable. He was content to walk beside her, letting her reside in her own thoughts. He hoped he hadn't pissed her off, asking about that, but after the hell he went through with his father, and then watching her pop pills that obviously meant more to her than she'd let on, he figured he had a right to know.

Max wanted to work at the park for solace for himself, not to watch somebody else succumb to the gut-wrenching process of addiction.

And now she tells me she's a junkie, he thought, somewhat wearily, and had to wonder just how far away she'd managed to get from it.

Kyler walked beside him in silence, knowing he was thinking about the tracks on her arm, probably the pills in the desk drawer at the park, and if she was telling the truth about the smack and the fact that she'd let go of it. A lot of his thinking and the conclusions he would eventually come to from that would depend on whether or not he stayed at the park, she knew.

She thought he might. He'd been around her enough by then to see that she didn't run to the bathroom every five minutes to shoot up, and the Percoset in the desk drawer hadn't been diminishing all that quickly.

Besides, she reflected, *he's still got that damaged look in his eyes, and the only time I don't see it is when he's skating or when he's working. He'll stay.*

They walked along quietly, and when the silence became a bit too long, Kyler opened her mouth to talk, but just then a hand shot out of the darkness of a recessed doorway, grabbing her shoulder as she went by. Her heart leaped up into her throat and she jerked back, slamming into Max and pinning him against the rough brick wall of a building. He felt the wind crushed out of him as something bit cruelly into his kidney.

In front of him, her back against his chest, he felt Kyler's body shaking violently. He started to put a hand on her arm, but then she moved away.

"Jesus," she gasped. "Carrie." She stopped and took a deep breath, trying to slow her pounding heart and still feeling the fear racing through her. "You scared the fuck outta me."

"Sorry," a raspy voice said somewhat absently, and Max witnessed a pale, gaunt zombie stepping out of the shadowed doorway. Even with the bright light of the street lamp shining on them from a half a block down, it still took him a minute to realize that it wasn't a zombie but a ravaged, ragged young woman. Her eyes were wild and insane, darting from his to Kyler's and back again.

Kyler took a step towards her and this time he did grab her arm. She shot him an unreadable look and shrugged off his hand.

"You're lookin' good," the girl said. Kyler nodded and just looked at her, waiting.

"So . . . uh . . ." the girl, Carrie, Max assumed, scratched the inside of one arm slowly, her jagged fingernails scraping along the raw track lines in a way that was turning Kyler's stomach. "You holding anything?"

"No," Kyler answered. "I'm done. I'm out."

The girl shot her eyes to Max's and then looked back at Kyler.

"Then ya got any money? It's close, you know? I gotta get somethin' quick or I'm gonna be hurtin' bad."

Kyler stared at her for a few long minutes before finally giving a short nod. Max watched her pull some bills from her pocket and separate a twenty.

"Ky—" he started, but cut off when her eyes met his.

"Here," she handed it to the girl. "Just make sure it's clean, all right?"

"Ain't nothin' clean out here, Kyler," Carrie muttered as she made the twenty disappear. "You know that."

"Yeah," she responded. "But taste it first anyway. There was some drain cleaner floatin' around here a while back."

The girl nodded a lie and started down the street. "Thanks," she called back over her shoulder, her voice indifferent now as her mind focused on her upcoming high.

Kyler took a deep breath and let it out slowly. With slightly shaking hands she lit a cigarette and looked at Max.

"C'mon," her voice was quiet. "Let's get outta here."

The silence surrounded them as they walked off, and Max just followed her aimless direction. When her cigarette burned down to the filter, she immediately lit another one from its butt. He watched her do this two more times before putting a light hand on her arm, stopping them alongside a graffiti-covered concrete culvert much like the one on the background of the computer back at the skate park.

This time Kyler didn't shrug him off or pull away, but she didn't look at him, either. Instead, she sat down on the edge of the culvert with her legs dangling over the side and her eyes staring at nothing in the ash-covered shadows.

"Your arms used to look like that." It wasn't a question but she winced just the same.

"My whole body used to look like that."

Max gazed at her profile in the moonlight, at the tight line of her jaw and the minute trembling in her hands.

"Heroin?"

"Mainly, yeah. For me, anyway. I don't know about her. But, you know . . ." she shrugged, still avoiding his sharp eyes, "like her, I'd do anything and everything—"

And everybody, her mind whispered.

"—to get high."

Kyler pressed the heel of her hand hard to her forehead and closed her eyes against the familiar shame and self-loathing.

"So it . . . you know," he began hesitantly. "You knew she was gonna get high, right? So why'd you give her the money?"

Now she did look at him, and he saw the hard edges of anger in her eyes.

"Christ, now you remind me of the doc," she growled. Standing up, she reached for her board and slipped smoothly over the side of the culvert, quickly disappearing into the shadows.

Without thinking, Max followed, straining to hear the almost-angry sound of her wheels on the concrete above his own.

A stream of brackish water ran down the middle at the bottom, and he jumped it effortlessly, catching a brief glimpse of her as she shot up the other side. She rode the edge as smoothly and easily as any line of coping on a ramp, and then back down fast, across the water, and back up the previous side. He stayed a constant distance behind her as they rode the culvert side to side, back and forth, for a good mile and a half north.

Finally he saw her fly over the top edge on one side and hit the ground, pulling her board out of the air. Following in her wake, he flew up the side and stepped off, spotting her a few yards away.

Kyler was standing with her hands on her hips, staring down at the ground and breathing hard. Walking towards her, he noticed a thin stream of blood running from her right calf.

"Kyler, look—" he started, but stopped when she whirled on him, dark eyes blazing with fury.

"I gave her that money because she needed it. She was desperate and jonesing and it's better than getting it lying on her back, ok? I've been in her place a million times and it ain't a good place to be."

She stopped and glared at him, defiance and shame mixing uneasily in her gaze.

Max held his hands up in surrender. "Wait. I don't know . . . what you . . . I don't know what jonesing means, Kyler, and I'm not condemning you for anything. I just . . . I just wanted to know . . ."

"What?" She snapped, lighting yet another cigarette. She was still all too aware of the fear coursing through her, but now it was mixed with another emotion . . . need. Seeing Carrie—despite her cadaver-like appearance—had awoken that rat, and Kyler found herself wishing she could be in her shoes for just one moment. That single, vital moment when the plunger was depressed and the sweet, numbing emptiness raced through her body towards her heart.

"About addiction," Max responded quietly.

Kyler regarded him for a long minute, her eyes piercing past the barrier he tried to hold up.

"Addiction," she repeated. "Why?"

"I . . ." he faltered, faltering under the weight of her stare. "I . . . just wanna know, Kyler."

She was silent, smoking her cigarette and feeling the anger dashing through her veins.

"What's it like?" He found his footing again and managed to hold up against her dark eyes. "Just—"

She grimaced. "Forget it, kid. I ain't gonna be your guinea pig." She started to walk away, but then something made her stop after only a few feet and glance back at him.

Max met her eyes and she was surprised to feel the squeeze on her heart at the sight of the tears running down his face.

"For me," he repeated. "I . . . had a friend who died . . . not too long ago. Addiction got him and I just wanna know why I couldn't save him."

Again her eyes bored into his, trying to find the lie or ulterior motive he had hidden. Max met her gaze head-on, not bothering to wipe the tears away. In his heart he felt the comparison between his father and the strung-out junkie he'd just seen. The wild light in her eyes was what got him the most and the similarities between them—along with the desperate and painful truth of addiction in any form—was enough to shake him to his core.

Finally, Kyler gave a slow shake of her head and a heavy sigh. Briefly she closed her eyes and then opened them to his raw, pure pain.

"All right," she said hoarsely. "What do you wanna know?"

Max stared at her for a long time. In his eyes she could see the massive amount of unrefined emotion, eating at him, driving him down to a point where she knew it wouldn't be too much longer before he was knocked to his knees. Again, she'd been there a million times, crawling from the huge weight of broken dreams and shattered faith.

She watched as the levels of emotions rose, painfully, mixing together until there was no clear line between them. Rage and fear mixed restlessly with grief and heartbreak, topped with utter hopelessness.

Kyler took a deep breath and held her hands out, palms up. "Max . . ."

"Shit," he growled, and looked away, swallowing hard. Without another word he grabbed up his board and went into the culvert, this time leaving Kyler standing on the edge. She sighed and shook her head, and then, like him just mere minutes before, followed him over into the now pitch-black concrete bowl.

With emotionally-fueled aggression, the two of them raced across the culvert, rode the edge hard, and flew back down the other side. Kyler stayed right on him, barely a second behind him, feeding off his anger and grief. Too much of what she saw his eyes she felt in her heart, and that hurt her, knowing that she could be that vulnerable, that weak.

Riding hard right behind him, she tried to channel her anger into the peace that usually came with skating, but his grief was greater, and as long as he had that grief shining from his eyes she felt it painfully in her heart.

Max felt her behind him, heard the angry sound of her wheels on the cracked and pitted concrete. "Fuck off," he muttered quietly, and flew up the slide, pulling a flip out of the slim air between them, trying to fly up and around her, needing more space and not finding any in the split second he had.

"Shit—" she started, sensing more than seeing the mistake in the darkness. In a flash she felt the crack of her board as it hit something hard, and then she was falling. She crashed down on her side, feeling the breath yanked out of her. Dimly she heard a skateboard—whether hers or Max's, she couldn't be sure—hit a few feet from her head.

Gasping, struggling for her lost air, Kyler reached out a hand in the darkness, feeling somewhat frantically for Max. As her fingers closed on his jeans-clad leg, she pulled herself to her hands and knees and worked her way over to him.

His body was shaking uncontrollably, but instinct rather than sight told her it was only from the adrenaline dump the high emotions and reckless run down the culvert had given him, rather than anything from a severe injury.

Wordlessly she sat beside him with a comforting hand on his side, not saying anything and just letting him take what he needed from her presence.

"Fuck," he groaned. "That fucking hurt."

"Yeah." She paused, and then asked softly, "You ok?"

"I don't know. I think so."

She looked towards the sound of his voice and wasn't surprised that she couldn't see him. Down in the bowl of the concrete drain it was pitch-black, far from any street light and with the moon nowhere to be found.

He rolled over on his back, grunting from the pain.

"Easy," Kyler said.

"I'm ok."

"Yeah?"

Max paused and she felt him moving beside her. "I can feel everything and nothing seems broken. I might be bleeding, though, on my head. Something hit me pretty hard."

She dug in her pocket and pulled out her lighter. "Mighta been my board. I felt it hit something right before I went down. Hold still." She thumbed the lighter and in the glow of the flickering flame saw that Max had blood running from a cut above his right eye. The blood flowed in and around his eye, making him looking like he'd been lacerated with a chainsaw.

"Yeah, you're bleeding. Lay still a minute, ok?"

Max lay back and stared up at the dark sky. Kyler put the lighter back in her pocket and darkness enfolded them once more. In the blanket of black his voice was soft, almost inaudible, and she had to lean close to hear him.

"I'm sorry, Kyler. I'm not lookin' to pick your brain, ok? It's just that . . ."

"No, it's all right," she responded quietly. "Some things hit close to home, you know?"

"Yeah, I know," he sighed. "Just seeing that look in that girl's eyes . . . like she was lost . . . haunted. Like there was a demon riding on her back, not letting go . . . and . . . it kinda reminded me of my . . . friend."

Kyler was silent, comfortable in the darkness, glad he couldn't see her face. Too many memories were too close to the surface, and she knew her eyes would betray her emotions.

"Shit," Max sighed and struggled to sit up.

"Whoa," she said. "Don't move."

"I'm ok," he muttered. "Just catch me if I start to fall."

With a hand on his arm, she helped him stand up. He put a hand to his forehead to try to slow the pounding in his head, but it didn't do any good.

"C'mon, I gotcha," Kyler slid an arm around his waist and kicked up his board. "Trucks're broken, I think."

"Damn. Those were brand new."

"Don't worry about it. We'll get you fixed up tomorrow and you'll be skating in no time."

Max shook his head and groaned at the pain. "This was stupid."

"Reckless," she agreed.

"Crazy."

"Fucking insane." He heard the grin in her voice. "Next time let's do this on a ramp, ok?"

"In the daylight."

"Exactly."

With him leaning on her for a change, they made their slow, careful way back up the side of the culvert. Kyler held both boards under one arm and supported him with her other. Once they were back on the street, she stopped under the cone of light from a streetlamp and surveyed his face again.

"It's not really too bad," she said hesitantly. "Let's find a bathroom and clean it up some."

Max leaned on her as they walked down the street, and when the bright light of a gas station appeared on a corner, she guided him around to the side, opening the door to the unisex bathroom.

He stared into the cloudy mirror, squinting against the bright light and painful sting of the cut. "Looks like I got hit with a brick."

"That's just the blood. Head wounds bleed a lot. Here, sit down," Kyler pointed to the toilet and pulled paper towels from the dispenser. She ran them under hot water and gently pressed them to the bloody area above his eye. He winced but held steady.

"Sorry," she muttered. "Lemme just try to get some of this blood off."

Max closed his eyes and gritted his teeth against the pain. Finally she leaned back and surveyed his head, brow furrowed.

"Yeah," Kyler said, almost to herself. "Ok."

"Ok, what?"

"I think you're gonna need stitches. It looks a lot better, but it's pretty deep." She looked at him with raised eyebrows.

"Shit . . ."

"It's alright. You're covered under the park's insurance. C'mon, let's find a phone."

She helped him up and led him back outside. He plopped down on the curb in front of a payphone and dropped his head gently in his hands. Kyler dug in her pockets for some change and dialed the phone.

Lamont's recorded voice picked up after the fourth ring, telling her to leave a message and he'd call back as soon as possible.

"Hey, Doc . . . it's me," she held the phone between her shoulder and ear, and reached into her pocket for her cigarettes. "I didn't know if you were still working or not. Uh . . . Max . . . well, Max and I were skating . . . at the park . . . and . . ."

Max shot her a sharp look but she waved him away.

"We collided on the ramp and I think my board cut him open, above his right eye. I cleaned it up some but I'm thinking he needs stitches. Um . . ." she took a deep draw off her smoke and thought about what to say next. "I guess we're gonna head over to the hospital. Right now we're at the Arco station on Rose and Venetian and it's on the bus line. We can be there in ten, fifteen minutes, I guess."

Without another word she hung up the phone and glanced at Max. His eyebrows were raised as he stared back at her.

"We were on the ramp?" He asked.

Kyler shrugged but her eyes were serious, gazing into his. "It's easier this way. Nobody has to know how fucking crazy we were."

"Insurance won't pay for it otherwise?"

"It's better this way."

Max waited a beat and then gave a slow nod. "All right."

Pitching her cigarette, Kyler looked out towards the bus stop. "Bus'll be here shortly. You ok?"

"Yeah. Hurts like hell, but it could be worse."

She offered a slight smile and sat down next to him. "Coulda been a lot worse."

They were silent for a few minutes, each thinking their own thoughts. Max saw the girl's eyes in his head again, and felt the weight of her demons on his own back.

Lamont stood leaning against his car, watching the meter on the gas pump climb higher and higher as the way over-priced fuel was drained into his tank. The phone on his belt vibrated against his hip but the number wasn't recognizable. He waited until he was done pumping the gas before he listened to the message on his voicemail.

His eyebrows shot up when he heard Kyler's voice and he looked out and up at the gas station sign, and then over at the street corner where the lighted sign showed he was on Rose Avenue.

His eyes roamed the parking lot and the store, searching for Max and Kyler, and he finally spotted two figures in the shadows along the side of the building. As he walked over they became clearer, with Kyler leaning close to Max, pressing something to his head.

"Shit," he remarked easily. "You mean it wasn't you that got hurt this time?"

Kyler glanced up, startled, relaxing when the light from the store fell on his face.

"Jesus, Doc, that was quick. I just called you."

Lamont jerked a thumb back over his shoulder. "I was here already, pumping gas. Lucky, huh?" He squatted down and looked with narrowed eyes at the cut above Max's eye.

"Hurt?"

"Yeah."

"You dizzy? Double vision?"

"No . . ."

Lamont shot him a look. "You don't sound too sure."

Max pulled his eyes away and looked at Kyler. "You think you could grab me a Coke or something? I'm dying of thirst." He reached into his pocket but she flapped a hand.

"I got it. Just a Coke? Anything else? Sandwich or anything?"

"No. Just a Coke, thanks."

"Doc?" Kyler glanced at him. "You want anything?"

"Nah," he shook his head. "I'm good, thanks."

She nodded and walked around the corner into the store. Max looked at Lamont and there was a kind of angry suspicion in his gaze.

Lamont sighed and moved to sit beside him on the curb. He was silent for a minute and then said softly, "You don't have to trust me, kid. You don't have to like me or—"

"Doc," Max's voice was very quiet, "I just . . . it still hurts, but I know it wasn't you who . . . I mean, you did all you could for my dad. It was, you know, too late, I guess, when he finally got to you."

Lamont was silent, feeling the kid's apprehension and slight fear. He waited, not pushing, not saying anything. Finally Max shook his head and pushed himself off the curb.

"Easy," Lamont grabbed his arm, stopping him from falling. "So I'm guessing you are dizzy?"

Max gave a careful shake of his head. "Just shaky, I guess. Fucking pounding headache."

"All right," Lamont said. "Walk with me, ok? Car's just right over there."

Kyler appeared silently on the other side of him and put a small plastic bag in his hand.

"I talked the lady into letting me have some ice," she said. "For your head." She slipped her arm around his waist again, adding her support to Lamont's while still managing to hold a fountain drink and both skateboards.

"Thanks," he said, putting the bag gingerly against his head.

"Yep. Still ok?"

"I guess."

Lamont opened the passenger side door of his car and they eased Max in. Kyler handed him the Coke and then slid in the back.

"How many, you think?" Kyler said to Lamont as he got in behind the wheel. "Stitches."

He glanced first at her and then at Max, giving a slight shrug. "I'd say five, maybe six . . . for him. Three or four for you."

She raised her eyebrows. "Me?"

"You got a cut on the back of your neck that looks pretty deep. It doesn't hurt?"

Kyler put a hand across her neck and winced. "It does now that I know it's there."

Lamont grunted and pulled out of the lot. "Both of you look like you've been run over by a train. Hit pretty hard, huh?"

"Yeah," they both said in unison. Kyler leaned back in the seat and finally began to feel the bumps and bruises that seemed to cover her whole body. Both her elbows were scraped raw, and her right calf, where she'd misjudged the lip of the culvert and slid in the gravel, was stinging in time to her heartbeat.

"Yeah, we hit hard," she repeated. "Got too close to each other, I guess."

"Working late?"

"We laid down some new boards and wanted to run 'em real quick to see how they were before we went home," Max cut in before she could respond.

Lamont nodded and pulled into the parking garage at the hospital. Looking into the rearview mirror at Kyler, he raised his eyebrows. "Floor three, ok?"

"Ok," she said. "You need help with him?"

"I can walk, Kyler," Max opened the door. "Go on, we'll meet you up there."

She got out without answering, but still walked with him over to the elevator, ready to catch him if he stumbled.

"I got him, kid," Lamont said, meeting her gaze.

Nodding somewhat reluctantly, she walked over to the staircase and started up. Behind her the elevator doors opened and Max and Lamont got on. As soon as the doors closed she pulled her smokes from her pocket and lit one, taking her time walking up the steps.

Inside the elevator, Max leaned against the wall and took a deep breath. Lamont looked at him with sharp eyes. "Dizzy?"

"Nah," he shook his head, and then winced from the pain. "Just . . ." he shrugged. "I don't know."

"Look," Lamont said quietly, then paused, trying to find the right words. "When he . . . when your dad died, I . . . uh . . . his alcoholism had just about eaten up all his major organs. It'd . . . been awhile . . . you know? I mean, even if he'd gotten here a month, even two, earlier, it . . . it wouldn't—"

"I know," Max blew his breath out angrily. "I already told you—"

Lamont reached out and hit the stop button and the elevator came to an abrupt halt, making Max grab for the rail that ran along the back three walls. The alarm sounded shrill and loud, seemingly directly inside his already pounding head.

"Jesus, Doc . . ."

"You either trust me or you don't," Lamont said. His voice was neutral but anger shot from his eyes like lightening. "Right now, I don't care. My main focus is getting stitches in your head, but you need to know that blaming me isn't—"

"I'm not blaming you," Max's voice was very quiet.

"Then what?"

Max shook his head, not meeting Lamont's eyes.

The silence was thick between them for a few very long minutes.

"I . . . I don't know," he finally sighed. "I just never thought I'd have to see you again, you know? Like it was getting to the point where it didn't feel like I was getting stabbed in the heart every fucking second, and then here you are, bringing it all back to the surface."

Lamont looked at him for a long moment. Finally he gave an aggravated shake of his head and hit the button, setting the elevator back in motion. "I didn't crawl out of the woodwork to bring up bad memories, kid," he muttered. "If it was up to me, I'd never look to see you again, either. The second hardest part of my job is telling families about the death of a loved one." His eyes were hard, glaring into Max's.

"You know what the hardest is?"

Max swallowed and leaned his head back against the wall, blinking back tears.

"Seeing those same family members again. Sometimes it's ok, 'cause you can tell they've moved on, they're doin' all right. And then sometimes I come across those that haven't moved on . . . that can't."

"'Course," he growled softly as the doors opened, "it helps to take advantage of those grief counselors' names we give you. We hand 'em out for a reason, you know."

Max didn't answer as he slid by him, wiping his palms across his eyes. Kyler was sitting on a bench watching as they stepped off the elevator and looking like she wasn't the least bit surprised she'd been waiting for a good ten minutes. Her eyes met first Max's and then Lamont's and she raised her eyebrows.

"Problem solved?"

He shrugged and then gave a slow shake of his head. "You all right?"

"Yeah," she stood up on shaky legs and he noticed the pale, waxy sheen of her face.

"What's wrong?"

"Nothin', why?"

"'Cause you look like shit," Max said shortly.

Kyler gave a wry grin and reached out a hand, touching the side of his head gently with her palm, forcing the cut eyebrow to the light. "So do you," she returned. "Feeling any better?"

"Got a headache," he grimaced and pulled away.

"I can imagine," she said. Beside her Lamont was staring at her, his eyes measuring.

"You throw up?" He asked.

She gave a half shrug and shot him a glance. "Something I ate, I guess."

"You ate?"

"IHOP earlier."

He arched an eyebrow at her, but then looked at Max. "Gonna let me stitch that up for you?"

Max sighed and stared down the hallway. "Sure, yeah, whatever."

"C'mon," Kyler slung an arm around his shoulders in a familiar gesture. "Won't hurt for long."

Despite himself, Max grinned and let her support him as they followed Lamont into a room.

"Sit up here," Lamont gestured to a low table. "I'll try to be careful, ok?" His eyes rested on Max's, calmer now, without the anger. "I gotta numb it and that's gonna hurt a little, but after that you shouldn't feel a thing."

"'Till the numbness wears off," Kyler added.

"Thanks," Max grumbled. "You're not really helping."

She offered a real grin this time and sat down on a stool. Lamont glanced back at her and saw she was less pale, slowly getting her color back.

"Hold still," he instructed, and Max flinched and squeezed his eyes shut as the needle pierced the tender area just to the inside of his eyebrow.

"Shit," he gasped.

"Ok," Lamont leaned back, watching him carefully. "It's done. I'm gonna give it a minute, all right, then stitch it up."

Max nodded and took a weak breath.

"You ok?"

"I guess so."

"Gonna pass out?"

He shook his head and winced. "No."

Lamont waited a few seconds and then ran a gentle gloved finger over the cut. "Anything?"

"No."

He nodded and reached into a drawer. Kyler looked away, unable to watch as he began sewing up Max's forehead. Her stomach was doing slow, lazy somersaults still, even without anything in it.

"*You* ok?" The doc's voice in her direction caused her to look over at him.

"Yeah, why?"

"Because you look like you're gonna puke again."

Kyler shook her head but didn't look at him. He quickly finished up with Max and taped a gauze pad over it.

"Still not dizzy? Seeing double?"

"No to both," Max slid down off the table. Lamont waited, ready to catch him if he stumbled, but he slid by him and walked over to Kyler.

"Your turn," he mumbled, and took the seat when she stood up.

"All right, Doc," she sighed, hopping up on the table. "Here we go again, right?"

"As always," he gave her a brief smile. "Least it doesn't look as bad some of the other cuts."

She bent her head forward, giving him access to the back of her neck, waiting for the ever-unforgiving sting of the needle. Prepared as she was, she still jerked when it pierced her skin.

"Easy," he put a hand on her head, holding it steady. "Sorry. I try to get it done quick, but it's never quick enough for the pain."

"That's all right," Kyler managed through her clenched jaw. "I should be used to it by now."

He didn't answer as he quickly sewed a couple of stitches into her skin. "How'd this happen, anyway? You hit the edge of the ramp?"

"Glass, probably," she answered, and then immediately gritted her teeth, shutting her eyes at the mistake.

Lamont didn't answer as he stripped off his gloves, but his eyes were hard, staring into hers. Finally he gave a slight nod and asked quietly, "Any problems walking? Dizzy?"

"No."

"Numbness or tingling anywhere?"

"Nope."

He nodded. "It's nowhere near close to your spine, but it never hurts to ask."

She grunted and slid off the table. "I didn't even know it was there until you mentioned it."

"It's not that wide," he stood up and reached for his jacket. "Just a little deep." His eyes found Max's. "Need a ride, I guess?"

"Why would you guess?"

"Because you might have a concussion and I'd like to keep an eye on you 'till we get you home rather than have you ride the bus."

"So . . . you're basically forcing me back into your car? Like I don't have a choice?" His voice grew hard.

"C'mon, kid," Kyler took his arm easily and pulled him to his feet. "Get in the damn car, ok? Quit this bullshit. You got a headache and now my neck hurts and I'm sure Doc just wants to go home, right?" She shot a look at Lamont. "Been here all day and he had to come back to patch both of us up—"

"It's all right, Kyler," Lamont said quietly, lending his support on Max's other side. "Let him be angry."

"I'm not angry," Max started. "I just—"

"I know," and now Lamont only sounded weary. "It's late. Let's let it go for tonight, ok?"

Max felt the anger melt away as quickly as it had come, and he slowly nodded. Together Lamont and Kyler guided him back out to the car, where he slid in the front seat.

Exhaustion and pain surrounded him, matched in intensity only by the vague anger still with him, which in turn was only a piece of the never-ending grief.

Lamont pulled out of the lot and onto the freeway. In the back seat Kyler leaned her head against the window and stared out at the night; he caught her reflection in the mirror and wondered why she'd lied to him.

The silence grew long in the car, as each of them felt the weight of the long day catching up with them. Lamont didn't know how to ease Max's ache and couldn't even begin to know where to try. Max, himself, felt trapped between both the doc and Kyler. With her drug-induced life and now battle-scarred body telling a tale of its own—something he wasn't sure he wanted to know in lieu of his own father's lost war with alcohol—and Lamont's connection with him through that war and subsequent heart-shattering loss, he felt backed up against a wall, caught between the problems of both of them while his own raged fierce inside.

Kyler, staring out at the night, felt the usual monstrous need roaring through her head, screaming for a fix, a line, a pill . . . *anything* to get her back up to where she needed to be. The sewn cut along the back of her neck pounded out its pain in rhythm to her heart, reminding her of other pains, other bad memories and the trash-filled gutter lows she'd driven herself down to.

Finally Lamont pulled into Max's driveway and shut off the car. He contemplated the dark house for a minute and then glanced at Max.

"Your mom home?"

"No," Max opened the door and started out. "She's out with some friends."

Lamont put a hand on his arm, stopping him. "Let Kyler stay with you, ok? Just 'till she gets home."

"Doc," Max favored him with a thin glare. "I'm not gonna fall asleep."

"Yeah . . . but . . ." he hesitated. "Just humor me, will ya? 'Cause it's not that hard to just say you're gonna lay down for a minute—just one minute—and then next thing you know you're sound asleep. And that's not good if you have a concussion."

"Jesus," Max sighed.

Behind him Kyler spoke up quietly, "It's no big deal, Max. I can stay as long as you need me to."

"That's just it," he snapped, feeling the pressure of being cornered. "I don't *need* you to."

Kyler scrubbed a hand across her face and met Lamont's eyes in the mirror before looking back at Max. "He's stubborn, kid," she said. "He won't give up. It'd be easier if you just let me stay."

"Fuck it," he growled. "Do whatever you want. I don't care." He pulled away from Lamont and got out, slamming the door hard.

Kyler heaved a heavy sigh and opened her own door. "I'll call you later, Doc."

Lamont nodded and said softly, "Thanks, Kyler. For this."

She gazed at him, reading uncertainty and slight pain in his eyes. Nodding, she got out and started up the walk. He waited until she went into the house before backing out of the drive.

CHAPTER 50

"There's Cokes in the fridge if you're thirsty," Max's voice came from the darkness just inside the living room. Kyler paused, pinpointing his direction. He switched on a light and she saw the furious look in his eyes.

"Or food or whatever if you're hungry."

"I'm not," she shook her head. "I puked, remember?"

He grunted and started up the stairs. "You really don't have to stay."

She didn't answer as she followed him. His room was under the eve of the house, giving the ceiling a slanting angle that made it comfortable. His bed was snug against the eve, with a computer desk off to one side and a bookshelf against the wall next to the bed. Not much else except clothes thrown here and there.

Max sat down at the computer desk and ran his hands through his hair. His eyes carried weariness and an unexplained pain, and Kyler felt her heart give a squeeze as she stared into them.

"I'm sorry," he muttered. "It's not you and it's not Doc. It's just . . . just something else."

Walking over to the small window, Kyler gazed out at the dark night, her mind working.

"Me giving that money to Carrie?"

He shrugged and then crawled up onto the bed. "Like Doc said, let it go. I don't understand why you did it and I don't care. My fuckin' head's killing me and I'm pretty pissed off right now. Doc . . . he . . ." Trailing off, Max pressed the heels of his hands against his eyes.

"Fuck," he muttered.

Kyler sat on a chair next to the window and ran a hand over the back of her neck, wincing when she scraped the gauze pad.

"Don't sleep," she said.

"I'm not."

"Mind if I smoke?"

Max hesitated, and then pointed a finger towards the computer desk. "Go ahead. You can use that Coke can for an ashtray."

She pulled her cigarettes from her pocket and lit one, inhaling deeply. Snagging the can off the desk, she took it back to the window.

"Can I open this?"

"Yeah," he rolled over and looked at her.

Opening the window, she relished the cool night air as it washed over her. Max watched as she closed her eyes and breathed deeply, smelling the ocean just a few miles away. His weariness was mirrored on her face, and he thought back to that reckless run up the darkened culvert.

"Tell me a story," his voice was very quiet. "Help me stay awake."

She glanced at him. "About what?"

"You."

For a second her eyes went rock hard, anger and something like humiliation shooting from her dark gaze.

"It's not today," he said, pointing to the clock. "You said you wouldn't tell me today, but it's tomorrow now."

Kyler noted the time at almost one in the morning, and shook her head angrily. "I didn't mean that literally, Max."

He didn't answer, but his eyes on hers were steady.

"Please?" The raw emotion in his voice tore at her heart again, and she gritted her teeth. Taking a deep draw off her cigarette, she gladly let the nicotine burn her lungs for a few long seconds before letting the smoke out in a long exhale.

"What do you wanna know?" She relented, stomach clenching.

"Whatever you wanna tell me."

She stared at him. "I don't want to tell you anything."

He watched her for a minute, then sighed heavily and turned on his back, staring at the ceiling. She saw a tear roll down his cheek before he brought a quick hand up to wipe it away.

Jesus, her mind moaned, and she brought her knees up and wrapped her arms around them, dropping her head on her forearms.

"Ok," she growled softly.

Max swallowed and didn't answer.

"Um . . ." she started, faltering. The cigarette burned down to the filter and she lit another from the butt. "I didn't have this . . ." she gestured around the room. "A house . . . or . . . or parents or any of this. So I . . . to survive on my own, on the streets . . . I did what I could, you know?"

Bile rose in her throat and she quickly swallowed it back down. "I . . . stole things, broke into houses and took what I thought would get me a couple quick bucks . . . enough to eat on or . . . whatever. I was . . . pretty good at it. Quick, in and out, you know? Never got caught 'till I was hooked on the smack . . ."

Kyler ran a hand through her hair, feeling the sweat in her temples. Swallowing again, she avoided looking at him. It was bad enough he had to know she was a thief; she absolutely could not bear to see contempt, pity, or revulsion on his face at what she was about to say.

"Let me turn the light off," she muttered. "Ok?"

Max nodded and stared into space as she got up and hit the switch. The room was swamped in darkness, settling down between them solid and silent.

"The first time I shot up I was hooked," her voice was back by the window, but he could tell she was speaking out into the dark night, not towards him. "Heroin had me by the balls with that first fix, and almost immediately I forgot about everything else."

Now he detected a catch in her voice, like she was fighting to hold back tears.

"Jesus Christ," she murmured, and there was a long pause before she continued.

"Then I was stealing for smack. Anything and everything. It was all for that next fix. And I got careless . . . desperate. It wasn't long before I was getting caught, and I'd find myself in jail more and more. I'd try to hit a place fucked up outta my head, so fucking high I was flying, and I couldn't comprehend the alarm systems any more.

"Or I'd try it when I was just starting to jones, shaking, even more desperate. Needing something so goddamned bad I'd raid the people's medicine cabinets first just to see if I could find anything to take the edge off. And that was wasted time right there, just begging the cops to show up and lock me up."

Kyler shook her head, gritting her teeth against the revulsion in her stomach. "It got so I was spending more time in jail than I was out on the streets, and I'd crash hard in there, in a cell. Curled up in a ball, puking . . . shitting . . . convulsing on the floor. Wanting to die . . . and . . ." she lit another cigarette with badly shaking hands, ". . . hoping I wouldn't just so I could get one more fix."

Max heard her take a deep, shaky breath, and he wanted to go to her but was held back by the weight of her words, sitting like a ton of concrete on his chest.

"I finally figured out that I couldn't pull any more B and E's because I couldn't stay straight long enough to do 'em right. At that point every time I tried to break in someplace I'd only end up in jail. So I . . . began to sell something else . . ."

She abruptly stood up. "I gotta use the bathroom, Max."

"Right across the hall," his voice was unreadable in the dark, and she was glad she couldn't see his eyes.

Kyler quickly slipped out of the room and into the bathroom, shutting the door behind her. Hitting her knees, she flipped up the toilet lid and violently threw up burning acid. Dry-heaving painfully for a few long minutes, she finally laid her sweating forehead against the cool porcelain, breathing heavily.

"Christ," she moaned softly.

In his room Max gripped the bedclothes in tight fists, hating himself for doing this to her, hating Doc for being there to bring up those bad memories, and hating even Kyler for being so fucking weak, letting that shit grab hold of her like that.

It was hard for him to equate the strong person he'd come to consider a friend to that gutter-crawling junkie whore—and he knew those would be her next words, that'd she'd started selling her own body for heroin—and the conflicting pictures were tearing him apart inside.

The door opened and Kyler stepped back into the dark. Silently she crossed the room to the window again and in the brief glow of her cigarette lighter he caught a glimpse of her haggard face. It twisted his heart.

"Still not sleeping?" Her voice was rough and jagged with shame and unshed tears.

"No."

There was silence again; thick between them, seeming to last a long time. Finally she cleared her throat and began again.

"I got strung out quick. It . . . I . . . couldn't steal anymore so I . . . started . . . hooking. Selling my body. For dope or money, whatever I could get the most of. It . . . Jesus, it hurt me. My pride, my heart. The only time I could bring myself to do it was when I was high or desperate, one step up from curling up in that ball feeling like I was being beat with a glass-covered baseball bat.

"'Course, by that time, I was one or the other all the time. Everything I'd ever had I'd thrown away 'cause my main focus was getting high and staying high. All the time."

Kyler paused, feeling the shaking in her body. "Anyway, I didn't last a year . . . living like that. I OD'd, like I said, in the ER at the hospital. Doc just happened to be there, saved my life, and got me into a six month program and then into a halfway house after. I was doing ok, but . . ." she swallowed. "Something happened and I . . . went out one night and snorted too much coke. Relapsed, as they say."

God, please don't ask me what that something was that happened, that sent me runnin' back out, her mind pleaded. *Please don't ask me that, Max.*

He didn't; didn't say anything, in fact. Just lay there, waiting for her to go on.

"So, then Doc helped me through that, too. Let me move in with him 'cause I didn't wanna do any more halfway houses. Actually, I really didn't have a choice. Like you thought he was forcing you back in his car and making me stay with you? I felt like he was forcing me to make a decision I didn't want to make. I didn't like either option and I felt like I was being backed into a corner.

"I fought him on that, but eventually gave in because I finally saw that I really *didn't* have a choice if I wanted to stay out of prison. Yeah, prison this time. The judge was tired of seeing me and figured the only way I'd finally get it was to head for the big time."

Kyler took a deep breath and let it out slowly. "Finally I gave in and moved in with Doc. It was either that or a halfway house, and . . . I couldn't do that. But it was a long time before I could trust him, you know? After . . . after everything I'd been through, with the guys I'd . . . done for drugs . . . I . . . well, it was hard and I hated it. But . . ." she shrugged. "I just . . . I didn't have a choice."

She stopped talking then and let the silence drift down around them again. The sound of a car outside the window drew her attention down to the driveway. She watched as a woman got out and walked around to the trunk, opening it.

"I think your mom's home," she said quietly.

Max took a deep breath. "Yeah, probably."

"I'm gonna go, all right? I'll tell your mom what happened. Don't . . . um . . . you don't have to come to work tomorrow. Just . . . take it easy, ok?"

She didn't wait for an answer as she started across the room.

"Hey, Kyler?" Max's voice stopped her.

Silently she waited, eyes closed, the all-too-familiar shame washing over her.

"Did they hurt you? Those guys?"

She gritted her teeth and shook her head. "Yeah," she responded softly and opened the door. "Take care, Max." She was gone before he could respond, slipping out quickly before the light from the hallway could fall on his face and show her his feelings.

Gliding downstairs, she paused just outside the kitchen door, listening to the sounds coming inside. Peeking around the jamb, she noticed an older woman with her back to her, putting away a small supply of groceries.

She cleared her throat and the woman jumped, startled, and whirled around to face her. Kyler held up her hands and spoke in a calm voice.

"Sorry, I didn't mean to scare you. I'm . . . uh . . . Kyler? Max's friend. From the skate park."

"Yeah," the woman said, somewhat shakily. "He's told me a lot about you. I didn't . . ." she glanced at the clock. "Didn't expect to meet you at two in the morning, though."

Kyler nodded. "Yeah . . . we . . . uh . . . well, Max and I were working late, skating the ramps. Basically we hit—collided—in mid-air." She gestured with her hands, trying to depict the picture she was trying to convey while trying not to alarm the woman too much.

"He got cut above the eyebrow. We stitched him up but my doctor wanted me here to try to keep him awake in case he has a concussion. He's still awake . . ." she jerked a thumb over her shoulder.

"And it was nobody's fault, Mom," Max's voice came from behind her. It was Kyler's turn to jerk in surprise, but she didn't turn to look. She was still terrified of seeing contempt on his face.

The woman slowly nodded her head. "I'm Betty Anderson," she stepped forward and held out her hand. Kyler shook it hesitantly, and then stepped back, towards the front door.

"Nice to meet you," she said softly. "Um . . . I gotta go, though, so . . . Max?" She finally turned to him, forcing herself to meet his eyes. "Just take it easy, ok? Like I said, don't worry about work tomorrow—"

"I'm ok, Kyler," he said calmly, his eyes steady and emotionless on hers. She didn't know if she was relieved or crushed at the deadpan look.

Nodding, she dropped her gaze and glanced back at Betty. "Sorry it's so late . . ."

"It's no problem," the woman said, finally seeming to get over her shock. Her eyes offered warmth and were minus the hostility Kyler expected in them.

"Thanks for staying with him."

Kyler nodded and shoved her hands in her pockets. "I, uh . . . gotta go," she repeated. Without another word she walked out the kitchen door and across the living room. Quietly she slipped out the front door and into the night, heart half a beat away from breaking, and still swamped with yet more shame and the world's weight of humiliation crushing her.

Max looked at his mother with exhaustion in his eyes. "I'm not hurt that bad," he said.

Betty nodded and ran a hand through his hair. "She seems nice."

He turned away. "She's . . . yeah, she's ok."

"But . . . ?"

He shrugged. "I don't know. Her doctor? The one who stitched me up? He works at the same hospital dad was in, and . . . he's the same guy . . ." he trailed off and shook his head.

"The one who told us . . ."

"Yeah."

Betty took a deep breath and let it out slowly. "You . . . uh . . . talked to him?"

"Couple times."

She gazed at him, waiting.

"He's . . . ok. Just . . . it's just hard, seeing him again. I just never thought I'd have to, you know?"

"Yeah," she said quietly. Putting her arms around her son, she pulled him into a strong embrace. "Just doesn't seem to get any easier some days."

"I know," he agreed. Finally he pulled away and wiped his eyes. "I'm goin' to bed, all right? I'm ok; I've been up for hours."

"I'll still check on you, all right?"

He offered a small smile. "I figured as much." He started out of the kitchen and she watched with sadness as he headed up the stairs.

Kyler finally slipped around the side of Lamont's house at almost six in the morning. She was surprised to see him sitting on the deck steps with his bare feet in the sand. The sun rising above the horizon played softly on his face, enhancing the weariness in his eyes as he turned to look at her.

"Hey," he said quietly. "You all right?"

"Yeah," she sighed, sitting beside him.

"His mom just get home?"

She shook her head. "No. She got home a couple hours ago. I was out skating."

He nodded and glanced down at his coffee cup. "There's coffee."

It sounded good to her, but Kyler knew her stomach probably wouldn't take it.

"Thanks, but my stomach's not too good right now."

Lamont grunted and gazed out over the water.

"How come you're not in bed?" She asked.

He shrugged. "Couldn't sleep. I'm off today, though, so it's no big deal."

Kyler lit a cigarette and stared at the sand between her feet. She let the silence between them drag on for a few minutes before she said softly,

"I lied to you, Doc."

He was quiet, thinking, and then said, "I know. I figured there's no way you'd let glass get near any of those ramps."

"I just . . . thought . . . I didn't want Max to get screwed on the insurance, and I thought it was probably best if you didn't know, anyway."

Lamont reached out and put a hand gently on the back of her neck. She flinched, but more out of reflex than from pain of the cut.

"I'd've stitched him up regardless," he responded in a quiet voice. "Without dealing with the insurance. I thought you knew that."

Kyler sighed and shook her head. "It's not that. I just thought . . . you know . . . shit . . ." she ran her hands through her hair.

"It's no big deal, kid. It's over, you're both patched up. It's another day."

She closed her eyes and tried to find some comfort from his words.

"Wanna tell me what *did* happen?"

She stared out at the ocean for a few long minutes, letting the ceaseless waves pound on her soul like they pounded on the packed sand.

"We ate . . . like I told you," she started. "After work. He . . . asked me what happened here . . ." she ran a finger through the air above the scars on the inside of her elbow. "And I told him it was from shooting up. It bothered him, I could tell, but I think because he thought I might still be doing it. When I told him I wasn't, he seemed to . . . accept it more, I guess, and I told him one day I might tell him about it."

Lamont remained silent, not saying a word.

"We were walking back from IHOP, and this girl I used to, uh . . ." she trailed off, shrugging. "You know . . . get high with . . ."

Lamont grunted, staring down into his coffee cup.

"She came out of, I don't know, this alley or doorway, or whatever. Scared the shit outta me, but . . ." she paused and said quietly, "I was with Max, so it wasn't . . . too bad."

"But she wanted money," Lamont said softly.

"Or dope," Kyler nodded. "Either or. I gave her a twenty and Max . . . I don't know," she shook her head and stood up, walking to the edge of the water. He waited as she watched the waves for a few minutes before coming back to sit beside him.

"He didn't understand. He knew—like I did—that she'd use it to get high. I tried to explain to him that . . . that it was better for me to give her that money. You know?" Her eyes implored the doc's to understand. "'Cause she'd just get it another way, and," she ran a hand across her face, feeling the exhaustion weighing on her, "she shouldn't have to do that. Not if . . . not if I could give it to her."

He put an arm around her shoulders and pulled her close. Kyler leaned against him, trying to find peace in his embrace. Finally she drew away and lit another cigarette.

"He asked me again about me . . . about my addiction. It . . . shit," she sighed. "I don't know. It felt like he was digging at me, trying to get too close, trying to pry open old wounds."

"Did he? Wanna know?" Lamont gazed at her. "Or was he just pissed you gave her the money?"

She shrugged. "He said he had a friend who died not too long ago from some kind of an addiction, and that he wanted to know why . . . why he couldn't save him."

"What'd you tell him?"

"I felt cornered," she responded flatly. "By this time we were at that old culvert, you know, behind that Seven-Eleven on Elias?"

Lamont gave a reluctant nod, only partway sure of where she was talking about.

"I dropped down into it and skated until I could think again. He followed me and when I finally came up on one side, he was still there, still wanting to know. Said he wasn't trying to hound me, but that . . . I don't know . . . I guess it really hurt him when his friend died.

"So then I said, yeah, sure, I'll tell ya, what do you wanna know?"

"And that's when he got pissed off, right?"

"I guess," she took a deep breath. "He has a lot of built up anger, though. And sadness. It's in his eyes," she shot him a glance.

"So then *he* dropped down in the culvert, only by this time it was all the way dark, and pitch-black down at the bottom. We were skating blind."

"And that's when you hit."

Kyler nodded. "I guess it was my board that caught him across the eyebrow, and like I said, probably some glass or something that got me."

Lamont was quiet for some time, thinking. He thought about Max's father and the crushing impact his death had on the boy. It was no wonder he wanted Kyler to tell him about it, as it was already evident he looked up to her, needing her as a friend and guide.

Whether it was to guide him through the finer points of addiction or overcoming his grief was hard to tell, but Lamont thought that her friendship was probably one of the best forms of grief counseling he could receive.

But on the other hand, pushing her to tell him something she wasn't ready to tell would only drive her further away, and in that respect it would end up a harsh blow to both of them. She needed him as much as he needed her.

"I told him," she finally muttered. "Tonight, when I was keeping him awake." Her eyes rested on the sun, now almost all the way above the horizon. "Or, rather, last night."

"Told him what?" But he thought he already knew.

"About me. About the smack, and . . . and what I finally ended up doing to get it." Kyler dropped her head and ran a hand along the back of her neck, rubbing especially hard over the stitched cut, relishing the white-hot pain that shot out.

"Stop," Lamont said gruffly, taking her hand. "That won't help. Besides masochism is just another form of addiction."

She took a deep breath and let it out slowly. Running a hand through her hair, she stared at the sand between her feet and didn't respond.

"You're not as low as you think you are," he murmured softly. "And you know that."

"Yeah," she finally said hoarsely. "I know."

"What're you afraid of, kid? That he's gonna look at you different? That he's just gonna go and not even come back to tell you he quit?"

"I just don't . . ." Kyler swallowed. "I just don't wanna see that look on his face . . . like . . . like he can't help but see me . . ." her voice caught and she stopped to clear her throat.

"Doing what I did just to get high . . ." her voice was very quiet, almost inaudible.

"Kyler . . ." Lamont said calmly. "*I* don't. And I've seen more of you than he ever will, ok? I've seen you when you begged me to either kill you or shoot you full of more dope, and you didn't care which one it was . . ."

She closed her eyes, swallowing back bile, feeling the intensity of those memories stabbing her like a thousand butcher knives.

"Doc . . ." she managed. "Don't, ok?"

"I won't," he conceded. "But just . . . just don't think that he's gonna turn his back on you."

Kyler was quiet, resting her head in her hands. He stared out over the water, watching as the first of the dolphins shot above the water out towards the horizon.

"Look," he said softly.

She raised her head and stared at the giant forms, curving out of the water, the sun reflecting off their shiny backs in bright pinpoints of light.

"That's peace out there," she muttered. "Freedom."

Lamont offered a small smile and briefly leaned against her. "Like when you skate," he pointed out. "C'mon, kid, you know that."

"Yeah," Kyler sighed.

He took her arm lightly and helped her to her feet. "Get some sleep, ok? It's only, what, not even seven yet. I'll wake you up in time to go to work."

"What about you?" She asked. "You gonna sleep?"

"Nah," he shook his head. "I got a little work I'm gonna do. Might take a nap later on if I don't get called in."

"All right," she gave in. Pausing at the door, she glanced at him. "Um . . . thanks, Doc. For that."

He didn't need to ask what she meant. He merely nodded his head and gestured towards the stairs. "Anytime, kid. You know that."

Kyler took the steps slowly, one at a time with her head down, feeling the heavy weight of exhaustion hard on her. Kicking off her shoes, she fell heavily on the bed and slipped almost immediately into a deep sleep.

CHAPTER 51

KYLER WAS SITTING in front of the computer barely two hours later entering invoices and letting the sounds of John Lee Hooker soothe the turmoil inside her. John Lee, among other blues greats, was another of the doc's musical contributions to her, and with the addition of a cheap yard-sale CD player to the office, she found it was easy to find the peace she seemed to be constantly seeking through the various musical avenues that had only recently been opened to her.

A shadow crossed the doorway and she looked up into Max's hazel eyes, bloodshot from pain and lack of sleep, but with otherwise none of the anticipated contempt or repulsed stare.

"Hey," he said slowly.

"Hey."

He walked in and sat down in the chair opposite the desk, his eyes still on hers. "Um . . . you ok?"

Kyler nodded. "Bruised up some . . . neck hurts . . . but . . ." she shrugged.

"Yeah."

"Aren't you, uh, supposed to be in school?"

Max ran a light hand over the gauze pad above his eye. "Mom wanted me to stay home, get some rest."

"Max," she glanced up at the clock, "it's nine o'clock. You coulda rested a little longer, don'tcha think?"

He shrugged and then slowly shook his head. "I couldn't sleep, Kyler. I wanted to come here and talk to you."

She felt her stomach clench and reached for her smokes with a slightly trembling hand.

"Come to tell me you quit?"

"What?" Genuine surprise crossed his face, and her stomach loosened up some. "Why would I quit?"

Kyler gazed at him. "Why wouldn't you?"

He stared down at his hands for a few long seconds, thinking. He'd noticed the pain in her own eyes, but knew that it didn't come from anything physical.

"What you told me last night . . ." he brought his eyes back up to hers and saw the pain spike, so much so that she winced as if anticipating a blow. "I . . . I'm not here to tell you that I'm quitting because of that, ok? I'm not here to judge you or . . . or pity you, or anything. I don't know what you went through, even though you told me, and it . . . it's hard for me to comprehend, but then I've never been addicted to anything other than skating.

"I just wanted to tell you that . . . I appreciate that . . . last night . . . you telling me. It helped me to see how my fa— . . . my friend could do the things he did." He swallowed heavily, seeing how close he'd come to saying "my father," and not sure if he was ready to put a face to the anonymous concept of his addicted "friend."

Kyler just looked at him through hooded eyes, trying to still the slow rolling of her stomach.

"I didn't want to tell you."

Max nodded and looked down at his hands again. "I know. I pushed you, and . . . and I'm sorry."

She shook her head and took a deep breath, letting it out slowly. "It . . . I don't wanna talk about it, ok? I told you because you were hurting, I saw that. And . . . and because nobody else I know besides me woulda been crazy enough to try that run up the culvert in the dark."

He shot her a glance and saw that she was serious.

"Yeah," he admitted, "It *was* dark."

Kyler took a deep draw off her cigarette and let the smoke filter out of her nose. The silence stretched out into long minutes, and finally she got up and stuck the invoices in the tray on the wall. "Guess I better get to work."

Max nodded. "I'm gonna head home for awhile, try to get some sleep. But I'll be back, though, ok?"

She gazed at him, noting the intensity in his eyes.

"Ok."

He walked out the door and she stood still until she saw him sit down on the bus stop bench across the street. Running a hand through her hair, Kyler gave a heavy sigh, still feeling the shame and humiliation crowding out everything else.

True to his word, Max was back right at four. Kyler was up on the railing on fifty-two, and she caught his now-familiar gait as he walked across the grass down below her. He looked up and nodded, and then she heard his footsteps on the wooded stairs.

"Hey," his head poked above the platform and with ease he pulled himself up.

"Hey, back," she pitched the butt of her smoke over the side and regarded him, still too leery of seeing condemnation in his hazel eyes.

"Been busy?" He walked over and handed her a bottle of water.

"Nah," she shrugged. "Just the usual repairs."

He nodded and stared down into the bowl. "My mom liked you," he said, somewhat thoughtfully. "Said you can come over for dinner sometime if you want."

"Really?" Kyler arched an eyebrow. "I'd've figured since it was so late she probably—"

"She's usually up late, anyway," Max pulled himself up on the railing beside her. "It was no big deal."

She was quiet for a moment, gazing out across the park. When she spoke, she turned her head and met his eyes. "All right. I'll come for dinner sometime. Tell her thanks."

"Sure." He took a deep breath and looked behind him at the other ramps. "What all'd you get today?"

She gave a small shrug and hopped down off the railing. "Everything."

"Everything? Even the bolts underneath those two little ramps?" He pointed.

"Yeah."

Max gazed at her. "I thought we said I'd do those, since you're . . . uh . . ."

"I didn't . . ." Kyler started and then stopped, gathering her words. "I wasn't entirely sure you'd be back," she admitted. "I mean, even though you said you would be, I just . . ."

"I'm not a liar," he said seriously. "If I wasn't coming back, I'd've told you this morning."

"I know," she nodded. "*Now*. But this morning . . . you know . . . I wasn't sure, so I just went ahead and did it all."

He was quiet for a brief minute, and then said quietly, "All right. But next time lemme get the shit underneath, ok? No sense you having to do it."

She shot him an unreadable look over her shoulder as she started down the steps. "I don't let my weaknesses stop me," she muttered. "Being claustrophobic's something I've lived with my whole life. It ain't gonna change and I'm not gonna change for it."

"Still," Max said, taking her arm and stopping her. "Just let me do it, all right?"

Kyler gazed at him for a long moment before gently taking her arm back. "Sometimes," she said. "You can do it sometimes. The other times . . . I'll do it."

He regarded her, confusion in his eyes.

"I'd feel like it was beating me if I didn't at least try, you know?"

"Kyler . . ." he sighed, but she just shook her head.

"It doesn't matter anyway. They're done for the time being."

Max took a deep breath but didn't respond. He fell into step beside her as they started across the grass. After a few long moments of silence he said quietly,

"Wanna come to dinner *tonight*? Mom's cooking her famous spaghetti."

Despite herself, Kyler smiled. "Yeah. Sure, I'll come."

"Yeah?" He grinned.

"Yeah. But just don't expect me to eat too much, ok?" Her smile faded somewhat. "My stomach, you know . . ."

Max nodded. "I know." He paused and then said softly, "Thanks, Kyler."

"For what?" She glanced at him with raised eyebrows.

He shrugged. "For just coming to dinner, I guess."

She plopped down at the chair in front of the computer and lit a cigarette. Her eyes were steady as they stared into his, but he detected a small amount of uncertainty in them.

"I should be the one thanking you," she said. "For . . ." she flapped a hand vaguely. "For not . . . you know . . . being too judgmental and—"

"I told you before I'm not gonna judge you," he said seriously.

"Yeah, but . . ." she trailed off and took a deep drag off her smoke.

Max shook his head. "Yeah, but nothing. We all got our demons, right? And we all do what we gotta do."

Kyler stared at him and then gave a slow nod. "Yeah, I guess," she said softly.

The office was quiet for a few minutes and then he gestured for her to get up out of the chair.

"Go skate," he said with a slight smile. "I'll put the invoices in."

She hesitated, but then reached for her board as a thin thread of anticipation started through her veins. "You sure?"

"Definitely. You did all the repairs today; I'd feel like I'm just drawing my check for free if I didn't do something."

"All right," she offered a grin that rested easily on his heart, beautiful in its weariness. "But you gotta come join me when you're done."

Max grinned back and gave her a gentle shove towards the door. "You got it."

CHAPTER 52

THE PHONE RANG harshly through the house, tearing into Kyler's sleep and dragging her back to awakening. She bolted up in bed, still too close to her old life to not think about inherent danger, even though she'd been completely clean for almost seven months.

"Fuck," she muttered, and ran a shaking hand across her face. The sky was pitch black outside the window; the clock on the nightstand read just past three in the morning.

Throwing back the covers, she got out of bed and crossed to the door in a few quick strides. Instinct told her that for once the phone wasn't for her, but still, at that hour, she knew it wasn't good news.

Slipping silently down the hallway, she stopped just outside of Lamont's bedroom, one ear cocked towards the two-inch crack between the jamb and the door. The sound of his voice was soft, the words intelligible, but the tone drilled right through her heart.

After a few minutes she heard him hang up the phone and with one hand she gently pushed the door open. Lamont glanced at her and she saw his eyes were deep set and haggard.

"That was Emily," he muttered. "She took Curtis off the respirator."

Kyler shut her eyes and leaned against the jamb. "Shit," she whispered. After a moment she straightened up and looked at him. He was still sitting on the bed, staring absently at the floor.

"You're goin'," it wasn't a question, but he nodded anyway.

"Yeah."

She nodded back, mainly to herself since he was still staring at the floor. "I'll put some coffee on." Without waiting for a response, she slipped away from the door and headed downstairs.

In the kitchen she pulled the coffee out of the refrigerator and filled the pot with water, dumping it into the urn. Her motions were automatic, her thoughts about a million miles away. The thought of Curtis lying there, now dead, put a lead ball in the pit of her stomach.

Jesus, that coulda been me a fucking hundred times.

She ran a hand across her face and watched absently as the coffee started to percolate, dripping slowly into the pot.

Upstairs she heard the shower in Lamont's bathroom start, and taking a deep breath, she had to shut her eyes briefly as real grief, surprising in its intensity, rushed over her. Without even ever having met Emily's son, she'd felt a kindred spirit towards him born of addiction and heartache.

Once again, drugs had claimed another life.

"Fuck," she muttered, and pulled a travel mug down out of the cabinet. Filling it to the brim and leaving it black and strong, she screwed on the top and left it on the kitchen table. Quickly she ran back upstairs and pulled on the same clothes she'd just taken off only a few hours before.

Lamont had an open suitcase on his bed and was packing it with clothes and toiletries when she walked back in his room. His eyes met hers and she saw a bone-deep weariness in them.

"I got a plane in an hour and a half. She's up in San Fran. Um . . . the funeral's the day after tomorrow, but I might stay the whole week."

Kyler nodded. "Ok. You want me to drive you? That way you won't have to pay to park."

He looked at her with raised eyebrows. "Yeah . . ." he said slowly. "Thanks."

"Sure."

"It's a stick, though. Can you . . ."

"Yeah," she nodded. "I can drive just about anything, Doc." Gesturing towards his suitcase, she asked, "You need any help?"

"Nah," he sighed, staring down at his suitcase as if he'd never seen it before. "I guess the only thing I really need is funeral clothes."

A deep silence fell between them, and then Kyler cleared her throat. "All right, then. I got your coffee in a travel cup on the table. If you drink it quick you can have it gone before you get to security."

Lamont looked at her and briefly wondered how he'd missed her making that transition from terror-ridden junkie to the confident person he now saw standing before him. As if reading his mind she gave a somewhat wry, bitter grin and offered,

"It's been almost a year, Doc. I'm slowly moving past it."

"You're doin' a helluva lot better," he said softly as he zipped up his suitcase and lifted it off the bed.

"Yeah, I know. You get everything?"

He shrugged as if it didn't matter, and she realized that it actually really didn't. Like he'd said, all he really needed was funeral clothes.

Throwing his suitcase in the trunk, Lamont slipped into the unfamiliar passenger seat as Kyler got behind the steering wheel. He waited for her to adjust the seat and mirrors, but she just started the car and expertly shifted into reverse and backed out of the driveway.

"It's funny," he murmured. "I just never thought about you driving. I don't know why . . . just never came up, I guess."

She glanced at him as she adjusted the seat while merging onto the freeway. "I'd rather be skating, Doc, but you know I *did* get a couple GTA beefs."

"Yeah," he nodded, staring out the window. "But still . . . I just never thought about it."

Kyler grunted and glanced in the side mirror. She waited a brief minute and then said quietly, "I'm really sorry, Doc. Will you . . . will you tell Emily that for me?"

He looked at her. "Yeah, kid, I will."

"Thanks," she chanced a glance at him before sliding over to the exit ramp for the airport. Pulling to the curb in front of his terminal, she had popped the trunk and was walking around to it before he even got out of the car.

"Shit," he said as he saw his suitcase already on the ground behind the car. "That's pretty fucking quick."

"GTA beefs," she repeated, somewhat bitterly. "Gotta be quick when you're ripping ofF a car, and I guess I still carry those habits."

Lamont stopped and looked at her, searching for the hidden meaning. She caught the look in his eyes and gave a slow shake of her head. "But not every bad habit, Doc."

"You gonna be ok?"

Kyler stared at him, reading uncertainty in his eyes. "Hey . . ." her voice was very quiet. "Yeah, Doc, I'm gonna be fine. Please don't worry about me, ok?"

He sighed and shook his head. "I don't know," he mumbled. "I just . . ."

She wrapped her arms around him in a now-familiar embrace. "Don't worry. I'm gonna be fine. You just take care of Emily, ok?" She felt him nod against her shoulder and then he pulled away, picking up his suitcase.

"Call me, though, if you need anything, all right?"

"I will."

"Um . . . here . . ." setting his suitcase back down, he pulled his wallet from his pocket.

"Doc . . ."

"Well, there's not much food in the house, Kyler," he pushed some money into her hand. "Order a pizza or something, but I don't wanna leave you without anything."

"I'm making my own money now," she said quietly. "And you know me; I'm never gonna starve."

"Please," he muttered. "Just take it, ok? Ease my mind a little."

Kyler sighed. "Shit." Shaking her head, she stuffed the money in her pocket without looking at it. "All right, Doc."

"Thanks," he managed to smile. He pulled her into another brief hug and then let her go, picking up his suitcase again. "I'll call you," he said over his shoulder, and she watched him disappear through the glass doors.

Slipping back in the car, Kyler pulled away from the curb and headed back to his house. She felt exhausted and somewhat empty, homesick for the doc already and grieving for Curtis and his addiction . . . the addiction that killed him.

And again—like always—there was that slight itch at the base of her skull, insanely begging her to get as high as she could, as quick as she could.

She gripped the wheel and gritted her teeth, feeling the weight of Lamont's money in her pocket.

Kyler booted up the computer in the office of the skate park and plopped wearily down in the chair. She knew she should be home in bed at the doc's, but after dropping off his car she'd known that sleep was over for the night.

Grabbing her board, she'd hit the streets once again, skating hard and aggressively, trying to dispel the demons yet once again. And now here it was, not even six in the morning, and her body was sore, her mind numb as she attempted to enter this week's invoices into the computer.

Her stomach gave a weak growl and she reached down to the bag beside her and pulled out the new coffee pot and small can of coffee she'd just bought with the money Lamont had given her. It was a needed purchase, she knew, and it got the tempting money out of her pocket and into something useful.

Setting the pot on the counter, she plugged it in and set the clock on it before starting to make her second pot of coffee for the day. As the aroma of it filled the room, she began to slowly wake up, her mind becoming more alert.

Coffee, she thought. *Coffee, and then work and then skating. In that order.* She knew if she kept moving, kept working, then her mind wouldn't have time to dwell on Curtis, Emily's grief, or the doc's lost eyes.

And it also wouldn't be given the chance to feel the need to feed her own addiction.

It was ten hours and four pots of coffee later and Kyler felt jittery to the point of screaming from all the caffeine. Her stomach was a hard, shriveled knot, protesting the thought of any more of the thick black stuff, and making any kind of food unappetizing and unthinkable.

She was lying under a ramp small enough so that the bottom boards of the bowl were pressing against her chest and awkwardly bolting in screws with the electric drill.

Max walked up to her and shook his head in aggravation. She was stuck under there in extremely tight quarters, and why the hell she just didn't let him do it was beyond all rational thought.

Her claustrophobia's gotta be blasting outta the top of her head by now, he thought, and carefully squatted next to her.

"Hey," he said quietly, touching her bare leg gently. "It's me."

He watched as her sunken stomach tightened up for a brief second before slowly relaxing. Kyler rolled out from underneath the ramp soaked in sweat and pale as a ghost.

"Jesus," he growled. "Why the fuck don't you let me do this shit?"

She lay on the grass and didn't answer. With her eyes closed against the sun, he could see her grabbing onto the open air with an almost physical gesture.

"It's done," she responded, and lit a cigarette without getting up or even opening her eyes.

He shook his head again and sat down beside her. "You're sweating."

"It's hot under there."

"It's more than that."

Finally she opened her eyes and looked at him with a bemused expression on her face. Max could see the total exhaustion in her gaze, made more prominent by the dark circles around her eyelids.

"Careful, kid. You're startin' to sound like the doc."

"Well, Kyler, shit, you know? Why do you put yourself through this?"

She sat up and drew her legs to her chest, resting her forearms across her knees. She stared at him a long moment and then finally gave a slight shrug.

"I don't know," she sighed. "I guess I'm just afraid that if I give in too easily it'll end up grabbing a hold of me."

He met her eyes, confused. "What, you mean by not forcing claustrophobic issues on yourself, the claustrophobia wins?"

Kyler took a deep draw off her smoke and stared across the park. "I don't know, Max," she answered tiredly. "It doesn't matter now. It's done, like I said."

Max was quiet for a few minutes, and then in an effort to change the subject, said, "I see we got a new coffee pot."

"Yeah," she stood up and held out a hand, pulling him to his feet. "I've been up almost all night and I really needed it. C'mon, I wanna show you something."

He fell into step beside her as they headed towards the office. "Why've you been up all night?"

"Hadta take Doc to the airport," she responded. "Early this morning, around four. Couldn't sleep after that."

Max waited a beat and then asked, "He went out of town?"

"Up to Frisco," she said. "For a funeral."

"Oh . . ." he said hesitantly. "Um . . . who passed away?"

She stopped by the desk and opened the bottom drawer, pulling out her Excedrin bottle. Pouring its contents into her palm, she selected a valium and popped it without meeting his eyes.

"His girlfriend's son."

Max watched her swallow the pill through narrowed eyes, but his voice showed surprise when he asked with raised eyebrows, "Doc's got a girlfriend?"

"Kinda, I guess," she shrugged, plopping down in the chair. "She . . . I think she lives up there now. Moved there to take care of her son, but . . ." she gestured vaguely. "Drugs. You know?" Her eyes were sharp and unreadable, staring into his. "Drugs got him."

Max watched her for a minute before reluctantly looking away.

"Anyway," Kyler sighed, "that's why I bought the coffee pot. Have some if you want. Fresh; just made it not even an hour ago."

"I might in a minute," he muttered.

"Well, here," she reached below her and pulled up a wrapped package whose shaped depicted it could only be one thing. "Happy birthday. Betcha can't guess what it is."

"What?" Max stared at her in surprise. "How'd you know it was my birthday?"

"I'm resourceful when I wanna be," she smiled. "Besides, it's on the forms you filled out when you started. I've been keeping track 'cause I wanted to see if you still wanted to work fulltime or not."

He slowly took the package, feeling the wheels of the skateboard as they tried to roll out of the paper. Offering a wry grin, he said,

"You didn't have to do this, Kyler."

She shrugged and got up to get some water out of the refrigerator. Handing him a bottle, she drank half of hers in one swallow; the cold water heaven as it went down her throat.

"Yeah, I did," she smiled, somewhat embarrassed. "I, uh . . . you know . . . just wanted to say thanks. For doing everything you do. You've really helped me."

Max shook his head and pulled the paper off the board. His breath caught as he stared down at it, running his eyes along the details as his mind recognized high-quality; a top-of-the-line product.

"Jesus . . ." he breathed. "Kyler, this . . ."

She sat back down across from him, watching him wordlessly.

"Shit, this is too much. How much . . . um . . ." he swallowed, tapping his fingers along the deck, feeling the new grip tape under his palm. From just the short time he'd been working with her, he knew and recognized her honesty, and knew that this new board—everything top-notch from the deck to the wheels—was bought and paid for by her. She never took anything from the park, and that included parts and materials for her own board.

He raised his eyes to hers. "How much did this cost?"

Kyler leaned back in the chair and looked at him, eyebrows slightly raised. She ran her hands across her face before lacing her fingers behind her neck. He was again struck by the hard exhaustion in her eyes, and found himself wanting to reach out to her, to try to ease it if he could.

"Shit, kid, you expect me to tell you that?" She grinned and lit a cigarette. "Anyway, don't worry about it. I mean, you know . . ." she shifted her eyes away and he witnessed the shame and the pain as they crossed her face. "Wasn't really all that long ago that I woulda spent it on dope. So . . ." she forced her gaze back to his. "I'm glad to do it. Really."

"Well," he relented reluctantly, "my old one *was* kinda beat up."

"And the grip tape was almost nonexistent," she added. He stared at her and she flapped a hand. "I saw you fall the other day . . . saw your foot slip off the board like it was on glass."

"And that's the third layer I've got on it. Keeps wearing through. Just too old."

Kyler took a deep breath and stared out the door into the park. "Yeah," she sighed. "Hell, I didn't want you to break your neck out there."

Max laid his new board carefully on the desk and met her eyes. "Thank you," he said seriously. "I really mean that, Kyler."

She nodded, stifling a yawn. "You're welcome, Max." She paused and crushed out her smoke, and then asked quietly, "So? You still wanna come on fulltime?"

"Yeah . . ." he started, then stopped, thinking. "I still can't come in before four during the week, though, 'cause of school. But I can pick up a few more hours on Saturdays and Sundays, if you want. I don't know how full time that is . . ."

Kyler flapped a hand. "It doesn't really matter, I don't guess. I'm still gonna be here, but . . ." she gave a tired smile. "Just good to have somebody else to talk to."

He nodded, letting the silence drift down around them for a minute. Finally she sat up and took the last drink of her water, watching him over the bottle.

"Go on out and skate," she said softly. "I know you gotta be dyin' to."

"Yeah," he admitted, and he really was. He thoroughly anticipated the feel of the smoother wheels racing along the wood; the new deck, lighter and stronger with the newest construction, and more stable with the new grip tape, riding easily beneath his feet.

Jesus, I can probably come damn near close to flyin' on this thing, he thought, as he again reached out and ran a hand down the length of the deck. But then his eyes found Kyler's, and the weight of sheer exhaustion shining from them cut him to his core.

"Yeah, I'm dyin' to try this thing out. But first . . ." he jerked a thumb towards the storage room. "Why don't you go take a nap?"

She looked at him for a long moment, not saying a word. True, she'd slept in the room before, and equally true was the fact that she desperately needed sleep. However, she'd held off sleeping in the room since Max had come to work with her, even for a short nap or two.

Since her trust in Lamont had grown, Kyler no longer found the need to sleep at the park, and hadn't used the storage room for that since she'd OD'd on the Nyquil months ago.

"C'mon, Kyler, you're exhausted," he murmured. "Besides," he hesitated a moment, "the valium's kicking in. I can tell."

Kyler regarded him with hooded eyes for what seemed like years to him. She neither affirmed nor denied the valium, but realized it didn't matter anyway.

It's not like I hid taking the damn thing.

"I'm all right," she muttered.

Now it was Max's turn to remain silent, his hazel eyes boring into hers.

"Bullshit," he finally said.

She pulled her gaze away and gave a heavy sigh. Now, not surprisingly, she felt the worn carpet calling to her. No pillow, she realized, and no blanket. But she was raised on the streets, where pillows and blankets were luxuries, not necessities.

"Shit," she growled softly. Looking back at him, he could see her indecision. "All right."

Max nodded and offered a slight grin. "I'll watch the place, no problem, ok?"

"Wake me up in an hour," Kyler pushed herself out of the chair, feeling the sudden pull of the valium.

"Sure."

"One hour, Max," she shot him a thin glare. "No longer."

He held up his hands in surrender. "One hour."

She stumbled around the desk and slid in the door to the storage room. It was dark and comfortable, and despite her reservations, Kyler curled up in a corner with her back to the wall and was asleep almost immediately.

CHAPTER 53

"HEY, KYLER," *A familiar voice came to her. She looked and saw an unfamiliar face standing beside her. "This shit's real." The young man had sandy blond hair that was tousled and dirty, but it wasn't the same color as Josh's, even if he spoke with Josh's voice.*

"This shit's real," he repeated, and it hurt her to hear that sweet voice again after all this time. It hurt even more, though, when he held up a spike with murky yellow liquid in it.

"Don't do it," she groaned.

"Too late," he grinned a horrible grin, and that was when she saw the hole in the upper left side of his chest. "Blew out my heart."

"Josh . . ." she felt her own heart skip a beat and then pause.

"Curtis," he responded. "My name's Curtis."

"Where's Josh?" Now her heart was having trouble beating again, and she gripped her left breast as panic began pounding in her brain.

"Don't know no Josh. But here, try some of this. It'll blow your heart out, too, but it's worth it. It's always worth it; you know that, right?"

Helplessly, she could only stand and watch as he inserted the needle in the scarred vein of her forearm. It was only seconds before she felt that angel/demon/lover/sinner race through her bloodstream.

"On its way," Curtis muttered. "Won't be long now."

"Shit," Kyler moaned, panic now lending the dope a hand, kick-starting her heart and forcing it to pound faster, rushing the poison through her body.

"Kyler," he said. "Hey, Kyler . . ."

"KYLER," THE VOICE was very close to her, almost next to her ear. "C'mon, wake up. Kyler." Max shook her shoulder lightly, and she bolted upright, just barely managing to bite back the scream.

"Easy," he said quietly. "It's just me."

Kyler stared at him though terrified eyes as her brain managed to register her friend beside her. Sweat covered every inch of her body; she felt it in her armpits and temples, and sliding in thick, oily strips down her back and sides.

"Fuck," she growled, scrubbing a hand across her face.

Max was still hunkered down beside her with his hand on her shoulder, lending the comfort he knew she needed.

"You ok?"

"Not yet," she said shakily. "Gimme a minute."

He nodded, but then laid the phone in her lap and stood up. "You have a call. I'll be outside, all right?"

Kyler managed to meet his gaze and saw the strange look he was giving her.

"I talked in my sleep," she sighed. "Didn't I?"

Max gave a slight shake of his head, more in agreement than disagreement. He pointed at the phone. "It's Doc."

She watched as he left, pulling the door gently closed behind him. Putting the phone to her ear, she fell back on the floor and watched the ceiling advance and recede in time to the erratic slamming of her heart against her ribs.

"Doc," she mumbled.

"Hey," his voice calmed her somewhat, but the strangling arms of the nightmare were still around her, choking.

"You ok?"

"Yeah. I was just . . . taking a short nap," she sat back up and pulled a battered pack of smokes from her pocket.

"Yeah, I kinda gathered that."

There was silence for a short minute before Kyler asked quietly, "Emily?"

"'Bout what you'd expect," and now his voice held a sorrow and exhaustion of its own. "Heartbroken. She can't stop blaming herself; thinking if . . . you know . . . she'd done something different . . ."

Kyler shut her eyes and rubbed her forehead. "Doc . . ." she started, then stopped, unable to find the words of comfort he needed to hear. "I'm sorry."

"Anyway, um . . ." Lamont cleared his throat. "I meant to call sooner, let you know I got here ok. But things've been . . . hectic . . . you know?"

"Yeah," she sighed. "I know."

"But I should be home early next week, I think. I plan on it anyway."

"Stay as long as you need to, Doc. Don't worry about things here, ok?"

There was silence for a long time, and then he finally spoke in a voice so soft she had to strain to hear.

"I can't help but worry, Kyler. You know that. Just . . . promise me you'll call, ok? It's tearing her apart up here. I don't wanna go through this shit."

Kyler was stunned into silence, plainly reading the implication in the doc's voice, noting the comparison between Emily and her son, and the doc and . . . herself.

Christ, does he really think of me like a daughter? And immediately she knew that was true. The similarities of Lamont and Emily, her with an addicted—and now *dead*—son, and the doc with a . . . surrogate? . . . daughter, who was just as addicted and who knew along with most of the rest of the world that it wouldn't take but one hit, pill, line, or fix to send her running right back out there.

"If it gets that bad, just promise me you'll call before you try to fix it on your own." Now his voice held anguish as well, and it was like a knife slashing away at her heart.

"Doc . . ."

"What was the dream about?"

"What?"

"The dream you just had. What was it about?"

"You know what it was about," she muttered. "Same shit it's always about."

"So promise. Don't make me go through this shit. She's stronger than me, Kyler. I . . . I don't think I could handle it."

"Doc, you're not making sense," Kyler snapped. *"I'm not Curtis. I'm not gonna go out and get fucked up just because* he *did. Have some fucking faith in me, will you?"*

The silence on the line was thick and heavy for a long time. Finally Lamont took a deep breath and let it out slowly, and when he spoke again, his voice was calmer. She sensed he was pulling on some inner self-control in order to regain a little sanity.

"Shit," he sighed. "I'm sorry, kid. You're right. I'm just . . . it's hell up here right now, and—"

"I know," she responded. "I'm sorry, too. It . . . shit like this, Doc . . . it . . . you know . . ." Taking a long drag off her cigarette, Kyler rubbed her forehead and shut her eyes against the headache forming above her left eyebrow.

"Yeah, I know," he said in a tired voice. "Look, I'm gonna get off here, all right? Uh . . . I'll have my phone on me . . ." he trailed off awkwardly.

"Ok," her voice was calm, somewhat soothing now, trying to ease both their heartaches. "And you can call me, too. It goes both ways, right?"

"Yeah. Take it easy."

"You, too." Kyler hit the off button and laid her head on her knees, still trying to calm the turmoil inside her. Finally she stood up and walked out into the office, noting immediately the shadows on the wall.

"Damn it," she growled, staring at the clock. Shoving the phone in her back pocket, she slipped out the door and into the park, looking around for Max and finally spotting him way over on the other side of the park.

He glanced up at her with a few nails in his mouth as she walked up. His eyes held uncertainty but he offered a small smile as she climbed up and sat on the coping.

"I said an hour," she said, somewhat accusingly. "Not three."

"You needed it," he responded casually, hopping up to sit beside her. "Besides, you did most of the work today. Felt like I had to give something back."

She grunted and lit a cigarette. "Tried out your board, yet?"

"Yeah," he grinned. "Smoothest run I ever made."

"I know," she glanced at him. "I tried it."

"I know. And I don't blame ya."

Kyler glanced up at the setting sun, smoking thoughtfully. Max cleared his throat and asked in a hesitant voice,

"Doc doin' all right?"

"I guess," she sighed. "'Bout as well as you'd expect. It hurts him, though. He loves her, and because she's hurting, it's tearing at him."

Max was quiet, thinking.

"But anyway," she hopped down into the bowl and looked up at him. "C'mon, it's closing time."

He nodded and walked with her as they headed towards the office. "You wanna come to dinner tonight? Mom's making me tacos for my birthday."

She shot him a sarcastic glance and threw an arm around his shoulders. "Sure, yeah, brand new board *and* tacos. What else you gonna get, huh?"

Max gave a small laugh shoved her away. "Gonna get you to skate with me on the way home. Show me how good you are on the street."

"You kidding? Shit, the street's my home ground."

"All right," he joked. "Prove it."

Once outside in the parking lot, Kyler shot him a look and then was off like a bullet down the street. Max didn't hesitate as he shot after her, but it soon became obvious that she was in a whole other league of street skating than he was.

Using everything she could, from the inch-thick backs of benches to the rough concrete barriers around the fountains in the park, Kyler skated hard and fast, scaring him at times with her fearless jumps and grinds.

Jesus, and even I *didn't think she was that good,* he thought as he fought to keep up with her, despite the fact that he was barely pulling any tricks; merely skating, four wheels on the asphalt as they made their way to his house.

In awe he watched as she jumped the hood of a car without even coming close to touching it, raced sideways along a guardrail, and then kicked up onto the slanting concrete underpinning of a viaduct. She came down easy, comfortable on her board.

"Wait," he shouted breathlessly, and Kyler gave a sharp twist, going against the grain of her wheels and coming to an abrupt stop. Kicking up her board and catching it out of the air with one hand, she waited like she wasn't even winded.

"Jesus," Max gasped as he finally caught up with her. "Aren't you even outta breath?"

"A little," she shrugged. "But I smoke, so I'm assuming it's normal."

"Great," he bent over and put his hands on his knees, fighting to breathe. "Sarcasm, that's great."

She smiled and lit a cigarette. "How'd you do?"

"You know how I did," he tried to smile in return but grimaced as a sharp pain raced across his ribs. "I could barely keep up with you."

Kyler was quiet for a couple minutes, watching him try to catch his breath. "Sorry. I'll go easy on you next time."

"Nah," he shook his head and stood up straight, stretching his back. "Don't. Don't ever let up, ok?" Now his eyes were serious, boring into hers.

She read the message in his gaze, felt it in her heart. Slowly she shook her head and let smoke filter out of her nose. "Yeah. You're right. I don't think I ever could. When I skate hard I'm at my best, you know? I can . . . let go . . ."

Max nodded and walked over to her, limping slightly. "Right."

They walked the last block in silence. Kyler felt lighter, freer, like she always did, and knew that Max felt the same way . . . even if he was severely winded. He glanced at her and grinned, and she felt relief in her heart.

"Tacos, huh?"

"Yeah, they're my favorite."

They walked in his front door and Betty poked her head out of the kitchen, smiling when she saw them. "Timed it just right, guys. Food's about ready."

"Awesome," Max draped an arm around his mom's waist and leaned over, smelling the seasoned beef. "I'm starving."

Betty shot Kyler a sarcastic glance and rolled her eyes. "What else is new?"

Kyler grinned and set her board down in a corner. "Can I help you with anything?"

"Hell, no," Betty set out three plates on the table. "You're a guest. Guests don't help."

"Sure?"

"Absolutely. Sit down, relax."

Max looked over at her. "Whatcha want to drink?"

"Uh, water's fine."

He brought her a glass of ice water and she took a drink, relishing the cold liquid as it rolled down her parched throat.

"Check out my new board, Mom," he plopped down in the chair beside her and gestured towards his skateboard in the doorway. "Kyler gave it to me for my birthday."

"Nice," Betty grinned. "Don't kill yourself on it, ok?"

"I won't," he winked at Kyler, who offered a small smile in return.

The dinner was excellent, though after two tacos Kyler felt her stomach start to protest. She leaned back and stretched, watching as they polished off the rest of the meal. "Thanks, Betty. That was really good."

"No problem," the woman answered. "You sure you got enough, though?"

"Yeah. I got kind of a weak stomach, and I don't like to push it."

Betty gazed at her for a moment, and Kyler read something in her eyes that said she knew a bit about weaknesses.

"Why don't you two go on out back, break in that new board? I'll throw these in the dishwasher and I'll be out in a minute."

"Here, lemme help you," Kyler picked up her own plate and a few bowls before Betty could protest.

"No, really—"

"No, you cooked," Kyler said quietly. "No reason you should have to do everything else, too."

"Well, all right," Betty relented. "I'm not gonna argue."

Together the three of them cleaned up the mess and then walked out on the back deck. There was a kidney-shaped pool in the backyard that had been empty, Max had told her, since he was about eight and fell in love with skateboarding. His parents had come home one evening and caught him siphoning the water out onto the lawn, flooding his mom's flower beds.

After a spanking and exile to his room, his parents laughingly agreed to drain the pool and let him skate in it, and hoped he wouldn't bash his head in on the concrete.

Now, as familiar as only somebody can be after another eight years, Max slipped over the side and rode his new skateboard with the ease and agility of one born to it. Kyler watched him for a few minutes, sensing Betty beside her, watching her son and still praying he wouldn't suffer a massive injury.

"He loves it 'bout as much as you do. Thanks for getting him that skateboard, Kyler. He's been wanting one for a long time, but . . ." she shrugged awkwardly. "They're not exactly cheap, you know?"

Kyler gazed at her for a long minute, and then gave a slow nod. "I built that one from the products we got at the park. He's been more of a help than I thought I needed, and I just wanted to, you know, say thanks. I figured he deserves the best of what's out there right now. He . . ." she swallowed, watching as Max skated the pool hard, using every inch of the concrete.

"He doesn't judge me," she finally said. "And that's more than I could find out of ten other people put together." She paused and shot Betty a sidelong look. "And I guess I got you to thank for that."

Betty was quiet, thinking. "Max . . . has changed a lot in the past couple of years. He's grown up a lot more than most boys his age, and his level of maturity is more grounded. He doesn't judge because he knows he has no right. There are . . ." she trailed of, gathering her words, "a lot of personalities that make up one person, and no one person has a right to judge another because of that fact, you understand?"

Kyler nodded, her eyes on Max.

"And he's learned that already. Most people don't ever learn it."

"Yeah," Kyler said shortly. "I know."

"So," Betty continued, "I guess I've got *you* to thank for being his friend. He . . . doesn't have a lot of those, and I was starting to get a little worried, if you want to know the truth."

She was surprised when Kyler gave her a bitter look. "Don't worry about him not having a lot of friends, Betty. I went a long time without having any, and the ones who claimed to be . . . actually were far from it. Friends are overrated."

Betty sensed the jaded tone in her voice and her eyes softened a bit. "No they're not," she muttered softly. "He's not. Your doctor's not, right?"

Kyler dropped her eyes and stared down into the pool. "Yeah," she sighed. "You're right. I didn't mean that."

"I know," Betty responded. "We all get tired, right? And bitter, sometimes. It's hard to always believe in the better times, even if we can remember them like it was yesterday."

Now it was Kyler's turn to stare at her, speculating, questioning, and concluding things better left unconcluded. Betty faltered under her heavy gaze and looked away.

"Go on," she gestured towards the pool. "Go skate with my boy. But do me one favor?"

Kyler merely waited, watching her.

"Don't hurt him, ok? He's already had enough of that."

Again that burning stare, trying to break through her defenses. Betty held her ground this time and stared back. Kyler was the first to look away, towards the pool. Grabbing her board from the ground at her feet, she jumped over the concrete lip and fell in behind Max, trailing him, this time at a safe distance, as they skated the entire surface of the pool.

"Tomorrow's Saturday," Max said as he walked her to the front door. "Why don't you sleep in and I'll open up."

Kyler gazed at him. "You sure?"

"Yeah," he shrugged. "I could use the money."

It was bullshit and she knew it, but she nodded anyway. "Ok. Thanks, Max."

CHAPTER 54

It was pushing almost eleven when Kyler finally left Max's house. She walked towards the bus stop and collapsed heavily on the bench, waiting for the next bus. Contemplating Max and his mother, she felt a piece of them was missing, and because of that she felt herself drawing reluctantly closer to them.

When the bus came she boarded it and sat in the back, watching the streets of her city flow by like liquid graffiti; street paint suddenly come alive and moving under and around the bus, rather than the bus moving through it.

"Fuck, I'm tired," she mumbled as she scrubbed a hand across her face. Stepping off the bus, she walked two blocks east and stopped in front of Barb's and Jimmy's building. She was relieved to see lights on through the drawn blinds, giving her renewed—though borrowed—energy.

Barb answered her light knock with a smile and a hug.

"Hey, Kyler. How ya doin'?"

"SSDD," Kyler grinned back and slipped by her to scoop Bailey up out of her playpen. "How's *this* kid doing?"

"Spoiled, thanks to you," Barb said wryly. "Can't hardly get her to sleep in the crib anymore."

Kyler held the girl up high in the air, feeling her heart lighten as Bailey screamed laughter. "Tell 'er, kid, tell 'er you ain't spoiled, right?"

Barb winced as Kyler tossed her up and caught her neatly, bringing her close in a hug.

"Besides," Kyler shot her a somewhat sheepish glance, "wouldn't hurt her to be maybe a *little* spoiled, would it? Just so she don't have to know the shit you and I know."

"She won't," Barb responded grimly. "Even if you *weren't* here to cater to her every whim. But, yeah, you're right. A *little* spoiling ain't all bad. C'mon in the kitchen; me an' Jimmy're playing cards. You want something to eat?"

"No thanks," Kyler sat down across from Jimmy. "Just got back from Max's. His mom made him tacos for his birthday."

"How's he working out?"

"Believe it or not, better than I ever thought possible. I didn't think I needed any help until he came along."

"More like too proud to admit it," Jimmy shot her a grin, looking at his cards. "Kyler, tell her a straight beats a four of a kind."

"Sorry, Jim, but it doesn't. Not unless it's a straight *flush*."

"No, just a straight. You're telling me my straight doesn't beat her four of a kind?"

"That's right," Kyler bounced Bailey on her lap and grinned at her.

"Since when?"

"Since as long as I've been playing." She picked a poker chip off the table and handed it to the child. Bailey stuck it in her mouth and then waved it around, laughing.

"You sure?" Jimmy looked confused.

"Yep," she tossed Bailey in the air again, making both Jimmy and Barb wince this time. "Who taught you how to play poker, anyway?"

"My brother," he muttered.

"Who is where?" Barb asked jokingly and poked him in the ribs.

"Prison," he affected a gruff tone and reached for her, but she jumped out of his way, laughing.

"Lemme guess," Kyler said. "Illegal gambling?"

"Not . . . really," he hesitated, watching Bailey as she watched him, chewing on her poker chip. He made a face at her and she burst out laughing.

"Tried to knock over a casino."

"Trying to beat the house?" Kyler raised her eyebrows.

"No," Jimmy managed to suppress a wild grin. "He just walked into one and started waving a gun around."

Kyler grunted and reached for the cards, gathering them into a neat stack. Bailey reached for them and she gave her a joker to play with. "He'd done better trying to cheat at cards."

"Well, I don't know," Barb said, winking at her while Jimmy rolled his eyes. "Not if he couldn't play to begin with."

"True," Kyler agreed, smiling. She put the stack in front of Jimmy. "Deal 'em, Jim."

He started to speak, but Barb cut him off. "Dealer's choice."

Relenting, he began to shuffle and then deal. "Five card draw, deuces wild."

For the next couple hours they played poker and talked. Steadily the plastic poker chips in front of Kyler grew, with her seemingly paying more attention to the child she still held in her arms than the play of her cards. Barb, who'd played with her before, wasn't surprised; Jimmy, however, found himself staring more and more at the cards as they were drawn, unconsciously trying to keep track in order to slow her down.

"No sense tryin' to count 'em, Jimmy," she looked up at him, grinning slightly.

"Why?"

"'Cause you're bottom-dealing every third or fourth card. You're only gonna confuse yourself."

"Cheater!" Barb lunged at him. She fell into his lap, laughing hard. "No wonder you're losing."

He tried to put a scowl on his face but broke down. "Well, hell, I'm just tryin' to figure out how she's winning every hand."

"Not every hand," Kyler looked down as Bailey settled her weight against her chest. "I let you win a couple."

"You *let* me win?"

She just grinned and stared back at the child. Bailey looked back calmly, but her eyes were getting heavy. Within minutes she was sleeping in Kyler's arms, settled against her chest with peaceful familiarity.

"See why we can't get her to sleep in her crib anymore?" Barb said softly, but her eyes were full of love as she gazed at her daughter.

"Yeah, yeah, blame it on me," Kyler replied, smiling at her friend. "Ok, so this one's my fault."

Barb shook her head and leaned back against Jimmy. "You're gonna have to teach him how to play. Or at least cheat where it's not so obvious."

"Was it really that obvious?" Jimmy leaned forward and snagged his smokes off the table.

"Not to me," Barb lit his with her lighter and then lit one for herself.

"And only to me 'cause I knew what to look for," Kyler stood up. "Plus," she grinned, "I was kinda expecting it."

Jimmy shook his head and offered a wry grin. "Guess I'll have to call up my brother. Have him teach me how to count cards."

"Then we can play for real money," Kyler joked as she gently laid the sleeping baby back in her playpen. "All right, I'm gonna go. Thanks for the card games."

"Anytime," Barb said as both her and Jimmy walked her to the door. "But it's late. You gonna be ok?"

"Sure," Kyler answered.

"You can crash on the couch if ya want," Jimmy offered. "'Cause, seriously, Kyler, there's a lotta bad things out there at night. You know that." He said it lightly, but his eyes were serious and hard, and conveyed that he knew the demons inside were all too often stronger and more violent than those outside.

"I know," she said quietly. "But I'll be all right."

Tearing her eyes away from his, she gave Barb a brief hug, smiling over her shoulder at the now-sleeping baby. "Look at her, Jim," she said. "Worth more than any drug I'll ever do."

"Yeah," he agreed, but his eyes were still searching, still trying to see past the wall of her pride. He wrapped his arms around her and held her tight. "Me, too. But be careful anyway, all right?"

"Always am," Kyler responded easily. "You guys come on by the park sometime. You can meet Max and see what we've done to the place."

"We will," Barb promised. "Soon."

Kyler left them then, standing there, watching her until she was out of sight. Both knew the temptations of the street would always be with her—with all of them—but there was no doubt she was better now, and her odds of surviving the monkey on her back had grown considerably.

As she walked with her board in her hand, she thought about things. Mostly about the doc and the fact that he was *that close* to thinking of her as the daughter he never had. For some reason, that bothered her. Kyler, deep in her heart, felt she didn't deserve to be anybody's daughter; let alone his.

"Jesus," she muttered. "It never shoulda came to this. I shoulda moved out when I finished my probation."

Another part of her felt the hesitation and fear that was new to her. This was a weakness that stemmed from a subtle dependency upon Lamont, grown so gradually over the past months that even she was unaware of it until now. It was obvious in the fact that she didn't want to go home; the thought of the empty house filled her with a lonesome feeling she wasn't accustomed to.

"I'm used to being alone. I'm used to crashing wherever and whenever I can, living and surviving on the streets with nobody to tell me anything." Kyler paused and scrubbed a hand hard across her face. "So why's it so hard for me to face an empty house I never shoulda stayed this long in anyways?"

Deep down she knew she trusted him, finally, and in every sense of the word. His generosity and unfailing stability had grown on her, instilling that trust until she felt it to the center of her core. But another emotion was there, as well, and this scared her more than anything. Until tonight, until he'd implied she was like a daughter to him, she'd been able to ignore it. Nonetheless, now it was rearing up, demanding to be noticed.

Love.

Christ, do I really love him like the father I never had?

"Hell, no," Kyler spoke quietly. "I'm too bitter for all that. Been through the grinder. Ain't got time for it."

Bullshit, her mind whispered. *He saved you, and never asked for nothin' in return. How many men have you known that you can say that about?*

"He would make the third," she sighed. "And I lost the first two and it almost killed me. If I lose him it probably will."

So I'll be the first to leave. It's better that way. Easier.

As she thought this, her eyes settled on a small sign in front of an apartment complex. It was bigger than Jimmy and Barb's, with six stories of apartments stacked side by side and on top of each other.

The sign said **For Rent, third floor, 1 bdrm 1 bath, w/d.**

It was pushing almost three in the morning, and she knew the office was closed. Committing the phone number to memory, Kyler slid on past it, not allowing herself to think anymore about it . . . at least not for the next couple of hours.

CHAPTER 55

MAX WASN'T IN the office when she walked in just before noon, so Kyler slid into the chair behind the desk and picked up the phone.

"Meade Realty, how can I help you?" A woman's voice answered.

"Uh, yes . . ." Kyler faltered. "I was wondering about the apartment for rent on Lancaster? The . . . uh . . . one bedroom, bath?"

"Oh, right," the woman replied. "What can I tell you about it?"

"Well, for starters," Kyler found her footing as she relived the anguish she'd heard in the doc's voice. *I'd only end up hurting him,* she thought. *Or driving him away.* "How much is rent per month?"

"$350," the woman answered. "It's got new carpeting and new appliances in the kitchen. A very nice unit for the price."

Unit, Kyler's mind moaned, and she again faltered, now thinking of the familiar feel of *home* the doc's house had become.

"The complex has an elevator at each end, as well as the stairs that run up the middle of each hallway," the voice on the other end of the line droned on, depicting the amenities of the apartment building.

Christ, am I really sure about this?

"Ma'am?"

"Yeah," Kyler jerked back to the present.

"Would you like to come see it?"

"Yeah. Yes," she said again, immediately. "When's a good time for you?"

"Oh, we're open today until six, and tomorrow until five. I can meet you at the apartment, if you'd like."

Kyler sighed and glanced out the door into the park. Across the grass she could see Max hammering boards down on a ramp. "I can be there in ten minutes," she muttered.

"Great, we'll see you then."

Hitting the off button, Kyler swallowed heavily. "They'll never rent to me, anyways. I have no credit."

She shut her eyes briefly and didn't know whether to be relieved or angry. Finally she pushed herself out of the chair and headed out the door, walking fast before she could change her mind.

"Here we are," the woman held the main door open for Kyler. "The elevators are this way . . ." she gestured, but Kyler shook her head, portraying a confidence she was far from feeling.

"Would you mind if I just took the stairs?"

"Of course," the woman said easily. "It's this way," she started up. "The apartment is about midway down the hallway, and the neighbors on either side are pretty easy-going. Of course, they all work, so if parties are your thing . . ." she trailed off, giving Kyler a sidelong look.

"No," Kyler shook her head. "I work seven days a week. Too busy to party," she smiled easily, hiding the sudden anger she felt. A year clean and she still had that look about her.

"Good," the woman looked relieved. "Where do you work?" She unlocked the door and gestured Kyler in ahead of her.

Ok. Here we go, Kyler thought as she walked into the apartment. *Here's where she's gonna start getting all the information she needs from me only to tell me my credit sucks and sorry 'bout my luck.*

Now that the chance to finally attempt to get her own place had arrived, she was suddenly all too aware of her past fuckups and irresponsible behavior.

"The skate park on Beaumont Avenue," she answered dully. By the look in the woman's eyes, Kyler knew she had no idea what or where she was talking about. But it didn't matter anyway; the chance had come and gone.

After an endless tour of the small apartment—during which Kyler found herself wanting it more and more—the woman suggested they go back to the real estate office and start on the paperwork.

"Sure," Kyler replied, now completely positive she didn't have a chance in hell of getting this place, but anxious to do what needed to be done so that later she wouldn't feel like she'd tried to fuck it up on purpose.

The paperwork was tedious at best, but there was nothing Kyler couldn't answer. After all, there was really nothing she could say; having no credit or previous employment history, everything basically consisted of both Lamont's and John's references.

"Great," she mumbled to herself as she left the office. "Not unexpected, though." She shook her head and shoved the whole thing out of her mind. Lamont would be home in a week or so, and whatever conflict she had raging inside her about him, she'd learn to deal with it and move on.

CHAPTER 56

THE PHONE IN her back pocket rang as she was holding a board steady for Max to nail down. Without letting go of her end, she snagged the phone out and hit the talk button, holding it between her ear and shoulder.

"Beaumont Skate Park."

"Hey," Lamont said hesitantly. "How's it going?"

"Ok," she answered slowly. "You?"

"Better. I wanted to call and say thanks for the flowers. How'd you know where to send them?"

"Read it in the paper," she responded.

"He didn't have Emily's last name."

"Yeah, I know. And that made it really hard to find out which funeral home he was in."

"But . . ."

"But I can be resourceful when I wanna be. I wasn't completely sure it was him, so I'm glad you got 'em." Kyler paused and then asked. "How's Emily doing?"

"She's doing better, too. I think . . . I think it really helped . . . you know . . . you sending those. It . . . kept her focused, I guess. Helped hold her together."

Kyler was silent for a long time, then said, "Hang on." Glancing up at Max, she gestured to the phone. "Mind if I take this real quick? It's Doc."

"Nah, go ahead. I'll grab us some water."

She watched him walk off towards the office and then put the phone to her ear again. "Doc . . . listen . . ."

"No," he muttered. "Lemme talk, ok? I . . . I don't know, kid," he sighed. "I'm sorry about what I said last week. You probably felt cornered again, right?" Now his voice was bitter and sarcastic. "Fuck."

Kyler remained silent, sensing his frustration and indecision. There was silence for a minute, and then he said softly,

"It was . . . not what I thought, you know? I mean, I've been around death for most of my adult life, telling family members their loved ones have passed, offering out numbers to grief counselors . . ." he trailed off, swallowing. "But this time it was also about the life Emily had pulled out of her. Like . . . like Curtis took her life, too, instead of just his own.

"And I guess I panicked. I saw this strong woman I thought I knew crumble to the ground, letting go of everything . . . even me."

She sensed the despair in his voice, but this time he managed to keep it in check

"Anyway," Lamont sighed, "I just wanna say I'm sorry and thanks for the flowers. And . . . I'm the last person who'd try to push you away, but . . ." and now something else entered his voice; something she couldn't quite grasp. "But . . . I'm not gonna hold you if you feel you gotta go, ok?"

"What?" Kyler stopped, confused. She lit a cigarette and inhaled deeply.

"I, um . . ." he took a deep breath and let it out slowly. "Listen, I'll be home day after tomorrow. My plane gets in around four-thirty in the afternoon. I know you'll be working then, so don't worry about picking me up. I'll get a cab."

"I'll pick you up," she murmured. "I'll get Max in here."

He was silent again, and she thought about that unknown emotion in his voice; that thing she couldn't grab hold of.

"All right," he finally said. "Thanks, kid. I'll see you then, ok?"

"Yeah." Kyler hung up and smoked thoughtfully, wondering about Lamont. Max headed towards her with the bottles of water, and she took one gratefully. It was hot and the sweat poured down her back, but it was also refreshing, like she was sweating out the toxins both in her body and soul.

"How's Doc doing?"

She shrugged. "I don't know. He's . . . different, I guess."

"Different how?" Max sat down next to her.

Kyler shook her head. "I'm not sure. But I think . . . I think this whole thing hurt him more than he thought it would. But he's coming home day after tomorrow. Think you can watch the park while I go pick him up? His plane gets in a little after four."

"Yeah," he nodded. "I'll just come straight from school."

She was silent for a minute, absently peeling the label off the water. Finally she took a final drag off her smoke and ground the butt into the grass. "All right, let's go. We're almost done."

Max reached behind him and picked up the hammer, then reached for another nail. For the next twenty minutes there was little talk between them as they finished up the ramp. The sun was sinking low by the time they put the tools back in the shed and locked it up.

"Mom's cooking again, if you wanna come over," he offered, though already instinctively knowing she'd decline.

"Thanks, kid, but I think I'm just gonna head on back to Doc's."

"Ok," he nodded. "See ya tomorrow, then?"

"Yep," Kyler held her hand up in a loose fist and he gently bumped her knuckles with his own. "Be careful."

"You, too," he said over his shoulder. She watched him for a moment as he headed towards the bus stop, then turned and started in the opposite direction.

Kyler pulled the blanket from the spare bed and carried it out to the deck. The sun had long since disappeared and the wind was cool, whipping off the ocean. She curled up on a lawn chair and wrapped the blanket around her, watching the whitecaps as they pounded the beach.

The tone in Lamont's voice was still with her, and his words . . . him saying if she had to go, he'd be the last to hold her. It didn't make sense to her on the forefront, but at the very back of her mind she wondered if the apartment complex had actually gone an extra step and called the references she'd put down on the application.

"Now *that* would make sense," she mumbled. "But I'd still bet a paycheck I got tossed in the trash the minute I walked out the door."

Snuggling farther down in the lawn chair, Kyler closed her eyes and let the wind wash over her, pulling away fears—past and present—and easing her gently down into sleep.

CHAPTER 57

LAMONT STEPPED THROUGH the jet way and into the terminal. His back ached from the flight in and his head pounded dully, circling around extreme exhaustion and a piercing heartsickness. Spotting Kyler leaning easily against the far wall flooded him with relief so powerful it was hard to keep from running to her.

"Hey," she wrapped her arms around him, pulling him into an easy hug.

"Hey," he muttered against her shoulder. "Thanks for coming."

"No problem," she pulled away and regarded him; face closed to the shock she felt inside at his haggard, beaten face. "C'mon, let's get you home."

Lamont let her lead the way down to the baggage claim, trailing behind automatically. He felt empty inside, carved out from anger, grief, and loneliness. Sensing his pain, Kyler leaned against him briefly as they watched the conveyor carry the bags around.

"I'm sorry, Doc," she said quietly.

Lamont shook his head and pulled away to snag his bag off the belt. "It's just been rough, kid. Nothing nobody coulda done."

She was quiet as they walked out to the parking lot. Hitting the key fob, she unlocked both front doors and popped the trunk. They rode in silence, each lost in their own thoughts as the car flowed along with the evening gridlock.

"I'm sorry about what I said," Lamont muttered at one point, staring out at the slowly passing scenery. "You're doing a helluva lot better and . . . and I had no right tryin' to compare you to Curtis."

"Forget it, Doc. It's no big deal."

He grunted and ran a hand across his face. He didn't say anything for a minute or two, and then said softly, "You ever been up there? San Francisco?"

"No," Kyler glanced at him. "Stayed down south mostly."

Lamont nodded. "It's cooler up there. Nice. We went to Alcatraz one day, just to get away. It was interesting."

She allowed a wry smile. "They let you go inside the cells?"

"Yeah," he shot her a look, and she was relieved to see some of the old Doc in it. "You'd've probably lost it."

"I'm sure. Bad enough to be stuck in a modern jail cell. I can't imagine how it'd be to be locked in something that old."

"They didn't lock us in, but you could get the feel of it. Small. Very, very small."

Kyler made a face and turned down his street. "I wouldn't last a half an hour."

"If that long," Lamont pushed open his door and stepped out into the garage. He stretched and took a deep breath, feeling a loosening in his chest. Gently, almost imperceptibly, he felt the grief lightening some, allowing him room to feel glad to be home.

"You're not working today, are you?"

"No," he unlocked the door and held it open for her. "I'm off the rest of the week. I think I'm gonna go lay down, though. I'm kinda tired."

"Ok," Kyler gazed at him. "I'm gonna head back to work. Call me, all right? If you need anything or . . ." she shrugged, but her eyes were steady on his. "Or if you just wanna talk or whatever."

"I'll be all right," he pulled her into a brief hug. "Thanks for picking me up. You can take the car if you want."

She smiled ruefully. "Thanks, but I got my board."

He gave a tired smile back. "I know. Why drive when you can skate, right?"

"Right," this time her grin was wider, and it eased the hurt in his heart.

Dusk was settling down around the park five hours later as Max sat on the low concrete wall surrounding the pool, watching as Kyler skated over the smooth concrete. Movement to his right caught his eye and he turned to regard Lamont as he walked up beside him.

"Hey," Lamont said, somewhat hesitantly. "How's it goin'?"

"Pretty good," Max gestured at Kyler. "We're finished for the day. Just thought we'd skate a bit."

Lamont nodded, watching as she flew from one end of the pool to the other. Silence stretched out between them for a few long seconds before Lamont cleared his throat and shot a glance at Max.

"I'm sorry, Max," he started softly. "All that shit about calling this number or that number . . . tryin' to get you to talk to somebody. It . . . it's not . . ." he shook his head and cleared his throat again, swallowing hard.

"Doc," Max said, shaking his head. "Let it go."

"I can't," Lamont's voice was somewhat gruff. "It just seems . . . real . . . *thin* . . . now. Now that I know the . . . now that I know what I know. I mean, seeing Emily losing her son, and . . . watching, you know . . . what it did to her . . ."

"Let it go," Max repeated brusquely. "Christ, Doc." He scrubbed a hand hard across his face. "Just . . . just realize that this . . ." he sighed and stared out at Kyler, still skating hard. "It hurts, Doc. It always hurts and it's always *gonna* hurt, just sometimes not as much as other times. And you were right, you know? Grief counselors *do* help." He gazed steadily at Lamont.

"I started going to one here awhile back. One of the ones in the book you gave me three years ago. And, yes, three years later, the pain don't seem to be so . . ." he held his hands apart, simulating pressure, "tight anymore." Max shrugged and raised his eyebrows. "Maybe it's got more to do with working here, hanging around and having fun with Kyler than any kinda therapy, or maybe not. I don't know. Don't care, either."

"You just feel you're getting better," Lamont said quietly.

"Yeah," Max stood up and looked at him. "Don't lose your faith, ok? They help."

Lamont took a deep breath and gazed out at Kyler for a long moment without responding. He watched as she did one final flip and stepped neatly off onto the concrete. Her eyes met his for a brief moment before she bent over her board, adjusting the front truck with a small tool she pulled from her pocket.

"Yeah," he sighed. "They do. I've just . . . never been on this side of the fence before, you know?"

Max offered a bitter grin, but his eyes were easy and forgiving. "I know. But it's not like you didn't know what you were talking about, right?"

"Right. I just didn't know . . . how bad the pain could actually get."

"But it gets better," Max responded softly. "You told me that, too."

Lamont looked at him for a moment before looking back over at Kyler. "C'mon," he said wearily. "Lemme buy you guys some dinner."

Kyler walked out on the deck later on and saw Lamont sitting on the steps, staring out at the ocean. Even from behind he looked haggard and worn, and she felt her heart give a squeeze.

"Hey," she touched his shoulder briefly as she plopped down beside him. "You ok?"

"Yeah," he sighed. "Tired. Been a rough week."

"Yeah," she agreed. Silence bore down on them for a moment, each lost in their own thoughts. Kyler watched the never-ending waves pound the packed sand, sending (as always) bittersweet memories through her head. Memories of endless homeless nights spent on beaches just like this one, where danger and pain were always close by . . . but yet somehow she was always able to fall asleep with the sound of those waves falling sweetly in her ears.

"I got a call," Lamont broke through her thoughts. "Couple days ago." He looked at her and she saw a kind of lost grief in his eyes. "From a real estate office, looking for a reference on you."

Kyler was silent, staring at him, but she felt her heart speed up behind her ribs.

"They said you applied for an apartment for rent. They needed another reference."

She gave a slow nod, her eyes never leaving his.

Lamont dropped his gaze for a brief second, and then looked back at her. "I gave them one. A good one. I think you'll get it."

Another moment of silence; this one lasting a lifetime. Kyler didn't look away, but as the grief in his eyes turned to hurt and then acceptance, she felt it harder and harder to meet his wounded stare.

"Doc . . ." she managed. "I . . ."

Lamont finally looked away, back towards the ocean. "It's ok," he said quietly. "I understand, kid. Gonna miss ya, though." His eyes back on hers were full of raw emotion, and she felt herself beginning to stumble. As if sensing this, Lamont said firmly, "But you're right; it's probably way past time. And you're gonna be ok. Living on your own doesn't necessarily have to come with that old baggage, you know?"

Kyler swallowed heavily and pulled a battered pack of smokes from her pocket. She lit one with a slightly trembling hand and dropped her head in her hands.

"I don't have it, Doc, not yet. And I probably won't get it. My credit's . . ."

"Nonexistent, I know," he said, somewhat gently. "So that's why they want references. I'm sure they called John, too, if you put him down."

"I did," she muttered. "And it was just a whim. I was walking by and saw the sign and just figured I'd throw it out there, give it a shot."

"That same day I was . . . kinda out of it, right? That day I talked about what Curtis was still doing to Emily, even in death?"

Kyler thought briefly about lying to this man, a small white lie that would throw his guilt off by a mere twenty-four hours. But his eyes were steady on hers, guilt replaced by resolution and steel, and she knew she'd rather take another needle in a vein than even try to alleviate some of his pain by lying to him.

Instead she gave a heavy sigh and stared down at the worn wood beneath her feet.

"Yeah."

Lamont put a gentle arm around her and pulled her close, even though he felt like somebody had punched him in the gut.

"It's ok," he repeated softly.

"But it all wasn't from what you said," Kyler looked back up at him. "It . . . I'm not . . . good at this, you now? And I shouldn't have let it go this long to where you . . . uh . . . felt . . . this close to me. I . . . I'm not . . ." she sighed and shook her head, staring across the ocean. "You shouldn'ta got this close to me," she muttered. "I always end up hurting the people who care about me the most."

"*Always?*" He offered a wry, sad smile. "Or just twice?"

Kyler was silent a minute. "Just twice . . . so far," she said quietly. "But I've had three people ever give a shit about me, and I fucked up and lost two of them." Her eyes met his. "I never wanted to get in that situation again where I'd . . . end up hurting somebody else."

Lamont squeezed the back of her neck. "I'm not goin' anywhere, kid," he responded. "Remember that, ok?"

She closed her eyes and shook her head. Taking a deep drag off her cigarette, she let it sit in her lungs until it burned, needing the pain. "I never thought . . . Josh would go anywhere, either," her voice was almost inaudible. "Or Ryan."

He swallowed and stared out at the whitecaps. The knob of bone at the top of her spine rested against his palm, and he was aware all over again of her battered, skinny body housing a somewhat fractured mental state and a nearly shattered sense of faith.

"Still, though," Lamont said very quietly, "you're a helluva lot better. And you know where to go now, right? When those demons come calling? It's been nearly a year, but I know it's still gonna get rough, right?"

Kyler ran a hand across her eyes and didn't answer.

"You got my key. Keep it; use it whenever you need to. Havin' your own place doesn't necessarily mean you need to move completely move out of mine."

"I know," she finally muttered. "Thanks."

He nodded. "That's what I'm here for, ok?"

"Yeah," she stood up and stretched her back. "I think I'm gonna head on to bed. Um . . . you gonna be all right?"

"Sure," Lamont replied. "I'll probably stay out here a while longer then I'll probably head on up, myself.

Kyler nodded and walked into the house, letting the screen door shut gently behind her. Her thoughts were scattered, ranging from one reasonable excuse to another, and she couldn't help but wonder if she'd made the right choice. Leaving the doc now would only hurt him at the worst possible time he could be hurt, and it would throw her into a state of vulnerability that she'd be lucky to come out of.

However, on the flip side, that apartment signified a new beginning; a chance to sever old ties and finally release old demons as she took this huge step forward. Almost twenty now, and approaching a year without any kind of drug, Kyler realized that as much as she honestly wanted to, she couldn't live with Lamont forever. He needed his house back to move on past the pain of losing Emily for the second time as much as she felt the need to move out on her own . . . to stand on her feet for the first time in her life.

"Jesus, I hope I'm doing the right thing," she muttered as she wearily climbed the steps. "Please don't let this be another fuckup."

CHAPTER 58

THE PHONE RANG early in the morning. Kyler slit open one eye and looked blearily at the clock, surprised it was pushing seven-thirty. She sat up and dug the heels of her hands deep into her eyes, forcing the sleep from her brain. Lamont peeked in the doorway and saw her staring at the carpet with her hands locked behind her neck. For a moment his gut clenched up as he pictured his house empty again save for him, and for the first time in a very long time.

"Hey," he said quietly.

Kyler glanced up at him with tired eyes that matched his own.

"You got a phone call."

For a moment she only looked at him, and then slowly got up and met him halfway across the room.

"Thanks," she said, taking the phone from his hand.

Lamont nodded and backed out the door, disappearing down the hall to his own bedroom. He felt torn, realizing the call and it's probable meaning, wanting her to stay but realizing with everything he had that she had to venture out . . . take that step on her own.

"Hello?" Kyler lit a cigarette and absently rubbed her knotted stomach.

"Ms. Maddox? This is Janet Clyde from Meade Realty. I just wanted to call and say congratulations, you've got the apartment."

Kyler shut her eyes, an emotion that was either relief or regret flooding through her. At that particular moment in time, with Lamont mere feet away down the hall, she honestly couldn't tell which one it was.

"Ms. Maddox?"

"Yeah," her voice came out a croak and she cleared her throat. "Yes, I'm here." She took a deep breath and forced her hands to stop trembling. "I really got it?"

"Yes," the woman answered. "However, there's just one thing . . . based on your credit, for the signing you're going to need a cosigner. Will that be a problem?"

Kyler looked out the door, holding the phone to her ear. Now it was real regret that swamped her and she gave up trying to stop the shaking in her hands.

"Ms. Maddox? Ma'am?"

"Sorry, yes, I'm here. I'm, uh . . . no, no that won't be a problem at all."

"Excellent. Do you think you can come down here around noon today?"

"Sure," she answered, having absolutely no intention of being anywhere near the real estate office at noon, and somehow managing to push this whole crazy idea out of her head and the sooner the better.

"Great. We'll see you then."

Kyler hit the off button and took a final drag off her cigarette before crushing it out in the ashtray. She got up and walked out into the hall, looking down towards Lamont's bedroom. Dimly she heard the sound of his shower filtering from the partially-closed door. She slipped back inside the spare room and quickly got dressed, then headed downstairs and out the front door.

Upstairs Lamont, ignoring the water running in his bathroom, poked his head out of the bedroom in time to hear the front door shut downstairs. He crossed over to the spare bedroom and walked over to the window, looking down at Kyler as she headed towards the bus stop on the corner. Without thinking about what he was doing, he picked the phone up and dialed back the real estate office from the caller I.D.

"Meade Realty," a female voice answered, and he was fairly sure it was the same person who had just called.

"Yes," he responded briskly. "My . . ." barely a pause, not enough to be noticeable, "daughter just spoke to someone there about signing on an apartment?"

"Right, Ms. Maddox?"

"Yes, that's right," Lamont's voice portrayed an efficient professionalism that he sure didn't feel. It hurt him to be going behind her back like this, but he'd seen something in her body movement as she walked towards the corner that hurt him even more . . . something that spoke of regret and defeat.

"And you're her father?" The woman didn't give him time to answer before she went on. "Will you be cosigning for her today?"

Lamont shut his eyes as the reason for her defeat became all too clear. "Yes," he answered, "but I was in the shower when she left and I was wondering if you can tell me what time I need to be there?"

"We settled for around noon, is that ok?"

"That's perfect. I'll see you then. Thanks so much." He hit the off button before she could reply and tossed the phone on the bed.

"Jesus, kid," he muttered to the empty room. "I wish you'd just talk to me sometimes." But in his heart he knew she couldn't; not about something like this. Kyler's pride was just as strong as it had ever been, and for her to ask him for a favor this big was something next to impossible for her.

Kyler stood up on the ramp she'd just got done repairing and looked across to see Max striding towards her. She raised her eyebrows as he hopped up next to her.

"It's Wednesday," she said. "Like maybe eleven-thirty."

"Yep," he replied. "Bomb scare at school. They let us out for the day."

"Seriously?" She stared at him.

"Seriously. I don't think they found anything, but they wanted to be safe so they sent us all home."

"Christ," Kyler shook her head. "What the fuck's this town coming to?"

"I don't know," Max said slowly. "Not cool, though, I know that. Mom was freaking out when she found out."

"Yeah, I'm sure she was," she lit a cigarette. "Jesus."

Max nodded and ran his hands through his hair. "Yeah. Anyway, I thought I might come into work early, if that's ok."

"Sure. I was just finishing up on this ramp. Seventeen over there's got a warped board along one side; thought I'd head over there next."

"Ok," Max reached for the hammer, then paused as movement from the corner of his eye caught his reflection. "There's Doc," he gestured.

Kyler glanced up and nodded. "Hope there wasn't a bomb scare at the hospital, too."

They both waited while Lamont walked towards them. There was something on his face that she couldn't quite read, and her first thought was that maybe there *had* been a bomb scare or something similar at the hospital.

"Hey," Lamont said easily when he got up to them. "Why aren't you in school?" He looked at Max.

"Bomb scare," he replied. "They let us go home for the day."

For a long moment Lamont only stared at him, and then he followed Kyler's response and shook his head. "Goddamn," he muttered softly.

"Seems to be the common thought on that right now," Kyler commented. "Why aren't *you* at work?"

He glanced at her and offered a half shrug. "I took off the rest of the day."

She nodded and rubbed the back of her neck, absently staring down at the various tools scattered around her feet. "Good day for it. Not too hot. You could maybe get some relaxation in."

Lamont's eyes bored into her for what seemed like a very long time. Finally he jerked a thumb over his shoulder and muttered softly, "You mind if I talk to you for a minute?"

For some reason she felt her stomach roll over. "Sure," she said slowly.

"I'll head on over to seventeen," Max offered. Without waiting for an answer, he gathered up the tools and hopped down off the ramp, walking across the grass away from them.

"What's up?" Kyler looked at Lamont with a raised eyebrow. "You ok?"

"Kyler…" he started, then stopped and sighed. "Aren't you supposed to be somewhere here in a couple of minutes?"

"Nope," she answered abruptly. "Not that I know of."

"Bullshit," he said quietly. "What about signing on the apartment?"

She stared at him, anger beginning to shine through her features. "Forget about that, Doc. It's a done deal. You were right; I'm better off staying with you."

"You really believe that?"

Shaking her head, Kyler glared out over the park, feeling the anger course through her. "It doesn't matter, Doc, you know that."

"It *always* matters," he offered gently. "Why didn't you tell me about the cosigner?"

Kyler cut her eyes to him, the anger raging full force through her now. "How'd you know about that?" She growled.

Lamont shrugged. "Like you, I'm resourceful when I wanna be."

She shook her head and stepped off the ramp. "Shit, Doc, what do you want me to say?"

"How 'bout, 'Hey, Doc, I got the apartment but they're gonna need somebody to cosign for me. Would you mind doin' it?'"

Kyler just stared at him for a long moment before turning around and walking towards the office.

"Hey, wait," Lamont reached out and snagged her arm. "Wait, kid, shit, I'm sorry. I didn't mean it like that, ok? I just …"

"What?" Kyler glared at him. "You what, Doc?"

He raised his hands in surrender, staring at her with a somewhat weary sadness in his eyes. "I'm gonna cosign for you, ok? Lemme do this for you."

"No," she started to walk again, but again he stopped her.

"Kyler."

She dug in her pockets for her cigarettes and lit one, not answering.

"Please."

Taking a deep breath, she pressed the heels of her hands hard against her eyes. "Doc," she sighed. "You didn't want me to leave anyway, right? So . . . it all works out this way. Just leave it alone, all right?"

"It doesn't work out for you," he replied quietly. "It's something you really want and I'm not gonna be your excuse not to get it."

"Cosigning's not like letting me crash in your spare bed for almost a year. Shit like this could really fuck up your credit."

"Only if you fuck up first," he said, then winced. "Shit, that didn't come out the way I meant it to."

"But it's true," Kyler said mildly. "I fuck up and it fucks you up. I don't wanna carry that responsibility, Doc. Thanks, but I'll pass."

He offered a smile that was small but genuine. "Listen, kid, it's not gonna fuck me up, ok? At the very least I'll owe rent for the year you signed your lease on. That's . . . what . . . ? Three-fifty times twelve months . . ." he trailed off, counting the numbers in his head. "Forty-two hundred. I think I can cover that."

"Yeah," she gave a short laugh and turned once more towards the office. "And then you're pissed at me and that'll only grow 'cause then I'll be back in your spare room and you'll feel too guilty to kick me out but you'll still be getting steadily more and more angry, and—"

"And you're overdramatizing," Lamont's smile grew. "C'mon, kid, have a little faith, will ya? Especially in yourself."

His smile faded and his eyes grew serious. "You can do this, ok? *I've* got faith in you, and I wouldn't offer to do this if I didn't."

Kyler took a deep breath and let it out slowly. She glanced over at Max, hammering down a board on ramp seventeen.

"He can watch the park while we're gone," Lamont read her mind.

She was quiet for a minute, thinking. "I've never done something this big before, Doc," her voice was soft. "This is . . ." she waved her arm in the air, gesturing absently. "This is the kinda responsibility that's for people who don't carry monkeys on their backs, you know? People who *get it*, people who keep it all together in *normal* ways."

"You'd be surprised, kid, at how many people there are out there, renting apartments, houses, whatever; cooking up meth or growing pot in closets while they shoot up on the couch and zone out in front of the TV night after night. People who get up in the morning and go to their jobs, snort up coke on their lunch hour and then come back home to these apartments and houses and do it all over again."

Kyler swallowed, feeling the small tendrils of fear that coiled in her gut from his words. *Jesus,* she thought, *how fucking easy would it be for me to spiral back down? There's no fucking way I can do this.*

Again Lamont seemed to read her mind. He wrapped his arms around her and brought her close in a hug. "It's a new life, kid; not an excuse to head back into the old one. How're you ever gonna know if you can do this if you don't try?"

"Lotta different fears," she growled softly.

"Sure," he responded. "And that's natural. But you gotta realize that you're not heading off alone, ok? Like I said, you got my key and use it whenever you want to. Taking this step is huge, yeah, but I promise you it's not always gonna be. Have faith, ok?"

She gave a heavy sigh and scrubbed a hand hard across her face. "Fuck," she muttered, staring across the park. "Doc, look . . ." her angry, haunted eyes swiveled to meet his. "This ain't about me . . . really . . . ok? I'm gonna do what I've always done, and whether that's bolt off into the darkness and get loaded or just stay straight and look for the simple things like my board or sitting by the ocean, well . . . I mean . . ." she shrugged half-heartedly. "I don't know. But I *do* know that this . . . for you . . . is too much, you understand? Don't put this kinda trust in me. I'm liable to do anything."

Lamont regarded her for a long moment, his eyes resting softly on hers. Finally he shook his head and put a hand on her arm, giving her a gentle push towards Max.

"Go on," he said softly. "Go tell him you'll be back in a half hour."

Kyler stared at him, feeling like she should be pressured again, pushed back into another corner. Only this time she *wanted* to be pushed; wanted to be guided in a specific direction. Even now, with the fear of using again hard on her, she wanted that apartment, wanted to see if she could stand on her own for once.

Besides, she thought, *if I was gonna use, I'd use. Bein' on my own, in my own place, don't have to warrant anything. I proved that not too long ago, with Jimmy in that hotel bathroom. Even with the doc puttin' up with me, giving me a place to stay . . . I still went out and got high.*

Without another word she turned around and walked towards Max, feeling Lamont's eyes on her back. "Please, God, let me be doing the right thing," she mumbled. "Just this once, let me do it right."

Max glanced up at her as she came up to the edge of the ramp. "Hey," he finished hammering in a nail, then stood up and stretched his back. "You ok?"

"Um . . ." Kyler chewed on a ragged fingernail. "Yeah. Listen . . . you think you can watch this place for a half-hour or so? I got . . . I got an apartment and I need to go sign on it."

His eyebrows shot up. "Seriously? Why?"

"Why what?" She lit a cigarette and inhaled deeply; using the smoke to still the trembling in her body.

"Well, I mean . . ." he shrugged. "I kinda thought you lived with Doc."

"I do. I did . . . I mean, I have since I got clean. But I just . . . you know . . . thought I'd try it on my own for once."

Max gazed at her and Kyler read his thoughts all too clear.

"I'm not doin' it to use again," she murmured. "But don't think that don't scare the fuck outta me."

"Hey," he held up his hands in surrender. "No, I know that, Kyler."

"And he'll be on my back, I'm sure," she jerked a thumb back over her shoulder with a pained smile.

Max didn't answer as he looked first at Lamont, waiting patiently by the office, and then back to her. "Yeah," he said quietly. "Yeah, go on, I got this."

Kyler nodded and turned, but stopped when he put a hand on her arm. She arched an eyebrow, hating that he could feel the shaking in her body.

"I know he's not gonna bar the door from you," he nodded towards Lamont. "He told you to come back, right? Whenever you need to?"

She was silent, thinking, for a brief moment, then gave a reluctant nod. "He said I could stay, yeah. When . . ." she swallowed. "When I get, you know, feeling kinda shaky."

Max found himself remembering his father again, and how that look would come into his eyes whenever the demon was back, clawing at him. When that happened, all the promises, debts owed, plans made, or love given would disappear with one swallow; one drop of the poison that so ruled his dad's—and thus, his own as well as his mother's—life.

"My house is open, too," he muttered, staring at her with hooded eyes. "Ok? Remember that, all right?"

Kyler met his eyes and saw the fervent pleading in them. Slowly she nodded, feeling sucker-punched and beaten. It was the same look Josh had all too often in those end days.

"Yeah. Ok, Max, I'll remember that."

He watched as she started back across the grass towards Lamont, his heart beating painfully against his ribs, pounding out the raw emotional heartbreak he'd already once endured. He was fairly certain he couldn't handle another.

Kyler's hand was shaking as she scrawled her name across the forms before passing them to Lamont, avoiding his eyes. Without hesitation, he signed next to her signature before handing the papers back across to the woman seated behind the desk.

She smiled and handed a set of keys over to Kyler. "Congratulations again, Ms. Maddox. The apartment's all yours. Feel free to move in whenever you like."

"Thanks," Kyler stood up and pocketed the keys. Lamont stood with her and reached across to shake the woman's hand.

"Thank you," he smiled, then put a comforting hand on Kyler's shoulder, guiding her out the door. Under his palm, he felt the trembling in her muscles but remained silent until they go back into his car.

Kyler slid into the passenger seat and sighed. He glanced at her as he got behind the wheel, offering a slight smile.

"Don't worry, kid."

"Hard not to do. The weight of those forms are pretty heavy."

He didn't respond as he pulled out into traffic. She stared out the window, seeing flashes of the ocean become sparse as they turned inland.

"If you miss it too much, come on over, all right?" Lamont finally said softly.

"Miss what?" She turned to him.

"The ocean," his eyes met hers. "If you miss sitting by it at night, you know. But don't think I'm just saying that to get you to come over, ok?"

"Don't worry," Kyler turned back to the window. "If I miss it you'll see me. Maybe a lot."

"But then," he slid into a spot in front of her apartment building, "maybe not so much." He shut off the engine and looked at her. "You're gonna be fine, kid, and you're gonna learn to love this place; call it home."

She stared at him for a moment before pushing out of the car. "How'd you know where it was?"

"I'm resourceful, like I said," Lamont fell into step beside her as they walked through the main door. "I just . . . don't get pissed, ok? But I just wanted to make sure it was an ok place. Ok neighborhood."

"Is it, you think?" Her dark eyes bored into his.

"I think so," he shrugged. "But it's really what *you* think."

Starting up the stairs, Kyler shot back over her shoulder, "If I thought I'd be able to get high right around the corner, I wouldn't've even bothered with this place."

"I know," he said neutrally, but they both knew that if she really wanted to get high, she probably could, and even closer than right around the corner.

"There's an elevator," she said absently. "Sorry, I forgot about it."

"I saw it," he said. "I'll probably use it when I help you move in, and I can just meet you up here at the top."

Kyler stared down at the keys in her hand, stopping outside the door that was now hers. "Doc," there was thin defiance and shame in her eyes that hurt his heart. "There's nothing to move in."

"Not yet," he agreed easily. "But there will be."

She took a deep breath and let it out slowly. Without answering, she unlocked the door and stepped in, looking around as if for the first time.

"This is it."

Lamont moved past her into the small living room. Off to the right was the kitchen with room enough for a small table if she wanted. To the left was a short hallway with a closet on one side that concealed the hookups for a washer and dryer; on the other side was the bathroom with the bedroom straight ahead at the end.

"Nice," he smiled. "I think you did good, kid."

Kyler looked at him for a moment before gesturing towards the bedroom. "The window lets out onto the fire escape. Not much out there but an alley, but . . ." she trailed off shrugging.

"But it's yours," he slung an arm around her shoulder.

"Yeah . . ." she said, somewhat reluctantly, but not quite regretfully. She watched as he walked to the bedroom then trailed slowly along behind him. Lamont stood in the center of the room, gazing around. Straight ahead, like she'd mentioned was the fire escape and he walked over and opened the window, leaning out.

"Do me a favor?" He shot her a look over his shoulder. "Keep this locked, ok?"

The look she favored him with was understandable, and he offered a feeble grin.

"I know. I don't have to tell you that, right?"

Kyler didn't answer as she lit a cigarette.

"Gonna have to get you a bed," he said. "No sense sleeping on the floor."

"Why?"

"Why?" He arched an eyebrow. "'Cause there ain't no point, kid, not if you don't have to."

She shrugged. "Floor's as good as a bed." A pause, then as brutally innocent as only a person raised on the streets can be, "Isn't it?"

"Not if you don't have to," he repeated.

Kyler gave a slow shake of her head. "It's not a matter of having to or not having to, Doc. It . . . it's just the way some chips fall."

"Jesus," he muttered gruffly. "I don't know if that's just a lackadaisical attitude you got or if you've just got a certain level of acceptance and you're afraid to reach above it."

His words stung her in a way that showed her she deserved it. Still . . . again . . . even now after signing for this apartment, he was still trying to save her, pick her up and show her yet another little small miracle.

"Sorry," she mumbled. "You're right. Three-fifty a month and I guess the least I can do is not sleep on the floor."

Lamont shrugged and gave a somewhat sheepish smile. "No, I'm sorry. I . . . keep forgetting sometimes that . . ." he trailed off and looked away.

"What?"

"I don't know. Just some things don't really . . . you don't think about some things the way I do, I guess."

Kyler gazed at him for a long moment, the anger gone now, replaced by curiousness.

"I never had a bed," she said softly. "Not 'till I came to live with you. You stack years against months and the years weigh pretty heavy."

"I know," he sighed.

"But I've learned a few things in those months," she went on, "and you're right. Life doesn't have to be as hard as I tend to make it out to be."

Lamont smiled and held out an arm. She went to him easily, letting him embrace her with the familiarity she'd come to feel for him over the last year. It amazed her still how different she'd become, where it wasn't all that long ago that she'd been terrified to even be in the same room as him, and now . . . well, now she felt a rock solid trust in him that was rare and honest and scary at times but well worth it a million times over.

"I'll get a bed," she muttered.

"Thank you," he replied. "It just makes me feel better, knowing you're not curled up in a corner."

"Yeah, I know," she pulled away and stared around her bedroom. "But you think I did ok? With this?"

"Yep," he answered immediately. "No question. I think this is good for you."

Kyler offered a slight grin. "But I can still come over, right?"

"Anytime," he said as they walked back into the living room. "Day or night, I don't care."

She locked the door behind them and then started down the steps. "Thanks. That helps." They walked a few steps down before she took the keys out of her pocket and took off the one extra she had.

"Here," Kyler handed it to him. "I want you to have the spare."

He took it gently and gave a slow nod. "Ok. But just so you know, I'm not gonna be popping in on you unexpectedly, all right?"

"You'd be lucky to catch me at home anyway. I work too much. Besides, I know I'll be at your house some, so . . . you know . . ." she shrugged.

Lamont shot her a brief look and asked quietly, "You gonna stay here tonight?"

Kyler hesitated, using the excuse to light a cigarette to gather her words. "Yeah . . ." she answered slowly.

He nodded and used the key fob to unlock the car doors as they approached it. "Ok," he said. "But call me, all right? If you need anything. I don't care what time it is."

"I will. But I'll be all right, I think."

"Yeah, I know you will." He shot her a genuine smile that was soothing to her mixed emotions, but inside he was heart-sore and sick, knowing he'd be missing her in the days to come.

CHAPTER 59

IT WAS NEARLY ten pm when Kyler came back to her new apartment. She'd closed the park with Max, and then skated the streets for awhile, alone and unconsciously putting off the time when she'd again open this door. She was homesick for the doc's house, and had been for a few hours now. Again, she wondered if she'd done the right thing.

Now, standing in her darkened living room, staring around at the shadows that didn't even conceal the nothingness she'd acquired materialistically, she felt the pang in her gut and the unshed tears in her eyes.

Slowly Kyler locked the door behind her and then made her way in the semi-darkness back to the bedroom. Dimly, in the back of her mind, she realized that not only did she have not one thing to stick in this apartment; she also didn't have a blanket or a pillow . . . not even a small piece of clothing to lay her head on.

"Great planning, kid," she muttered as she slid down the wall. She started to light a cigarette and gritted her teeth when she looked around and saw again, *nothing*, in which to flick her ashes. "Real great planning."

Briefly she thought about going back to Lamont's, at least for that night, and then doing some better packing early in the morning. But then she thought better of it, instinctively knowing that it would only make it that much harder to leave.

Better to crash without a pillow or blanket tonight than to get to the point where his safety beats out my independence.

But it was more than that, and she knew it. Nothing in the world told her that she'd be better off without him, especially since time and again he'd picked her up when he didn't have to. But her damn pride couldn't handle it, and because of that Kyler knew she'd most likely spend the night curled up on the floor without even a blanket.

She took a deep breath and let it out slowly, pressing her hands hard against the floor. Under her palms she felt the rough Berber carpet and felt the wall hard against her back.

"Not even a stereo to listen to," she muttered. "Nothing to make the time go by faster. Not even a fucking clock . . . Jesus, I don't even know what time it is." Kyler scrubbed a hand across her face and gritted her teeth.

And then suddenly she felt something more than the emptiness of her new apartment or homesickness for the doc. Now, those feelings were secondary as very real, very raw panic began to descend on her, sending tendrils of fear through her veins like the heroin once did.

"Oh . . . Christ . . ." Kyler gave a choked moan and squeezed her eyes shut. The panic slammed into her, full-force against her chest, wrapping her lungs in a claustrophobic vise grip and making breathing next to impossible. She thought of chrome and glass

(smack and water, mixing too easily in the spike, and I wouldn't even have to get the water from a rain puddle this time. Or from the

tank of a gas station toilet) and then looked dazedly around her new crib, her eyes resting on the kitchen sink.

"I've got clean water," she mumbled. "A safe place to crash . . ."

The itch at the base of her skull was maddening, and Kyler raked at her skin, trying to dig it out. She felt half on the verge of insanity, knowing full well the frustration of trichotillomaniacs but unable to stop. One ragged fingernail, still not quite grown out smooth and solid from the compulsive chewing heroin had instilled upon her, scraped along the still-tender spot on the back of her neck where she'd cut it open on glass in the culvert . . . on that night that seemed years ago now.

Absently she felt blood trickle from the cut but the pain was very distant. Everything was distant except the overwhelming need that had her in a chokehold; the track on her right arm was an itch that defied any sense of reason, screaming for the prick of a heroin-filled needle.

Kyler curled up in a ball, as far back against the wall as she could get, and clenched her jaw around the howl that wanted to rip out of her throat.

Call me, all right? Lamont's voice whispered teasingly in her ravaged brain. *I don't care what time it is.*

"And neither one of us thought to think that I don't have a phone," she muttered shakily, her heart pounding against her sternum. "Christ."

She lay there, hitching in one ragged breath after another, trying not to go completely crazy from a feeling of withdrawal that hadn't been this strong in months. It was terrifying in its physical aspects, sending her heart rate racing, shooting both her blood pressure and body temperature way up. Kyler felt the slick sweat on her skin cover the millions of goose bumps that covered every inch of her, felt her stomach do a slow, lazy somersault before exploding in a ball of acid.

Moaning, unaware of the tears rolling down her cheeks or of the erratic pounding of her heart that shot spears of pain across her chest and back, she bolted up off the floor and ran to the bathroom, crashing to her knees in front of the toilet. She heaved painfully; vomit racing up her throat and splashing into the water with the violence of a projectile.

You know what it would take to feel better, that fucking rat spoke up in her head. *Just one fix, one little taste and you could get your feet back under you, stand up again. Face the world again.*

Kyler shut her eyes and gave a soft groan, reaching blindly for the flush with a badly shaking hand. "God, get me through this," she whispered. "Please, just get me through this."

And then, softly, in the back of her mind, Emily's voice whispered soothingly; a cool salve against her raw, battered mind.

Breathe, Kyler. Just breathe.

"Breathe," she croaked.

One breath at a time, in and out.

She felt the cool porcelain against her heated skin, fighting back the fevered insanity.

Slowly . . . too, too slowly . . . the claws around her throat began to loosen. Reason, though thin and shaky, once more reasserted itself and her vision cleared.

"All right," she said softly. "Hold on, kid." She took another deep breath, let it out in a long exhale. She took another, and then another, slowly gaining back strength and sanity. With an effort Kyler finally managed to gain her feet, holding desperately to the side of the sink. Without even bothering to look at her face in the mirror, she turned and shuffled out of the bathroom, suddenly way too old for her young age.

Not thinking or wondering where she was headed, Kyler left her apartment, locking the door behind her and heading off into the dark night.

Across town Lamont lay in bed and stared up at the ceiling, wondering about the kid, missing her. Hoping she was ok.

Kyler pushed open the door of the twenty-four hour CVS pharmacy and headed down an aisle. She found herself staring at a row of alarm clock radios and picked one up at random. The description on one side of the box stated it featured an AM/FM radio as well as various other alarm sounds, one of which was a "soothing ocean sound."

She offered a bitter smile and tucked it under her arm. Passing by the liquor aisle, she halted so abruptly she almost dropped the clock. Staring down the aisle, row after row of booze-filled bottles filled her vision, and she was suddenly aware that if she didn't do something soon to alleviate the raging need inside her, then it would eventually wind up swallowing her alive.

Booze, mind whispered. *Better than nothing.*

Kyler slid down the aisle and picked out a half-pint of Jack Daniels. Walking over to the cooler, she pulled out a twelve-pack of Budweiser and balanced it easily under one arm. Almost imperceptibility she began to feel better, knowing that she was *doing* something, *getting through* without shooting up.

The woman behind the counter didn't even ask for an I.D., and with thin hope Kyler was able to see past the endless seconds in her dark apartment and focus on making it a home, a place livable and without fear.

CHAPTER 60

KYLER CAME TO early the next morning to the sounds of southern rock coming out of the tiny speaker on her new radio. She was sprawled out on the floor with her head mere inches away from the radio plugged into the outlet above the baseboard. The time read just after seven in the a.m., and staring blearily at the pale light shining through her bedroom window, she figured that was about right.

"Survived the first night," Kyler muttered, and winced as the sound of her own voice sent her headache spiking up to a near intolerable point. "In my new bedroom."

Groaning softly, she pulled herself to her feet and ran a gentle hand over her knotted stomach. Hungover and hurting, she got in the shower and let the hot water wash away as much of the past night's fears as possible. No soap, of course, or towels, so she used her clothes to dry off with as best as she could before she put them back on.

"Make a list," she mumbled to herself. "Towels, soap. Fucking Excedrin."

Kyler ran her hands under the cold water tap in the sink and splashed water on her face, working the water across her forehead and around her eyes where the headache seemed to be centered. Raking her hands through her hair, she took a deep breath and let it out, then lit a cigarette, feeling more in control than she thought possible.

It was a wonder what one small item such as a clock radio could do as far as easing her over that first rough patch. And of course, the booze didn't hurt, either. As hungover as she was, Kyler was able to realize that and feel at least moderately saved, considering how close she'd come to using again.

She was skating hard through the early morning streets, thinking she would either go into work early or stop by to see the doc, and then out of nowhere the music hit her hard. She skidded to a stop and looked around, spotting the small yard sale on a lawn across the street. The music was coming from a stereo laid out on a card table . . . or rather, a receiver with a turntable stacked on top, plugged into an extension cord that trailed into the house.

Listening to the gruff sounds coming out of the small speakers on the grass, she felt the words wash over her in pure rock and roll sound.

—*"Well, there's a hundred miles of desert lies between his hide and mine. I don't need no food and no water, Lord, 'cause I'm runnin' out of time—"*

Kyler waited, leaning against a tree. She lit a cigarette and watched as the family across the street continued setting up their yard sale. A small cardboard sign was propped against the base of the card table, and she saw a price of twenty-five dollars. Whether that was for everything on the table or just the album playing, she had no idea, but in the back of her mind she heard Lamont say most albums could be found at yard sales such as this for less than a dollar.

—*"So I stood on a ridge and shunned religion, thinking the world was mine. I made my break and big mistake, stealin' when I should've been buyin'—"*

A man came out of the house carrying a milk carton full of more albums, which he put down beside the card table. Then he went back inside the house, only to emerge a moment later with a crock pot and a blender, which he put on another folding table off to the side.

She hesitated, glancing at the time on a bank sign. Twenty after eight. Time to make a decision or else she was liable to be late for work. Taking a final drag off her smoke, Kyler dropped the butt and crushed it beneath her foot.

"Shit," she sighed. The music was just too hard to ignore, and without thinking anymore, she grabbed up her board and trotted across the street.

The man shot her a glance as she ambled up to the card table. "Take it all," he said. "My wife's tired of tripping over it."

Kyler stared at him with raised eyebrows. "She's makin' you sell all this?"

"All of it," a woman grinned as she came out of the house carrying another box of stuff. "That's why God made CDs. The smaller, the better, right, hon?" She winked at her husband."

"I guess," he grumbled. "High price to pay for losin' my youth, though."

"Your youth was lost a long time ago," she responded good-naturedly. Turning back to Kyler, she winked again. "Sign says twenty-five, but make me an offer."

"Make *me* an offer," the husband corrected. "They're my albums, right?"

The wife smiled. "Sure, dear." She went on into the house and left Kyler standing on the lawn thinking of an offer that would include the sound system, plus the carton full of albums.

"Ah, hell," the husband muttered. "Make it ten for everything, ok? It'll get 'em off the lawn and out of my wife's hair. That sound good?"

Slowly Kyler reached into her pocket and pulled out a wad of crumpled bills. She wasn't exactly sure how much had been spent on the booze the previous night, but she spotted a bunch of ones and a five.

"Everything? Including the albums?"

"Everything," the man repeated, sweeping his arm in a gesture that encompassed the receiver, turntable, speakers, and milk carton full of albums. "That way I can sell 'em early and won't have to worry about them sitting in the sun all day."

"Deal," Kyler counted out the five and five ones. "One thing, though . . ."

The man waited, eyebrows raised.

"About them sitting in the sun . . . I'm actually on my way to work right now, and . . . I was wondering if I could maybe leave them here?"

"Yeah, sure. No problem. Here . . ." he pulled a piece of paper from his pocket and a pen from off one of the tables. "Here's my number. I'll be here all day; just call when you're gonna come back by. In the meantime, I'll put everything back in the garage. That way it'll still be outta the sun."

"Thanks," she said. "I can help you put it up real quick."

"Nah, don't worry about it. Between me, you, and the gatepost, I hate to see 'em go. I might listen to a few more songs while I finish setting up."

"Ok," Kyler smiled. She started off down the sidewalk, ten bucks less in her pocket but with a sense of peace lying lightly on her heart. She figured every little thing she could put into her new place to make it more her own would be another shield against having nights like the one she'd just had.

Max walked up to her as she skated the flatland, and waited patiently until she finished her run. Like always, he loved watching her, her movements as fluid as liquid; her body as completely at ease as it ever was.

Today, though, as she stepped off the mini ramp and came towards him, he saw the pale sickness of a hangover on her face—easy enough for him to spot—and his stomach clenched.

"Hey," she sat down heavily beside him, lighting a cigarette with a slightly trembling hand. "You're early."

He shrugged. "Not too early. Just now four."

Kyler nodded and stretched out her back, staring down at the worn boards.

"You ok?" He asked.

"Yeah. Tired. Long night." She sighed and offered a somewhat bitter smile. "Doc spoiled me. Not used to waking up with nobody around."

"Lonely?"

She shot him a sidelong glance and gave a sarcastic grin. "Hell, no. I'm a lone wolf, kid. I thought you knew that."

"Liar," he said amicably. "Strange place, right? Empty rooms . . . too empty. Nothin' to do."

Kyler shifted her eyes away, not liking the way he was reading her. "C'mon," she stood up and offered a hand. "Help me fix these boards real quick. Then I wanna ask you a favor."

Max gave a mock groan, but allowed her to pull him up. "What do I gotta do now?"

She grinned. "I bought a sound system at a yard sale this morning, but I couldn't drag it all here by myself. I was wondering if you can help me take it to my place after we close."

He looked at her skeptically. "What kinda sound system?"

"Turntable, receiver, speakers. Milk carton full of albums."

She waited for what seemed like a long time while he stared at her. Finally he gave a slow shake of his head and said carefully, as if speaking to a child,

"You know about CDs, right? And smaller, more compact stereos that weigh less than five pounds. And do they even make milk cartons anymore?"

"So is that a yes or a no?" Kyler waited, smiling, knowing he'd help her.

"Jesus," he scrubbed a hand across his face. "Yeah, it's a fuckin' yes, ok? But seriously, maybe you could think about getting some current technology."

"Maybe," she agreed. "But I just like the sound of albums. It's better, more rugged."

Max gave a smile and another shake of his head. "Yeah, you're right. Doc spoiled you. Truthfully, you never thought about this shit before you lived with him, right?"

"Yeah," Kyler said slowly, turning away so he wouldn't see the shame in her eyes. "Never really had time to . . . you know?"

Shit, he thought. "Hey, wait," he reached out and grasped her arm lightly. "Hey, I'm sorry, ok? I . . . I didn't mean it like that. I was just . . ."

"No, it's ok," she mumbled. "It . . ."

"C'mon," he interrupted, draping an arm around her shoulder. "Let's get these ramps done and then I'll help you with your stuff. And feel free to hit me. I got a big mouth sometimes."

"Nah," she gave a wan smile that he was glad to see. "I'm just . . . some things just hit hard, you know? It's not you."

Max didn't answer, but he didn't take his arm away, either. He sensed she needed the comfort and that the previous night was far worse than she was letting on. Even her mild hungover state proclaimed that, but he was the last person to pass judgement.

Together, with the help of both skateboards rolling on the sidewalk and carrying most of the weight, Max and Kyler finally managed to get the system to her apartment building.

"You take the elevator, all right?" She stood, hands on her hips, breathing hard. "I'll meet you up there. Three, ok?"

"You gonna be able to make the stairs?" Max hit the button and waited, watching her. "You're outta breath as it is."

"Halfway hungover, too many cigarettes," she said. "But I can handle these steps better than that elevator."

"All right," he conceded, rolling the skateboards into the elevator when the doors opened. Three, you said?"

"Yeah."

Max nodded and let the doors close between them, thinking that was the first time all day she'd admitted to drinking the night before. He wondered if she knew how much weight that laid on him; how much it twisted his gut.

She was waiting outside the elevator when the doors opened, and gestured towards the door standing open halfway down the hall.

"That's it. Just help me get it in there and then you can get on home."

"I can help you set it up if you want," he responded, grasping a skateboard and pushing it ahead of him. "I know you're going to, anyway."

"What about school tomorrow?"

Max shrugged. "It's no problem. Probably won't take us that long."

"All right," Kyler followed and locked the door behind them once they were inside. "Thanks. I guess we can just put it over there for now," she pointed to a wall in the living room. "Just 'till I can find a table or something to put it on."

He grunted as he lifted the heavy carton off the skateboard and set it on the carpet. "We might have an old stereo stand up in our attic, if you want it. It's real sturdy and it'll hold all this weight."

"Really?" She looked at him with raised eyebrows, smiling a hopeful smile that eased his heart.

"Yeah. It's been up there for awhile, but I'm sure it's still in pretty good shape."

"Thanks." Looking around, she gave an absent gesture. "I figure . . ." Kyler paused, thinking. "You know, the more I fill this place up, the easier it'll be to get used to it." She shook her head and ran a hand through her hair. "I mean, I'm glad I got it, but . . ." she shrugged, embarrassed. "It's just *empty*."

"You miss Doc," Max gave her a playful shove. "Go on, admit it."

She gave a faint smile but didn't answer. Instead, she began to slowly sort the various components of her new system, separating the wires and plugging the turntable and speakers into the receiver.

"Seriously," he squatted down to help her, "they sell killer systems now that are more compact, without all these wires."

"Sound's not the same. Hand me that top album there, would ya?"

Max pulled the album out of the milk carton and looked at it dubiously. "Uriah Heap?"

"Yeah. There's this one song on there that kinda stuck out at me." She took the album and pulled it from its jacket, placing it carefully on the turntable.

"And lemme guess, it was the one playing when you found this stuff."

"Yep," she adjusted the needle carefully over the record like Lamont had shown her, and then hit the switch that slowly lowered it. In mere seconds the rough, rugged sounds of the song came clearly through the speakers.

Max sat back on his heels and nodded approvingly. "Sounds good, anyway. How much'd you pay for all this?"

"Ten dollars. Guy's wife wanted him to get rid of it, ASAP." She looked at him and gave a smirk. "Said that's why God made CDs."

He offered a smile in return and gave a shrug. "Yeah, they're definitely smaller. But . . . this don't sound half bad. And all this for ten bucks, I think you got a pretty good deal."

"Yeah," Kyler nodded. "I thought so, too."

They were quiet for a moment, listening to the song, and then Max pushed himself to his feet, grimacing as his knees popped.

"Mind if I use your bathroom?"

She shook her head. "Down the hall on the right."

"Thanks."

Lying back on the floor, Kyler lit a cigarette and blew the smoke towards the ceiling, letting the soothing music roll over her. The words to this song hit her hard, knowing how many times during her life she'd been stealing when she should've been buying, and that not necessarily being in the literal sense.

"Well, I see you got a bed anyway," Max said, as he came back into the room. "So your bedroom's 'bout half-filled."

"What?" She sat up and stared at him. "I don't have a bed."

He gazed at her. "Well," he started slowly, "there's one back there."

"Shit," Kyler sighed and got up. She walked to the bedroom with Max behind her, and stopped just inside the doorway, looking at the brand new full-sized bed in the middle of the room, complete with pillows, sheets, and blanket.

There was a piece of paper in the middle of it, held down by what she recognized as Lamont's cell phone.

"Goddamn it, Doc," she growled, reaching for the note.

Saw the radio on the floor and figured you were right next to it all night long. Don't get pissed. Just think of it as a housewarming gift. Humor me, all right? Also, it hit me late last nite that you need a phone, so use my cell to call the phone company. Here's the number and you shouldn't have any problems getting hooked up, but they may need a deposit so I left you a blank check (I know you'll get pissed over that one). Just take it down to their office—corner of Aiken and Jared in the old bank building—and let me know how much it is.

Call me later, let me know how your first night went.

Kyler took a deep breath and let it out in an exasperated sigh. Max squeezed her shoulder.

"Relax. He just doesn't want you sleeping on the floor, and he knows how stubborn you can be."

She shook her head. "He didn't have to buy me a whole fucking bed."

"Why?" He said seriously, his eyes staring into hers. "Don't think you owe him for this, Kyler."

She regarded him for a long moment before turning away, her jaw tight with anger. Rubbing the heel of one hand across her forehead, Kyler tried to fight the conflicting emotions within her.

"Hey," Max's voice was quiet. "Don't be pissed at him, ok?"

"He knows I got the money," she muttered. "For that fucking phone. So why'd he leave me a blank check? And who the hell would leave a goddamn junkie a blank fucking check anyway?"

"Ok, first of all, the phone company won't take cash. I know that for a fact from when I tried to pay our bill there one time. It's check or money order only because they gotta have a paper trail. Cash is too easy to lose."

Kyler looked at him, impressed despite her anger. "They told you that?"

He favored her with a sarcastic look. "Yeah, but only after I hounded them for a week about it."

She sighed and sat on the edge of the bed. "Ok, but that still doesn't mean he's gotta pay for it."

"So pay him back," he said. "Write the check for the amount, get a receipt, and pay him back in cash. That way, since it's bothering you so goddamn much you two'd be square. And anyway, you need a phone."

"Why?"

He gestured around him. "Because you got this place. C'mon, Kyler, now you're just tryin' to be stubborn."

She dropped her head in her hands, running her fingers through her hair. "No. I'm really not, Max. It's just . . . even this . . . this place is more than I coulda hoped for. You gotta realize I spent my whole life on the streets, without a place to live, without a phone, without all the shit that you guys live by. And . . . for me, it's kinda all coming at once. The apartment, now the bed, and the phone . . ."

She lay back on the bed, grudgingly admitting to herself that it actually was very comfortable, and that only served to enhance her feeling of claustrophobic panic. The mattress shifted as Max sat down beside her. She waited but he remained silent.

"You're right," Kyler finally admitted. "I don't owe him for this. He's just . . . tryin' to get me up off the floor."

He lay back beside her, starting at the ceiling. "A lot of this is your pride," he said quietly. "The fact that you've fought through so much and come out scarred but surviving. And over the course of time you've found it's easier not to expect any help from anyone, 'cause most times you don't get it anyway."

Max turned his head to look at her. "Too many years of thinking like that and you developed a certain amount of pride in relying on nobody but yourself."

Kyler sighed and sat up, shaking her head. "Doc's already done all this analyzing, kid. No point in you doing it, too." She felt him put a gentle hand in the middle of her back and immediately tensed before forcing herself to relax.

"I'm not analyzing," he muttered. "I'm stating facts." He sat back up and stared at her. "Honestly, Kyler, if he hadn't done this how long do you think it woulda took you to do this? If ever? Maybe over time you woulda gotten at least a pillow or blanket, but an actual bed?"

"I'm not used to this," she growled softly.

"I know. So take it slow, ok? The bed's already here; no sense stressing over that. Besides, it's the *doc*. You oughtta know by now he's not gonna expect nothin' in return."

"Yeah, but you don't know exactly *how much* I already owe him."

"Do you?" His eyes bored into hers.

Kyler swallowed and slid her gaze away. "More than I'll ever be able to repay."

"So don't worry about," he said abruptly, as if that solved the whole problem. "You can only do what you can do."

"I'm not used to owing people."

Max gave an aggravated sigh and threw an arm around her shoulders, pulling her close in a brief, gruff hug. "You ever think maybe you've already given him more than you owe?"

She pulled away and stared at the floor. "I'm not wired that way, Max. It's hard for me to think in anything but plain terms. I can't imagine I've given him what I owe, plus the risk he took in giving me a blank check."

"Ok," he agreed easily, "so just quit thinking about everything, all right? Quit fucking stressing over this shit you can't control, no matter how much you *wanna* control it. You can't change it; it's a done deal. So if you want, tomorrow I'll go with you to the phone company, help you set up an account, and get you at least a line of communication with the world outside these walls."

He paused and gave her neck a brief squeeze, thinking how important a phone was when the demons wouldn't quit coming in the dead hours of the night.

"You'll need it one day," his voice was quiet. "And Doc aside, *I'd* feel better if I could talk to you, maybe call you if I got a problem."

Kyler shot him a bitter, sarcastic look. "Or rather, you mean, if I could call out when *I* got a problem."

"Whatever," Max shrugged. "It goes both ways."

She shook her head and ran a hand through her hair. Taking a deep breath, she glanced at the time on her new clock and stood up.

"C'mon, it's getting late. You got school tomorrow and I'm tired. Might as well try to get used to my new bed."

He offered a slight smile and stood up beside her. "Tomorrow, ok? I'll go with you and set you up with a phone line."

Grudgingly she gave in and nodded. "All right. Keep me from runnin' off and blowing his check on dope, anyway."

Max wrapped both arms around her and pulled her close in a longer hug this time. "I'd hunt you down, Kyler. Drag your ass outta the gutter if I have to."

His voice carried a jagged truth that was more real to her than anything else he'd said, and Kyler was grateful for that. That, at least, was something she could understand; something to carry off to her first sleep in her new bed with her.

Shutting the door behind him, Kyler walked back to her bedroom and stared at the clock. It was only a little after ten, and the long hours of the night loomed up before her.

"Christ," she mumbled, scrubbing a hand hard across her eyes. Taking a long, deep breath, Kyler came to a decision.

"One last night," she said softly. "Just get enough liquor to get me through the night, and then tomorrow I'll drop those walls enough to let Max and Doc help me learn to live in the real world."

Than was the last coherent thought she had before the booze carried her off on a swift, mind-erasing ride. Like sand scouring the shells and rocks clean on the beach, Kyler pushed the alcohol into her system in a harsh effort to scour her mind and soul clean; trying desperately to find a niche, a path, that would allow her to ultimately get through the days without counting out each second, without always fighting to stay away from the demons clutching her neck, from the monkey that always rode her back with its incredible weight.

CHAPTER 61

SLITTING HER EYES open, Kyler stared blearily around the room, lost in unfamiliarity for a minute before reality came crashing back. The Who came softly through the tiny speaker of her clock radio, singing about teenage wastelands, and she rolled over with a painful groan.

Half on and half off the bed, Kyler finally slid all the way off, looking up at the ceiling. The hangover roared through her, worse than the day before, and she pressed her hands into the carpet, gritting her teeth. Though her bladder was full, it felt like a ball of lead in her lower belly and her head pounded with a sickening thud, sending shards of painful bright light pulsing across her vision.

Dimly she heard a soft knocking on her door, and with a low moan pushed herself to her feet. The room swayed alarmingly for a brief second before righting itself, and Kyler, stumbling down the short hallway, leaned against the wall for support.

The knocking continued, and she shut her eyes around the spikes of dull pain it caused in her head. When she opened up the door and regarded Max's hazel eyes, she found she wasn't too surprised to see him.

"Christ, you look like shit," he muttered softly.

"I just got up. What time's it?"

"A little after seven," he stood there, his eyes hard on hers and anger coursing through his veins. "What time did you go to bed?"

Kyler shrugged. "I don't know. Why aren't you in school?"

He looked at her for a long moment and then cocked his head. "Some bad habits start small, and I know you know that."

"That doesn't answer my question," she growled.

"School can wait."

"Oh, yeah? Since when?" Now she was the one who felt anger, fueled by the monstrous hangover and topped off with the underlying pity she sensed in him.

"Since you're having a rough go of it and you think the booze is gonna solve your problems." Max glared at her. "I had a feeling you were gonna do this again."

"Christ, do *what*?" Kyler snapped.

"Fall back on the booze," he muttered bluntly. "Like you did the night before last. Too many long hours to get through, right?"

"Fuck, that's better than getting high," and now she was really angry; raging, actually, and ready to fight. Shame and humiliation cascaded around her with the knowledge that Max had known probably even before she did that she was going to get loaded again last night. Max and his fucking sense of perception, delving further into her thoughts and actions than she wanted anybody to be.

He shrugged, standing solid, ready for the blow he figured she'd lash out. "That's a matter of opinion, I guess," he said. "You gonna let me in or what?"

Kyler clenched her jaw and looked away, swallowing heavily. In a desperate move, she reined in her anger, recognizing the damage she could potentially do . . . to him, to her, to their friendship . . . most of all, to his faith and own jagged innocence.

"Fuck," she groaned, scrubbing a hand hard across her face. "Don't do this again, all right? Don't come here looking for a fight when I'm this hungover. I . . . I got a bad temper and it's hard to pull it back sometimes. Don't tempt it, ok?"

Max slid around her, pushing a plastic bag into her arms as he did so. "I didn't come lookin' for a fight. I came to go with you to the phone company. Go take a shower; I'll wait."

"What about school?" Kyler repeated, glaring at him.

He sighed, standing with his back to her for a long moment, regarding the parade of empty beer bottles standing on the counter. At least twelve, he counted, and with an empty half-pint of Jack Daniels shoved in the back, almost like an afterthought.

"I had Mom call me in sick," he answered. Turning to look at her, she read anger and resolve in his eyes. "You need me more."

"Me?" Her eyebrows shot up. "I don't need you."

Max gestured at the counter with a tired nod. "So, what? You're gonna do this shit every night? If that's the case, why didn't you just stay with Doc?"

"Fuck you," she said brusquely. "I'm an addict, Max. I can see you comin' in here with an attitude if I had a counter full of spikes, ok? But that's just beer, just something I did to relax. I'm not an alcoholic and I'm not gonna run to the bank every payday, cash my check, and spend it on booze.

"You," she pointed a trembling finger at him, "need to fucking realize that and quit making accusations before you even know what the fuck is goin' on."

Real fury raced through him, and it was only by sheer will that he managed to keep it in check. He clenched his jaw, feeling the tension in his body reach full pitch. "I'm not accusing," he managed through gritted teeth. "I'm stating facts. It's too easy to come to depend on this."

Kyler stared at him, her dark eyes full of a deep anger. "You think I can't recognize when I'm falling?" She asked softly. "Like I'd just willing give up a year of being clean, knowing what it'd lead me back to?"

"I'm just saying that sometimes shit like this sneaks up on you. That it's there before you know it."

"I'd know it," she responded sharply. "There'd be no way I couldn't see it coming. But what I'm asking from you is a little patience . . . a little tolerance. I got this place on my own, yeah, but now that I'm here it's like you and Doc want all this shit within the first week. A bed, a phone, a . . . what next, a couch and a TV?

"Just because it might take me a little longer to settle in don't mean it won't happen, ok? I'm movin' slow, Max, 'cause this is new territory for me, but movin' slow ain't stopping. Back off. I'm doin' what you guys're wanting me to do. The phone'll be hooked up today, I got that bed . . ." she flapped an angry hand back towards the bedroom.

"Don't think I'm gonna pay three hundred and fifty bucks a month to drown myself in alcohol, or to use it as a gateway to use again."

Pausing, Kyler took a deep breath. "I'm asking for faith, I guess, more than anything, all right?"

Max rested his eyes on hers for a long moment, feeling his resolve start to crumble. The solid steel in her gaze was more than enough to convince him, but on top of that was the incredible anger . . . anger that bordered on near-hatred, and he couldn't help but wonder if he'd pushed her too far.

Kyler saw his indecision, and felt her own anger start to ebb. This was Max, after all, and despite his own wars, he was still a kid. He didn't deserve her unleashing a wall of insane memories and past deeds on him.

She shook her head and dropped her eyes. "Fuck," she sighed, turning away. Walking over to her new stereo, she turned it on, letting the soft music try to mend the ragged edges of her soul. Behind her, Max stared at her back, feeling low and beaten. He watched her light a cigarette and let the smoke slowly filter out of her nose while she stared at the floor.

Finally she took a deep breath and lifted the seemingly forgotten plastic bag in her hand, still standing with her back to him.

"What's this?"

He swallowed. "I . . . towels. Shampoo and stuff. I stopped at the Family Dollar on my way over here. Yesterday I . . . when I was using your bathroom, I went to wash my hands and saw you didn't have any of that stuff, so I . . . you know . . ."

"Yeah . . . I know." Kyler finally turned to look at him, all hint of anger gone from her eyes. "Thanks."

Max gave a hesitant nod.

"Lemme take a shower, and then we can go." She started to walk back to the bathroom, but stopped when he said her name.

"There's . . . uh . . . some Excedrin in there, too. I just . . . figured you'd need it."

Without answering and feeling like she was drowning in shame, Kyler locked herself in the bathroom without responding. She leaned against the door and shut her eyes, feeling exhausted and hungover and torn up from the inside out.

"Goddamn it," she said softly. Digging through the bag, she pulled out the bottle of Excedrin and swallowed three with a small sip of water from the faucet. Praying they would start to work fast and knock back the pounding headache, she quickly pulled the rest of the stuff from the bag and set it on the counter.

Pulling off the same clothes she'd had on the day before, Kyler turned on the shower and stepped into a wall of steaming hot water. She stood there for a long moment, letting the heat and steam wash away the dirt, sweat, and booze from her body.

Briefly—again . . . as always—Josh's deep blue eyes flashed across her vision, and she felt another piece of her heart break off.

"Miss ya, boy," she mumbled into the water. "God, do I miss you."

The tears were there before she could stop them, mixing with the water running down her face. Kyler stood, letting the water pound between her shoulder blades for a long moment, trying to come to grips with her shaky mental state, with the fact that she needed another drink despite the hangover, and with the thought of Max, waiting for her in the living room, already scarred enough without her . . . and scarred more from knowing her.

Finally with a huge effort, she managed to find a deep steel inside that allowed her to pull herself together. It never was in her to break down, to just let go and give up, and it wasn't in her now. Whether it be Josh and Ryan or Doc and Max, she'd had people who'd leaned on her before as much as she leaned on them. People who gave strength when she needed it . . . and when she took it despite her pride.

And she wasn't about to lose it now. Somehow Kyler knew she had to pull it together, pull away from the anger and rage, from the addiction and constant need for *something* . . . *anything* . . . that thrummed through her veins.

Taking a deep breath, she quickly dried off with one of her new towels and then wrapped it around her. Walking into her bedroom, Kyler pulled some clean clothes from a plastic bag and got dressed. Her stomach was a shriveled knot but at least the headache had abated some, and she was able to allow herself to feel halfway ok again ... somewhat sane and in control.

Max was slowly gathering up the empty beer bottles and putting them carefully back in the cardboard pack they'd come in when she walked back in the room. His eyes met hers briefly before he glanced away.

"I'm sorry," she muttered.

"No," he said softly. "It's my fault. You're right; I shouldn't've come here wanting to jump down your throat."

Kyler sighed and lit a cigarette. "Let's go. Maybe we'll all feel better once I get a phone in here."

Wordlessly he picked up the carton of empty bottles and walked ahead of her out of the apartment. Still letting the silence build between them, she waited while he threw the carton in the dumpster on the side of the building, and then the two of them started walking in the general direction of the phone company.

After an endless ten minutes of still solid silence, Max finally cleared his throat.

"Kyler ..."

"No," she put a hand on his arm, stopping him. "Let's just sit, ok? Just for a minute."

Plopping heavily down on a low stone wall in front of a house, he watched as she took a deep, shuddering breath and ran her hands through her hair.

"You ok?"

Kyler didn't answer as she lit a cigarette with a badly shaking hand. Max wanted to tell her that the phone company was right around the corner, and that they were getting pressed for time if they wanted to make it to work by nine, but one look at her haggard face was like a spike through his heart.

Slowly he sat beside her and waited, watching as she stared at the ground between her feet, the hangover roaring through her. Finally she swallowed and looked at him.

"You remember that day you asked me if we were hiring at the park? That day you saw I had a . . ." she paused and ran her fingers lightly over her lower stomach. "Something here? I was . . . I was cut up pretty bad and you . . ." she stopped and took a deep breath. For the first time he saw how badly she was shaking.

"You helped me bandage it up after I tore some stitches."

"I remember," Max responded quietly.

"I never told you what happened that made me get those stitches."

"You don't have to."

"Yeah," Kyler's eyes were full of a dark defiance as they stared into his. "I do."

He reached for her but she pulled away, shaking her head.

"There was a guy I used to . . . uh . . . back when I was using, I used to go to him when I really needed something. When I needed to get high so fucking bad I'd do anything. *Anything*, Max, you understand?"

He didn't answer, but he knew she wasn't expecting him to. She was shaking harder now, and it wasn't because of the hangover.

"He was the worst out of all of them," her voice was a hoarse mutter. "He . . . really liked to hurt me, in any way he could. When I uh . . . got clean and I was slowly getting better . . . up here," Kyler tapped her head, "I ran into this guy again. It was late, I had just left the park, and he jumped me. Beat me up pretty bad."

She shut her eyes and took a jagged breath. The cigarette trembled between her fingers and Max felt his heart crumbling.

"He's insane. He likes violence, especially on women. He gets off on it, and the bloodier, the better. When I was shooting up, it got really bad with him sometimes. I can't tell you how many times I just wanted to fucking end it all 'cause I just couldn't do it, you know? Not one more time.

"And I tried. I shot up more and more . . . anything and everything . . . trying to fucking kill myself, trying to find a way out so that I wouldn't need the shit so bad that I'd let him do all that to me . . . over and over."

Kyler stared at the ground, trying to bore a hole into it with her burning gaze big enough to fall in.

"'Course that only made it easier for him to do what he wanted. I was a goddamn zombie most of the time, and as long as I was in that zone I was free. I didn't have to think, I didn't have to feel . . . The more he did what he did, the more I shot up. The more I shot up the easier it got for him."

"Christ," Max growled and tried once more to reach for her, but again she pulled away.

"That night . . ." Kyler pressed the heels of both hands hard against her eyes, trying to physically push the memories out of her head. "That night I'd been clean for awhile. I was living with Doc and he was helping me to *stay* clean. I . . . well, he came outta nowhere and smashed a big glass jar against my head, 'bout knocked me out.

"I fought him as best as I could, but he still managed to get a piece of glass down my pants, cutting me up. He was trying to . . . uh . . ."

"Stop," Max said gruffly, his voice hoarse with unshed tears. He wrapped both arms around her, pulling her against him. "Just stop, ok?"

Kyler let him hold her for a minute before gently pulling away and standing up, walking a few feet from him. "You don't need this baggage," she muttered. Her eyes were hooded and dull, defeated in a way that cut him deeply.

He scrubbed a hand across his face and didn't answer.

"I would know," she continued softly. "For me to go that low over an addiction . . . I would know if I was headed down that same path."

She shrugged and gazed at him with miserable eyes. "So I got drunk for two nights in a row. That don't mean I'm gonna do it tonight or tomorrow." She paused, trying to find the right words. "Sometimes . . . sometimes, Max, I get scared, 'cause I know that shit's still got me. Clean almost a year and I still see myself going out and scoring some smack and shooting up . . . and *not* seeing anything wrong with that.

"And that's what scares me, you know? There's a fucking shitload of things wrong with that, but it's all too easy to pick up where I left off, and when I think about it, it ain't even about me or what I'd do to keep on getting what I need."

Looking at him, Kyler read the fear in his eyes, and it weighed on her that she could mean that much to somebody.

"I think about you and I think about Doc, and my job and the good I think I do those kids at the park. Right there's enough reasons *not* to do it, and those're the reasons that keep me hanging on. But it's just really hard sometimes, especially late at night . . . in an empty apartment. I get to thinking about things I've done, things I've lost, things I've driven my pride and spirit and dignity into the ground for.

"And then you guys take a back seat to the shame, and all I want is to just quit thinking about everything, and I know the only way to completely erase my mind is to just find some potent shit . . . stuff that'll just blast through my veins and blow my head off. And all the stuff I did to get it makes me . . . it just kills me so much that I can only think of doing it again just to forget about everything."

Max stared at her for a long moment. Finally he shook his head and looked away, swallowing heavily. "Jesus, Kyler."

"But I'd still know," she repeated quietly. "Shit like that's hard to lose."

"You'd know," he muttered. "If the booze started to take you, you'd see that path stretching out in front of you. But . . ." he paused, pleading with his eyes. "Would you tell me? Or Doc?"

Kyler gazed at him for a long moment; dark eyes locked on hazel ones. "I don't know," she finally admitted. "But truth be told you guys would probably recognize it."

"And you'd let us help you? Or get you help?"

She sighed and rubbed her forehead. "Right now I can't tell you what you wanna hear, Max. I'm just trying to help you understand. Just . . . please try to understand, all right?"

Max stared at her, then finally got up. She let him walk by her without trying to stop him before falling into place at his side. The silence once more dropped down between them, and stayed that way . . . a wordless, heavy weight . . . until they got to the phone company.

Max waited with her through the paperwork, the writing of the blank check (which was somewhat of a relief to Kyler), and the issuing of a new phone number but still didn't say a word. Kyler felt the heaviness in her heart, pulling her down.

As they left the phone company and headed towards the park, he remained silent beside her. He waited while she unlocked the gate and then the office door before finally muttering,

"I'm gonna start on the repairs on the far side. You just take it easy, all right? It's small shit; no need for both of us out there."

Silently Kyler headed over to the computer and booted it up as he slipped by out into the park. She knew he was just trying to accommodate her hangover, but she couldn't help but feel ashamed. Ashamed to be in the air-conditioning while he was out in the heat, ashamed to let him do the work she should be doing, and more than anything just wishing—for about the millionth time—that everything would just *stop*. Just *stop* for a little while and let her have a little breathing room.

Kyler plopped down in the chair and reached into the bottom drawer, finding her Excedrin bottle amid jumbled office supplies. She popped a Percoset and leaned back, pressing the heels of her hands hard against her eyes. She understood Max's frustration; the feeling of wanting something good to come out of fucking shit was something she'd been experiencing for too long now. But Kyler knew he couldn't save her, and she hated to see him try so hard only to feel the sharp pang of disappointment and regret in the end.

"He was probably better off never knowing me," her voice was a soft mutter. "Christ." Depression washed over her in waves, only enhancing the hangover and both physical and emotional pain.

The longest day Kyler'd had in a long time finally began to come to an end. Over the last twelve hours Max had barely spoken to her, and then it was only to communicate something about the park. The hangover had finally abated, but she was heartsick and depressed, knowing that her earlier thoughts were still correct.

"He'd've been better off not ever knowing me."

"Who?" Max's voice came from behind her at the top of the steps. Kyler was sitting on the edge of the huge ramp, letting her legs dangle down into the bowl, and she felt her heart leap up into her throat.

"Me?" He sat down beside her.

"Fuck, you scared the shit outta me," she said shakily.

"Who you talkin' about?" He persisted, looking at her.

"Nobody," Kyler ran a hand through her hair. "I didn't know I said that out loud."

Max grunted and stared down into the bowl. He was quiet a minute and then said, "I finished up and went ahead and locked the tools up. Front gate's locked, too. Everybody's already gone."

Kyler gave an absent nod but didn't answer.

"And for the record," she heard his voice catch and it was like he cut off a piece of her heart, "if you're talking about me, you're wrong. Ain't no way I'd been better off not knowing you."

She shut her eyes and swallowed hard. "You can't save me," she said softly. "I'm gonna fuck up and I'm gonna rip your heart out, Max. It's a given with me."

"So . . . what? You want me to just walk away?" His eyes blazed with anger and sadness. "Just say 'fuck you, Kyler' and walk on outta here like it don't even matter? Like nothing fucking matters?"

Everything matters, she heard Lamont whisper in her head, and suddenly Kyler knew she'd rather cut off her own hand than cause this kid anymore heartache.

"You should," she muttered. Meeting his hurting gaze, Kyler felt lower than ever. "You thought I was gonna hit you this morning. I saw it in your eyes. And, Jesus, kid, just the fact that you thought that should tell you something."

"Would you?" His eyes blazed. "Ever hit me?"

She regarded him for a long time before dropping her eyes back to the bowl. Max waited, feeling the pain and anger of the conflict between them.

"Lock the gate after me, ok?" Her voice was hoarse with unshed emotions. "I'm going home." Sliding down into the bowl, Kyler felt the depression swamp her, overlying every positive thing around her. She stepped off into the grass and wished she was stepping into hell.

"Jesus, Kyler, wait!" Max yelled. He scrambled over the coping and hit the bowl hard, barely feeling the burn of bare skin against raw wood in his anger and pain. She stopped and looked back, feeling the spike of pain at the blood running from his leg.

"You think I'm gonna look at you differently?" He snarled, furious. *"You think I'm gonna see you as that junkie whore, treat you like shit on the bottom of my shoe?"*

Kyler winced and scrubbed her hands across her face and through her hair, locking her fingers at the base of her neck as she tried to stare a hole into the ground.

"As long as you've known me, I'd think you'd know me a little better than that." His voice was back to normal level, but she could sense the rage just beneath the surface. "After all this shit, Kyler . . . Christ . . ." Max took a deep breath and glared across the park. "You told me before, remember? About this? When you thought I'd quit?"

Kyler didn't answer and she felt his hand on her shoulder, forcing her to look at him.

"I didn't quit, though, right? And I didn't walk away from you. You can tell me things like this all day long and—"

"I didn't wanna tell you," she growled. "None of it."

"I know," he responded softly. "But you did and I accepted it as who you used to be, ok? Not who you are now. Shit . . ." Max sighed, trying to find rational words around the pain and anger.

"Look," he muttered. "I'm sorry about this morning. I . . . I jumped all over you and I didn't have any right to. It was like I expected you to understand without . . . without really knowing why I was so upset and . . ." he trailed off, shrugging.

"The difference between you and me," she said quietly, cupping a gentle hand around his neck, "is that I'll always have this monkey on my back, and it'll always control me. People like you and the doc, though, are like . . . counterparts to my misery. You hold me up when that monkey wants to pull me down . . . and . . ." Kyler swallowed. "I don't wanna be carried like that."

"So what're you saying?"

She shook her head and gave a heavy sigh. "I don't know. I'm just tired, Max . . . of everything, and . . . I can't help but think that as you carry me, hold me up, keep me going . . . maybe I'm just too much of a burden. I'm gonna get heavier every day."

"And you want me to let go."

Kyler met his eyes and felt the pain in them mirrored in her heart. "I don't know," she repeated. "Look . . . it's just been a hell of a day. I'm tired, all right? I'll see you in the morning."

She turned away and started towards the gate, but stopped when he laid a hand on her arm.

"I'm not gonna drink," her voice was quiet, but hard. "If that's what you're thinking."

"That's not what I'm thinking."

She took a deep breath and let it out slowly. "So . . ."

"So be careful. And call me if you need anything, and I don't care what time it is."

Kyler looked at him and smiled a beautiful, exhausted smile that both hurt and elated him. "Jesus, you're sounding more like Doc every day."

CHAPTER 62

SPEAKING OF LAMONT made her change her direction from headed to her place to his. It'd been two days since she'd last seen him and Kyler was surprised to find herself missing him as much as she was.

The sound of the ocean, soothing in its ever-present roar, greeted her long before she reached his street. As dusk gave way to full darkness, she walked up the driveway and slipped around to the back of his house. The railing on the deck blocked her view of the deck itself, and she didn't see him until she was almost upon him.

"I figured if I sat here with my feet buried in the sand long enough, you'd come around that corner." Lamont's voice was quiet, barely heard above the pounding of the surf.

Kyler offered a wan smile and sat down on the steps beside him. "You're missing out on all that nice, expensive deck furniture."

"Expensive, yes. Nice? Maybe, but not too comfortable," he slung an arm around her shoulders and pulled her close in a hug. "Been missing you."

"Yeah," she sighed. "I know. I meant to come by sooner, but . . ."

"New place, new things," he said. "I understand."

Digging in her front pocket, Kyler pulled out his cell phone. "Been missing this, too, I bet."

"Nah, not too much," he took it from her and shoved it absently into his own pocket. "Been nice and quiet without it." His eyes met hers. "You get your own phone hooked up?"

"Yeah," she held out a hand with a slip of paper tweezed between two fingers. "Your receipt," her eyes were darker with a distant anger. "And I'm paying you back."

Lamont smiled easily. "I knew you'd be mad."

Kyler took a deep breath and stared out at the water. "Jesus, Doc, what the fuck were you thinking, giving me a blank check? With that much unlimited cash, no telling how much smack I coulda bought."

He leaned back on the steps, stretching. "I have faith in you," she felt him tap the middle of her spine gently. "I keep telling you you've come a long way."

She dropped her head into her hands. "It's hard, having this much faith put in me," her voice was a hoarse mutter. "Between you and Max, I feel it's just only a matter of time . . ." She paused, lighting a cigarette with a slightly trembling hand.

"Matter of time before what?" Lamont asked softly. His hand on her back was calming and familiar, fighting back the demons within.

"Before I fuck up again. And then you two are left with nothing but anger and resentment, and I'm back with a spike in my arm."

"I doubt that," he sat up and drew her close to him. "You just gotta give yourself a chance, kid."

Kyler took a deep drag off her smoke and stared at the ocean. "I feel like he's skinning me," her voice was a soft growl. "Like he's peeling off one layer at a time, letting these fucking . . ." she gestured. "All this bad shit out and leaving raw flesh underneath."

Lamont sat silent beside her, watching the waves pound the beach.

"He fucking needs to know everything, but I don't think he should carry all this weight."

"So why're you telling him?" He looked at her. "Why not just say 'Fuck off, Max, that ain't none of your business?'"

Now it was her turn to be quiet, thinking.

"I don't want him to judge me," Kyler mumbled. "So I'm trying to explain it all to him, only . . ." she swallowed and gave a slow shake of her head. "Only knowing the more I tell him the more he's gonna judge me."

"Kyler, I don't think—"

"He doesn't need to carry this," she repeated, looking at him. "He's just a kid; he doesn't need my nightmares keeping him awake at night."

Lamont took a deep breath and looked out at the waves for a moment. "Where were you at sixteen?" He asked. "Not strung out on dope."

"But not completely innocent, either. I was raised on the streets, Doc. I wasn't like Max . . . I didn't have a mom to watch out for me and a house to go home to every night."

He shot her an unreadable look in the dim light. "But that doesn't mean he's been protected from the rougher side of the world, either. Max has . . . he's had his bad times, Kyler, and he's not as green as you think he is."

Kyler stared down at the worn boards between her feet, feeling tired throughout her body. Max, angry outside her doorway that morning flashed across her memory, and she gritted her teeth against the raw emotion it brought her.

"Still," she growled softly, "he's a good kid. He doesn't need this."

"What?" Lamont asked quietly. "You being haggard and hungover, and him thinking it's only a start to another addiction?"

She looked at him sharply. "You talked to him." It wasn't a question.

He hesitated. "He called me."

Running a hand through her hair, Kyler sighed and leaned back on the steps. He saw the anger in the tightness of the jaw as she stared hard at the crashing waves.

"I kinda thought he had issues," she turned her dark gaze on him. "With you. I'm surprised he did that."

Lamont was quiet for a long moment, giving her time to regret her words.

"His issues," he finally murmured, "have less to do with me than the, uh . . . situation that brought us both together. It was hard and he hasn't gotten over it yet."

Kyler stood up and walked out into the ocean without answering. He watched as she walked straight in, only stopping when the water got just above her knees. He tried to swallow his heart back down, but it seemed like it was stuck in his throat.

"Jesus," Lamont said gruffly.

She shot him a look and then relented, walking back to him. Her eyes were calmer now, staring steadily into his. "I'm not about to just walk out there and let it take me, Doc."

He just shook his head and didn't answer. Kyler shut her eyes and breathed deep of the salty air. She felt the drag of her wet jeans hanging low on her hips, and the seawater on her skin. Lamont's eyes on hers were shot with an underlying fear that hurt her heart, and she finally conceded, holding up her hands in surrender.

"I'm sorry," she said. "I'm hungover and tired . . . feeling like Max hollowed me out but I know that ain't his fault." Kyler paused as she sat beside him again, briefly leaning against his side. "And I know it ain't fair for me to keep doing this to you," she muttered.

Lamont held her to him and they sat in silence for a long moment before he finally responded, "I didn't know I was signing on for this when I was fighting to keep you alive in that ER, Kyler. I didn't know I was gonna open my home and . . . and my heart . . . to someone who'd literally crawled out of the gutter . . ."

Kyler clenched her teeth and pulled away from him, shame raining down on her.

"But . . ." he put a gentle hand on the back of her neck, "I don't regret any of it, ok? I'd do it all again in a heartbeat, kid, 'cause you've given me far more than what I could ever give you.

"You think you're gonna crush me if you go back out there?" Lamont gestured vaguely towards the front of the house and the street. "Yeah, you will, and I'll freely admit that to anybody. So this weight you're carrying from all the faith I got in you . . . and Max, too . . ." he stared hard into her eyes. "Get used to it, all right? 'Cause it ain't goin' away."

She lit another cigarette and didn't answer.

"And if you *do* go back out there, don't think I'm just gonna give up on you. I won't stop looking for you."

"You'd just find heartache."

He rubbed the bridge of his nose, giving her a sidelong look. "I'm not that green, either," he said quietly. "You oughtta know that by know."

"Yeah," Kyler sighed, running her hands through her hair. "You're right." She waited a beat and then looked directly at him. "I'm sorry."

Lamont hooked an arm around her neck in a loose headlock, feeling the sharpness of her collarbone beneath her thin shirt. "Nothin' for you to be sorry about," he responded easily. "I'm just glad to see you. How's the apartment coming?"

She ducked her head beneath his arm, giving him a slightly exasperated look. "You oughtta know . . . you were there."

"Once again, I knew you'd be mad," he smiled.

"Nah . . ." Kyler shook her head. "I was at first, but I'm over it now. The bed's too comfortable to stay mad for long."

"Glad you like it. I figured you liked the one upstairs so I tried to get it as close as I could."

She nodded absently, looking out across the ocean. "Thanks." A pause, then, "How much did it cost?"

Lamont stared at her and then gave a heavy sigh. "Kyler . . ." he started, then paused, giving a slow shake of his head. "Look, I know you, ok? More than you'd like me to 'cause you're too damn full of pride, but you've lived here for a year now. I've learned a lot, and I know this move is scary for you, but I also know how important it is. You're clean, got a little money in your pocket, and once again your pride kicks in, tellin' you you can't live here forever, right?"

She looked at him but didn't answer.

"So you try this, living on your own . . . *in your own place.* A place that ain't in some alley somewhere or hiding in a shelter when there're too many people after you."

She gritted her teeth, still remaining silent but hating that he *did* know that much about her.

"So you got an apartment, right? But that doesn't mean you're gonna go out and buy a bunch of stuff for it. That's not you, and even less you now that you got a steady paycheck coming in. A pillow and a blanket would do for you . . . once you got around to getting one or both. And hell, you'd still be sleeping on the floor a year from now; tell me I'm wrong."

Her eyes, dark with anger again, glared hard into his.

"There's nothing wrong with wanting a little bit more, kid, ok?" Lamont said quietly.

"The only thing I ever wanted more of was dope," she growled. "I was always fine with what I had . . ."

". . . or didn't have," he finished for her. Kyler swallowed heavily and stared out at the ocean, feeling the harsh tang of the nicotine bite into her lungs as she held the smoke in as long as she could.

"Be mad all you want," he said, "but the bed's there now. It'd be more trouble moving it back out then for you to accept it. But then . . ." his eyes held a tired amusement, "that's not too big of a deal for you, is it?"

Shame washed over her and she dropped her head. "It's not that I'm ungrateful," her voice trembled slightly, and she stopped, hating it, trying to get herself together.

"I know," Lamont gave her a brief, gentle hug. "I know, Kyler. I'm sorry. That came out all wrong."

"No," Kyler pulled away once more and took a deep breath. "It's just that . . . like I was telling Max this morning, I kinda feel pressured . . ." she looked at him. "By him and by you. It's like since I got this place—that I've only had for a couple days now—everything has to be done at once. Hook the phone up, get some furniture . . . couch, TV . . . bed . . . like me taking this step scares both of you more than it does me, and you're wanting me to get settled in as quick as possible so I'm less likely to be off runnin' the streets.

"And I'm *not* gonna go running the streets, Doc, but I'm not the type to hurry up and buy a bunch of shit to get settled in, either. I can be slow sometimes but I get the shit done. And I know it bothers you to think I'd still be sleeping on the floor in a year and it'll probably bother you even more to know that I'm fine with that but only because I'm not used to all this shit. Not used to having a phone or my own bed or . . . or anything, you know?"

She stopped and looked at him, dark eyes imploring him to understand.

"Fuck," she growled. "I don't wanna fight with you tonight, Doc. It's just that . . . I don't think I can be what you and Max want me to be."

Lamont regarded her for a long, long moment before finally turning his eyes back to the ocean. "I can't speak for him, kid," he said quietly, "but . . . here," he took her hand and pulled her to her feet. "Walk with me."

"Where?"

"Out there," he pointed. "You're calmer out there."

Without waiting for an answer he guided her into the rough waves, gritting his teeth as the cold water rushed over his knees and then his calves, numbing him down to his toes. Kyler showed no sign that the freezing waves were pushing them back even as it pulled them forward; didn't give an inch or show any emotion when the water reached her waist.

Lamont stopped and she stopped with him, waiting.

"I watched you crawl out of the gutter," he repeated. "Watched you crawl a little bit more before you were able to walk again. Watched you stumble and then fall again, surrendering to that monkey on your back after you were raped."

Kyler shut her eyes and in the darkness he could just barely make out the tight line of her jaw.

"And then I saw you get back up again, stronger than ever. That day you came to my house, scared, high, and lost?

Don't you think that if there ever was a time when I wanted to change you, it would've been then?

"Truth of the matter is, Kyler, addiction and rape are common generalities, and it doesn't matter who you are, where you're from, or the wars you've been through or haven't been through. I'm the last person in the world to tell you to change, to make you what I *want* you to be. It's impossible to begin with, and I wouldn't try it even if I could."

She was quiet beside him, swaying gently with the waves. Her eyes were on the invisible horizon, reflecting the moonlight but hiding her emotions . . . as always. Finally she took a deep breath and put an arm around his waist, giving him a brief hug at the same time she guided him back towards shore.

"C'mon, it's cold out here."

Lamont hung back, looking at her. "I'm not lookin' to change you," he repeated. "And I'm not lookin' to shove all this shit on you, make you more settled in than you wanna be. I just . . ." he sighed. "I just wanted the phone, ok? Just so . . . so you had a way to talk to me or . . . or somebody . . . you know, if you needed to."

Kyler looked at him, waiting.

"The bed . . ." he shrugged. "I just kept thinking back to you sleeping on the floor in the storage room at the park, and I'm sorry, but it broke my heart, ok? I just wanted you to not have to do that, but you're right. From your eyes I can see how you're feeling cornered."

The waves pushed around them, colder by the minute, and she felt ashamed again, and hungover, and way too much exhaustion digging at her core. She felt the weight of her past clinging to her, pressing down on her, and thought back to all the times Lamont had been there for her, pulling her back from that edge, guiding her back to sanity with a gentleness she hadn't seen in any man since Josh.

She'd realized long ago that he didn't have to do that, but it was only recently that she'd begun to see there was no ulterior motive in it for him. He'd pulled her back because that's what he did: he saved lives. He'd guided her in a new direction, away from her demons and the humiliating things she'd done to feed them, and he didn't want anything in return except to offer a bed so she wouldn't have to sleep on the floor.

Kyler raised her eyes to his and realized for the first time how much her being in his life impacted him. How much faith and confidence he'd put into her at the risk of his own heartbreak, and thought again of him saying she had to carry the weight of that faith, and to get used to it because it wasn't going away.

"You'd come looking for me?" She asked softly. "If I went back out?"

"I'd never *stop* looking for you," Lamont answered seriously, and then waited for the explosion of pride in her eyes, denying his words.

She took a deep breath and scrubbed a hand hard across her face. "All right, Doc," she sighed. "Ok."

He stared at her for a moment, and then relented and walked towards her, wrapping an arm around her. She was now shivering from the cold and he felt the goose bumps along her bare arms.

Together they walked back to the beach and up onto his deck. He pulled some towels off the table and handed her one.

"Th-thanks," she stuttered, the freezing cold sinking deep into her core. "Sorry I . . . I made you go out there."

Lamont gave a tired smile. "I made *you* go out there, remember? C'mon, let's go inside."

Kyler pulled the towel tight around her and stepped into the warm air of the kitchen. The coffee pot was on and she found herself suddenly longing for a cup.

"Good thing I made a full pot," he grinned, reaching for two cups.

"Like you were really thirsty or were expecting company." She offered a smile in return.

He shrugged. "Figured you'd stop by eventually. Hoping sooner than later."

There was silence for a few moments as they sat at the table, each lost in their own thoughts. Lamont absently stirred sugar in his coffee and then took a sip, gazing at her over the rim of his cup. Kyler raised her eyebrows and waited.

"You, uh . . ." he started, "gonna stay here tonight or are you goin' home?"

She glanced at the clock on the wall; it was pushing ten-thirty and she was tired. Exhausted, really, and wet and cold.

"Spare bed's still available," he gave a small smile.

Kyler paused a moment and then gave a slow nod. "Ok. Thanks."

"Anytime, you know that. Think you even have some clothes still here."

"Yeah," she rubbed an eye with the heel of one hand. "Think I can use your shower, too?"

"You don't have to ask," Lamont got up to refill his cup. "I keep telling you that."

"I know," she sighed, stepping up behind him and putting hers in the dishwasher. "I just don't like taking things for granted."

He glanced at her. "Seriously, kid, when did *you* ever take anything for granted?"

Kyler met his eyes. "Once. With Josh. And Ryan." She shrugged. "They were my family, and I guess I just thought they'd always be there. I didn't realize how much the smack was . . . you know, tearing all of us apart."

She lifted one shoulder in another half-hearted shrug and slipped out of the kitchen before he could answer. A few minutes later he heard the bath water start to run upstairs.

CHAPTER 63

KYLER PULLED ON the baggy sweats and t-shirt she'd found in the spare bedroom and then glanced at Lamont's open bedroom door as she stepped out into the hall. She hesitated, torn between her pride and fear, and then gave in and walked lightly down the hallway.

She saw him reflected in the bathroom mirror, shirtless, wearing pajama bottoms and brushing his teeth, and then his eyes found hers and he nodded before dipping his head to rinse his mouth out with the faucet. She waited while he dried his mouth and turned to face her, pulling a long string from a roll of floss.

"Hey."

"Hey . . ." Kyler hesitated, her eyes dropping to the floor by the tub, where it seemed not too long ago she'd almost bled to death. Lamont watched the fear cross her face at the memory, but waited, saying nothing. He began to floss slowly, eyebrows raised in question when she finally looked at him.

"You ok?"

"Yeah . . ." she leaned against the doorjamb. "I just . . . wanted to say thanks . . . for everything."

Lamont waited a beat while he finished flossing and then dropped the string in the trash. He looked back at her and saw pride battling humility in her gaze.

"I don't want to take you . . . and this . . ." she waved her hand in the air, indicating—he assumed—his house with her in it, and the safety and security that came with it, "for granted. Like I did with Josh and Ryan. I know it won't last . . ." Kyler swallowed and he saw fear jump into her dark eyes; fear fueled by the monkey's need that was still clinging to her back.

"It'll last," he said quietly. "For as long as you need it to, Kyler."

She took a deep breath and looked away, gritting her teeth.

"Can I talk to you?"

Lamont only just managed to keep the surprise out of his eyes. "Yeah," he answered, his voice soft. Instinctively he knew that he had to tread lightly, that one wrong move and she'd close back up.

"Here," he extended a hand towards the bedroom. "Let's sit down, ok?"

Kyler took a step back, relieved to get out of the bathroom and its walls that were closing in on her. She sat gently on one corner at the foot of the bed, drawing her legs up to her chest and resting her chin on her knees.

Knowing her like he did, Lamont sat up against the headboard, giving her the distance he knew she needed and just waited. He thought back to that day she'd come to his door, high on coke and looking as lost as he'd ever seen anybody look, and then he flashed to that night he'd gotten the call from Emily, and how Kyler'd been there to be a rock he could lean on during that long drive to the airport.

The psychiatrist part of him was curious at the yo-yo of her emotions, flowing one from end of the spectrum to the other with seemingly no glitches or pauses; level-headed one minute, steady as a rock, and then the next full of white-hot rage and hatred, and then still the next minute ready to bolt and run like her world was full of demons.

Which it is, he thought, *and who can blame her for having this wild swing of emotions?*

"I, uh . . ." Kyler swallowed, looking at him with hooded eyes. "I don't like having to depend on people."

"I know you don't," he responded gently.

"But I was thinking that I've probably done that more times in my life than I haven't. I was real young when I left the orphanage, so I don't remember much of it, or my life on my own out there on the streets after, you know? It seems my life started the day I met Josh, and . . . uh . . . I know now that I depended on him more than I thought I did at the time."

He watched her trace a line in the design on the comforter with a slightly trembling finger.

"It's like this, Doc." She ran her finger down the line. "It's like my whole life there's been this line in me; one side's safe . . . love, happiness, freedom . . . and the other side's a suicidal, drug-addicted mind-freak." Her eyes on his were filled with a mixture of emotions, most conflicting.

"With Josh and Ryan I was always on this side of the line . . . *way over* on this side. I had them to support me, protect me . . . walk with me, you know, as we struggled through day to day life. Josh and I . . ." her eyes grew distant as she looked back over the years. "We did a few things . . . pot here and there, sometimes a line or two of coke, pills, maybe.

"Little things," she looked at him, "and not too much of anything. I know that every time I did it I walked a little closer to that line, but I never crossed it. I didn't need to; I didn't *need* any of it, you know? Not like I do now."

Lamont gazed at her, trying to see past that wall. "Ryan never got high?"

Kyler shook her head. "He didn't like it; didn't need it. He surfed . . . I told you that, right?"

He nodded.

She shrugged. "That was all he needed to get high. A good wave and his surfboard. He . . . would stay with us, though, when we'd get a little crazy. Just to make sure we didn't walk in front of a train or fall down a fire escape or anything."

She was quiet for a few minutes, thinking, and Lamont let her. It was rare for her to open up like this about those two guys and her life before the smack, and he didn't want to do or say anything that would make her stop talking. Plus, more than anything he knew that she wouldn't be talking at all if this wasn't something she felt she had to get out.

"Then one day I went from here," her finger touched one side of the line and then jumped far over the line to the other side, "to here."

"The first time you shot up."

Kyler looked at him and nodded. "And I didn't even pop it . . . just went straight for the needle. I'd been doing coke a lot longer and had never shot it up. Still haven't." She looked away and took a deep breath. "But I sure went for that needle . . . and didn't even flinch."

Swallowing hard, she scrubbed a hand hard across her face. "From then 'till the day you stopped me from dying on the floor in the ER, I couldn't get back across that line."

Lamont wanted to go to her and pull her in his arms but he held back.

"Josh tried to pull me back, and so did Ryan, but I couldn't let the heroin go. I mean, I tried, but it took me, Doc, and held on. The first time I skated it was the same way . . . something that had me by the proverbial balls and wasn't letting go. Skating's the positive side to heroin's negative, but in the end it was the heroin that won.

"I quit skating, quit loving life. I quit Josh and Ryan, too, although they held onto me long after I'd let go of them. But finally, you know . . . they couldn't hold on any longer."

Kyler's eyes were full of unshed emotion, breaking his heart.

"The thing was, though, by that time I only lived to shoot up, and I was shooting up more and more. I hadn't started . . ." she flapped a hand vaguely, not looking at him, "doing the things I eventually did to get high, but only because Josh kept giving me money. I think he knew how far it would go if he didn't, so he did what he could and kept giving what he could.

"But I know it was hard." A tear slipped from the corner of one eye and she wiped it away absently. "You might be able to panhandle enough money in a day to get a halfway decent meal somewhere, but shooting dope's a fucking expensive habit. I have no idea what he had to do to keep giving me all that money . . . for all I know he coulda been selling himself."

Kyler swallowed hard again and gritted her teeth. Lamont saw the tight line of her jaw and the trembling in her rock hard muscles.

"Finally he just couldn't do it anymore. Him and Ryan left, and even though I was fucking dying inside, you know what my main emotion was?"

Lamont knew but remained silent.

"I held onto him as long as I could but I was relieved when he finally walked away. It was like I was saying, 'Fuck, go. Go.' Like I'd been trying to do something for a long time and he'd been standing in the way. I wanted to get higher and higher each time I shot up but couldn't do that because I loved him, and because of that love I couldn't do what I needed to do to get as high as I needed to get."

She ran her hands through her hair and dropped her forehead to her knees, locking her fingers behind her neck. "Fuck, I hated that part of me, Doc. I hated it and I wanted to kill it so in order to do that I just gave it what it wanted."

"You fed it what it needed," he murmured.

"Higher and higher, doing whatever I could—whatever was *necessary*—to keep me that way. I didn't care anymore about anything except getting high or dying, whichever came first. You hadn't've saved me that night I'd've been dead the next morning."

Lamont couldn't agree more but he merely nodded.

Kyler stared out the window for a moment before turning her eyes back to his. "So then there you came along, trying to save me when I didn't want to be saved. But . . . after awhile, you know, the physical pain left, leaving me with just the shit up here," she tapped her head.

"You got me my board and I found myself watching those shows again . . . X Games, the Amateurs up in Venice Beach, Sk8 TV . . . and I remembered . . ." she swallowed. "I remembered what it felt like to skate, to . . . to be alive. To love that ocean out there.

"Treatment worked well enough and I made some good friends there. Got a really good job where all I do all day long is just what I love to do. Starting finding more to life than getting high."

There was silence between them for a few long moments and then Kyler dropped her head, staring at the bedspread between her knees.

"And then that night at the halfway house . . ." her voice was barely audible but Lamont heard her just fine. He remained outwardly calm, but his heart was pounding and inside he was shouting with relief.

The girl was finally going to talk about it; finally going to get it out of herself where it was doing nothing but poisoning her.

"Up 'till then I was starting to feel things again. *Positive* things. I could wake up in the morning and I just knew that if I did everything right I could get through the day without a fix. I *knew* that, Doc," her dark eyes were a mass of rage and fury. "Just knowing that . . . that I didn't *have* to reach for a needle, that I *could* make it without getting high . . . it was . . ." Kyler swallowed, struggling for words. "It was a strength I'd been without for a long time.

"He took that all away from me," now her voice was a whisper. "He came in and threw me on the ground and I couldn't move. He was on me before I really knew what was happening, and then he . . . then he was *in* me and I felt like I was gonna go crazy right there.

"Everything good was gone and I felt like all that bad shit was crashing down on me again. Like I was going through all this fucked up shit and I didn't even want it this time.

"I th-ought I was doin' good, Doc," Kyler looked at him, her voice trembling. He saw her whole body shaking from the memory. "I wanted to do it right this time, to stay clean and not go back to that shit."

She ran a hand across her eyes.

"When he, uh . . . when he raped me I just didn't see the point in all of that anymore. I'd been pushed back into that same old life and it seemed I'd lost everything again. I couldn't face all that without getting high . . . so I did." Kyler shrugged but it was miserable and half-hearted.

"I guess I figured if I had some asshole fucking me that I didn't even know then I might as well get something out of it for myself."

"But you came back," Lamont said softly. "You didn't give up completely, Kyler, because you came back."

"Yeah," she sighed, looking away and wiping the tears from her eyes. "I came back." A pause and then she looked at him. "And you picked me up again."

"You're stronger now, kid."

Kyler dropped her forehead on her knees again, suddenly exhausted. "That night Lewis almost killed me, Doc, I was in an area of town I shouldn't've been in and I don't know what would've happened if he hadn't attacked me."

The silence between them was longer this time, and heavier.

"It was that night John called me to tell me I was off the city's time. I wasn't sleeping then so I thought I'd celebrate by getting some valium and hopefully sleep through the whole night for once. Only . . . only I'm not sure I woulda ended up with just valium."

"Jesus . . ." Lamont growled.

"It was a fucking thought that just came out of nowhere and, you know, it made perfect sense to me . . . at the time. Later on, though, after all that shit happened, I wanted to kill myself, Doc. For turning my back on you . . . on Emily . . . on everything I tried so hard to hold on to."

She took a deep breath and closed her eyes. "It's a fucking circle for me. Always letting go of all the things that keep me sane, things I'd die for, just to catch a high. I'm tired of running that circle; tired of playing Russian roulette with my life."

Lamont looked at her and his gaze softened. Again he wanted to go to her and comfort her, but again held back.

"Kyler, look—"

"Shit," she pressed the heels of her hands hard against her eyes, then turned and rolled off the bed. "I need a cigarette." Pausing at the door she stared down for a long moment before raising her gaze back to his.

"But I . . . I need to come back, ok? I, uh . . . there's something I need to tell you."

Her dark eyes on his were hard enough to ignore in any normal circumstance, but now they were almost black with a mixture of harsh emotions.

"Sure," he mumbled. "You can smoke in here if you want."

Kyler shook her head. "I'm just gonna go out back. I'll be back in a minute." Without waiting for a response she slipped out the door. Lamont raked a hand through his hair and took a deep breath.

Ten minutes later she was back and looking more haggard than before. He sensed it was more than the hangover; more than her opening up to him. He waited while she sat on the bed in the same corner; waited again for what seemed like an eternity while she pulled her words together.

Finally she looked at him and he saw a hopelessness in her eyes that reminded him far too much of that beaten down kid who'd collapsed on his porch nearly a year before.

"You remember the day Bailey was born?"

"How could I forget?" He asked quietly.

"Shoulda been a really good day . . . for all of us. But we were scared, Doc," Kyler muttered. "And pissed off. I didn't know if Barb was gonna die right alongside her daughter; she didn't know how she'd make it if Bailey died." She paused. "Jimmy was right up to that edge," her finger found the line on the comforter again and slowly traced it, "and it wasn't gonna take much to send him over."

"And I was up there, pissed as hell 'cause you'd left the county," he offered. "And that only made it worse for you."

She looked at him. "Looking back now, you were the sanest part of that whole day."

Lamont regarded her for a long moment. Finally he shook his head and took a deep breath. "What happened?" He asked.

Kyler briefly managed to meet his eyes before looking away. "After Bailey was born and stabilized, the doctor said I could see Barb for a few minutes. She was still scared but relieved, too, you know? She hadn't died . . . neither one of them had, and for a second it seemed like everything was gonna be ok.

"She told me Jimmy was pissed off but hadn't told her what about. I knew what it was about but I wasn't about to tell her. Anyway, she asked me to check on him; said he'd checked into this motel down the road 'cause he was planning on staying a day or two 'til everything got figured out."

Kyler stopped for a moment and swallowed, trying to stop her roiling stomach.

"He didn't answer the door when I knocked," she said hoarsely. "I really thought he was dead, Doc. O'D'd in the fucking room or something."

"Bailey'd just been born," Lamont said quietly.

"And he was as mad as I've ever seen him," she countered gently. "Bailey woulda saved him, yeah, but at that point he hadn't even gotten to hold her yet. Impulse mixed with that rage would've sent him back out in a heartbeat, leaving Barb and Bailey like I left Josh and Ryan."

He stared at her for a few long minutes before giving a vague gesture with his hand.

"So what happened?"

"I picked the lock on the door. The only light on in the room was the bathroom, but the door was closed. I pictured him in the bathtub with his wrists cut or something, and I didn't wanna look, Doc, but there was nobody else to do it."

Kyler stopped and ran a shaking hand across her face. "He was kneeling on the floor in front of the toilet. The lid was down and he'd laid out lines of coke on a little mirror."

Lamont hissed in a breath and only just managed to clamp his mouth against the shout of rage that wanted to come out, because suddenly he knew what happened . . . what she'd done.

"Jimmy told me to turn around and leave, Doc. That it was the best thing I could do."

"But you didn't," his voice was thick with anger and Kyler winced, feeling her stomach twist.

"I didn't even think about it. I didn't even try to back up or turn around. It . . . it never even crossed my mind. One minute I'm standing there in shock and the next I'm crawling across the floor towards him."

He stared at her and she saw his eyes cloud over with a rage so deep it could have bordered on hatred. Her own stomach twisted more and she felt the acid start to gather in her chest.

"Jesus . . . fucking . . . Christ," his words were slow and deliberate; his voice hoarse with that anger. "And here I thought you were just exhausted that next day when I saw you. Well, fuck, yeah you were exhausted 'cause you'd been up all fucking night doing coke, right?" His eyes blazed with a fury unlike him and Kyler cringed from shame and despair.

"How much?" He managed around the bowling ball–sized mass of anger in his gut. "How much did you do?"

"Enough," she mumbled.

He glared at her. "Fuck, it's never enough for you, Kyler. There ain't that much coke in the whole fucking world for it to ever be enough for you."

Lamont abruptly got off the bed and stormed out the door, leaving Kyler swamped with that hopelessness again. A few minutes later she heard the stereo start up in the basement and just had time to recognize Neil Young's voice before the bile streaked up her throat. She rolled off the bed and raced towards the bathroom, just barely making the toilet in time as the vomit exploded from her throat and mouth with painful intensity.

She laid her head on her arm, feeling her heart beat erratically in her temples and behind her sternum.

"God help me," her voice was a gruff whisper. "Please help me to quit fucking up all the good things in my life."

Kyler sat there for a few minutes more before she managed to pull herself to her feet, swaying from the sheer range of emotions still coursing through her. Finally she pulled on that steel will that had been ingrained in her since birth and gritting her teeth, forced herself to walk downstairs to the basement.

She sat on the bottom two steps and surveyed Lamont, sitting on the couch with his elbows on his knees. He stared at her for an eternity and she tried to gauge the depth of his rage. It was deep she knew, but how deep would be the measurement of his friendship and trust in her.

The silence between them was as thick as it had ever been, pressing against her chest and making it hard to breathe.

"What else?" Lamont snapped.

"What else what?"

"What else have you done?"

Kyler waited a beat, feeling the distrust in the room like hot liquid and knowing she deserved every bit of it.

"Valium and Percoset."

"What else?" He flapped a hand impatiently. "I know you did *that*, Kyler. Fuck, I gave that to you. What else did you do that I don't know about?"

She shook her head. "Nothing."

His gaze burned into hers. "Nothing," he repeated, his voice heavily laden with sarcasm.

Kyler spread her hands in surrender, feeling her stomach twist again at the anger in his eyes. "Test me," she said. "Right now."

Lamont glared at her, feeling the rage roaring through him. Shaking his head he raked both hands through his hair, trying hard to get a grip on this insanity, on his anger, and on the fact that this girl he'd trusted with everything had betrayed him.

"Doc," Kyler's voice was quiet. "I'm sorry. I . . . I didn't even know how to tell you this, or even if I should. It . . . it was months ago and even though that doesn't really matter, I know, I just . . ." she swallowed back more bile, trying to calm her ravaged stomach.

"I've learned a lot since then. I think . . . I hope I'm stronger now. Jimmy's clean and so's Barb. They haven't done anything since that day and neither have I."

Lamont raised his eyes to hers again and she held up a hand.

"You can't trust me on that and don't blame you. So test me, ok? Right now."

The silence dropped down them again, weighted with a much-needed friendship existing on a razor-thin wire.

"Fuck," he growled.

Kyler sat where she was, miserable, filled with self-loathing.

"I'm goin' to bed, kid," the anger was still there, but now it was mixed with a bone-deep weariness. "Turn the stereo off, will ya?"

She was silent as he slipped by her up the stairs, not waiting for an answer. On the turntable the Godfather of Grunge rasped out to whoever was listening that rock and roll would never die.

CHAPTER 64

KYLER LOOKED IN on Lamont before she left around four a.m. He was facing the far wall and she would've bet money he wasn't asleep.

Silently she made her way downstairs and out the back door, needing the freedom of miles of asphalt to wash away the glass-pitted hell her life had suddenly become.

Two hours later, dragging from exhaustion and still feeling half-sick with shame and the uncertainty of losing Lamont for good, she forced her battered body up the three flights of stairs to her apartment. Her mind was numb from the constant battling of emotions, and she was almost tripping over the still form sitting outside her door before she saw him.

"Max?" Kyler rubbed her eyes.

He looked up, his own eyes weary and circled with the dark rings of fatigue. "Hey."

"What's up?" She squatted down next to him. "You all right?"

"Yeah," he struggled to stand up and she grasped his upper arm, helping him.

"You don't look all right."

He gestured at the cardboard carrier with two cups of coffee in it at his feet. "I brought some coffee. You can have both; I'm not feeling so good."

"C'mon," Kyler picked up the coffee and unlocked the door, guiding him in. "What's wrong?"

"Nothing. I just ate some bad food, I guess. Been throwing up half the night."

"So why aren't you at home in bed?"

"I couldn't sleep."

"Well, no, not if you're puking, I guess."

"No, I mean," he looked at her, "I'm sorry about yesterday and you said you were sorry and everything's, I guess, ok again, but I still just couldn't stop thinking about it, you know? Everything, I mean."

"That's probably why you're sick," she responded. "Too much thinking."

"I think it was the Mexican I had after I left the park. I ate at that little place in that strip mall next to the Holiday Inn."

"Jesus, hasn't that place been shut down a couple times?"

"Has it? Look, you mind if I lay down for a minute? Just here on the floor's fine. I think I'm either gonna puke or pass out if I don't."

"C'mon," Kyler slipped an arm around his waist. "You can lay in the bed."

"I'm not gonna take your bed," Max hung back.

"I'm up for the duration anyway," she said. "I just skated the streets pretty hard so I'm kinda wired right now. Besides, I'm gonna hook up this CD player I bought. You sleep, all right? Don't worry about work; I'll take care of it."

All this time she was slowly maneuvering him down the hall towards the bedroom, and now Max collapsed gratefully on the bed, pulling the covers around him. Kyler noticed the sheen of sweat on his face and the goose bumps along his neck and arms.

"Here," he reached behind him and pulled a CD from his back pocket. "Speaking of CD players, I made this for you. Rock mix."

Kyler took it from him and looked at it. It was plain on one side with the words "Classic Rock" in his handwriting on the other. "You made this? How?"

Max managed a slight grin. "One day I'm gonna make you computer savvy."

"Ok, just try to get some sleep, all right? I'll be right out here if you need anything, and you know where the bathroom's at if you gotta puke again."

"Yeah," Max pulled the covers around him, shivering. "Thanks, Kyler."

"Sure." She watched him for a minute, feeling the gratitude of being able to help him ease the shame she felt of hurting the doc; betraying the trust and faith that he'd had in her.

Silently she slipped out of the room, shutting the door partway behind her. In the living room she pulled the CD player from the closet and set it underneath the turntable. It was another yard sale acquisition, but she knew enough about music equipment by now to be able to realize it was in decent condition.

So she was surprised when it wouldn't play the CD Max had made for her.

Another half-hour, another connecting and reconnecting of wires, and it still wouldn't play, and Kyler sat back on her heels and lit a cigarette, giving her mind a break. Glancing at the clock on the wall she was surprised it was barely after seven; it felt closer to eight or nine.

A sound from the hallway told her Max was up, and then she heard the telltale signs of vomiting coming from the bathroom.

"Shit," she sighed and got up, heading down the hallway.

He was kneeling before that familiar god, his body tight and shaking and his eyes closed against the exertion. Kyler sat on the edge of the tub and put a calming hand on his back.

"Fuck," Max coughed. "What the fuck did I eat?" He sniffed and laid his cheek against the cool porcelain.

"Want me to call somebody? Your mom or . . ." she swallowed, "or Doc?"

"No," he muttered. "I'll be all right. I don't think I can puke up much more." He paused. "But yeah, will you call my mom? Just to let her know where I'm at."

"Yeah." She hesitated and then ran a hand through his sweaty hair, brushing his bangs back from his forehead. "Sure you're all right?"

"Yeah."

"Ok." Kyler got up and walked back to the living room, snagging her new phone off the charger as she passed it. Dialing Max's home phone from memory, she waited through three rings before the answering machine picked up.

"Hey, Betty, it's Kyler. Max is here at my house and he wanted me to call so you wouldn't worry. He's . . . not feeling too good; said he must've had some bad Mexican. Right now he's between puking and sleeping, so I guess you're gonna worry anyway. My address is 3917 Bay Pine, number seven . . . third floor. You can come by anytime, but I'll be at work after nine. He'll probably still be here though."

She punched the off button and put it back on the charger. Looking back at the stereo, she lit another cigarette and was contemplating where she must have gone wrong when there was a soft knock on her door. She pulled it open and regarded Lamont's eyes gazing back into her own, solemn and cautious.

"Hey," he said quietly. "I figured you'd be here."

"You figured or you hoped?" Kyler moved aside and waved him in.

He slipped by her and stepped into the kitchen. "I guess I . . . I just hoped."

Kyler rubbed the back of her neck and gave a small nod. She watched as he emptied the two plastic bags he had, putting cans and boxes into her previously bare cabinets.

"Just some dry goods," he said, somewhat apologetically. "You know . . ." he shrugged, "just in case you get hungry. Ginger Ale," he put a two-liter in her refrigerator. "It's good for settling stomachs."

Straightening up, Lamont turned to face her. "I heard you leave this morning, and I kept thinking about how you said Jimmy took off that day . . ."

"He was pissed off," she said softly. "If anybody should be mad here," she gestured, indicating the space between them, "I would think it would be you. I mean . . . shit, Doc, if I could take all that back I'd do it in a heartbeat. There's not . . ." she swallowed and turned away, running a hand through her hair. *"Fuck,"* she growled, feeling too much emotion . . . and fearing too much had already been lost.

"I'm sorry," she turned to him. "I'm really sorry, Doc."

He stared at her for a few long minutes, and then gave a slow nod. "What, uh . . . what made you tell me? Now, I mean. Or . . . you know, ever?"

Kyler sighed and walked back over to the stereo. "I told you before I'm not a liar. And I'm not. It . . . was eating at me, even though it was months ago." She turned to face him from across the room. "You opened up your home to me . . .

a . . ." she waved a hand in front of her torso. "A thief and . . . a junkie. You gave me a key to your fucking house, for Christ sakes."

Lamont was quiet, watching her, not saying anything.

"Last night you said you'd come after me if . . . if I ever slipped. That kinda scared me, Doc. I started thinking . . . shit that makes no sense."

"Like what?" He asked gently.

"Like having you as a safety net for me; that you'd be there to catch me when I fall."

"*If* you fall."

"No," she said. "*When*, Doc . . . *when*. Don't you see? If you're there to catch me, why wouldn't I try to fly?"

"Jesus, Kyler . . ." he gave a tired sigh. "So you *don't* want that security? You don't *want* that knowledge, that . . . that . . ."

"I'm just saying I got scared, and that I wanted you to know about the coke so you'd—"

"What, push you away on my own? Give you no reason to even *think* you have a safety net?"

Kyler sank to the floor in front of the stereo and draped her arms over her knees. Her eyes were on the current problem with the wiring, but her heart and mind were on the man behind her.

"I don't know," she admitted quietly. "I really don't know."

He moved to sit facing her, his left calf touching hers. Reaching out, he tapped the center of her forehead gently. "You think too much," he said. "Maybe we both do."

She shook her head. "I went skating this morning . . . you know, to clear my head, I guess. And I got to thinking that . . . Jesus, Doc, you gave me everything. You've saved my life a hundred times over." Her eyes met his. "You made me want to live again, *taught* me how to live again, without the dope and all that crazy shit that went with it."

Kyler pinched the corners of her tired eyes. "I think that if I'm gonna go back out, it's not gonna be because you'll be there to save me again . . . although it's comforting to know that."

"So . . ." he started, but she cut him off.

"So maybe you being there to catch me *won't* be the reason I'd try to fly again. I did a lot of thinking this morning, a lot of trying to figure all this shit out, and basically it comes down to this: I'm clean, Doc, right now. I don't need the Percosets anymore and I've even dropped down on the valium. I don't *need* this shit anymore, and God knows I don't want it."

Lamont was quiet for a few long moments; his leg touching hers was a symbol of his still-strong faith in her, and it was a strong shield against the demons both inside and out. Finally he took a deep breath and let it out slowly, looking at her.

"I did some thinking, too, and I realized I was angry at something that happened almost a year ago, and that there were too many things that happened between then and now that I was forgetting about. Like how you handled Lewis, for instance, and the pain you suffered because of him, and how you stayed clean throughout it all.

"You've helped Max gain back a faith he'd lost, made a positive impact on that park, and even helped me get through Curtis's death. Jimmy and Barb needed help spoiling that kid and you've definitely done that," he allowed a small smile.

"Yeah," Kyler sighed.

"You're strong," he said softly. "And every day you stay clean you become a little stronger. I'm sorry I didn't realize that before I flew off the handle last night."

"I'm sorry I didn't tell you sooner," she responded.

The silence between them this time was smoother, easier to carry, and wasn't weighed down with unspoken accusations. Lamont gazed at her and asked quietly,

"Does Barb know?"

"She knew the minute we walked in the room the next morning," Kyler answered. "I guess it's true what they say, you know?" She looked at him. "An addict knows."

"What'd she say? Was she mad?"

Kyler laid back on the floor, trying to stretch out her knotted stomach. Lamont's brow furrowed at the way her hips and ribs stuck out; too much bone and not enough meat.

"More than I've ever seen her," she said softly. "I don't know why she didn't just tell both of us to get lost."

"'Cause she loves you."

She pressed the heels of her hands against her eyes and took a deep breath. "Love really doesn't stand a chance against addiction, Doc."

"Call it faith, then," he conceded. "Or hope. Maybe it was one or the other that made her try to hang on just a little bit longer."

The phone rang and without looking Kyler reached out to her side and snagged it up off the carpet.

"Hello?"

Lamont watched her as she lay with one arm across her eyes. Her clothes were baggy on her, sinking in the hollows between her bones, pooling on the carpet on each side of her skinny frame. He shook his head in frustration but managed to keep it out of his eyes.

"No, he's still here," Kyler said. "Little better, I guess, but still throwing up occasionally. Might be sleeping now but you want me to check? See if he's awake?"

Lamont raised his eyebrows in question but her eyes were still closed and she didn't see him.

"Ok, yeah. Yeah, that Mexican place? I know, I told him." She felt Lamont's hand on her knee as he pushed himself to his feet, and then the carpet shifted under her head as he walked behind her towards the hall.

"I'll tell him. Ok, yeah I should still be here." She hit the off button and sighed, feeling tired and worn out. Alone now in the living room, Kyler got to her feet and walked into the kitchen. In the bedroom Lamont was staring at Max as he lay curled up on the bed. His face was pale but his breathing was regular and even.

"Damn, kid," he put a hand on his forehead, "you eat something you shouldn't have?"

"Apparently," Max said hoarsely. "Over at the Mexican place by the Holiday Inn."

Lamont arched an eyebrow and squatted down next to him. "I think the health department shut that place down not too long ago."

Max shot him a thin glare. "Seems that's a piece of information I missed out on, Doc."

Offering an easy smile, Lamont leaned back and shrugged. "I don't think you're gonna die if you still got that sarcastic streak in you."

"He's too hardheaded to die," Kyler said as she slid behind him and picked up Max's hand, wrapping it around a glass. "Here, drink this. Ginger Ale. Recommended by both the doc here and your mom."

Max sat partway up and managed to take a small sip. She saw the relief in his eyes when he realized it might actually stay down.

"Thanks," he said hoarsely. "But I don't wanna take too much, though. Don't wanna puke in your new bed."

"I'd appreciate that," Kyler gave a small smile as she sat beside him. "He got a fever?" She looked at Lamont.

He shrugged. "A little . . . not too much. My diagnosis?" He smirked. "Sleep and liquids. Lots of both."

"Well, that's good," Max closed his eyes and settled farther into the bed. "'Cause I'm really tired and just about dyin' of thirst."

Kyler held up the glass and let him take another small drink. Lamont just barely held back his surprise as she ran a hand through his hair again, moving his shaggy bangs back from his eyes. It was a gesture totally unlike her and he began to see for the first time the protectiveness she had over the kid.

"Just take it easy, all right?" She said. "Your mom's on her way but you can stay here as long as you want."

Max grunted. "She say where she was at?"

"No, but I didn't ask either. Just said she was about a half hour away."

He gave a small nod. "Ok. I think I'll feel better if I just lay here for a while. Moving around makes me wanna puke."

Kyler set the ginger ale by the leg of the bed and pushed herself to her feet using Lamont's shoulder. "It's right here, all right? And I'm gonna be out in the living room if you need me."

"Me, too," Lamont stood up with her.

Max nodded weakly and they left him alone in the semidarkness. Kyler rolled her head on her neck as she squatted down in front of the stereo again. The lack of sleep was catching up with her and Lamont noticed as he kneeled beside her.

"Why don't you take a quick nap yourself?" He asked softly. "I'll wake you up in time for work."

"Nah," she ran a hand through her hair. "I'm all right."

"Sure? I mean, uh . . ." he looked around, trying to find a place she could lay down, knowing she wouldn't share the bed with Max.

"You know me," she offered a crooked smile. "If I really needed to lay down I'd find a place."

"Even after giving him your bed."

Kyler shrugged. "He's sick. I'm not."

"How long's he been here?"

"Since I got home, I guess. He was sitting outside the door when I came up the steps."

"Why?"

She glanced at him, her eyes unreadable. "Yesterday was a bad day for all of us, Doc. I was hungover and he knew it. We didn't get along real well and I guess that bothered him. He said he couldn't sleep, thinking about it, and figured he'd come over." Kyler paused, thinking, then murmured, "I hate that he felt he had to come here even after puking all night."

"Maybe he just wanted to say he was sorry."

"He didn't do anything."

Maybe he felt panicked, thinking you'd just take off . . . the way I felt when you first started hanging around in my life, he thought but didn't say.

Lamont watched her for a few minutes as she began checking her connections once again. As she laid on the floor along the wall, meticulously working her way down the wires, he was again painfully aware of the loose way her clothes sat on her body.

"Hungry?" His voice was somewhat cautious.

She glanced at him, reading his emotions in his eyes. "I'll eat if you want me to."

Lamont sighed, but then shook his head. "It's not what I want, you know."

Kyler took a deep breath and let it out slowly. She was more tired than anything, and food was probably the last thing on her mind. Still, though, she wasn't about to get into another argument with the doc. Stubbornness, pride, anger . . . or even just lack of hunger . . . none of it was worth it.

"Sure," she muttered, staring at the wire in her hand. There was silence for a minute between them and then she scrubbed a hand across her face. "Shit," her voice was a soft groan, squeezing Lamont's heart. She started to stand up but he put a hand on her arm, stopping her.

"Forget it," he said gently. "I'm sorry."

Kyler sat up next to him and looked at the stereo. "I hate fighting with you. Hate fucking fighting in general."

"Me, too," he murmured, and put an arm across her shoulders. "Let's not do it anymore, ok?"

She offered a wan smile. "Deal."

"So whatcha got goin' on here?" Lamont gestured towards the stereo.

"Max made me a CD. I bought this CD player at a yard sale last week and I know it works 'cause I tried it out before I even unhooked it from the guy's extension cord but it's not playing it," Kyler gestured towards the homemade disc laying on top of the turntable.

"Figured I had it hooked up wrong, although I'm pretty sure I got it right."

"You got it right," Lamont said. "That player's just too new, I think."

"What?" She looked at him. "Too new? For what?"

"For the CD," he smiled. "Here," he handed her his car keys. "Run down and get one out of my car. Make sure it's a store bought one and not one like that, ok? I'm pretty sure it'll play it."

"Well . . ." Kyler hesitated, "why would it play one and not the other?"

"I'll show you. You go get one and I'm gonna double check everything and then if it plays the one of mine I'll tell you why it won't play yours, ok?"

She looked at him skeptically but took the keys out of his hand and walked out the door. Lamont gave a cursory glance over the wires but knew it was hooked up correctly. A few minutes later Kyler walked back into the apartment and handed him *The Best of the Monkees.*

"Good choice," he grinned and inserted it into the player. A few seconds later the sweet alternative rock beat was pouring out of the speakers. "Love the sound you got out of this system. How much you pay for it?"

"Yard sale price," she said absently, staring at the CD player. "So what went wrong with mine?"

"I would guess nothing. Max made it? I'm sure he knows what he's doing. It's just the player itself. Sometimes—especially with the new technology and being able to download songs online—some of the newer players won't play homemade CDs because the music industry is trying to discourage illegal downloads. Singers, producers . . . practically the whole industry can't make any money if there's a huge popular virtual black-market on songs."

Kyler was staring at him, confusion on her face.

"Tell you what," Lamont said easily, "I think I may have an older player at my house. I'll trade you, ok? I'll take this one and you can have the one I've got that I'm pretty sure'll play Max's CD."

"O . . . k," she said slowly. "But I just don't understand how . . ." she trailed off, confused.

He smiled. "Don't worry about it. Between me and Max, we'll teach you."

She squatted down beside him and stared at the CD player. "Not if it's illegal," she muttered. "I'm not goin' to jail."

He slung an arm around her and gave a small laugh. "It's not . . . too illegal. I mean, there're actual legal sites you can go to . . . you have to pay a certain amount a month, but it's usually not much. And there're sites that are . . . legalish; you know, not *as* illegal as some."

"Illegal is illegal, Doc," she responded.

"You're thinking too much again," he replied amicably. "You wanna trade or not?"

"Yeah, ok."

"And you wouldn't go to jail just by having this," he indicated her CD. "This is not the possessing stolen property you're probably used to."

Kyler gazed at him wordlessly before looking back at the stereo. They sat there in silence for a few minutes before Lamont said gently,

"It's goin' on ten 'till."

She sat back on her heels and scrubbed her hands across her eyes. She was exhausted, he knew, but she'd never say it.

"Shit," she muttered. "I thought Betty'd be here by now."

There was another round of silence between them before she looked at him, eyes red-rimmed and weary.

"Can you stay? Just 'till she gets here?"

Lamont paused just a moment too long and Kyler caught it but she merely waited.

"You worried about him stealing your system here?" he said half-jokingly.

She offered a tired smile. "I trust him as much as I trust you, Doc. Besides, I get the feeling he's more of a CD man . . . the smaller, the better." She paused and then pushed herself to her feet, stretching. Her shorts hung too low on her skinny hips and she seemed all but swimming in her T-shirt. He grimaced but remained silent.

"He's sick," she said, looking at him. "I just . . . you know . . . I'd feel better if he wasn't alone. But if you gotta go to work . . ."

Lamont shook his head. "Not 'till later. I'll stay with him."

She nodded and he saw the relief in her dark eyes.

"I'm really sorry," Kyler's voice was hoarse with rare emotion. "About all that before."

Lamont gazed at her and slowly nodded. "Yeah," he said softly. "Me, too." He stood up and pulled her into a gentle hug. "I'll call you later, all right?"

She nodded against his chest and then slowly pulled away. Lamont watched her leave and then giving a heavy sigh, sat down in front of the stereo and began absently flipping through her albums.

"Have to find her a couch, I guess." But then he gave a wry grin as he selected a Doors record and dropped it on the turntable. "And she'd probably get pissed about that, too."

His glance slid to the hallway, where beyond, Max lay in the bedroom, sick as hell after eating some bad food probably, and under the umbrella of Kyler's fierce protection.

Rare, he thought, for her, but then he paused, reflecting back on the year. Perhaps not so uncommon considering his own brutal attachment for her that had come on so quick . . . definitely atypical, especially for him.

He reflected on her words

". . . I trust him as much as I trust you . . ." and remembered the long, hard road it took her—both of them—to get to that point; where she could say those words and not think twice about them.

That terrified, broken kid who'd showed up on his doorstep . . . addicted and lost . . . well, Kyler had found her feet again and managed to stand back up. He'd never in a million years thought he'd have that much to give . . . that much of himself to bring the kid back from the literal brink of death.

"But I think she brought it out of me," he murmured softly. "And now she can find trust for me." Lamont stared absently at the spinning record, thinking of Kyler . . . and from her to Max sleeping in the bedroom. Emily flashed across his mind in a brief spurt of bittersweet memory, and again he was thankful for Kyler's support during the time of Curtis's death.

He shook his head, thinking of all the times she'd said he'd saved her . . . guided her . . . held her up . . . and knew that as much as he'd done that for her, she'd done it for him tenfold.

". . . as much as I trust you . . ."

It was fucking amazing, really . . . everything. Him, her . . . watching her skate, stitching her up. Seeing her pick Max up and put that light back in his eye, take charge of the park and turn it around . . . everything . . . just fucking *everything*.

Again he gave a shake of his head and reached up to turn the record over, but stopped at the soft knock on the door. When he opened it Betty's familiar face was there to greet him, though now three years older and lined with deep groves that had only just begun to appear the last time he'd seen her.

Her eyes widened in shock, and then his heart gave a squeeze as she winced, as if he'd reached out and physically slapped her.

"Max was right," she muttered hoarsely. "Seeing you brings the hurt back all over again."

Lamont dipped his head in a gesture of surrender. "Mrs. Anderson," he responded quietly, extending one hand in an invitation to come in.

Betty slid past him, her heart pounding. It hurt him to see her clutching her purse like she was; like he might snatch it from her at any time.

"Kyler's not here?" Now her eyes were heavy with a dark, smoldering anger; barely controlled.

"She left for work not too long ago."

Betty checked the watch on one thin wrist . . . a nervous gesture that seemed to cut right through him.

"I tried to hurry. Traffic on the Five was horrible."

Lamont nodded. "It usually is this time of day."

She glared at him for a long moment. "Max . . . ?"

"He's back there," he pointed. "In the bedroom."

Betty offered a slow nod but remained where she was for a moment longer, watching him. Lamont got the feeling she was gathering her emotions together, checking them, trying to put them in some kind of order.

Finally without another word she headed down the small hallway. He took a deep breath and pulled The Doors off the turntable, replacing it at random with the first album his hand fell on. Then he slid down the wall to the floor and draped his elbows across his knees, his gaze on the hall.

After a few minutes Betty walked back into his line of sight. The lines around her eyes had faded some but there was a new weariness across her face. It deepened momentarily for just a brief instant when she heard the song on the stereo, but with a resolve that was admirable she straightened up and looked directly at him.

"This was my husband's favorite song," her tone was hard, almost accusatory. "We played it at his funeral."

With a start Lamont realized Simon and Garfunkel's current "Bridge Over Troubled Waters" was a horrible coincidence, and that he couldn't have played it at a worse time.

"I . . . I'm sorry," he stammered. "I wasn't even looking . . . I just . . . threw it on."

As soon as the words were out of his mouth he realized how lame they sounded. But he knew he couldn't explain that he'd had no idea Kyler even *liked* Simon and Garfunkel, or that his random pick of the album really was that . . . just random.

Betty's hazel eyes—so much like Max's—just stared at him. Lamont didn't even try for another record; just switched to tuner and hoped that whatever was playing on the radio was neutral and unemotional.

The silence stretched out between them, growing more uncomfortable by the second. Finally she shook her head, defeated, and jerked a thumb back over her shoulder.

"He wants to stay," she murmured quietly. "Says whenever he moves he feels like throwing up so he just wants to try to sleep it off."

Lamont watched her for a moment . . . her tired faced surrounding hurt, defeated eyes.

"He can stay," he responded quietly. "And you can too, if you want. I, uh . . . I have to get to work but you're welcome to stay as long as you want."

Relief flashed for an instant across her features but then it was gone. She merely nodded and shifted her gaze to the stereo and multiple albums stacked around it.

"She just moved in, right?"

"Yeah . . ." Lamont hesitated. "I brought her some food and stuff earlier and you can help yourself to that, too. If you're hungry." He paused and then gestured around the living room. "She hasn't really had time to get a whole of anything else . . ."

Betty just nodded. "I'll be fine. "I may not stay long . . . he'll be ok here by himself?" Her eyes drilled into his.

"Kyler'll call throughout the day," he assured her. "I'll call her and tell her."

Again just the nod. Her eyes, when they met his, were full of such raw emotion it was hard for him to look at them. So he was glad when she chose to stare at the albums instead.

Slowly he pulled one of his business cards from his wallet and laid it gently on the bar between the living room and the kitchen.

"Here's my cell and office numbers," he said softly. "And Kyler's at the park if you need her."

Betty didn't answer; didn't acknowledge him in any way. Hesitantly Lamont walked to the door and allowed himself one last look at her turned back before he slipped quietly out of the apartment.

Grimacing, shaking his head, he headed for the stairway. He had a few hours yet before he had to be at work, but he knew Betty wasn't quite ready to spend more than a few minutes with him.

"Still, though," he mumbled, "that could've gone a whole lot worse."

For a moment he wanted to be angry at Kyler for putting both him and Betty into that situation, but he realized it would be as irrational as the anger that had flowed between them the night before. It was nobody's fault, nobody's weight to carry, and *besides,* he figured, *Kyler didn't know about the history he shared with Max and his mother.* The grief and the heartache that they felt justified in laying on him. Maybe not rightfully so, but Lamont couldn't judge them; couldn't blame them.

Max, he knew, had managed to somewhat come to terms with his grief and blame, but . . . Betty . . .

"Hell, she came there expecting Kyler to answer the door. Probably already worried with Max being sick . . . the last thing she expected was to see me opening the door.

"Shit," Lamont ran a hand through his hair, knowing how much her seeing him had hurt; bringing back too many bad memories of her husband dying three years ago . . . of her world finally falling apart after she'd tried so long and so hard to hold it together.

CHAPTER 65

"BEAUMONT SKATE PARK," Kyler wedged the phone between her shoulder and ear as she hammered a nail into a board.

"Hey," Max's voice came weak over the line.

"Hey, back," she responded. "How're you feeling?"

"Better, I guess. Don't know how I'm still throwing up, though. I don't have anything left in there."

"Acid. There's continual acid buildup in your stomach."

He grimaced. "Good to know."

"Where you at, my place, still?"

"Yeah, I'm laying the middle of your living room, listening to the radio."

"Why aren't you in bed?"

"I'm working my way home. I just have to move in small distances right now."

Kyler gave a small shake of her head. "You don't have to go home. You can stay there as long as you need to."

"I know, but . . . I just figured I wouldn't spread any more of my germs around. Besides," he paused, somewhat embarrassed, "I think Mom wants to take care of me."

Kyler'd never had a mother and she wondered what it felt like to have a mother's cool hand placed on a fevered forehead.

"Sure," she responded. "You want me to call her, or maybe Doc, to come get you?"

"I already did; she's on her way. I just called to tell you . . . remember that stereo stand I said you could have?"

"Yeah."

"Well, I forgot all about it until I got to laying here on the floor and I'm eye level with your receiver. Tonight or tomorrow or whenever I feel better, if you can help me get it down out of the attic, you can have it."

"Oh, sure. Yeah, ok. Thanks."

"You're welcome," he replied. "And if I'm feeling better later on I'll come on in, ok?"

"Don't worry about it. It's no big deal, Max. Just get better."

"I'm gonna try. Hopefully it'll be soon."

"All right. I'll call you later, ok?"

"Yeah. Thanks again, Kyler, for . . . you know, letting me stay here and everything."

"Anytime, kid." Kyler hit the off button and sat back on her heels, lighting a cigarette. She gazed up at the blameless blue sky and wondered absently about life with parents, and how different her own life would've been if she'd had a mother or father growing up. Then she thought of the doc and how he was there, taking care of her when she needed it and always without judgment.

"Maybe it's kinda like that," she mumbled softly. "Him being there when I need him to be."

She smoked in thoughtful silence for a few more minutes before pitching her cigarette in the grass and reaching for the hammer once more.

CHAPTER 66

"How big is it?" Kyler asked Max as they walked into his house. The smell of tomato sauce and hamburger wafted through the air, making even her weak stomach grumble.

"Uh . . . ," Max hesitated. "Not too big, I don't guess. We may have trouble, though, rolling it down the sidewalk on our skateboards."

Kyler was quiet for a moment, thinking. "I can probably figure something out," she said finally.

"Yeah, maybe we can fit it in the car," he responded, but she heard the doubt in his voice.

"Well, Doc's got the SUV. I'm sure we can fit it in the back."

"Yeah, that'd probably work better."

They walked into the kitchen where Betty was at the stove, stirring a pot of spaghetti.

"Hey, Mom," Max pulled two bottles of water from the refrigerator and handed one to Kyler. "That smells good."

"Thank you," she smiled at them. "Thought about tacos but figured you'd starve if I did that." Betty winked at Kyler as Max grimaced and rubbed his stomach. "I think he gave up on Mexican."

"Maybe just for awhile," he admitted. "I love it but I don't like being sick like that."

"I'm sure your mom's tacos are a far cry from that rat hole you ate at."

"I know they are, but it's just the whole concept, you know?"

Kyler grinned and took a long drink of her water. The cold liquid felt good running down her throat, pushing back the heat of the day.

"Hey, Mom?" Max said hesitantly. "Kyler was thinking about calling Doc over here, see if that stereo stand will fit in his SUV. That ok?"

Betty gazed at her son for a long moment, during which Kyler felt something private pass between them.

"Sure," she said finally. "That's fine. You wanna get it tonight?" She looked at Kyler.

"Maybe," she gave a small shrug. "I guess it depends on if he can do it tonight."

Betty nodded. "Ok. You can call him if you want. See if he might want to stay for supper, too."

Max's eyebrows shot up but he remained silent.

"All right," Kyler met her eyes, sensing damage and redemption somewhere beneath the surface. "Thanks." Snagging the phone off the charger, she walked into the living room to call Lamont.

In the kitchen, still seated at the table, Max stared at his mother. She gave a weary shrug.

"It's been three years. And he saved *her*," she jerked a thumb over her shoulder. "Right?"

He didn't answer, and a minute later Kyler came back into the kitchen.

"He said tonight's fine," she set the phone gently back on the charger. "And he said he might stay for supper if I do."

"And you're gonna, right?" Max got up and slipped an arm around his mother's waist, kissing her temple. "Mom's spaghetti's pretty good. And besides," he regarded her with a measuring look. "You're too damn skinny."

Kyler gave a wan smile and flapped a hand. "Yeah, yeah. I know."

He looked at his mother. "Can we go skate for awhile? Till the food's done and then maybe Doc'll be here and he can help us get this thing down out of the attic."

"Sure, go ahead," Betty offered a genuine smile. "Just don't kill yourselves."

"Sure?" Kyler hung back. "You need any help with anything?"

"Nope," she ushered them out the back door. "You guys go. I'll call you when it's ready."

She watched them for a few long moments, and it never ceased to amaze her how free Max seemed when he was skating. He'd stopped doing a lot of things when his father passed away, but skating wasn't one of them, and she'd suspected for a long time that it was the one thing that had kept him sane.

Turning back to the stove she began absently stirring the spaghetti again, lost in thought. Years ago, when it was just her and Nathan, life was good and it seemed that it could only get better. They'd spent countless hours lying in each other's arms on the basement floor, listening to his records . . . the receiver and turntable on the very same stand Kyler was about to take . . .

Betty allowed a small absent smile that didn't touch her eyes. She was going to miss that thing in a bittersweet way, but she also realized the importance of letting it go. Kyler needed it; it was only taking up space in the attic . . . and essentially it was because Max wanted her to have it; wanted her to have something of her own that could hopefully *mean* something to her . . . keep her grounded and allow her some sort of pride that didn't come from the streets.

A knock on the front door startled her out of her thoughts, and she glanced towards the living room, hesitating. Finally, taking a deep breath, Betty made her way slowly out of the kitchen.

Lamont stood quietly on the front porch, waiting with his heart pounding behind his rib cage. He wasn't sure of this at all, but Kyler had asked him to come. In a distant way he hoped Betty wouldn't be home because he wasn't sure he wanted to face her again. Two days ago in Kyler's apartment had been hard enough and truth be told he wasn't ready for another round of her anger and resentment pounding him in the face.

Her eyes met his when the door was finally opened, and he felt his gut twist up.

"Hello, Mrs. Anderson," he said quietly. "Um . . . did Kyler tell you I was coming?"

"She did, and you can call me Betty," she stood aside and gestured him in. "I . . . uh . . ." she glanced away and bit her lip. "I want to apologize for the other day. It . . . it was just a shock . . ."

"Yeah," Lamont ran a hand through his hair. "I know. And I'm sorry, too. And I swear to God I didn't mean to play that song."

Betty nodded and didn't answer. The silence between them was almost too long but then she nodded towards the kitchen. "You like spaghetti?"

"Sure," he offered a small smile. "But I don't want to impose. I mean . . ."

"C'mon," she smiled back. "It won't be ready for awhile. How 'bout coffee while you decide?"

"Yeah. That sounds good."

She led the way into the kitchen and flapped a hand at the table. "Have a seat if you want." Lamont picked a chair and slowly sat down. He watched as she pulled the coffee out of the fridge and started it brewing. "Sugar? Cream?"

"Um . . . yeah. Both, thanks. Are they—?"

"Outside. Skating in the pool," Betty finished for him and pointed out the window.

He got up and looked out at the huge kidney-shaped pool in the backyard. Kyler and Max were running up and down the length of it, and from side to side, sometimes chasing each other and sometimes following passively.

"I hope they don't collide again," he muttered.

"You and me, both. Here," she handed him a cup. "There's sugar and cream on the table. I'm gonna—" She cut off as the phone rang. "Excuse me."

Lamont watched her leave the kitchen and then he looked out the window again. Kyler was standing on the lip of the pool, waiting for Max to complete his run. As he shot up the side one final time, she reached out a hand to steady him and then pointed to the large area beside the pool.

He watched as she gestured, obviously explaining something. Max nodded and said something back, and even from twenty feet away Lamont was conscious of the ease between them . . . like they'd been friends for far longer than a year.

Another sign that the kid was really finding her footing again, and able to let people in, if even for only a short distance and a short while.

He was suddenly aware of Betty standing beside him.

"For the last couple years I've been living with a stranger," she said softly. "Just a shell of the fun-loving boy I raised. The fight was gone out of him and I watched him just exist day by day."

Lamont was silent, waiting, as she took a sip of her coffee.

"Then one day he comes home and tells me the old park over on Beaumont opened back up. I have to admit that I was less than fazed because southern California is shot through with skate parks, right?" Her eyes rested on his a moment before she looked back out the window.

"But for some reason that light was back in his eyes and that was all I cared about." Betty paused, smiling. "And then he tells me he got a job there. I was surprised, of course, 'cause I didn't know he was ever looking for one. But again," she faced him, the smile gone now, her eyes intent. "I didn't care because I saw my son start to come back."

Lamont looked at her and didn't respond.

"For what it's worth, thank you for saving that girl's life so she could save his."

He was silent for a long time, regarding her for a moment before turning back to the window.

"Kyler literally collapsed into my life," he said quietly. "I'd just gotten off work one night and was headed out the door when she came into the ER and passed out on the floor. She'd OD'd on some bad shit and she wasn't breathing." He stopped and stared into his coffee cup.

"I was just trying to do my job. I wasn't about to become a social worker or a drug counselor."

"Yet somehow you got roped into it, huh?" Betty asked with a small half-smile. Lamont offered a wan smile in return and gestured to the table.

"Wanna sit?"

"You gonna tell me a story?"

"Ah . . . sure," he said slowly.

Betty sat down and regarded him with her hazel eyes. Lamont slid into a seat across from her and tried to pull his words together.

"I'm in love with a woman," he started slowly, "whose life parallels mine in a way I never thought possible. She had a son who passed away not too long ago, as a direct result of drug addiction. I went to the funeral . . ." he stopped and took a deep breath. "And I watched this strong woman crumble. She'd lost her only son, and working every day with drug addicted patients, counseling them, guiding them back to sanity—to lead clean lives, productive lives . . . well, I think . . ." Lamont stopped, faltering.

"I think, being this was a battle she couldn't win, and being so personal . . . I think it took something out of her. Something vital. And something in her died."

He trailed off, thinking, realizing perhaps that very same thing had happened to Betty—and Max—three years ago.

"I got scared," he muttered. "Watching her break down like that." He stared at her and she saw defiance and fear battling each other in his eyes. "And you know why?"

Betty watched him for a long moment before giving a slow nod. "Because you were seeing yourself if Kyler were to ever lay in a casket."

He nodded and looked away, swallowing heavily. "And what scared me even more was that I *could* get scared over that. I'm not a father. I'm not a counselor or a social worker. I'm just a doctor and that's it."

"Except this girl comes along and turns you into all three, right?"

Lamont took a deep breath and let it out slowly. He leaned back in his chair and drummed his fingers restlessly on the table.

"The kid's nineteen," he said shortly. "She's used to being on her own and doing things her own way 'cause that's all she's ever done. She lived with me for almost a year and I've watched her go through some hell. I've held her up when I could, but mostly it's been her holding me up . . . especially through Curtis's funeral and Emily leaving."

He shook his head and clenched his teeth. "I just . . . I hate worrying about her, you know? I don't like not knowing where she is and I really don't like the fact that I worry about shit like that."

Sighing, he glanced back out the window. "She's been on her own her whole life, and I'm inherently self-motivated. I like things calm and quiet and done my own way . . ."

Lamont was quiet for a minute and Betty raised her eyebrows in question.

"So?"

"So, but . . . yeah," he murmured. "As self-sufficient as she is, she still needs to crash at my place every once in a while."

"And you need to worry about her when she doesn't," she finished for him.

Lamont gazed at her and gave a slow nod.

"And for what it's worth to *you*?" His voice was soft, nearly inaudible. "Because of her . . . and from watching Emily as she lost her son . . ." he swallowed. "I know the true power of death now. And . . . and it was wrong of me—trivial—to hand you a bunch of numbers to call to strangers to help get you through it.

"She's got that much power over me," he pointed out the window, "that losing her would destroy me. It would take much more than a phone call and a few kind words to save my sanity."

Lamont met her eyes.

"I'm sorry for that . . . for doing that to you."

Betty was silent for a long time, staring at him. Finally she reached over and gently took the empty coffee cup from his hands and stood up.

"Welcome to parenthood," she said kindly as the back door burst open and Kyler and Max came in. Max went to the stove by his mother and Kyler plopped down in the chair next to him. As his eyes settled on hers, he felt a sharp, painful squeeze on his heart and knew that, for better or worse, he'd finally gotten a chance to be a father.

THE END

CPSIA information can be obtained at www.ICGtesting.com
Printed in the USA
LVOW111730170212

269209LV00001B/1/P